Ravi K. Thiara
Stephanie A. Condon
Monika Schröttle (eds.)

Violence against Women and Ethnicity: Commonalities and Differences across Europe

Barbara Budrich Publishers
Opladen • Berlin • Farmington Hills, MI 2011

A CIP catalogue record for this book is available from
Die Deutsche Bibliothek (The German Library)

www.barbara-budrich.net

ISBN 978-3-86649-409-1

Die Deutsche Bibliothek – CIP-Einheitsaufnahme
Ein Titeldatensatz für die Publikation ist bei Der Deutschen Bibliothek erhältlich.

Verlag Barbara Budrich Barbara Budrich Publishers
Stauffenbergstr. 7. D-51379 Leverkusen Opladen, Germany

28347 Ridgebrook. Farmington Hills, MI 48334. USA
www.barbara-budrich.net

Jacket illustration by disegno, Wuppertal, Germany – www.disenjo.de
Typesetting by R + S Beate Glaubitz, Leverkusen, Germany
Printed in Europe on acid-free paper by
paper&tinta, Warsaw

Violence against Women and Ethnicity: Commonalities and Differences across Europe

Dedication

Thaibaran, for the ongoing love and support and for being there (RT).

As well as to 'my three', a special dedication and thanks for their guidance to two 'great feminists': Maryse J and my mum (SC).

For my courageous mother and for all mothers who teach their daughters self-respect, justice and pride (MS).

Acknowledgements

Putting together this Reader took us more than three years and the project would not have been successful without the intensive work and support of many people.

First of all we would like to thank the authors of this book for their stimulating and elaborate contributions and for their patience during the production process of the book, somewhat lengthened by the finalisation of the English versions of the chapters written in French or German.

The dedication and hard work of Renate Klein and Carol Hagemann-White in building up and organizing European research networks on VAW were central in the international cooperation that led to this Reader. Without their network activities, bringing the three of us together and giving us the opportunity to discuss the theme of gender, violence and ethnicity/discrimination, this project would never have launched.

We would also like to thank our publisher, Barbara Budrich, and her team for their support during this project and for their patience whilst awaiting the full manuscript, never placing pressure on us nor losing faith that one day the Reader would be completed.

WAVE was another important European partner for this Reader, as Rosa Logar, Maria Rösslhumer and Felice Drott helped us in searching for funding for translations and in preparing a framework for the dissemination of the contents of this book during the annual WAVE conference in October 2011. Our colleague and friend Nancy Gage-Lindner gave us important ideas for possible funders and for the realisation of the project, in addition to revision work on the German to English translations.

Without the generous support given by INED (the French National Demographic Studies Institute) toward our meetings in Paris over the past four years and its contribution to funding the translation of the French-language chapters, the Reader would still be awaiting completion. INED has supported research on VAW since becoming a partner in the first French survey on the topic, coordinated by Maryse Jaspard in 2000. It must be said that it is extremely difficult to convince institutions of the importance of high quality translation in scientific exchange within Europe. The particular theme we are dealing with in the Reader made the challenge even greater.

The excellent work of the translators Harriet Coleman (France) and Ulrike Mietz (Germany) has been an invaluable component of the production process for the English version of the Reader.

Kathrin Vogt from the University of Bielefeld assisted us in the final stage of the project, particularly for the literature reference checks.

We also thank our partners, families and close colleagues who gave us support by showing understanding that our shared time and energy was often sapped by the additional work that this project demanded.

Last but not least, we would like to dedicate this book to the many migrant and minority women in Europe who have struggled against violence in the past and those that are still working to stop all violence against women, as well as to those who are fighting for the full bodily and personal integrity of migrant/minority women in Europe and elsewhere in the world.

Contents

Part 3: Forms and Effects of Violence Against Women

Preface

Renate Klein

In the early 1990s, I moved from Germany to the United States. One consequence of this move was a change in my perspective on European research on Violence Against Women (VAW). As long as I had been in Germany differences between European countries had stood out but viewed from the U.S. they receded into the background. Instead, now the whole of Europe came into clearer relief as a large, complex, and diverse entity. I became increasingly interested in a European voice on VAW and began to organize a network of like-minded scholars and practitioners. It was during meetings of this European Network on Conflict, Gender, and Violence that I met the editors of this book and many of its contributors. They bring to this volume knowledge, awareness, and integrity.

The 1990s were a period of intense international and European networking related to VAW, by researchers and practitioners alike; it was infused with energy by the fall of the Berlin Wall and the unprecedented opening and subsequent integration of Europe, punctuated by the large women-focused UN conferences – 1993 in Vienna, 1995 in Beijing – and reflected in the VAW-related initiatives over the past two decades by the Council of Europe and the European Union.

Networking thrives on the discovery of shared interests and concerns and the ability to join forces in the pursuit of a common goal. In terms of practice this was perhaps most obvious in the development of Europe-wide standards for intervention in VAW, led by the WAVE network out of Vienna. In terms of research, the Co-ordination Action on Human Rights Violations out of the University Osnabrück pushed the integration of European prevalence and evaluation research to a new level. Networking also reveals topics that have received less attention than they deserve. The role of ethnicity in VAW is one of these areas. It is to the great credit of the editors of this book to present, to an international readership, the first comprehensive Reader on VAW and ethnicity in Europe. They are exceptionally well-suited to do this.

Established scholars in their respective disciplines, the editors have assembled an excellent group of authors. Working in different European countries, the contributors approach ethnicity and VAW in Europe within a broad and comprehensive framework. Ethnicity and VAW is not a homogenous phenomenon. Women from ethnic and racial minorities face different legal, cultural, and economic circumstances depending on which European country they live in. Public debates about women, gender, ethnicity and violence are shaped by national discourses about citizenship. For instance, while the notion (in Britain) of multi-culturalism emphasizes the presence of multiple cultural identities within a British nation state, the emphasis in France is on the integration within a French nation of individual citizens sharing French citizenship and identity.

Public and scholarly debates also reflect different histories. In the U.S. the category of race is predominantly and inextricably linked to the system of slavery and the civil rights movement, whereas ethnicity appears more often in relation to immigration, and Native Americans tend to be ignored in either discourse. In Europe, categories of ethnicity and race are linked to different histories again. They include the legacies of colonialism and the Nazi dictatorship. They also include the contemporary immigration and migration of people across Europe and the treatment of Roma, Sinti, and other traditionally nomadic groups.

A thoughtful analysis of VAW within these complex contexts presents a major challenge, which the editors and their authors have taken up with gusto. Empirical accounts of diverse experiences of VAW are balanced with analyses of similar structural problems. Underlying this balancing act is recognition that VAW reflects compound vulnerabilities in terms of how women suffer and how they seek help and redress. This is also a matter of how societies construct this suffering and help-seeking and how researchers can move to intellectually honest accounts of the diversity of VAW. The book offers a much needed broadening of intersectional approaches from the early focus on race, class, and gender to accounts that incorporate the challenges of cultural relativism and national security discourses.

These analyses have been lacking until now. The book is essential reading for anybody interested in a fuller story of VAW, one that neither excludes ethnic minority women nor simplifies or exoticizes their stories. The book's unique contribution is that it addresses issues of ethnicity and VAW within and across national contexts, and thus makes visible how ethnicity and VAW are at once situated and discursively constructed in these. In doing so, the book also breaks through the habit of framing VAW as something that can happen to any woman. While this may be true in theory, in practice some women are more vulnerable than others, some have more money, political and social clout than others, and some live in precarious circumstances at the margin of society.

As I am writing this, Dominique Strauss-Kahn, former head of the International Monetary Fund and potential contender for the French presidency in 2012, is under house arrest in New York City for alleged sex crimes against a hotel maid. Strauss-Kahn is a wealthy white male and, until his resignation a couple of days ago, held one of the world economy's most influential posts. The maid is a low-paid black immigrant from West Africa holding one of the world's countless dead-end jobs. Regardless of the outcomes of the case, the press coverage about it already is a case study of how VAW reporting is entwined with sexist discourses about women, men, and national character. In order to move beyond simplistic accounts, we need careful and accessible scholarship. Within the cacophony of blogs and tweets this book sounds a reasoned voice for the thinking person.

Newburgh, Maine, May 2011
Professor in Applied Social Sciences, London Metropolitan University
Associate Professor in Human Development & Family Studies,
University of Maine

Introduction

Ravi K. Thiara, Stephanie Condon and *Monika Schröttle*

This Reader, the first ever to bring together research and writing on issues of violence against women (VAW) and ethnicity across Europe, was born out of conversations that began between the editors during the pan-European project entitled Co-ordination Action on Human Rights and Violence (CAHRV) in 2005. At this time, academic and policy work on VAW and ethnicity in many European countries was still in its infancy or marginal to wider discussions on gendered violence. Hence, this volume was motivated by a concern about the lack of visibility of VAW and minority ethnic and migrant (MEM) women's issues and the absence of MEM women articulating these issues within European conferences and events on VAW.

As has been established by extensive research and policy development, VAW is extremely widespread, and costs health, welfare and criminal justice services billions each year. More pronounced than even the economic costs are the human costs of the problem, which range from chronic physical health issues, severe injury, mental and emotional distress, and death. The recognition of VAW as an enduring problem, its costs to society, concerted activism by women's movements, as well as international developments, within the United Nations (UN) in particular, began to shape responses to the issue across Europe. The recognition of VAW as a human rights concern within the UN, in the early 1990s, following after CEDAW, and the adoption of the Declaration on the Elimination of Violence Against Women culminated in the creation of the United Nations Special Rapporteur on Violence Against Women (UNSRVAW) to monitor VAW worldwide (UN SRVAW 2009). Not without its challenges, the Special Rapporteur mandate established in 1994 has provided the necessary push and a momentum in the requirement of national governments to address VAW, the definition and scope of which has evolved over the years. In addition to these developments, the Council of Europe, since the Ministerial Conference in Rome in 1993, has explicitly recognized that the elimination of VAW is central to ensuring democracy and human rights. In general, although VAW is now no longer regarded as a private family affair, it remains an intractable problem, despite important developments and progress in addressing it across many countries, including in Europe.

While ethnicity and gender are not reducible to either minority ethnic groups or women, in this Reader our concern with ethnicity and VAW is focused on issues for MEM women experiencing gendered violence. Since the Reader is the first of its kind, bringing together much of the existing work on this issue, it presents a challenge to the hitherto absence and marginality and the fragmentary knowledge base about MEM women within academic, policy, and practice debates across much of Europe.

Migration and ethnicity

Migration of people from MEM communities is common across much of Europe where the presence of a younger generation of minority ethnic groups who are European citizens, along with more recent migrations, are now an established fact. There are, of course, important differences in terms of periods of migration and the range of minority ethnic groups that have migrated and settled in each national context. This trajectory of migration is influenced, among other factors, by historical links between colonial powers and the colonized, which saw the movement of people from ex-colonies to colonial centres. Women's role within these migration processes has not always received extensive academic and research attention even though the feminization of migration to many countries in Europe has been highlighted since the early 1980s (Morokvasic 1984; Phizaclea 1983; 2003; Andall 2003).

Just as the migration and settlement of minority ethnic groups across Europe has differed, so have policy and political discourses about their incorporation into the host society, frequently dominated by the assimilation/integration versus multi-culturalism argument, and the reception given to them by the majority community (Favell 1998). The structural location of MEM groups has in turn shaped their own responses in terms of self organization and activism to challenge their marginality. For instance, in the UK, drawing on their experiences of anti-colonial struggles, black migrants began very early on to self organize and set up political organizations that provided a challenge to their discriminatory treatment. Within this movement, black feminists also began to forge their own autonomous organizations from the 1970s onwards, a few of which continue to exist even today and have been a crucial part of the challenge to VAW within MEM communities. Across many European countries, however, organization by MEM has not been as strong as in the UK and issues have remained rather marginalized. Despite such important differences, many similarities can also be seen in the construction of the immigrant as 'other' and related discourses.

Gender, ethnicity and violence against women

With few exceptions, theoretical and empirical separation in the study of gender and ethnicity across Europe has been noted by numerous researchers[1]. There has been some important work on gender and ethnicity, influenced by theoretical developments in 'race' and ethnic studies and post colonial feminism, which has sought to challenge the negative and homogenous construction of MEM women (see Lutz 1997). Within the wider scholarship on ethnicity and on gender across much of Europe, despite extensive literature on immigration and ethnicity, the links between gender, ethnicity and VAW has been a particularly marked absence (Condon 2005).

VAW, not always so termed, has been at the forefront of feminist struggles across Europe since the 1970s. However, the form this has taken has varied, shaped as it was by local and international impetus, as has the content and goals of VAW and women's movements. Developments, including legislation, legal and support measures, to address VAW also vary across European countries where the main focus has been on domestic violence (see Martinez and Schröttle et al., CAHRV Reports 2006–2007). Interventions to support victims of VAW vary across countries. For instance, in Austria and Germany intervention centres for survivors of domestic violence are run by non-governmental organizations (NGOs) but are funded by the Federal Ministries of the Interior, Social and Family Affairs. In the Netherlands, victims are supported through general Victim Support Centres within which specialist domestic violence support is provided. In the UK, Women's Aid, a federation of local independent refuge and other domestic violence support services, along with Refuge, a national organization with local services, remain the largest providers of support (Humphreys and Carter et al. 2006, CAHRV Reports: 11). Rather than being concerned with the details of VAW and immigration responses across Europe, however, this Reader is concerned with the impact of these at both symbolic and material levels on MEM women experiencing VAW in all its forms.

---

1 See Lloyd, 2000; and Andall's book on gender, ethnicity and migration provided an important early contribution to linking these issues by giving recognition to minority ethnic women's social, cultural and political experiences in Europe.

There are numerous studies across Europe that focus on issues of VAW in different European national contexts and provide an important insight (see Martinez and Schröttle et al., CAHRV Reports 2006–2007). Much of these, with few exceptions (see chapter by Condon, Lesne and Schröttle in this Reader), do not substantively address the location of MEM women within these debates and developments. The Daphne Programme, which has funded numerous research initiatives on domestic violence and VAW, also provides some useful information (European Commission 2009). Overall, in much of the debates about ethnicity and immigration as well as gender and VAW, MEM women have either been absent and marginal or more recently constructed and represented in particular ways. It is only recently that some researchers have begun to focus on the particular issues encountered by MEM women facing gendered violence, work that has resulted in publications that have begun to foreground these linkages and intersections (Hovarth and Kelly 2007; Sokoloff and Pratt 2005; Thiara and Gill 2010). Indeed, it is true to say that, with the exception of those in this Reader, there is extremely limited research and information available across Europe, making the knowledge base across different contexts very uneven. What is available often focuses on women's experiences of culturally specific forms of harm or constructs VAW as an issue of culture rather than gender. The UK, where the history of settlement and activism is longer for MEM women, perhaps provides a richer source of information and knowledge.

In addressing VAW across different groups and national contexts, the SRVAW has been significant in expanding and nuancing the debate about the causes and consequences of VAW and the accountability of states to address its wide ranging effects on different groups of women. For instance, in challenging the public/private divide and 'expanding state accountability[2] beyond private actors for private acts of violence', the SRVAW has asked states to address the external pressures that exacerbate domestic violence for particular groups, including racism, socio-economic marginalization and restrictive immigration policies (UNSRVAW 2009: 12). This has led to a call for countries such as Sweden, with established gender-equality policies, to address the remaining gaps in terms of gender inequality as well as protection gaps for particular groups of women, including immigrant, refugee or

2 The due diligence standard has been central to developing state responsibility for violence perpetrated by private actors in public and private arenas. It imposes on the state the responsibility for illegal acts that are not directly committed by the state or its agents but by private actors on account of state failure to take sufficient steps to prevent the illegal acts from occurring. Equally, once an illegal act has occurred, the state's inaction and failure to investigate, prosecute or punish the act perpetrated by a private actor amounts to neglect of the state obligation to be duly diligent (UNSRVAW 2009: 25).

asylum seeking. In the Netherlands, attention has been drawn not only to gender-neutral state responses (as part of gender mainstreaming) but the 'cultural essentialist responses' (p.13) to violence in migrant communities. In general, it is underlined that effective responses to VAW require 'multifaceted strategies' to tackle multiple violence forms, including addressing laws that exclude women from accessing support and protection because of their immigration status (UNSRVAW 2009; Roy 2008; Thiara and Gill 2010).

The Reader integrates parallel discourses on VAW and ethnicity in Europe to examine the particular issue for MEM women. Although some countries have a stronger evidence base than others, in selecting contributions attempts were made to give voice to all countries, though some disparity may still remain. Consequently, debates differ and in some countries the experiences of MEM are only starting to be highlighted whilst in others debate is inextricably linked with wider critiques of politics, policy and practice – both mainstream and within the VAW sector. Although research evidence is extremely limited on MEM women's experiences of VAW and their access to legal and other support, research shows that they experience greater exclusion and vastly reduced access to legal solutions for violence when compared with women who have secure immigration status. An Austrian study shows that immigrant women are often unable to contact the police because they do not speak the language or are afraid of involving authorities (see Humphreys and Carter et al. 2006). Consequently, many MEM seek assistance from refuges or women's shelters, where they are often over-represented (see chapter by Creazzo et al. in this Reader). This has led some to argue that this over-representation means that MEM women face few barriers to accessing help. However, such arguments ignore that majority (white) European women have often more recourse to other actions and measures when compared with MEM women, who are socially and economically marginalized, with greater dependency on men and families, and whose options are likely to be reduced. Thus, immigration status, or lack of citizenship, continues to be a major cause of unequal access to protection for women experiencing VAW across Europe. Different laws and legislations exist across the countries to shape this. For instance, the CAHRV study viewed immigration as a fourth planet in determining women's access to justice and protection (Humphreys and Carter et al. 2006). Indeed, immigration status breaches human rights and fails to offer women protection against violence. Moreover, in the name of protecting women from actual or potential violence, including forced marriage, government responses have been to restrict immigration (Bredal 2005).

However, there is still no European wide study documenting the range and nature of responses to MEM women. Without this, it is hard to say, with any certainty, if the support and protection needs of such women are being met adequately. Even in those countries that provide some insight into effective responses to some MEM groups, recent developments suggest that these are being eroded rather than being strengthened. The aim of this Reader is to provide a more cohesive knowledge base about the intersection of ethnicity, gender and VAW whilst aiming to give primacy to MEM women's specificity within VAW discourses. It further seeks to foreground the complexity and interconnections between different categories of VAW. The contributions to this Reader also highlight the current absence of MEM women themselves writing about these issues across many countries in Europe. Whilst gaps remain and there is much more research to be done to explore the specificity of MEM women's experiences of VAW, along with the responses to this, this Reader provides some insight into the particular aspects of a number of European contexts in constructing discourses around VAW and ethnicity. Discourses have taken distinct forms across Europe, though there is also some commonality, and more recently the intersectional discrimination which compounds risks for women from marginalized or racialised communities has increasingly been emphasized, albeit in essentialist ways.

Violence against women and ethnicity

The intersection of VAW and ethnicity has generated interesting debate in recent years. VAW within MEM communities and especially violence experienced by MEM women and their descendents has become a significant issue in politics, policy, and media debates. Much of this has been critiqued for essentialising minority/migrant cultures and communities and for seeing them as inherently violent (see chapter by Manier in this volume). Indeed, the SRVAW has problematised this approach arguing that

> The particularization of domestic violence among non-Western immigrants as a cultural problem…[is] problematic, as it discounted the relationship of socio-economic disadvantage and restrictive immigrant policies to domestic violence. (UNSRVAW 2009: 13).

The growth of religious fundamentalism and 'Muslim terrorism' with its accompanying security agenda since 9/11 and the conservative political trends fuelled by this has added a particular angle to debates about violence against MEM women. The greater polarization between countries and communities created after 9/11 has provided fertile ground for cultural discourses, which pose a serious challenge to gender equality and MEM women's rights, both from within their communities and from external nationalist discourses (see Patel and Siddiqui in this volume). Thus, discourses on 'harmful traditional practices', such as forced marriage, honour-based violence, and female genital mutilation, have at times become parallel discourses to that of VAW in some national contexts, despite the attempts by many MEM and other feminists to resist this and conceptualise these practices as gendered violence where the intersection of culture and gender are given primacy (Bredal 2005; 2011; Gill and Anitha 2011).

Two trends within cultural discourses can be discerned and have been problematised (see Chantler and Gangoli in this volume; Welchmann and Hossain 2005). On the one hand are arguments, underpinned by cultural relativism, which reject universal human rights and undermine women's equality (articulated from within cultural communities). On the other hand are cultural essentialist approaches which, in the process of 'othering', view some cultures, communities and countries as inherently and uniformly toxic for women, a view that has taken a stranglehold in the popular imagination across much of Europe. It also serves to view violence in majority societies as individualized aberrations (see Chantler and Gangoli in this volume). Both place MEM women, subjectively and structurally, in extremely difficult and contradictory positions. Moreover, such responses have failed to improve the situation for MEM women, who frequently find themselves having to negate the valued aspects of their traditions and cultures to be constructed as victims of traditional and patriarchal violence. This leaves women with restricted options as many want to be protected against male violence without making the choice of 'exit' from their communities (see Gill and Mitra-Khan 2010). Together, both perspectives fail to address the underlying causes of VAW. To make connections within and between different women and VAW, the importance of exposing patterns of domination within rather than differences between cultures, interrogating hegemonic interpretations of culture, and addressing the patriarchal socio-economic and political interests within and outside that benefit from such interpretations has been emphasised. In some countries, MEM have carved out a third space for their voices and indeed were the first critics of the increasing move towards religious fundamentalism (as in the UK through the Women Against Fundamentalism group).

Thus, cultural discourses (cultural relativists and cultural essentialists) resist women's rights and uphold patriarchal order, on the one hand, and 'fix', through homogenizing constructions, cultural communities, on the other. This is further explored in 'their' culture, 'our' honour section of the Reader. Indeed, as can be seen from a number of countries in Europe, cultural essentialism serves to justify state action or inaction on VAW against MEM women. By highlighting discourses that reinforce a view of MEM as experiencing greater levels of VAW, some European state responses to addressing violence against MEM women have involved the tightening of immigration controls which have been couched as protecting MEM women and outlining requirements for social and cultural integration, but which fail to address their socio-economic and political marginality (see Hester et al. 2008).

Culture versus gender

As noted above, the utilisation of 'culture' by particular religious-cultural political projects, where cultural justifications are used to limit women's rights, has been increasingly documented and critiqued. Of particular concern to feminist writers has been the acceptance by government and political players, and sometimes feminists, of not only the dominant patriarchal voices within communities which marginalize women's (dissenting) voices but a viewpoint which privileges culture in justifying violence against MEM women (as in the UK for instance; see Patel and Siddiqui in this volume). Indeed, the importance and value of foregrounding women's voices as a counter narrative, which highlight the contestation within communities and disrupt homogenizing explanations of culture, to hegemonic interpretations of culture and identity and which serve to limit secular spaces, has been urged (Patel and Siddiqui 2010). Such competing narratives from women highlight the fact that: *the threat to women's human rights comes from the monopoly over the interpretation and representation of culture by the powerful few rather than from culture per se'*. (UNSRVAW 2009: 29)

Writers have for some time now pointed to the role that women play as cultural entrepreneurs in their constant negotiation and renegotiation of cultural norms and values which leads, in migration settings, to hybrid or syncretic cultural forms. This has highlighted the importance of seeing culture not as a static but as a constantly evolving, contested and re/negotiated terrain. To only see MEM women as 'victims' of their cultures, a view widely challenged, then is to do a disservice to the positive role that culture also plays in many MEM women's lives. Moreover, the simplistic view of women as victims of their cultures from which they need protection, a logical outcome of the acceptance of the 'harmful traditional practices' argument, has been widely challenged, as essentialising MEM communities as backward and uncivilised. For these reasons, for instance, the SRVAW rejected the term 'harmful traditional practices' in favour of 'harmful practices' in relation to cultural practices that erode women's rights (see UNSRVAW 2009).

To only see VAW as a facet of cultural communities is also to separate VAW from structural inequalities underpinning 'race', class, and gender systems and results in inadequate conceptual explanations. At an international level, the emphasis placed on addressing the causes and consequences of VAW through the UN has enabled emphasis to be placed on gender inequality and an interrogation of approaches that de-link VAW from the overall subordination of women. Thus, when VAW is viewed as an outcome of gender discrimination it becomes an inevitable outcome of unequal socio-economic, cultural and political structures. This perspective enables us to see women not simply as vulnerable victims in need of protection but VAW as an outcome of a gendered order, frequently challenged at individual and collective levels, that privileges male violence, individual and collective, which is used to ensure women's compliance. This is further compounded for MEM women who are located at the intersection of multiple axes of oppression and discrimination. However, discourses on honour-based violence and forced marriage, as highlighted by a number of contributions to this volume, have tended to privilege culture rather than gender in explanations which draw on essentialized notions of culture and tradition and serve to stigmatise MEM women and their communities. Such discourses have created a binary of the emancipated white woman and the oppressed MEM woman, both of which serve to normalize the violence and discrimination of white women and to marginalize MEM women (UNSRVAW 2009: 36).

Honour-based violence as an explanation for the high levels of control and violence in MEM women's lives has become commonplace in recent years. The potency of the forced marriage/honour-based violence discourse is evident when practitioners and policy makers are found to use 'honour' to explain what would have been termed as domestic violence not so long ago. This re-packaging of the range of violence experiences of MEM women can serve to de-link their experiences from wider VAW issues and ghettoize them into their 'cultural and traditional practices' enclaves. As a counter to such cultural explanations, honour-based violence and its links to control over women's sexuality has been pointed out by several writers, who have highlighted the ways in which religious and cultural arguments view women as markers and custodians of community honour, thereby coercing women to conform to notions of the ideal/honourable woman and avoid male violence through any sexual transgressions (Sen 2005; Welchmann and Hossain 2005). It has thus been argued that gender has to feature large in any explanation of such forms of VAW. Although there are some differences, this form of control is not just specific to MEM women as most forms of VAW are often used as an instrument to control and regulate women's sexual behaviour. This is reflected in much of the research on domestic violence where women frequently speak of sexual jealousy as being a root cause or justification for men's violence.

Intersectionality

> being oppressed….is always constructed and intermeshed in other social divisions (Yuval-Davis 2006: 195).

Whilst critiques of those who use culture as an explanation/justification for VAW help us to shift attention towards gender as the dominant explanation, intersectionality allows for the particularity of violence against MEM women to be understood as well as shape responses. The importance of using an intersectional approach to identify and to address the effects of the simultaneous operation of multiple systems of oppression/discrimination rather than addressing each in isolation has been underlined by several writers (Sauer 2011; Thiara and Gill 2010; Verloo 2006; Yuval-Davis 2006). Whilst there has been a rich debate about intersectionality among feminist writers, it is not our purpose here to rehearse this. However, we, along with several contributors to this volume, utilize the concept of intersectionality as our preferred explanatory tool for unpacking the complexity of VAW issues as they impact on the lives and experiences of MEM women who are located within overlapping and interconnected structures of discrimination and power.

In short, 'intersectionality' or an intersectional analysis suggests that in a society based on multiple systems of domination, individual experiences are not shaped by single identities/locations (as a woman or a minority ethnic person). Thus, it recognises that some women's experiences are marked by multiple forms of oppression and subject positions, and that individual social categories can be further broken down so that 'women' can be situated in powerful/less ways to one another (Crenshaw 1991). This involves looking at how power is inscribed *within* individual systems of oppression and *between* them (Razack 1998; Thiara and Gill 2010), and which can create both oppression and opportunity (Collins 1990; Zin and Dill 1996). Intersectionality or intersectional analysis has recently been used to examine VAW in the UK, US and Canada (see Sokoloff and Pratt 2005), although debate about whether some of this reproduces additive notions of oppression, especially when used in a limited way within political mobilisation, still remains rife (Yuval-Davis 2006).

Whereas many explanations of VAW or ethnicity and gender either homogenize the diverse experiences of women or fragment the experience of violence of individual women, intersectionality allows for the universality of VAW without losing these particularities in women's experiences, whether individual or collective. Through its focus on intersecting social divisions and multiple systems of domination/oppression, intersectionality has the potential to explain complexity and difference without resorting to essentialist explanations (Phoenix and Pattynama 2006).

A note on translation and terminology

Given the complexity of streamlining terms and definitions – of ethnicity and of violence against women – across the Reader and to avoid imposing our definitions and academic disciplines, a first decision made was to allow authors to speak for themselves in the terms used in the national contexts in which they are writing and using their local policy and political frames. This has resulted in a volume that includes contributions from activists and researchers rooted in various social science disciplines which is invariably reflected in concepts and terms used. It also lends to a more nuanced and richer insight into current debates about VAW and MEM women across the different European contexts.

Second, a belief in the necessity of bringing these writings on MEM women and VAW closer to people working in the field of violence prevention and victim support, as well as to academics, led us to the idea of producing the volume in the three main European languages, French, German and English. Authors were invited to write in the language with which they felt most comfortable. This was to raise various challenges, not only for the co-ordination and funding of the translation work but also in terms of agreeing equivalent terms for concepts and categories socially and politically located in specific national contexts. Collaboration within the CAHRV programme had made us aware of semantic issues involved when comparing research findings and also of the complexities of translating terms into English. The question of which 'English' also arose, as many European researchers outside the UK publish in English whilst not necessarily using terms used by researchers writing in the UK. Knowing the various standpoints in Europe on how to categorize im/migrants and their descendents, we had anticipated that the translation of chapters written in French or in German would throw up a number of problems. We opted against generalizing the use of a single terminology, such as ethnic minorites, for instance, which not only does not correspond to academic or political conceptualisations of integration and referring to immigrants and their descendants but is also inappropriate in contexts such as Germany, where many im/migrants from Eastern Europe or Russia are considered to be 'German ethnics'.

Organisation of the Reader

Our invitation to colleagues who responded to the call for contributions was to focus on a particular aspect of gender violence against women and its intersections with ethnicity or racism and to set it within a national context. The Reader aimed to reflect the growing body of knowledge and thinking on these politically sensitive issues. After much discussion among the editors, four themes were identified for the Reader and when the call for contributions was made, potential contributors were asked to indicate which theme their papers would address. Although some modifications took place when we became clearer about the range of research that was in existence and the continuing gaps, these themes are reflected in the four sections of the Reader.

In seeking to share knowledge about VAW in Europe, the first section outlines the progress made in addressing VAW and the challenges that remain in tackling this complex issue across all countries. The second section, making the links, discusses the ways in which the inter-connections between gender, ethnicity and violence can be conceptualized (through the concept of intersectionality for example) and outlines the different forms of violence against minority women (as a continuum for example). The forms and effects of gender-based violence, the third section, includes writing about the ways in which racialised and gendered processes generate and influence different forms of violence against women. In the fourth section, responses to gender-based violence, contributors look critically at different responses to the issue of ethnicity and violence against women in the different contexts and examine legal reform and policy responses, support services, NGO/community responses and autonomous organization by women from MEM communities. How these link with debates on integration, multi-culturalism and cohesion are also explored as is the role of the state in the construction and representation of minority communities and 'culture'. The ways in which MEM women are figured into these debates and what implications this has for practice responses to gender-based violence are some further issues considered by the authors. The final section, is it a question of (their) 'culture' and (our) 'honour', looks critically at some of the debates that use 'culture' to justify non-intervention or greater scrutiny of communities as well as discourses that use 'honour' to argue for or against intervention in issues of VAW. How different players use both 'culture' and 'honour' to justify a particular position and how these arguments impact on the situation of MEM women affected by gender-based violence is also considered.

This Reader is an important initial step in synthesizing writing and debate on ethnicity, racism and VAW across Europe. We hope that it will be used by researchers, policy makers and practitioners to inform the future development of effective responses to MEM affected by gender-based violence. Beyond this, we hope that it will act as an inspiration for others to continue the process, begun here, of exploring these complex mechanisms and processes and their effects at individual, collective, and societal levels.

References

Andall, Jacqueline (ed.) (2003): Gender and Ethnicity in Contemporary Europe. Oxford: Berg.

Bredal, Anja (2005): Tackling Forced Marriages in the Nordic Countries: Between Women's Rights and Immigration Control. In: Welchmann, Lynn/Hossain, Sara (eds.) (2005): 'Honour': Crimes, Paradigms, and Violence Against Women. London and New York: Zed Books, pp. 332–353.

Bredal, Anja (2011): Border control to prevent forced marriages: Choosing between protecting women and protecting the nation. In: Gill, Aisha/Anitha, Sundari (eds.) (2011): Forced Marriage: Introducing a social justice and human rights perspective. London: Zed Books.

CAHRV, reports of Co-ordination Action on Human Rights Violations. Internet: http://www.cahrv.uni-osnabrueck.de/reddot/190.htm

Collins, Patricia Hill (1990): Black Feminist Thought. London: Unwin Hyman.

Condon, Stephanie (2005): Violence against Women in France: Issues of Ethnicity. In: Smeenk, Wilma/Malsch, Marijke (eds.) (2005): Family Violence and Police Response: Learning from Research Policy and Practice. Alderhot: Ashgate.

Crenshaw, Kimberle (1991): Mapping the Margins: Intersectionality, Identity Politics and Violence Against Women of Color. In: Stanford Law Review 43, pp. 1241–1245.

European Commission (2009): From Classical Myth to Cutting Edge Action: More Than a Decade of Daphne. European Commission Directorate-General Justice, freedom and Security.

Favell, Adrian (1998): Philosophies of integration: immigration and the idea of citizenship in France and Britain. Basingstoke, UK: Macmillan.

Gill, Aisha K./Anitha, Sundari (2011): Forced Marriage: Introducing a Social Justice and Human Rights Perspective. London: Zed Books.

Gill, Aisha K./Mitra-Kahn, Trishima (2010): 'Moving Towards a Multiculturalism without Culture': Constructing a Victim-Friendly Human Rights Approach to Forced Marriage in the UK. In: Thiara, Ravi K./Gill, Aisha K. (eds.) (2010): Violence Against Women in South Asian Communities: Issues for Policy and Practice. London: Jessica Kingsley Publishers, pp.128–155.

Hester, Marianne/Chantler, Khatidja/Gangoli, Geetanjali/Devgon, Jaswinder/Sharma, Sandya/Singleton, Ann (2008): Forced Marriage: The Risk Factors and the Effects of Raising the Minimum Age for a Sponsor, and Leave to Enter the UK as a Sponsor or Fiance(e). Available at: www.bristol.ac.uk/sps/downloads/FPCW/forcedmarriageresearchsummary08.pdf.

Hovarth, Miranda/Kelly, Liz (2007): From the Outset: Why Violence Should be a Core Cross-strand Priority Theme for the Commission for Equality and Human Rights. London: End Violence Against Women Campaign.

Humphreys, Cathy/Carter, Rachel (2006): The Justice System as an arena for the protection of human rights for women and children experiencing violence and abuse. CAHRV Report. Available at: http://www.cahrv.uni-osnabrueck.de/reddot/190.htm

Lloyd, Cathie (2000): Genre, migration et ethnicité: perspectives féministes en Grande Bretagne. In: Cahiers du CEDREF, 8/9, Femmes en migrations. Aperçus de recherche, pp. 17–42.

Lutz, Helma (1997): The Limits of European-ness: Immigrant women in Fortress Europe. In: Feminist Review, 57, pp. 93–111.

Martinez, Manuela/Schröttle, Monika et al. (2006a): State of European research on the prevalence of interpersonal violence and its impact on health and human rights. CAHRV – Report 2006. Co-ordination Action on Human Rights Violations funded through the European Commission, 6th Framework Programme, Project No. 506348. Internet: www.cahrv.uni-osnabrueck.de/reddot/190.htm (01.05.2011)

Martinez, Manuela/Schröttle, Monika et al. (2006b): Comparative reanalysis of prevalence of violence against women and health impact data in Europe – obstacles and possible solutions. Testing a comparative approach on selected studies. CAHRV – Report 2006. Co-ordination Action on Human Rights Violations funded through the European Commission, 6th Framework Programme, Project No. 506348. Internet: www.cahrv.uni-osnabrueck.de/reddot/190.htm (01.05.2011)

Martinez, Manuela/Schröttle, Monika et al. (2007): Perspectives and standards for good practice in data collection on interpersonal violence at European level. CAHRV – Report 2006. Co-ordination Action on Human Rights Violations funded through the European Commission, 6th Framework Programme, Project No. 506348. Internet: www.cahrv.uni-osnabrueck.de/reddot/190.htm (01.05.2011)

Morokvasic, Mirjana (1984): Birds of passage are also women…. In: International Migration Review (Special issue, Women in Migration), 18(4), pp.1–29.

Morokvasic, Mirjana (1983): Women in Migration: Beyond the Reductionist Outlook. In: Phizacklea, Annie (ed.) (1983): One Way Ticket: Migration and Female Labour. London: Routledge.

Patel, Pragna/Siddiqui, Hannana (2010): Shrinking Secular Spaces: Asian Women at the Intersect of Race, Religion and Gender. In: Thiara, Ravi K./Gill, Aisha K. (eds.) (2010): Violence Against Women in South Asian Communities: Issues for Policy and Practice. London: Jessica Kingsley Publishers, pp.102–127.

Phizacklea, Annie (ed.) (1983): One Way Ticket: Migration and Female Labour. London: Routledge and Kegan Paul.

Phizacklea, Annie (2003): Gendered Actors in Migration. In: Andall, Jacqueline (ed.) (2003): Gender and Ethnicity in Contemporary Europe. Oxford: Berg, pp. 23–38.

Phoenix, Anne/Pattynama, P. (2006): Intersectionality. In: European Journal of Women's Studies 13, 3, pp. 187–192.

Razack, Sherene (1998): What is to gained by Looking White people in the Eye? Race in Sexual Violence Cases. In: Razack, S. (ed.) (1998): Looking White People in the Eye: Gender, Race and Culture in Courtrooms and Classrooms. Toronto: University of Toronto Press.

Roy, Sumanta (2008): No Recourse – No Duty to Care – Experiences of BAMER Women and Children affected by Domestic Violence and Insecure Immigration Status in the UK. London: Imkaan.

Sauer, Birgit (2011): Migration, Geschlecht, Gewalt. Überlegungen zu einem intersektionellen Gewaltbegriff. In: GENDER, 2/2011.

Sen, Purna (2005): Crimes of Honour, value and meaning. In: Welchmann, Lynn/Hossain, Sara (eds.) (2005): 'Honour': Crimes, Paradigms, and Violence Against Women. London and New York: Zed Books, pp. 42–63.

Sokoloff, Natalie/Pratt, Christina (eds.) (2005): Domestic Violence at the Margins: Readings on Race, Class, Gender and Culture. New Brunswick: Rutgers University Press.

Thiara, Ravi K./Gill, Aisha K. (eds.) (2010): Violence Against Women in South Asian Communities: Issues for Policy and Practice. London: Jessica Kingsley Publishers.

United Nations Special Rapporteur on Violence Against Women (2009): 15 Years of the United Nations Special Rapporteur on Violence Against Women, Its Causes and Consequences (1994–2009): A Critical Review.

United Nations Special Rapporteur on Violence Against Women: Country mission report on the Netherlands, A/HRC/4/34/Add.4.

Verloo, Mieke (2006): Multiple Inequalities, Intersectionality and the European Union. In: European Journal of Women's Studies 13, 3, pp. 211–228.

Welchmann, Lynn/Hossain, Sara (eds.) (2005): 'Honour': Crimes, Paradigms, and Violence Against Women. London and New York: Zed Books.

Yuval-Davis, Nira (2006): Intersectionality and Feminist Politics. In: European Journal of Women's Studies 13, 3, pp. 193–209.

Zin, M./Dill, B. (1996): Theorising Difference from Multiracial Feminsm. In: Zin, M. Baca/Hondagneu-Sotelo, P./Messner, M.A. (eds.) (1996): Through the Prism of Difference: Readings on Sex and Gender. Needham Heights, MA: Allyn and Bacon.

Part 1: Building and Sharing Knowledge about Violence Against Women in Europe

Violence Against Women: Still a Political Problem Throughout Europe

Rosa Logar

> It is incumbent upon those of us who already have power and prestige to shoulder the responsibility of expanding models, examining our practices, and giving voice to those who are silenced among us. This cannot be done without fear and discouragement: those of us who live in safe contexts experience the risk of speaking out, and we understand more clearly how in the lives of the invisible, the marginal, and the disenfranchised, every move toward safety entails risk and may intensify danger. It is sobering and distressing to realize that, although anti-domestic violence work has promoted greater safety for some individuals, many remain in a position as dangerous and vulnerable as ever (Richie 1996). The words of the Jewish Talmud remind us: It is not your job to finish the work, but you are not free to walk away from it. (Bograd 2007:34)

Introduction

Violence against women, which was made an issue of public discussion by the second wave women's movement in the early 1970s, continues to be a severe problem in Europe. According to a prevalence study carried out in Germany, one out of four women have experienced physical or sexual violence (or both) by current or former intimate partners and this is mirrored across much of Europe (Schröttle and Müller 2004a: 7). In particular, immigrant women of Turkish origin are suffering physical and sexual violence significantly more often than the average female population (Schröttle and Müller 2004b: 27). Violence has massive effects on health, which is already in a poor state among a section of immigrant women, apparently in connection with their difficult social situation, characterised by low wages as well as inadequate and insecure occupational integration (Schröttle and Khelaifat 2008: 19f).

The purpose of this article is to highlight that while it has been possible, to a certain extent, to raise the awareness of violence against women as an issue of social relevance, many problems still remain and not all groups of women benefit from the measures taken so far. Immigrants and minority ethnic women face multiple discrimination, and in recent years they have also been confronted with cultural relativism: violence is perceived as a part of their culture, and thus as a normal occurrence. Parallel to this, increasing attention has been given to violence in immigrant/ethnic minority communities, in particular forms of violence that are attributed to certain cultures such as honour killings or forced marriage. Batsleer et al. 2002 (cited in Thiara 2008: 144) have pointed out that violence for 'cultural' reasons either tends to be ignored (homogenised absence) or overemphasised (pathologised presence). As a result of such contradictory discourses on culture and violence, immigrant and minority ethnic women are becoming stigmatised, they are inadequately protected against violence, and have to overcome considerable barriers in order to find help.

The women's movement has identified violence against women as part of inequality and an indication of men's dominance over women. Although their approach encompassed all forms of violence against women, in practice the women's movement has tended to focus on domestic violence against women and sexual violence in the public sphere. Establishing women's shelters to which women abused by their husbands or partners may turn with their children, as well as phone hotlines for women who have become victims of rape, have been among the first steps taken by the women's movement to respond to the issue of violence against women. Other forms of violence such as trafficking in women, female genital mutilation, sex determination and abortion of female foetuses, violence against women during and after wars and armed conflicts, or violence in the form of forced marriage and dowry murders were put on the agenda of the women's movement only at a much later stage. The Women's Rights are Human Rights campaign, launched by the international women's movement which reached its apex at the United Nations Human Rights Conference in 1993, played an essential role in this respect (see Bunch/Reilly 1994). The views predominant until then were also shaken when rape of women was systematically used as a military technique during the wars in former Yugoslavia in the 1990s (Nikolic-Ristanovic 1999).

Violence against BAMER[1] women has always been a significant issue in the women's movement against violence: in some European contexts it is

1 In this article, the term BAMER will be used to refer to immigrant women, minority ethnic women, black women, refugees and asylum seekers. Using one single term for these women should not lead to the assumption, however, that they form a homogeneous group. This is not the case: the term BAMER includes different groups in different historical, social and political contexts, and also within the individual groups, diversity is found: for instance, it makes a considerable difference whether an immigrant woman has a secure residence status

evident that these women disproportionately often flee to women's shelters, because they have fewer options, compared to dominant ethnic women. Still, the main discourse continues to underline that women of any ethnic and social origin, of any class and any age, may suffer violence committed by men. On the one hand, this has been important in order to position the issue of violence against women in the political mainstream, but on the other, such a homogenising approach includes the risk of obscuring and ignoring the ethnic and social dimension of violence against women (Crenshaw 1994; Burman and Chantler 2005). Lehman (2008: 85) states that Germany still lacks a systematic intersectional perspective of domestic violence against women which recognises that gender is always linked to other distinguishing categories such as class or ethnic origin (see Thiara and Gill 2010). This applies to both theoretical and practical approaches, and most likely to the entire European region. It is imperative to revise current approaches to ensure that issues for all groups of women affected by violence are addressed. As Bograd emphasises, this is not an abstract discussion of high-brow concepts such as intersectionality but it has very real, life-threatening consequences if the trauma of violence is further aggravated by other forms of discrimination and violence (Bograd 2007: 32). At the end of this article two cases will be described to illustrate how racist prejudice may exclude BAMER women and their children from protection against violence.

Other developments in the discussion of the theme of violence against women give reason for concern, too: the past decade has seen a pronounced shift of the discourse away from violence against women towards domestic violence. This might be read as a positive sign and as extending protection to include other groups of people, and also in the sense of intersectionality, so that victims are no longer solely defined along gender lines, i.e. it is not only women who are affected by violence but also men and other criteria such as age, disability, etc. are also taken into account. Still, this development entails the problem that violence against women is ignored or qualified ('women may also commit violence'), and even the need for support services targeting women is questioned (see, for instance, the campaign to abolish women's shelters initiated by a male sociologist and published via the WELT Online website[2]). The present tendencies may well be expressions of a new upsurge

---

or has not been granted a residence permit. Women 'without papers' are among the group of people whose situation is extremely vulnerable, and thus their risk of suffering all possible forms of violence or exploitation is particularly high. In the UK, apart from BAMER (Black, Asian, Minority Ethnic and Refugee; see IMKAAN 2009), the abbreviation BME (Black and Minority Ethnic women) is also used; it especially refers to South-Asian, African and African-Caribbean communities (see Thiara 2008).

2 Welt Online: http://debatte.welt.de/kommentare/146073/wir+brauchen+frauenhaeuser, 30 July 2009 (text in German)

of family values, accompanied by a disregard for women's rights: it is held that the family should be protected, not women as individuals. Even representatives of women's organisations have started to contribute to the gender-neutral approaches to the problem and tend to use terms such as domestic violence or violence in families instead of violence against women in the hope of finding greater acceptance and of obtaining financial support more easily.

As a result, the category of gender is made invisible, and violence against women as a specific form of violence is denied. This tendency is contrary to agreements under international law which underlines that violence against women is a violation of human rights and that states have to take measures to prevent, investigate and punish it (United Nations 1992: para 9).[3] In its general recommendations, the Committee on the Elimination of Discrimination against Women (CEDAW Committee) adopts a clear position, stating that 'the definition of discrimination includes gender-based violence, that is, violence that is directed against a woman because she is a woman or that affects women disproportionately' (United Nations 1992: para 6). This definition explicitly characterises violence against women as a specific form of violence which women suffer because of their gender and by which women are affected especially often. It is an important definition which, regrettably, is not observed to an appropriate extent at national level and is rarely used to explain why violence against women differs from other forms of violence and why specific interventions are needed in order to eliminate violence against women. Its weakness is that it is one-dimensional and presents gender as the sole reason for violence while disregarding other mechanisms of discrimination and oppression. Still, there are other developments in international law that increasingly take into account the complexity of multiple discrimination and violence. For instance, the CEDAW Committee's General Recommendation 26 on women migrant workers adopted in 2008 addresses the problem of specific and multiple discriminations that labour migrants face (United Nations 2008). The Committee's recommendations relate to both the political and economic empowerment of migrant workers and their protection against violence and access to justice, and the states that have ratified CEDAW are obliged to implement these recommendations.

In other words, the point is not to abandon the approach of gender-related violence but to expand it. Women experience violence and discrimination because they are women, but at the same time also because they are immi-

3 CEDAW Committee General Recommendation 19, para 9: 'Under general international law and specific human rights covenants, States may also be responsible for private acts if they fail to act with due diligence to prevent violations of rights or to investigate and punish acts of violence, and for providing compensation'.

grants, or minority ethnic women, or because they are poor, or for other reasons. Such multiple discrimination results in very specific forms of discrimination and oppression which have to be identified, pointed out and changed. In particular, it is important to ask one question again and again: 'Who is excluded and why?' (see Kanuha 1996, quoted in Bograd 2007: 33).

New interventions to respond to violence against women: who benefits and who is excluded

In the past two decades, many European countries have increased their efforts to prevent violence against women and in particular domestic violence (European Commission 2008; Hagemann-White 2008; Council of Europe 2008b; Federal Chancellery and Federal Ministry for Women 2008). These have included, for example: the Zero Tolerance campaign was launched in 1992 in Scotland and has continually been advanced and also specifically addresses young people (Federal Chancellery 2008: 263ff.); in 1997 Austria adopted an act under which the police is obliged, in cases of imminent danger, to make a perpetrator leave the home immediately and to prohibit his return to the flat and its neighbourhood for a period of seven days[4] (Logar 2000); in Spain an act covering a wide range of provisions took effect in 2004 and includes women's protection against violence (Organic Law 2004, quoted in: Council of Europe 2007b: 163); in 2005 Bulgaria saw the adoption of an act on the protection against domestic violence, according to which victims may apply for civil law protection orders under which perpetrators must keep away from certain places (Council of Europe 2007a: 97); in 2007 Germany's Federal Government adopted the second Action Plan on Violence against Women, which also includes interventions to respond to violence against immigrant women and women with disabilities (Bundesministerium für Familie, Senioren, Frauen und Jugend 2007); in Sweden, the new offence of gross violation of a woman's integrity was defined in 1998, under which repeated acts of violence against a partner are punished more severely than individual acts (Council of Europe 2007: 177).

This small number of examples is not sufficient by far to illustrate the numerous changes and improvements in the prevention of violence against women that have taken place. Regarding assistance and support to women

4 The act has seen several amendments so far and when the second Act on Protection Against Violence entered into force in June 2009 the period of eviction under orders issued by the police was extended to two weeks. The new act also includes a number of other relevant improvements regarding protection against violence; see Logar 2009.

and their children, many new centres have been established and new programmes implemented which include, for instance, national women's telephone helplines, proactive counselling by intervention centres, mobile support or independent domestic violence advisors. The women's movement against violence has succeeded in counteracting the marginalisation of this issue and helped to integrate it in political programmes and legislation. Research activities focusing on violence against women have also increased, although research at university level is lagging behind and there are very few university institutes and chairs that focus on gender and violence.

In recent years, international organisations such as the Council of Europe have also intensified their activities in this field. For instance, the United Nations published a study on violence against women (United Nations 2006). The Council of Europe launched the campaign Stop domestic violence against women, which was implemented from 2006 to 2008, and at present, the Council is discussing the introduction of a legally binding Draft Convention on preventing and combating violence against women and domestic violence (CAHVIO 2009). At the level of the European Union, legislation aimed at preventing gender-related violence exists only in individual areas such as sexual harassment at work or trafficking in women, but there are numerous activities and recommendations (soft law) that reflect an intensified commitment and the European Union's triggering function in this regard (Kantola 2006; Krizsan and Popa 2009).

Progress has thus been made in a number of fields regarding the prevention of violence against women and domestic violence. Still, it must not be overlooked that the extent of violence against women continues to be high and that it has not been possible so far to reduce, let alone eliminate, violence against women. In the absence of systematic evaluation and monitoring, it is difficult or impossible to derive statements on the effects of measures taken.

Who then benefits from the new measures and who might be excluded? Below, this question will be discussed with regard to BAMER women, and it will be shown that they benefit from the new measures to a small extent only and that new tendencies and discourses such as cultural relativism or the minoritisation of violence (Burman and Chantler 2005) involve risks for these women. Problems have been identified in the following areas: 1) The protection of BAMER women has hardly been considered in political programmes and measures such as plans of action, which primarily focus on domestic violence; 2) New measures are found especially with regard to protection against violence under civil law and criminal law, while social and economic rights, which are necessary to be able to leave a violent relationship, have hardly been considered; 3) Restrictive alien laws and discrimination of BAMER women contribute to their dependence on violent perpetrators and this especially affects women who have no legal residence status; 4) There are gaps in the support system, and for BAMER women these gaps are especially wide since their access to support is often difficult, and they are excluded from several types of assistance; 5) As a result of the tendency towards and the discussion of the cultural relativism of violence, combined with the existing prejudice against BAMER women, government authorities that are in charge of protecting women against violence do not take adequate protection measures and thus BAMER women do not get as much protection as women from the majority population.

It is not possible in the context of this article to address problem areas such as insufficient or non-existent laws on protection against violence, lack of or inadequate implementation and evaluation, as well as the continuing problem, underlined again and again, that violence against women is not punished in a large number of cases (see, e.g., Hester 2003, quoted in Humphreys and Charter et al. 2006; Kelly, Lovett and Seith 2009).

National plans of action lack comprehensive measures to prevent violence against BAMER women

A study conducted on behalf of the Council of Europe which investigated the implementation of Recommendation 2002–5 on the protection of women against violence has shown that an increasing number of states have adopted plans of action on violence against women in recent years (Hagemann-White 2008). The quality of the plans of action and their implementation cannot be analysed in detail here, but there is reason for doubt about the effectiveness of many action plans which often are just noble words. In this chapter, the extent to which plans of action take account of the situation of BAMER women will be discussed. What is typical of the majority of action plans is that they are still focused on the areas of domestic violence and sexual violence (Hagemann-White 2008: 9), with only very few also dealing with other forms of violence mentioned in the Council of Europe Recommendation (2002: 5): violence in institutions, forced marriage, violence in situations of conflict, murder in the name of honour, female genital mutilation and failure to respect freedom of choice with regard to reproduction. This indicates a trend towards marginalisation of forms of violence that are regarded as typical of other cultures and it is a questionable contradiction to the overriding emphasis on violence in BAMER communities that is often found but does not lead to what might be expected, namely intensified measures against violence laid down in plans of action. This may be the result of an attitude that sees violence as an inherent characteristic of certain cultures, which thus cannot be changed. And it points to the view that the women concerned are passively putting up with violence so that interventions would be useless anyway (Burman and Chantler 2005: 63). Such attitudes are a form of discrimination as a result of which support and assistance are not made available.

Even where the situation of BAMER women is discussed and included in action plans it is interesting to note the ways in which this is done. For instance, an analysis of Germany's second Plan of Action to combat violence against women acknowledges the fact that especially women of Turkish and East European origin are suffering physical and sexual violence considerably more often, and in more severe forms, than the average German female population and that these women are also affected by specific forms of violence, such as forced marriage (Bundesministerium für Familie, Senioren, Frauen und Jugend 2007: 7). It is also pointed out that there is a greater need for support and a number of model projects are listed. The necessity of integration is frequently pointed out and the wish that immigrants should integrate themselves through learning German is also evident. Experience of violence, however, tends to be regarded as an individual phenomenon or is linked to certain cultures. The Plan of Action does not mention structural problems and discrimination or racist prejudice against immigrants, which are additional barriers when they are seeking protection and support. Furthermore, the barriers created by lack of residence rights or lack of social and economic security are not addressed, and the chapter on support services does not mention the need for specific centres for immigrant women affected by violence.

It has to be conceded as a positive point of Germany's Plan of Action, however, that the situation of immigrant women suffering violence has in fact been recognised as a focal issue. Still, the way in which this area is treated is less than perfect. The Plan pursues an individualised approach and does not see the problem in all its aspects and only certain fragments are covered. The focus is placed on individual deficits, while deficits in the system are hardly made visible. It is implied that immigrants have to change, not the system. Pursuing such approaches certainly is not limited to Germany, as the analysis by Roggebrand and Verloo (2007) of the Netherlands' immigration policy shows.

Similar problems can be found in the UK's new National strategy to end violence against women and girls. Imkaan, a second tier organisation representing minority ethnic domestic violence support services in the UK, welcomes the National strategy which encompasses many fields but also has concerns: while the strategy mentions problems such as forced marriage and honour-based violence it lacks reference to the extremely vulnerable situation of BAMER women who want to leave a violent relationship and have no recourse to public funds (Imkaan 2009: 2).

Thus, the national action plans and policies lack comprehensive approaches to the situation of BAMER women. The intersectional aspects of experience – of discrimination and violence – are insufficiently taken into account, which may result in inadequate measures and lack of support for BAMER women and their children. Therefore it is of vital importance to integrate in national plans of action and other policy documents comprehensive measures for BAMER women and their children who have suffered violence, and to orient them towards the specific needs of different groups (immigrant women with precarious residence status, refugee and asylum seekers immigrant women without residence permits). For the latter group the barriers to seeking help are high because when they turn to government authorities they may be identified as people who live in the country illegally and eventually be deported.

Gaps in the statutory protection against violence

In recent years, many European countries have adopted laws on protection against violence that include measures under civil and criminal law such as civil law injunctions and barring orders against perpetrators, or defining marital rape and stalking as criminal offences. This undoubtedly is a positive development and shows that domestic violence against women is no longer considered a private matter but its prevention is regarded as a duty of the State. The process of adopting statutory protection measures has not yet been concluded and deficits regarding statutory regulations and their implementation can still be seen in many countries (Council of Europe 2007c; European Commission 2008; Council of Europe 2008a).

Measures under civil law and criminal law aimed at protection against violence are absolutely necessary but prevention has to go beyond that. Complementary measures are needed so that the women affected and their children actually have access to these rights and may benefit from them. Intervention centres that support victims, mobile counselling services or independent domestic violence advisors have proved to be essential in order to enable women to make use of their rights. However, support services such as those mentioned above are not available in many countries and regions because the corresponding laws were passed without ensuring the financial means needed for implementation.

Another problem is that statutory measures are not harmonised and may even be contradictory. This may be the case with regard to the protection of children against domestic violence. Hester (2006) developed the Three Planet Model (Planet A: violence against the partner; Planet B: violence against children; Planet C: fathers' rights) to illustrate this situation. This shows that if the three areas dealing with the problem of domestic violence are treated as separate issues, as a result children, because of family law provisions, may insufficiently be protected after the mother has separated from a violent partner and may be exposed to further violence. Therefore, it is essential for protecting children against violence that statutory measures are aligned and that, in accordance with the 1989 United Nations Convention on the Rights of the Child, the rights of children to physical and mental health should supersede the father's right to have contact with his children.

Thus, comprehensive, well-aligned statutory measures are needed to ensure effective protection against violence (see United Nations 2008; Council of Europe Task Force 2008). In addition, thorough implementation, secure access to law, and regular evaluation of measures are important elements to ensure that laws are more than fig leaves, adopted to have something to show when reports have to be written.

Residence laws versus anti-violence laws

To what extent do BAMER women and their children actually benefit from the new measures of protection against violence? This primarily depends on their status of residence: the less secure it is or the less information on this aspect of their situation women have, the less likely it is that BAMER women will turn to the police or justice authorities to seek protection. Women who do not have a legal residence title are almost always reluctant to contact authorities because they cannot expect protection but may face sanctions and deportation. Because of the provisions of alien law, women may become (more) dependent on the abuser if they are not granted residence rights independent of their partners, and recently, the corresponding regulations have become more restrictive in many countries.

A few examples will illustrate the situation: the UK applied the one-year rule for many years- women entering the country had to remain in marriage with their spouse for at least one year before they could apply to stay in the UK permanently and thus divorce him without having to leave the country. This also applied when a woman was abused by her husband. Women's organisations such as Southall Black Sisters[5] repeatedly pointed to the detrimental effects of this regulation for women depending on their partners with regard to their leave to remain in the UK. Eventually a few concessions were introduced from which women suffering violence could benefit under certain conditions. However, it was not possible to prevent the extension to two years of this regulation in 2003. In addition, under the no recourse to public funds requirement, persons coming to the UK have to be supported by their spouses and are not entitled to social benefits, which makes it very difficult or impossible for women in violent relationships to leave their violent partners (Kelly and Sen 2007).

In Germany also women have to live with their husbands for two years before they may apply for an independent residence permit, which at first grants residence for one year only.[6] For women suffering violence a hardship regulation was introduced. However, it includes the requirement that massive acts of violence must have been committed and that they must have been reported to the police.

In Austria, the residence status of immigrant women who have no sufficient income of their own depends on their husbands for five years.[7] Exceptions applying to women suffering violence are also granted in Austria but the requirements for this are strict and cannot easily be met. For instance, women must have applied for an interim injunction because of the violence committed. The chances of being granted an interim injunction are good especially in those cases in which eviction orders have previously been issued by the police. However, many immigrant women are reluctant to turn to the police and rather resort to relatives, friends or a women's shelter. This significantly reduces their chances of obtaining an interim injunction.

In order to be granted an independent residence permit for Austria, women have to overcome other obstacles as well. Their stay in the country must not involve expenses for the state, and therefore they cannot take up state financial support. In addition, they have to prove an accommodation in accordance with local custom as well as a minimum monthly income of EUR 770 for themselves. As many immigrant women do not have employment or (have to) work in low-wage jobs it is difficult to prove such an income. Childcare duties are not taken into account and immigrant women thus have to prove an income at the required level independent of the question of how old their children are, if childcare services are available and whether the

5 Southal Black Sisters http://www.southallblacksisters.org.uk/campaign_oneyearrule.html 31 July 2009
6 Section 31 of the Act on Residence
7 Section 27 of the Act on Settlement and Residence

woman in question will find employment at all. Here immigrants face multiple discriminations: as women, as mothers and because of their origin.

Asylum seekers have no access to the labour market in Austria, and they are not entitled to welfare assistance either. As the laws have been restricted also in Austria in order to prevent 'immigration by marriage', not even asylum seekers who have married an Austrian are granted residence permits following the marriage. They have to leave Austria and apply for a residence permit in their country of origin. This is in fact impossible for asylum seekers, and when they are in a violent marriage they are forced to continue living with their husbands because it is not possible for them to ensure their existence independently.

These examples illustrate that many BAMER women who suffer violence have no choice but to stay with the abuser, as they would otherwise risk their very existence, especially if they are asylum seekers or depend on their husbands or have no legal residence status because the laws on residence and asylum are getting increasingly restrictive. A study carried out in Scandinavia, which interviewed immigrant women living in women's shelters, arrived at the same conclusions:

> In this report, we have used the women's narratives to illustrate how abused foreign women are literally trapped between law and life, as the report title indicates. The women can either choose to stay in violent marriages until becoming eligible for permanent residence. Or they can leave their abusive husbands and hope to be among the few elected who are granted residence permits – both potentially life-threatening options. If the women stay in the violent marriage, they expose themselves and their children to great danger, as most women in the report talk of brutal violence. If they leave their husbands, they risk expulsion and possibly exposing themselves to violence and, in the extreme, honour killing by their own or their husband's families. Alternatively, they risk ending up in prostitution or being married off to old men and/or generally having to live in wretched circumstances, unable to support themselves. In other words, the women are locked in a no-win situation, and the Nordic countries' legislative provisions fail to offer the necessary protection.' (The Danish Research Centre on Gender Equality 2005: 63)

A violent man may use the insecure residence status of his partner to put her under pressure and to intimidate her. He may threaten to inform the authorities and in this way makes her keep quiet about the violence committed. And if women make public the fact that they are suffering violence, violence committed by a partner may be replaced by violence on the part of the state. A group of British researchers conclude that violence against women is tolerated by the state in order to control access to citizenship – 'what this illustrates is that what is most important to the state is to regulate citizenship even at the expense of terrible abuse to women. In this sense, the state can be seen to be an active partner in the violence against women' (Burman and Chantler 2005: 65).

This approach by the state is a violation of the obligation under international law to protect all women who have suffered violence and to make possible for them a life free of violence. The current Council of Europe activities to draft a legally binding Convention on preventing and combating violence against women recognizes BAMER women's right to a life free of violence. The Interim Report reads:

> Thus women and children of foreign nationality who have been, or who are, victims of such violence could be granted a specific legal status in their host country, particularly in respect of the right of residence and the right to work, so as to enable them to lead a life free of violence (Council of Europe 2009: para 45).

It will be of great importance over the coming two years that women's and human rights organisations engage in lobbying to ensure that not only the Interim Report but also the final text of the Convention will definitely oblige states to grant to women and children affected by violence residence rights that are independent of those of the perpetrator, and as well as rights that secure their livelihood so that they are indeed in a position to lead lives free of violence and without having to fear for their existence.

Lack of social and economic rights

As has already been mentioned, anti-violence laws alone are not enough, nor are new regulations for residence permits, if women are not granted social and economic rights that permit them and their children a life under their own control. The Council of Europe Recommendation 2002–5 says that the member states shall take necessary measures 'to ensure that women are able to exercise freely and effectively their economic and social rights' (Council of Europe 2002: para II).

In recent years, numerous legal reforms have taken place, but only in few cases have they included social and economic rights for women who have become victims of violence. Frequently, provisions have not been harmonised, and while women may turn to the courts and apply for orders under which their violent partner has to leave their home immediately, the legal processes that are necessary to obtain maintenance take weeks or months. Interim injunctions and eviction orders do not feed women and children, therefore it is essential to include in the anti-violence laws also provisions that ensure immediate maintenance payments and grant those concerned non-bureaucratic access to welfare assistance until maintenance is paid. Spain's legislation (Organic Law 2004, quoted in: Council of Europe 2007b: 163) is a good practice example in this regard. It defines special courts for cases of violence against women, which are competent not only for ordering protection measures but also for settling maintenance claims. Other provisions of the act prevent discrimination at work of women experiencing violence and guarantees them labour rights as well as financial support.

The majority of recent new acts also lack provisions under which women affected by violence and their children are granted the right to affordable housing. Being unable to find adequate, affordable housing is the most frequent reason why women stay in shelters for longer periods or return to precarious living conditions after they stay in the shelters. Violence often means losing one's home, therefore many women are forced to go on living with the perpetrator, also after a separation (Council of Europe 2007c: 25).

In other words, what BAMER women and their children need to live free of violence is not only laws that protect them against violence but also laws that ensure their existence including housing, easier access to the labour market, education and training as well as childcare. In addition, there must be labour laws which guarantee that women who have become victims of violence will not lose their work, and eventually also other social and economic rights are required.

Massive gaps in the network of support services

In Europe, as of the 1970s – in Central and Eastern Europe as of the 1990s, after the collapse of Communism – women's organisations have opened women's shelters, provided advice by phone as well as other services for women and their children who have become victims of male violence, and the women's organisations have fought for obtaining government funds to finance these services. A network of support services was thus built, but in many countries and regions this network has massive gaps (European Commission 2008; WAVE 2008; Kelly and Dubois 2008). The deficits that show are both quantitative (insufficient number of support centres) and qualitative (no specific services, e.g. for women who have become victims of sexual violence), and this does not apply to Eastern Europe only but also to other countries of the European Union.

A number of studies drawn up on behalf of the Council of Europe have revealed that many countries cannot even say precisely how many women's shelters they have (Council of Europe 2008), and moreover, the figures given by governments differ from those communicated by women's organisations.

For instance, in the 2007 report, the Czech Republic indicated a capacity of 1 147 places in women's shelters, while women's organisation said that only 27 places existed (OSI/Network Women's Program 2007). In Slovakia, the figures the Government gave for the 2008 report mentioned 517 available places (Council of Europe 2008: 16), while women's organisations said that 46 places existed and 539 places were lacking (WAVE 2008). The Council of Europe Task Force recommends a minimum standard of one family place[8] in a women's shelter per 10 000 of population (Council of Europe 2008b: 84). According to the countries' own information, this standard of supply has so far been met by few of the 33 countries that took part in the survey (Luxembourg, Norway, Andorra, Ireland and Liechtenstein). Many countries have less than half the number of places in women's shelters that would be necessary, and there are states where the number of places in shelters is so small that one cannot at all speak of adequate supply (Italy, Cyprus, Hungary, Romania, Georgia, Turkey, Bulgaria).

Women's shelters are essential for protecting women and children against violence. A lack of shelters brings about a very difficult situation, as many countries do not have effective legal measures of protection against violence and many women have little confidence in government authorities. Often, there are no other service providers, such as counselling centres for women affected by sexual violence either, and only a minority of countries operate cost-free 24-hour phone helplines for women which the Council of Europe Task Force indicates as part of the minimum standards for the support of victims. A report prepared for the Council of Europe on minimum standards for support services mentions one counselling centre for victims of sexual violence per 200 000 women and one counselling centre per 50 000 women where various services such as court assistance or outreach are provided (Kelly and Dubois 2008: 38). A central function of support services for women is to help women suffering violence and their children get access to justice. The obligation under international law for states to protect women against violence and to prevent violence includes the right to support and access to justice. At present, these rights are available to a small number of women affected only, indicating an urgent need for action on the part of political decision-makers.

In addition to quantitative gaps, problems in the quality of support services have also been shown. It is widely recognised among experts that women who suffer violence need specific support services for women, provided by staff with a specialised knowledge and skill base for counselling and support services for women and their children and who act in the inter-

8 Family place = a bed space for the mother and her children

ests of their clients (WAVE 2004; Kelly and Dubois 2008). The goal of these services is to empower women and enable them to gain autonomy, i.e., take control of their lives, and to prevent them from further violence as well as new traumatisation resulting from inappropriate interventions by state agencies and institutions.

Many countries and regions have no specialised support centres and general social service providers, such as social welfare departments, are hardly in a position to provide adequate support. As a rule, they cannot ensure advocacy, i.e., acting in the interests of victims, and many of them even have power and control over victims, for instance, the power to remove children from the family or to control financial support. Therefore they cannot pursue the aim of empowering the victim, which has to be focused on helping victims lead independent lives. It is important to have social service providers that are trained in the field of violence against women, but they cannot replace specialised, autonomous women's organisations. Children also need independent support and advocacy, which, regrettably, is also lacking in many cases (Eriksson 2005; Kavemann and Kreyssig 2005).

So, what is the situation of BAMER women and their children with regard to support services? There are many indications of marginalisation and manifold barriers making it difficult to get support, in a network of services providers that is inadequate as such. There are studies pointing out that BAMER women tend to have little information on support services (Schröttle and Khelaifat 2008) and that they turn to support centres less often than women in general (Batsleer et al 2002, quoted in Thiara 2008). In other words, they are a target group that is not, or insufficiently, addressed. This is a contradiction to the Council of Europe report according to which 24 out of 38 governments have stated that information on rights and support services for women are available in all relevant languages (Council of Europe 2008a: 38). The survey does not specify the criteria for defining languages as relevant, but obviously it is safe to assume that the views of the governments may have been overly optimistic.

Apart from access to information, there are also other, hard barriers that BAMER women are facing with regard to access to services, especially if, apart from the problem of violence, their residence titles are insecure as well. This particularly affects women and children who have no legal status of residence or who risk losing their right of residence. They are hardly welcomed by providers of support services because their cases involve much more work or because support centres do not feel competent to handle such cases: they regard themselves as specialists in violence problems, not in residence problems. Here, the lack of intersectional approaches results in the exclusion of BAMER women and their children.

They are 'the wrong target group', and the problem of violence tends to be ignored or not given priority.

Shelters that admit BAMER women whose residence status is insecure or who have no residence title, often face the problem that they cannot take up public funds for these women and their children because they are not entitled to social benefits (Burman and Chantler 2005). Fund-raising among private sponsors is necessary to be able to ensure the protection of these women and their children in the women's shelter, which in turn requires much time and effort. There is the risk that support centres make BAMER women feel that they are 'a burden', and they are personally made responsible for this, while it is in fact the system and racist as well as sexist discrimination that cause additional work. This divides the women concerned, which in turn has negative effects on BAMER women and their children due to the prejudice they face. There is reason to assume that BAMER women and their children are refused help by support centres in Europe and also in the European Union every day because they have no, or no secure, residence titles. Women living in shelters are not safe from deportation either, and regulations according to which women without residence titles may not be admitted are frequent. There are no exact figures and studies at European level that link the residence status of BAMER women who suffer violence to possible consequences with regard to access to justice and to service provision. Research in this field would be of great importance.

Support services that are specifically oriented towards BAMER women and their children, such as Southall Black Sisters in London or Berlin's emergency shelter of Interkulturelle Initiative, are the exception rather than the rule and are usually found only in larger cities. This is another considerable gap in the support system, as research has shown that BAMER women are very positive about being able to talk to a worker from a similar background who speaks her language (Thiara 2008: 147; Parmar et al 2005). In spite of this fact, support centres that specialise in services for BAMER women frequently face the danger of being closed down and cannot be expanded either, and a typical reason given is that such a specialisation would not be desirable as it prevents integration. This is contrary to the needs and wishes of many BAMER women, which unfortunately is not deemed to be relevant by many policy makers.

In sum, BAMER women and their children whose stay in the country is not based on a legal residence title form the low end of society: they have no rights and as a result have no access to adequate protection and support. This does not conform to international law, which, as mentioned above, obliges states to ensure effective protection against violence of all women, irrespective of their origin, nationality, ethnic group, etc. It will be imperative in the future to defend and implement the right to adequate support as well as access to support for all women, also BAMER women. Political players are called upon to adopt measures to this end and to provide the resources needed.

Lack of protection against violence

As described at the outset, racist prejudice and cultural relativism in the field of prevention may be a danger to the life, health and freedom of women. To illustrate this, two cases will be described in more detail. In 2002 and 2003, respectively, Şahide und Fatma, two women of Turkish origin who lived in Austria, were killed after many years of suffering abuse by their husbands (Citak 2008). Both women had been clients of the Domestic Abuse Intervention Centre of Vienna, a support centre that provides services to victims of domestic violence after eviction orders have been issued against the perpetrators. The staff of the Intervention Centre were shocked and upset about the murder of the two women, and in their opinion, the state authorities had failed to act with due diligence and had not done everything in their power to protect the lives of the two women. In 2005, the Intervention Centre and the Association of Women's Access to Justice submitted a complaint to the CEDAW Committee on the Elimination of Discrimination against Women of the United Nations[9] (United Nations CEDAW Committee 2007 a, b; Logar 2009).

The authors of the complaint underlined that the murders of Şahide und Fatma were two tragic examples of the fact that violence against immigrant women in Austria still was not taken seriously enough by state authorities and institutions, that the criminal law system, especially Public Prosecutors and judges, continued to regard violence against women as a social or domestic problem of little importance, found only in certain social classes and cultures, that criminal law provisions were not applied because violence against women was not taken seriously and the victim's fear was ignored by the criminal law authorities. In both cases, the perpetrators had not been detained in spite of repeated threats of murder.

In its comments on the complaint regarding the case of Şahide, Austria used an argument that was explicitly racist in order to justify why the Public Prosecutors had withdrawn the charges of making criminal dangerous threats

9 The CEDAW Committee monitors the implementation of the 1979 UN Convention on the Elimination of All Forms of Discrimination against Women, a major agreement under international law.

of murder. Austria submitted that 'it could not be proved with sufficient certainty that Mustafa was guilty of making criminal dangerous threats against his wife that went beyond the harsh statements resulting from his background' (United Nations CEDAW Committee 2007a). In other words, it was doubted whether the threats of murder actually were 'real' or rather came from the perpetrator's 'background', i.e., his Turkish origin, suggesting that such threats were normal occurrences in this culture and might be regarded as rude but did not violate any law. Thus, a certain cultural background is assumed as a reason for qualifying an act that is punishable under the applicable law (which is a discrimination), and double standards are thus introduced: threats made in this culture have to be judged in a different way to threats made in an 'Austrian' culture. As a consequence of this reasoning, victims are refused protection against such a threat as they are no longer regarded as victims.

The CEDAW Committee did not follow the view of the Republic of Austria, and in 2007, it decided that Austria had violated the rights of the two women to protection of their lives and physical and mental integrity according to the CEDAW Convention. The Committee considered that there had been sufficient indications of the danger of the perpetrators to which the authorities had not reacted by taking all appropriate protection measures.

In both cases, the CEDAW Committee acknowledged that Austria had established a comprehensive model to address domestic violence but also stated that this was not enough:

> In order for the individual woman victim of domestic violence to enjoy the practical realization of the principle of equality of men and women and of her human rights and fundamental freedoms, the political will that is expressed in the aforementioned comprehensive system of Austria must be supported by State actors, who adhere to the State party's due diligence obligations (CEDAW 2007a and b: para 12.1.2).

In other words, it is not enough to have good laws; they also have to be practised in each case and by all actors.

Austria also maintained that detention would have been disproportionate because it would have been too massive an interference in the perpetrator's basic rights and fundamental freedoms. The Committee stated in both cases that the perpetrators' rights cannot supersede women's human rights to life and to physical and mental integrity (CEDAW 2007a: para 12.1.5 and CEDAW 2007b: para 12.1.5). It was recommended that Austria adopt a series of measures in order to ensure that the state and its actors act with due diligence to prevent and respond to violence against women and adequately provide for sanctions for the failure to do so (CEDAW 2007a and b: para

12.3 a–d). These two decisions are of great relevance for all states that have ratified CEDAW and may directly be applied in national law. Women's and human rights organisations can use these decisions for lobbying at national level in order to improve the protection of women, in particular BAMER women, and to point to gaps in legal and support structures. In this way, international rights may become an effective instrument that is more than noble words but has practical relevance for the realisation of women's rights.

Conclusions

This article has shown that in spite of what has been achieved in the past four decades to improve the prevention of gender-related violence against women, there continue to be massive gaps in the legal and support structures which, due to sexist and racist prejudice, primarily affect immigrant and minority ethnic women, and refugees and asylum seekers. As the intersection of simultaneous multiple forms of discrimination, in theory and in practice, because of gender and ethnic and social origin, has not been analysed properly, the situation of the women concerned remains invisible. In this way, they are marginalised and experience further discrimination. In order to respond to this, intersectional perspectives have to be included in political programmes such as national plans of action, based on the question of who is in danger of being excluded and why, and how the groups of women affected can be integrated in the relevant measures.

The majority of new measures aimed at the protection against violence that have been adopted in recent decades concern protection orders under civil law and criminal law. There is no doubt that these are important instruments but they do not cover everything that is necessary as they are based on individualised approaches and ignore the structural causes of why women live in violent relationships which can be difficult for them to leave. Future activities need to focus on improving the social and economic rights of women experiencing violence, in particular, the right to housing of their own, the right to financial independence and access to the labour market as well as education and training. Laws that discriminate BAMER women and force them to continue to live in dependence on violent partners are highly dubious from an ethical point of view because the state thus acts as an accomplice of perpetrators. Such laws should be abolished. BAMER women whose residence status has become illegal because of violence suffered or discrimination by law should be granted residence permits for humanitarian reasons and should not face the risk of deportation.

Another cause for concern is discrimination and marginalisation of BAMER women in support service provision: they are denied support, and the barriers preventing access to help are growing. An essential point in this regard is to implement the principle to grant support and assistance to **all** women and their children, independent of origin and status, and not to refuse any woman access to women's shelters or other support centres or provide unrestricted support. Furthermore, it is necessary to establish and expand specialised centres for BAMER women in order to ensure adequate support. Public relations activities have to be intensified in order to inform all communities of the right to support and assistance. Eventually, it is of vital importance that the state agencies in charge of protecting women against violence are aware of possible discrimination and prejudice with regard to BAMER communities and take steps to change this so that their actions are not guided by discrimination and prejudice.

Under international law, such as the Convention on the Elimination of All Forms of Discrimination against Women, as well as the decisions by the Committee in charge of monitoring the implementation of the Convention, it definitely is a task of states to act with due diligence to protect all women against violence. It is essential to propagate these two decisions, which are milestones in the field of preventing violence, and to use them as arguments in favour of initiatives aimed at closing the gaps in the support system and with regard to the protection of immigrant and minority ethnic women, refugees and asylum seekers as well as their children.

References

Bograd, Michele (2007): Strengthening Domestic Violence Theories: Intersections of Race, Class, Sexual Orientation and Gender. In: Sokoloff, Natalia J. (ed.) (2007): Domestic Violence at the Margins. Readings on Race, Class, Gender, and Culture, Rutgers University Press, New Brunswick, New Jersey and London, pp. 25–38.

Bundesministerium für Familie, Senioren, Frauen und Jugend (ed.) (2007): Aktionsplan II der Bundesregierung zur Bekämpfung von Gewalt gegen Frauen. Berlin.

Burman, Erica/Chantler, Khatidja (2005): Domestic violence and minoritisation: Legal and policy barriers facing minoritized women leaving violent relationships. In: International Journal of Law and Psychiatry, 2005, 28, pp. 59–74.

Citak, Tamar (2008): Protection of Immigrant Women in Austria Against Violence. In: Federal Chancillery of Austria/Federal Ministry for Women, Media and Regional Policy (eds.): 10 Years of Austrian Anti-violence Legislation. Vienna: Published by the editors, pp. 145–148.

Council of Europe (2002): Recommendation Rec(2002)5 of the Committee of Ministers to member States on the protection of women against violence adopted on 30 April 2002 and Explanatory Memorandum. Strasbourg.

Council of Europe (2007a): Legislation in the Member States of the Council of Europe in the Field of Violence against Women, Volume I: Albania to Ireland. Strasbourg.

Council of Europe (2007b): Legislation in the Member States of the Council of Europe in the Field of Violence against Women, Volume II: Italy to United Kingdom. Strasbourg.

Council of Europe (2007c): Protecting women against violence. Analytical study on the effective implementation of Recommendations Rec(2002)5 on the protection of women against violence in Council of Europe member States, prepared by Carol Hagemann-White and Sabine Bohne/University Osnabrück, on behalf of the Gender Equality and Anti-Trafficking Division/Directorate General of Human Rights and Legal Affairs. Strasbourg.

Council of Europe (2008a): Protecting women against violence. Analytical study of the results of the second round of monitoring the implementation of Recommendation, Rec (2002)5 on the protection of women against violence in Council of Europe member states. Prepared by Carol Hagemann-White, University of Osnabrück. Strasbourg.

Council of Europe (2008b): Council of Europe Task Force to Combat Violence against Women, including Domestic Violence (EG-TFV), Final Activity Report. Strasbourg, September 2008.

Council of Europe (2009): Ad Hoc Committee on Preventing and Combating Violence against Women and Domestic Violence (CAHVIO). Interim Report. Strasbourg.

Crenshaw, Kimberly (1994): Mapping the margins. Intersectionality, identity politics and violence against women of color. In: Fineman M./Mykitiuk R.(eds.): The Public Nature of Private Violence. New York: Routledge, pp. 93–118.

Eriksson, Maria/Hester, Marianne/Keskinen, Suvi/Pringle, Keith (2005): Tackling Men's Violence in Families. Nordic issues and dilemmas. Bristol: The Policy Press.

European Commission (ed.) (2008): Gendering Human Rights Violations: The case of interpersonal violence. Research Project Coordination Action on Human Rights Violations (CAHRV). Final Report 2004–2007. Brussels: Office for Official Publications of the European Communities.

Federal Chancillery/Federal Ministry for Women, Media and Regional Policy (eds.) (2008): 10 Years of Austrian Anti-violence Legislation. International Conference in the Context of the Council of Europe Campaign to Combat Violence Against Women. 5 to 7 November 2007. Vienna: published by the editors.

Fineman, M./Mykitiuk, R.(eds.) (1994): The Public Nature of Private Violence. New York: Routledge.

Hagemann-White, Carol (2008): Measuring Progress in Addressing Violence Against Women Across Europe. In: IJCACJ, 2008: Vol. 32, Iss. 2, pp. 149–172.

Hester, Marianne/Radford, Lorraine (2006): Mothering Through Domestic Violence. London: Jessica Kingsley.

Humphreys, Cathy/Carter, Rachel et al. (2006): The justice system as an arena for the protection of human rights for women and children experiencing violence and abuse, European Research Project CAHRV, University of Osnabrück, research report (unpublished). http://www.cahrv.uni-osnabrueck.de/reddot/190.htm (July 2009)

Imkaan (2009): Response to the Home Office Consultation Paper Together We Can End Violence against Women and Girls, London (unpublished).

Kantola, Johanna (2006): Transnational and National Gender Equality Politics: The European Unions's Impact on Domestic Violence Debates in Britain and Finland. In: Hellsten, Sirkku K./Holli, Anne Maria (eds.): Women's Citizenship and Political Rights. New York: Palgrave Macmillan, pp. 154–178.

Kavemann, Barbara/Kreyssig, Ulrike (eds.) (2005): Handbuch Kinder und häusliche Gewalt. Berlin: VS Verlag für Sozialwissenschaften.

Kelly, Liz/Dubois, Lorna (2008): Combating violence against women: minimum standards for support services, report prepared for the Council of Europe/Gender Equality and Anti-Trafficking Division/Directorate General of Human Rights and Legal Affairs. Strasbourg.

Kelly, Liz/Purna, Sen (2007): Violence against women in the UK. Shadow thematic report to the Committee on the Elimination of all Forms of Discrimination against Women, Report (unpublished).

Krizsan, Andrea/Popa, Raluca (2009): Stretching EU Conditionality: Mechanisms of Europeanization in Making Domestic Violence Policies in Central and Eastern Europe. Report in the frame of the European Commission Sixth Framework Programme Integrated Project QUING (Quality in Gender+Equality Policies). Vienna, research report (unpublished).

Lehmann, Nadja (2008): Migrantinnen im Frauenhaus. Biographische Perspektiven auf Gewalterfahrungen. Opladen & Framington Hills: Verlag Barbara Budrich.

Logar, Rosa (2000): Feministinnen und Staat gegen Männergewalt. In: Schwarzer, Alice (ed.): Man wird nicht als Frau geboren. Köln: Verlag Kiepenheuer & Witsch Köln, pp. 191–204.

Logar, Rosa (2009): Die UNO-Frauenrechtskonvention CEDAW als Instrument zur Bekämpfung der Gewalt an Frauen: zwei Beispiele aus Österreich. In: Frauenfragen, Frauenfragen der Eidgenössischen Kommission für Frauenfragen Schweiz, Nr 1.2009, Bern, pp. 22–38.

Miller, Edgar G. (2004): Postmodern Terrorism. Buxtehude: Rubbish Publishers.

Nikolic-Ristanovic (1999): Violence Against Women in Former Yugoslavia. In: Violence Against Women, Vol. 5, No. 1, pp. 63–80.

OSI/Network Women's Program/Violence against Women (VAW) Monitoring Program (2007): Violence against Women. Does the Government Care in the Czech Republic? Report. Budapest/New York.

Parmar, Alpa/Sampson, Alice/Diamond, Alana (2005): Tackling Domestic Violence: Providing advocacy and support to survivors of domestic violence, UK Home Office, London.

Roggeband, Conny/Verloo, Mieke (2007): Dutch Women are Liberated, Migrant Women are a Problem: The Evolution of Policy Frames on Gender and Migration in the Netherlands, 1995–2005. In: Social Policy & Administration, 2007, Vol. 41, pp. 271–288.

Schröttle, Monika/Müller, Ursula (2004a): Lebenssituation, Sicherheit und Gesundheit von Frauen in Deutschland. Eine repräsentative Untersuchung zu Gewalt gegen Frauen in Deutschland. Im Auftrag des Bundesministeriums für Familie, Senioren, Frauen und Jugend. Berlin: published by the authors. http://www.bmfsfj.de/Kategorien/Publikationen/Publikationen,did=20530.html (31.07.2009)

Schröttle, Monika/Müller, Ursula (2004b): Eine repräsentative Untersuchung zu Gewalt gegen Frauen in Deutschland. Zusammenfassung zentraler Studienergebnisse. Auftrag des Bundesministeriums für Familie, Senioren, Frauen und Jugend. Berlin: published by the authors.

Schröttle, Monik/Khelaifat, Nadia (2008): Gesundheit-Gewalt-Migration. Eine vergleichende Sekundäranalyse zur gesundheitlichen und Gewaltsituation von Frauen mit und ohne Migrationshintergrund in Deutschland. Kurzzusammenfassung zentraler Ergebnisse. Studie im Auftrag des Bundesministeriums für Familie, Senioren, Frauen und Jugend (ed.). Berlin: published by the editor.

Seith, Corinna/Lovett, Jo/Kelly, Liz (2009): Different systems, similar outcomes? Tracking attrition in reported rape cases in eleven European countries. Country report Austria (summary), London, research report (unpublished).

Sokoloff, Natalia J. (ed.) (2007): Domestic Violence at the Margins. Readings on Race, Class, Gender and Culture. New Brunswick, New Jersey, and London: Rutgers University Press.

The Danish Research Centre on Gender Equality (ed.) (2005): Trapped between Law and Life. Report on Abused Minority Women in the Nordic Countries, Roskilde/Denmark: The Danish Research Centre on Gender Equality.

Thiara, Ravi K. (2008): Building Good Practices in Responses to Black and Minority Ethnic Women Affected by Domestic Violence: Issues from the UK. In: Federal Chancillery/Federal Ministry for Women, Media and Regional Policy (eds.): 10 Years of Austrian Anti-violence Legislation. Vienna: Published by the editors, pp. 130–140.

Thiara, Ravi K./Gill, Aisha K. (eds.) (2010): Violence Against Women in South Asian Communities: Issues for Policy and Practice. London: Jessica Kingsley Publishers.

United Nations (1992): General Recommendation No. 19 on Violence against Women, Committee on the Elimination of Discrimination against Women (CEDAW) 11th session, 1992, New York.

United Nations/GA (2006): In-depth study on all forms of violence against women. Report of the Secretary-General, Doc A761/122/Add.1, New York.

United Nations/CEDAW Committee (2007a): Views of the CEDAW Committee under Article 7, Para. 3, of the Optional Protocol to the CEDAW Convention (thirty-ninth session), Communication No. 5/2005, No. CEDAW/C/39/D/5/2005. www.un.org/womenwatch/daw/cedaw/protocol/dec-views.htm (28.02.2009)

United Nations/CEDAW Committee (2007b): Views of the CEDAW Committee under Article 7, Para. 3, of the Optional Protocol to the CEDAW Convention (thirty-ninth session), Communication No. 56/2005, No. CEDAW/C/39/D/6/2005. www.un.org/womenwatch/daw/cedaw/protocol/dec-views.htm (28.02.2009)

United Nations (2008): Good practice in legislation on violence against women. Report of the Expert group meeting organized by United Nations Division for the Advancement of Women United Nations Office on Drugs and Crime. Vienna.

UN-Kinderrechtskonvention (1989): Übereinkommen über die Rechte des Kindes. Internet: http://tychsen.homepage.t-online.de/ksb/rechte/00.htm (6.6.2011)

WAVE (2004): Away from Violence. European Guidelines for Setting up and Running a Women's Refuge. Vienna.

WAVE (2008): Country Report 2008. Reality Check on European Services for Women and Children Victims of Violence. Vienna.

What Do We Know About Gendered Violence and Ethnicity Across Europe From Surveys?

Stephanie Condon, Maud Lesné and *Monika Schröttle*

In recent years, political and academic debate on VAW in Europe has been appropriated by an almost obsessive focus on immigrants and their descendants. The media have played a key role in relaying statements by politicians and reports of sexual harassment and rape, murder, forced marriage and honour crimes, and female genital mutilation. In the spotlight have been the victims: young women of immigrant parentage, born in Western Europe or having arrived there during childhood or adolescence, living very often in metropolitan housing estates. Most often, their assigned 'origins' (resulting from their parents' migration histories) are North or Sub-Saharan African, Turkish or South Asian. Meanwhile, in the near background are, on the one hand, the perpetrators of the violence – generally understood to be the men of 'their' groups – and, on the other hand, 'their culture'. The chapters in this Reader investigate the reasons for the sudden focus on these populations, and on the 'specific' forms of violence seen to be socially acceptable by their communities, as well as the consequences of such perceptions and representations. In many ways, the beliefs and assumptions underpinning discourse – and much social practice and policy – have established themselves without recourse to representative data. Local and national governments have sought scientific validation for their policies by requesting 'hard', statistical (i.e. 'reliable') data. Yet these requests are usually made with little knowledge about how prevalence is measured, how population statistics are compiled or how relationships between various factors, characteristics and acts are inferred. There are also assumptions regarding the boundaries of immigrant or ethnic minority categories.

A certain number of European prevalence studies have attempted to take on board these issues. Very often, the reports indicate that, whilst violence against women is a universal social problem that concerns women of all social backgrounds, ethnic groups and age groups, migrant women and black and ethnic minority women are at higher risk of experiencing violence within and outside partner and family relationships (Jaspard et al. 2003; Müller and Schröttle 2004; CAHRV 2006). The studies conclude that this greater vulnerability is linked to women's less favourable socio-economic situations in relation to most of the majority population in the countries in which they live, racism, discrimination and social isolation. Since they are designed to analyse prevalence, using indicators describing the current situation of women, these surveys contain very little information on the migration trajectories or background of the women, or on cultural practices. Using examples of results from the major prevalence surveys, this chapter investigates the specificity or universality of different forms of violence, gives a critical viewpoint of statistical measurement of risks facing some groups of women and discusses important methodological considerations for future quantitative research on the subject.

Prevalence research on violence against women in Europe

Over the last decade or so, many countries around the world have started to collect data about violence against women (Gautier 2004; Hagemann-White 2001; Heise et al. 1999; Martinez and Schröttle et al. 2006a; Jaspard and Condon 2007). This was in response to the Beijing Platform call for the gathering of statistical data on the prevalence and forms of violence experienced by women throughout the world. It was clear that official crime statistics could only give a glimpse of the tip of the iceberg in relation to the scope and intensity of interpersonal violence, not just because they revealed only convictions or reporting to the police, but also because the categories used to describe acts corresponding to certain forms of violence recognised as 'crimes' (Hagemann-White 2001; Jaspard et al. 2003). These definitions of course vary from one national context to another. Whilst criminological surveys have produced detailed information on victimisation through different crimes on a national or international basis, they often cannot produce data on violence in close relationships, such as violence through partners or other family members. This is because the framework of crime victimisation is usually not an adequate framework to remember or to report cases of violence through very close persons as these are often not felt to be crimes or violent acts. One exception is the British Crime Survey with its specific self-completion module on domestic violence, sexual assault and stalking (Mirrlees-Black 1999; Walby and Allen 2004). Hence the move towards VAW prevalence surveys, whose aim was to measure the extent and types of violence experienced. Setting these acts or situations within their context contributed to developing international standards of what constituted violence and intolerable behaviour, to be condemned by state and legal institutions. Publications by the WHO, bringing together results from the DHS surveys conducted in many countries in the South (Heise et al. 1999; Ambrosetti et al. 2011), and international research networks on VAW like the EU Co-ordination Action on Human Rights Violations (CAHRV) have revealed the efficiency of certain indicators and reports from national surveys have contributed to building a substantial body of knowledge on the contexts and forms of violence against women.

Violence against women takes many forms. There is now a wide international consensus that it includes not only physical and sexual violence but also psychological. Another aspect of variation in the types of violence is the context in which it takes place. Earlier surveys in Europe focussed on married or cohabiting couple relationships (Römkens 1989; Gillioz, De Puy and Ducret 1997), or alternatively on the household. Violence in this context is often referred to as 'domestic violence,' although the use of this term is questioned by some who claim that it confuses violence against a partner and that towards children (as well as other violent family relationships). Studies from 1996 onwards extended the perspective to also include other contexts of violence against women in various life situations, e.g. in public space, in the work place and/or by other family members and acquaintances (Heiskanen and Piispa 1997; Jaspard et al. 2003; Lundgren and Westerstrand 2000; Müller and Schröttle 2004; Reingardiene 2003).

During this period, methodology on VAW research has improved, enabling disclosure of hitherto unreported forms of violence. For example, summarizing questions on experience of violence have been supplemented by lists of items referring to specific acts or behaviour – including a move to no longer using the term 'violence' – and combined measures of questioning (e.g. face-to-face interviews and additional written questionnaires on sensitive topics). Researchers sought to design instruments that would facilitate the reporting of violence. Furthermore, VAW research nowadays uses only specially trained (mostly female) interviewers and aims to ensure that the respondent is alone with the interviewer. Other factors, including those relating to ethical issues and to the safety of the interviewees, intervene in the design of current research instruments (Hagemann-White 2000; 2001; CAHRV Reports 2006–2007).

Another trend within current prevalence research is to examine the different levels of severity of violence as well as the patterns and consequences of violence, not only throughout the life span, but also within one partner relationship (see CAHRV 2007; Schröttle and Ansorge 2009). A fragmented view of violence that differentiates only between forms of violence experienced by women cannot adequately reflect the reality of violence through the life course as well as within intimate relationships, as both are often marked by a combination and accumulation of various violent forms and actions. Therefore, all three forms of violence (psychological, physical and sexual) in combination as well as their severity levels and frequency have to be considered to assess whether specific *patterns* of violence and their consequences on social and economic participation, and health and so on, produce further victimisation. This makes it possible to distinguish, for example, severe forms of continued violence and abuse from less severe and/or isolated violent incidents and to quantify them.

Overall, prevalence data from several European surveys show that one in five to more than one in three women in several European countries have experienced at least one act of physical and/or sexual violence by a current and/or former partner. Also that one in 10 to more than one in 4 women were affected by several forms of psychological violence (Martinez and Schröttle et al. 2006b: 12–13, 23–24). A high level of overlapping of forms of violence by partners was found in all the European studies (ibid.: 29). Though domestic violence experienced by current or former partners is the most common form of violence reported in all the European studies, significant rates of violence by other (known/unknown) perpetrators were also reported: 3–11% of women reported physical violence through others than partners/ex-partners during their adult life and 5–8% sexual violence through other perpetrators than partners (ibid.: 33– 35).

Although the methods of recording and measuring violence against women and the understanding of this complex and long invisible phenomenon have progressed, surveys carried out within the general population do not allow us to know whether the results are valid for minority groups. Most studies on prevalence of interpersonal violence in Europe have focused on violence against women, children and adolescents. There have been very few prevalence studies with a focus on violence against older people or against especially vulnerable groups such as disabled persons, homosexuals/bisexuals, and migrants. With respect to migrants and the minorities composed of immigrants and their descendants, definitions of groups involved in the samples of the studies vary from country to country, owing to differences relating to citizenship status, language spoken or ethnic backgrounds of the interviewees. Detailed results are not always published in the survey reports. Yet the projection of migrant and black/ethnic minority women to the front stage of debate on violence against women means that further effort is necessary to produce data to inform this debate. Do women migrants face specific risks in relation to violence? Do their daughters face similar risks? How can representative surveys be improved to enable us to examine such processes?

Prevalence of violence against migrant and ethnic minority women

Statistical studies of violence against women in migrant/ethnic minority communities in Europe are very rare, as are national level studies including data enabling us to situate the experiences of such groups. Accounts of violence revealed in anthropological studies or local monographs on migration are analyzed in relation to the societies in which these women – or their mothers – spent their childhood and youth and to often so-called 'traditional' values that remain intact after migration to more modern societies. These values, and their impact on women's lives, are seen as an obstacle to social integration in the 'host society'. Thus, differences in levels of fertility, in labour market participation and so on between migrant groups or ethnic minorities and the general population have been explained in terms of the maintenance or loss of such values – and their corollary, the stagnation or improvement in gender status. In the case of violence against women, few data sources have been available in order for such comparisons to be made.

During the CAHRV programme[1], which brought together various European prevalence researchers who had conducted national surveys on violence against women, an exploratory comparison of violence against migrant and non-migrant women in Germany and France was set up (Condon and Schröttle 2006). Both national surveys had collected data on violence against migrant women and their descendants[2]. The originality of the German survey was that it included specific samples of what were defined as 'Turkish' women (that is, women born in Turkey or descendants of migrants) and women from countries of the former Soviet Union interviewed in their mother tongue language. Questionnaires were translated into French and Russian languages and interviews were conducted by mother tongue language interviewers who were of Turkish and Russian origin. Conversely, the French survey was based on a representative sample of women living in France and the analysis of violence experienced by migrant women or descendants of migrants could only be achieved by constructing sub-populations, using the questions on nationality at birth and country of birth.[3] Moreover,

1 www.cahrv-osnabruck

2 The German sample for this secondary analysis included 4,768 women of German origin, 259 Turkish-origin women and 317 women from Eastern European countries who had a current partner at the time of the interview. The French sample included 186 women of North-African origin and 6,300 women of mostly French origin.

3 Condon S, 2005, 'Violence against women in France and issues of ethnicity' in Malsch M et Smeenk W, *Family violence and police reaction*, London, Ashgate Publishers, pp.59–82.

since the survey was conducted by telephone, only women with a sufficient command of French could be interviewed.

There are differences, of course, in the French and German immigration contexts. Post-colonial migrations represent a large part of immigration flows from the 1960s to the present day, particularly from North and Sub-Saharan Africa, whilst Germany's main immigration route was from Turkey, through the *gastarbeiter* programme. Nevertheless, present discourses in each country, constructed through the media and by politicians, bear many similarities and reveal the profound conviction – partly based on representations of the inferior status of women within these groups leading to a 'cultural' justification of violence against women – that these 'foreign' populations cannot integrate. The aim of this analysis was to inform public debate by providing some indication of the prevalence and forms of violence against certain groups of migrant or ethnic minority women at the same time as setting their experiences within the overall context of violence against women in France and Germany. Comparison of rates of reported violence between these groups and the majority group in each country, thus, goes some way to contextualising the phenomenon. Given the substantial differences in the questionnaires, the survey methods, the definition of the intimate partner relationship and also the period of reference used to measure the violence, the rates per se were not to be compared. Rather, what was analysed was the internal comparison within each data set. Higher rates and levels of violence were found for migrant women or women of immigrant parentage in both countries. A breakdown of the different forms of violence suggests that some forms present a specific risk to migrant women and their descendants.

Fewer significant differences between the minority and majority populations were observed in relation to psychological or verbal violence but here results were in part contradictory as the German survey found more differences with respect to psychological violence than the French survey. However, the results from the German as well as from the French survey show significantly higher rates of male dominance and control reported by migrant women in couples or their descendants than within the majority population. Items relating to jealousy, dominance and restriction of outside contacts showed higher rates for these groups of women in both contexts. But though male dominance and control is reported significantly more often by these groups in both surveys, the surveys show that this problem is relevant for women of the majority group too and cannot be reduced simply to the experience of migrant women or their descendants.

Various items were proposed in the two surveys with the objective of exploring the extent of threats of violence. Very similar results on threats are to be found in each survey, as migrant women or women of immigrant parentage reported significantly higher rates of threat with a weapon, and threats to kill, especially within the younger age groups. The higher rates of threats of violence against immigrant minority women in both countries may reflect the higher rates of manifest and severe violence perpetrated against women by their partners. Women of Turkish origin tend to stay longer in violent relationships than women of German origin, whose divorce-rate is generally higher. Not being able to escape such relationships has been shown to contribute to higher reported rates of violence generally (Jaspard et al. 2003).

Without casting doubt on the fact that these higher rates of violence are a problem that has to be addressed, it must be stressed that the majority of the North African or Turkish minority women in each sample did not report violence at the hands of their partners. Many factors intervene, generating higher or lower levels of reporting. Sunita Kishor (2005) has long warned against taking prevalence differentials at face value. These differentials doubtless include differentials in reporting, as some women are more likely to under-report, thus complicating the observation of actual differences. We still do not know, for example, whether migrant women living in surroundings of high acceptance of VAW tend to report violence in surveys more openly or whether, on the contrary, they report less violence because of feelings of guilt and shame or of simply not wanting to disclose intimate information to the interviewer. Social and cultural differences between interviewer and respondent may certainly intervene. It must be noted that there are high taboos regarding the reporting of experiences of violence within the majority populations of women, too, especially among more highly educated women. Whatever the national context, the shame attached to talking about violence to which one 'should not be exposed' may prevent women from reporting (Ambrosetti, Abu Amara and Condon 2011). What needs to be thoroughly investigated are the risk factors, meaning that some women are more at risk of being victims of violence than others, and also which forms of violence are specific to migrant and ethnic minority women?

Risk factors and specific vulnerability of ethnic minority women to gender-based violence

Ambivalence of certain results makes the identification of 'risk factors' difficult

Risk factor analysis with respect to VAW aims to find out which groups of women are more vulnerable than others, which men tend to perpetrate violence against women and which factors might support the development of violence within couple relationships. There is growing interest in research and in practice in identifying risk and protective factors.

Many studies have collected relevant information, but in most cases limited resources have not permitted multi-dimensional analysis of factors that are likely to increase or reduce the risk of experiencing violence and the risk of staying in violent situations or relationships (Martinez and Schröttle et al. 2006a, 2006b, 2007). Thus, systematic research on risk and protective factors in relation to partner violence is still limited. A number of correlates emerge from these studies but it is impossible to show which factors are most important, how factors are interconnected and how the direction and interplay of various risk factors with victimisation can be identified (Schröttle and Khelaifat in this Reader). It must be stressed that if one factor is correlated with violence, this does not mean that the factor can be seen as an isolated variable. Rather, it is likely to be related to other, more relevant factors. Similarly, it cannot be deduced that the violence experienced by a majority of women is related to this factor; and in turn, nor can it be deduced that respondents giving a positive answer to the question exploring this factor have experienced violence (Schröttle and Ansorge 2009). For example, the German survey showed that although unemployment of one or both partners might be a risk factor for VAW, in most relationships in which (severe) violence had occurred, neither partner had experienced unemployment; nor had most unemployed women or men experienced or perpetrated violence within their relationship (ibid). Further research must to be carried out in order to find out under which circumstances and within which combination of factors certain risk factors lead to a higher likelihood of violence. Combining multi-dimensional quantitative research with qualitative research about the history of violence in women's/men's lives and couple relationships is certainly the most fruitful path towards understanding the role and interdependency of risk factors as well as of protective factors for VAW.

From the universal to the specific

The German survey offered the opportunity of exploring the reasons for higher levels of violence recorded in previous studies. The two groups of women studied (migrant women from Turkey, or having parents born there, or women born in the former Soviet republics) are affected twice as frequently by patterns of severe psychological abuse by their current partners than German women with no migration background. This suggests that, as far as psychological abuse is concerned, not ethnicity but the consequences of migration and the accompanying social tensions and strains on gender roles play a role in amplifying the risk of violence. Thus, more information about migration history – both for women and their partners (where these have migrated) – is necessary to go beyond a purely ethnicized perspective on the risk of being subjected to violence.

Before detailing the various factors that make the migration context particularly favourable to an increased experience of violence, we need to outline aspects of women's lives which, in any context, augment the risk of violence. Both the French and German surveys found that women who had suffered violence and different forms of hardship (including witnessing violence within the family) during childhood and youth were more likely to be subjected to violence during adulthood (Jaspard et al. 2003; Schröttle and Müller 2004). According to the German study, the most powerful risk factor for severe violence against women in couple relationships was childhood experience of violence. Women who had experienced violence during childhood and/or adolescence had a two to threefold risk of suffering partner violence in later life; women who had been sexually abused before their 15th birthday had a fourfold risk of suffering sexual abuse in adult life. Three quarters of women affected by severe violence in current relationships had experienced physical, sexual and/or psychological assaults during childhood or adolescence and, as a consequence, are intensely affected psychologically and physically. Similar results were found in a local study[4] conducted by Maryse Jaspard and Maud Lesné in 2007 in one of the northern Paris suburbs: having suffered hardship or acts of violence, or being a witness to serious family conflict or violence, were principal factors in adult experiences of violence, whatever the geographical origins of respondents. This emphasises the key role of inter-generational transmission of violence. Although identified as a key factor in experiencing violence, this does not imply that all women who have lived through hardship or been subjected to violence during childhood will experience it later. Other factors and events often act in combination to increase the risk of experiencing violence. Migration or being part of a minoritized/ethnicized group produce specific circumstances and place women in a more vulnerable position with respect to violence.

4 Survey conducted in the Seine-Saint-Denis district north of Paris, in 2007, commissioned by the local authority. Detailed results from the survey relating to migration or ethnicity have not yet been published. For further information, see internet source: cooperation-territoriale.seine-saint-denis.fr/.../A154_07_Premiers_resultats_d_enquete_sur_les_comportements_sexistes_et_violents.pdf

Migration and minority status as factors of vulnerability

Migration is often perceived as a positive phenomenon, offering individuals the chance of social and economic betterment. At the same time, the process can generate a certain amount of upheaval, as people are uprooted from familiar surroundings and make their way to a destination, usually unknown or at best, imagined. Women migrants have increasingly begun to be seen as actors in the migration process, participating in family decision-making or planning their own autonomous emigration. Migration, nonetheless, continues to be a hazardous experience for many women, whether they are primary instigators of their departure or not. Encounters with immigration services in the destination, employers, housing gatekeepers, and so on can be difficult, especially when women have limited knowledge of or skills in the majority language of the destination country. Women who travel to join partners may have their immigration status settled in advance. Yet, with the passing of time and as their legal residency approaches it's end, they can find themselves in a vulnerable position – particularly if relations with their partner have become tense or violent. Those who lack resources in terms of education or capital may find themselves in great difficulty. The question of social isolation is of prime importance since many women may not have access to social networks, either compatriot networks or ones formed in the neighbourhood. Thus, they may not be aware of support facilities for women experiencing intimate partner or other types of interpersonal violence. Once again, knowledge of the majority language of the country is important for accessing information about their rights and the ways of finding their way around an administrative system about whose institutions and legal framework they remain ignorant.

The legal arrangements governing the settlement of immigrants in a state may also be a vulnerability factor for women by amplifying inequality in the marital relationship and limiting the autonomy of women. For example, in the context of family reunion in France, the conditions of obtaining and maintaining legal residence in essence limit the autonomy of women because the permit is inherently linked to the sustainability of their marital and legal status and, up until recently, have placed them[5] in a situation of dependency vis-à-vis their partners during the two years after their arrival in France. In Germany, the duration necessary for independent legal status has recently been

5 Law change in July 2010: Loi du 210–769 du 9 juillet 2010 art 12. This text aims to give legal protection to foreigners with respect to intimate partner violence through the creation of a specific residence permit. At the time of writing this chapter, it is too early to know what the impact of the law has been in protecting im/migrant women against partner violence.

expanded from two to three years and thus lengthens the time during which women remain dependent. Many forms of control may be exercised by the partner, including the confiscation of identity papers or any official papers necessary in obtaining a residence permit or its renewal, barring of access to financial resources and women being made to feel that they owe an allegiance to their husband for making their migration possible. Control may be exercised in other cases by a partner who has stayed in the woman's country of origin and uses the children for transnational blackmail.

As regards women born in the country of immigration or who migrated at an early age, their vulnerability is more specifically related to the social segregation and stigmatization endured by considerable proportions of minorities, as well as being victims of discrimination themselves. A recent German study found that a significant proportion of migrant women in Germany are affected by violence and health problems and have more difficulties in leaving abusive situations, also because they are undermined by social and racial discrimination within German society (see chapter of Schröttle and Khelaifat in this Reader). Despite increased awareness of discrimination and racism suffered by visible minorities, only very few surveys on violence against women, to date, have included these factors in the analysis of violence against women systematically (see chapter by Romito et al. in this Reader). Generally, in Europe, regional variations in intimate partner violence have not been a focus for attention. Media reports and declarations made by some women's associations tend to suggest, however, that in some areas of countries such as France, social deprivation and social exclusion combines with gender and ethnicity to increase the risk of interpersonal violence.[6] Accounts of sexist and sexual violence experienced by young and often adolescent women reveal a heightened vulnerability of these groups. The issue of strict social control – exemplified by the wearing of the Islamic veil by some women – has become incorporated into debates on gender, 'race' and religion (Gaspard and Khosrokhavar 1995; Amiraux 2003).

Discrimination and racism, by limiting access to goods and essential services such as improved housing or employment, serve to socially exclude minority women and discourage them to report violence, making them more vulnerable. Moreover, the trend towards the racialization of violence against

6 *Ni putes ni soumises* (*Neither tarts nor submissive women*) is the name that has been given to the movement in protest against two images of young immigrant women and their descendants; the former, attributed by those criticizing their right to dressing as most young women of their age group and to choosing to go out alone, the latter, stereotyped view of these women as being dominated – and accepting this domination – by husbands, fathers and other male family members. The former representation is said to be a product of local 'community', the latter, the outsider view.

women belonging to visible minorities establishes a distrust of women vis-à-vis institutions. Women may face a cultural relativism questioning the abnormality and the unacceptability of violence they endure (Batsleer et al. 2002; Thiara in this Reader). Racism and discrimination can exacerbate the reluctance to confront the official institutions whose assistance is often perceived as inappropriate.

Critical points of the measurement of violence against ethnic minority women

The lack of data and the persistence of stereotypes hamper the development of strategies adapted to assist minority women in the context of policies to combat violence against women. The construction of appropriate tools for collecting data on violence against immigrant and descendants of immigrants is essential to carry out a thorough study and combat the stigma attached to certain groups and also interpretations that overlook or disregard the pervasiveness of violence against women throughout society.

Considerations for sample size and composition

If the necessary categorization of respondents depending on their migration background, their country of origin or that of their parents, as well as that of their partners, has begun to be standard in some surveys, building a sample adapted to detailed analysis is a more sensitive issue. Additionally, the choice of data collection method is linked to numerous constraints, such as residential instability or limited knowledge of the official language of the country in which the respondents live and reduce our capacity to reach a sufficient heterogeneity of women's situations. The quality of the measurement will also depend on the capacity to record the multiple forms and the dynamism of violence, depending upon the context in which they take place.

Owing to insufficient numbers, most surveys conducted in Europe have not been able to pursue analysis of results by taking account of these numerous risk factors. Studying minority groups by origin, and often what are relatively marginal situations, impose constraints of size and composition for using a representative sample of the population. A first alternative is to over-represent randomly selected immigrants and the descendants of immigrants in general or for specific origins in the preparation of the sample. This method, already tested in the German survey, enables us to produce higher case numbers together with the ethnic minority women from the main survey and is an important basis for further investigation within target populations groups. The constraints of composition and size of the sample surveys, as well as protocols including questionnaire translation, generate extra cost and time in their implementation. Moreover, in some countries, the identification of descendants of immigrants for their over-representation may be complex. An important consideration is that the commissioners of surveys must allow sufficient time for the survey instrument to be developed and the protocol to be implemented.

Beyond these efforts in terms of sampling, we need to identify the factors that lead to the under-representation of immigrant women and their descendants in surveys. What obstacles contribute to this under-representation and how can we overcome them? In order to reach immigrants and the descendants of immigrants in the diversity of their situations, the method chosen should compensate for two difficulties: the residential instability that characterizes parts of recent migrants and also the problem in reaching young people, and people who are more isolated because of language or other problems. Indeed, considering the difficulties of settling in a new country requires extending the coverage beyond a household sample. As an illustration, the study on violence in the Seine Saint Denis local authority, mentioned earlier, attempted to widen the scope of reaching respondents using an innovative method. Face-to-face interviews were carried out with 1,600 young women aged 18–21 years contacted through universities, colleges, training centres, local job information centres, hostels for young workers, or encountered in the street or in shopping malls. Since household samples have tended to under-represent the younger populations, the aim was to find a way of minimizing selection bias and to reach women from a broad range of backgrounds. Such methods could be appropriate for contacting migrant or other mobile populations.

These two difficulties are compounded by the lack of knowledge of the majority language. However, one problem is that many migrant women, particularly those recently arrived or those suffering from social isolation or exclusion from the labour market, do not speak the language well enough to take part in the interviews conducted in the majority language. Not many surveys have been able to adopt the procedure followed by the German survey, which conducted interviews in different languages in order to increase the participation of migrant women. Such techniques may help to reduce obstacles such as the refusal to participate in surveys by women who are unlikely to respond at the time of the first contact with interviewers owing to diminished personal autonomy and thus a lack of confidence in the ability to take part (Jaspard et al. 2003).

Furthermore, as has been widely discussed in literature on empirical methods in social sciences, the social positioning and distance between interviewer and respondent is an issue to be considered. There is no real consensus on the question. Some studies have found that choosing interviewers from similar geographical origins or who also have a migration background encourages the disclosure of violence (Müller and Schröttle 2004). One argument is that it may be easier for the respondent to confidentially report about her own experience if she does not fear prejudice or stigmatisation by the interviewer. At the same time, interviewers have to be trained adequately to avoid over-identification with the respondents and insure neutral interviewing. Conversely, other studies have found that migrant or minority women may feel more comfortable about discussing intimate details (such as sexuality, virginity, female genital cutting) with women outside their community or not from the same geographical background (for example, the above-mentioned Paris suburbs study). Social differences between interviewers and respondents certainly intervene in the disclosure process, and it may be that similarity in age plays a more important role in encouraging reporting.

Questions aimed at gaining more relevant information about 'specific' vulnerability

The categorization of women according to their migration background requires systematic questioning about their country of birth and nationality at birth, as well as about other aspects of their migration trajectory (e.g. length of stay in the country of immigration). The identification of descendants of immigrants means that information on their parents' background and their own experiences in relation to this background is necessary. For a more detailed analysis that takes into account the heterogeneity of the situations of immigrant women, it is necessary to gather information on the conditions of arrival (age, marital status, residence, knowledge of the majority language) but also on their changing residency status since migration, their family circumstances and their paid work experiences. Also, despite the sensitivity of this issue, it is essential to distinguish between undocumented women and women awaiting regularization. These women living clandestinely represent a population at risk and face particular difficulties in undertaking protective action against violence.

As well as categorizing women, information must also be gathered on their partners, both present and past. Enriching the available data on former partners or marital history implies the sometimes unsettling or painful memorizing of past relationships. Indeed, collecting data for different partners increases all the time spent on completing the questionnaire and therefore the cost of the investigation. However, limiting the questions to the current partner relationships neglects essential contextual information on violence experienced in the past particularly as a common trend found in European surveys is for higher rates of (more severe) violence experienced at the hands of a former partner. Furthermore, such information, along with questions relating to consent to marriage, would be vital in the study of arranged or forced marriage (Hamel 2008) and how some women escape from such marriages and form new partnerships (Collet 2008). Thus marital histories must be linked up to the migration histories of both partners. Similarly, questions on aspects of family relations must be posed in order to grasp how strict social control might put women, both migrants and their descendants, at greater risk of violence.

Surveys on violence against migrant women should always include questions about discrimination through institutions and society and factors that reduce their ability to leave violent situations. They, furthermore, have to include questions on violence and social control within their families by other family members and not just partners, in order to better describe the context in which violence has been experienced and which might detain women from leaving violent situations.

Incorporating questions on the above themes into survey instruments will go some way to identifying what specific forms of violence are experienced by migrant women and their descendants, inside or outside the family home or in other interpersonal relationships. It will then be possible to locate more easily those forms of violence which are considered specific to certain national or regional groups. Immigrant women and their descendants are not a homogeneous group, neither in social terms nor in their representations of gender relations. Thus, the challenge is to track down particularizing assumptions – conscious or unconscious – while allowing the description of all types of violence in their various forms and the different risk factors. This brings up issues in relation to specific factors for different groups (questions on residency status for foreign nationals, on racial discrimination for visible minorities) and must be reconciled with a need to account for macro, contextual factors that increase risk of experiencing violence. Thus, the development of the questionnaire becomes a real challenge.

Conclusion

Despite progress in identifying the types and degrees of victimization with the development of sophisticated methods constantly refined over successive surveys conducted in Europe, research is still limited when it comes to counting and analyzing violence against women from minority groups. This lack of data is a major obstacle. It renders analysis and communication on these issues particularly sensitive. Cases reported in the media admittedly give subjective viewpoints but are no less real. Despite the existence of many localized surveys in Europe showing the universality of domestic and intimate partner violence, the risk remains that the results of such studies can be instrumentalized to reinforce racist and sexist essentialist perspectives.

Methodological precautions are essential to limit and counter the biased interpretations of the results that would only convey a stereotypical view and increase stigmatization of immigrant groups and descendants of immigrants, regarding the levels of violence they experience. Deciphering the frequency and forms of violence suffered by ethnic minority women without participating in the process of *othering* is a major challenge. We need to question assumptions at the same time as rendering visible the specific vulnerabilities placing migrant and ethnic minority women at risk of violence. Analysis of their social, family and economic circumstances, their education, work and migration histories must be set in context using other micro variables, such as indicators of gender relations in the household, health status, sexuality, experience of discrimination and racism, as well as using macro indicators describing the political and social context in relation to the research object (majority attitudes regarding gender roles, gender sensitive policies, level of awareness of laws protecting women against violence, anti-discrimination laws, immigration policy). The broadening of the context in which data is analysed is important to shift the focus away from women's 'cultural characteristics', enabling a more balanced perspective that brings in the characteristics of the society in which they live their lives. We need to produce the means by which to study violence against women in its various forms and to participate in a global reflection towards its eradication. This is an essential part of progressing towards gender equality.

References

Amiraux, Valérie (2003): Discours voilés sur les musulmanes en Europe. Comment les musulmans sont-ils devenus des musulmanes. In: Social Compass, vol.50, n°1, pp. 85–96.

Ambrosetti, Elena/Abu Amara, Nisrin/Condon, Stephanie (2011): Gender based violence in Egypt: analysing impacts of political reforms, social and demographic change, In: Violence against Women; Sage Publications (forthcoming).

CAHRV (2006a): State of European research on the prevalence of interpersonal violence and its impact on health and human rights. CAHRV – Report 2005. Co-ordination Action on Human Rights Violations funded through the European Commission, 6th Framework Programme, Project No. 506348. Published online: www.cahrv.uni-osnabrueck.de

CAHRV (2006b): Comparative reanalysis of prevalence of violence against women and health impact data in Europe – obstacles and possible solutions. Testing a comparative approach on selected studies. CAHRV – Report 2006. Co-ordination Action on Human Rights Violations funded through the European Commission, 6th Framework Programme, Project No. 506348. Published online: http://www.cahrv.uni-osnabrueck.de/reddot/190.htm

CAHRV (2007): Perspectives and standards for good practice in data collection on interpersonal violence at European Level. CAHRV – Report 2007. Co-ordination Action on Human Rights Violations funded through the European Commission, 6th Framework Programme, Project No. 506348. Published online: www.cahrv.uni-osnabrueck.de;Stichwort: Publikationen

Collet, Beate (2008): Refuser un 'mariage forcés' ou comment les femmes réagissent-elles face à l'imposition parentale. In: Migrations société, Vol. 20, n° 119, pp. 209–227.

Condon, Stéphanie/Schröttle, Monika (2006): Violence against immigrant women and their daughters: a first comparative study using data from the French and German national surveys on violence against women. In: Martinez, Manuela/Schröttle, Monika et al. (2006b): Comparative reanalysis of prevalence of violence against women and health impact data in Europe – obstacles and possible solutions. Testing a comparative approach on selected studies. CAHRV – Report 2006. Co-ordination Action on Human Rights Violations funded through the European Commission, 6th Framework Programme, Project No. 506348. Internet: www.cahrv.uni-osnabrueck.de/reddot/190.htm (01.05.2011)

Gaspard, Françoise/Khosrokhavar, Farhad (1995): Le foulard et la République. Paris: La Découverte.

Gautier, Arlette (2004): Les violences au sein de la famille. In: Quesnel, A. (ed.): Rapport des experts français à la 35e session Population et développement, Paris, Ministère de l'emploi et de la solidarité, Direction de la population et des migrations, CEPED.

Gillioz, L./De Puy, J./Ducret, V. (1997): Domination et violence envers la femme dans le couple. [Domination and violence towards women within the couple]. Lausanne: Editions Payot. In French.

Hagemann-White, C. (2001): European Research on the Prevalence of Violence against Women. In: Violence against Women, Vol 7, No. 7, Juli 2001, pp. 732–759.

Hagemann-White, C. (2000): Male violence and control. Constructing a comparative European Perspective. In: Duncan, Simon/Pfau-Effinger, Birgit (eds.): Gender, Economy and Culture in the European Union. London.

Hamel, Ch. (2008): Mesurer les mariages forcés. L'appréhension du consentement dans deux enquêtes quantitatives. In: Migrations société, Vol 20, n°119, n°55, pp. 59–81.

Heise, L./Ellsberg, M./Gottemoeller, M. (1999): Ending violence against women. In: Population Reports, 27, n° 4, pp. 1–44.

Jaspard, Maryse et al. (2003): Les violences envers les femmes en France: une enquête nationale. Paris: La Documentation française.

Jaspard, Maryse/Brown, Elizabeth/Lhomond, Brigitte/Saurel-Cubizolles, Marie-Josèphe (2003): Reproduction ou résilience: les situations vécues dans l'enfance ont-elles une incidence sur les violences subies par les femmes à l'âge adulte? In:Revue Française des Affaires Sociales, n°3.

Jaspard, Maryse/Condon, Stephanie (Eds.) (2007): Nommer et compter les violences envers les femmes en Europe: enjeux scientifiques et politiques, Conference proceedings, European conference coorganised by Institut Démographique de l'Université de Paris 1 (IDUP), INED, CAHRV, La Sorbonne [Paris], 26 Septembre 2005/Paris: IDUP.

Kishor, Sunita (2005): 'Domestic violence measurement in the demographic and health surveys: The history and the challenges'. Expert group meeting paper. Violence against women: a statistical overview, challenges and gaps in data collection and methodology and approaches for overcoming them. Organized by the UN Division for the Advancement of Women in collaboration with: Economic Commission for Europe (ECE) and World Health Organization (WHO). 11–14 April, 2005, Geneva.

Lundgren, E./Heimer, G./Westerstrand, J./Kalliokoski, A.M. (2002): Captured queen. Men's violence against women in "equal" Sweden: a prevalence study. Univ. Uppsala.

Mirrlees-Black, C. (1999): Domestic violence: Findings from a new British Crime Survey self completion questionnaire. London: Home Office Research Study 191.

Müller, Ursula/Schröttle, Monika (2004): Lebenssituation, Sicherheit und Gesundheit von Frauen in Deutschland. Eine repräsentative Untersuchung zu Gewalt gegen Frauen in Deutschland. [Health, well-being and personal safety of women in Germany: a representative study on violence against women in Germany.] Federal Ministry for Family Affairs, Senior Citizens, Women and Youth. Long version in German. Short version in German and English. See Internet: http://www.bmfsfj.de, Publikationen.

Reingardiene, J. (2003): "Dilemmas in Private/Public Discourse: Contexts for Gender-based Violence against Women in Lithuania". In: Journal of Baltic Studies, XXXIV (3), pp. 354–368.

Römkens, R. (1989): Onder ons gezegd en gezwegen. Geweld tegen vrouwen in man-vrouwrelaties. [Let's keep it between us. Violence against women by male intimates]. Rijswijk: Department of Welfare and Health. In Dutch.

Schröttle, Monika/Khelaifat Nadia (2008): Gesundheit – Gewalt – Migration: Eine vergleichende Sekundäranalyse zur gesundheitlichen und sozialen Situation und Gewaltbetroffenheit von Frauen mit und ohne Migrationshintergrund in Deutschland. [Health – violence – migration: a comparative secondary analysis of the health and social situation as well as victimisation of migrant an non-migrant-women in Germany. A research project of the Intercisciplinary Centre for Women's and Gender Studies (IFF) of Bielefeld University, funded by the Federal Ministry for Family, Senior Citizens, Women and Youth (BMFSFJ)].

Schröttle, Monika/Ansorge,Nicole (2009): Gewalt gegen Frauen in Paarbeziehungen – eine sekundäranalytische Auswertung zur Differenzierung von Schweregraden, Mustern, Risikofaktoren und Unterstützung nach erlebter Gewalt. [Violence against women in couple relationships – a secondary analyses on differentiate levels of severity, patterns, risk factors and support after the experience of violence. A research project of the Interdisciplinary Centre for Women's and Gender Studies (IFF) of Bielefeld University, funded by the Federal Ministry for Family, Senior Citizens, Women and Youth (BMFSFJ)].

Walby S./Allen J. (2004): Domestic Violence, sexual assault and stalking. Findings from the British Crime Survey. Home Office Research Study 276. Home Office Research, Development and Statistics Directorate. London. www.leeds.ac.uk/sociology/people/sw.htm

Part 2:
Making the Links

Particularly Violent? The Construction of Muslim Culture as a Risk Factor for Domestic Violence

Renée Römkens with *Esmah Lahlah*

> In 2007 a 24-year-old, highly educated woman of Turkish descent, born and raised in the Netherlands, married a Turkish young man from her parents' native village. Her parents had arranged for her to meet him while visiting Turkey so she could make her own choice. She liked him and agreed to marry him. After the wedding, the husband moved to live with his wife in the Netherlands. She was the wage earner. The husband had no job and hardly spoke any Dutch and was in a dependent position. He became violent and abusive towards his wife. When the wife wanted to divorce, her family convinced her to return and try again. She did. Soon the violence resumed. She then convinced her parents that a separation was necessary and they took her in. While the application for the divorce was pending, the young woman was shot by her husband on the way to work while waiting for her train. The husband was arrested. The woman died on the train platform.

This tragic event was extensively portrayed in the Dutch media as a culturally motivated murder (see *Noord Hollands Dagblad* 25 June, 2007; *NRC* 24 May, 2008). The fact that both victim and perpetrator were Turkish and Muslim and that they had been introduced to each other as potential marriage candidates, led to a construction of a narrative in which the victim had been 'forced' to marry, and the perpetrator's motive was 'honour-related'. This reconstruction of both the killing and the couple's marital history is illustrative of the culturalist discourse on violence against women (VAW) among Muslim minorities that is currently evolving in a multi-cultural society that is facing increasingly discriminatory attitudes towards Muslims. Stereotypical images of 'culturally' based violence are growing in popularity and contribute to the discursive construction of Muslim minorities as *particularly* violent, especially towards women, and notably as *more* violent than the native Dutch. This paper critically addresses how this tendency is playing out in Dutch research.

There is a growing concern about violent *public* crime (robbery, burglary, assault) by young males from minority migrant communities, not only in the

Netherlands. It reflects a complex problem where discrimination and social isolation play a role (FRA 2010). Against a backdrop of intensifying discrimination of Muslims in general across Europe (FRA 2009), and ongoing negative stereotyping of Muslim communities, the discrimination reflects a clear gendered dynamic. Muslim women have become the subject of particular concern in categorizing all Muslim women representing the ultimate victims of women's oppression and notably domestic violence as typical for the Muslim community (Roggeband & Verloo 2007). In the Netherlands, the Turkish and Moroccan communities, predominantly Muslim, are the focal subjects of this discourse. Although they constitute a minority of 4.3% (Garssen and Van Duin 2009)[1] they have become emblematic of a wider anti-migration and anti-Muslim/anti- Islam discourse that is evolving, also across Europe (European Monitoring Centre on Racism and Xenophobia 2006; Fundamental Rights Agency 2009; 2010).

Globalization and migration imply a confrontation with forms of VAW that most European societies are less familiar with, like forced marriages, female genital mutilation, and so-called honor-related violence. It is not surprising that such manifestations of violence can be interpreted as the emblematic examples of the violent and oppressive characteristics of some migrant communities, leading to a representation of both perpetrators and victims as the 'other', as 'them', who are unlike 'us' in Western cultures (Okin 1999). In this chapter, we will present the Netherlands as a case study for this kind of rhetorical dynamic. We focus, however, on the most common forms of violence that is not culturally specific: domestic violence and spouse killing. Despite its cross-cultural nature we will point out how a discursive construction of the cultural specificity still takes place when these forms of violence occur within ethnic minorities. From a post-colonial and feminist theoretical perspective, we argue that this rhetorical othering, illustrates that multicultural Europe faces a profound challenge: how to acknowledge the epidemic prevalence of VAW in its midst, notably domestic violence against women, and avoid the trap of an ethnocentric rhetoric in which VAW is used

---

1 The Netherlands has 16.5 million inhabitants, of which migrants constitute 18%. Over half of them (10%) are non-Western migrants. The category migrant includes individuals born outside the Netherlands (first generation) or who have at least one non-Dutch parent (second generation). In this chapter, we focus on the two largest non-European migrant communities: Turkish and Moroccan labour migrants (who moved to the Netherlands from the early 1970s onwards) who together constitute 4.3% of the population. This figure does not fully cover the proportion of people who would identify themselves culturally speaking as (partially or predominantly) Turkish or Moroccan. Since the figure is based on a demographic census-based definition, not on a social-cultural definition, it excludes the third generation, born and educated in the Netherlands (therefore technically not migrants), yet raised in a social and cultural context that is marked by the culture of origin of the first generation.

as a device to position 'the west' (the 'old' Europe) hegemonically against 'the rest', the 'new' Europe (Mohanty 1991; 2004).

First we address the empirical question, whether cultural minorities, mainly the Turkish and Moroccan communities, differ from the native Dutch population in relation to the prevalence of intimate partner violence and spouse killing. Then we reflect on how Dutch research contributed to a selective construction of cultural difference. Finally, we contextualize this discursive shift within two wider concurring trends: a growing anti-migration rhetoric in the Netherlands and an increasing trend towards portraying domestic violence among the native Dutch as a gender neutral phenomenon, affecting men and women alike and not structurally related to any form of inequality or discrimination between men and women.

A brief note on terminology: The first generation of Turks and Moroccans (mostly male) were labour migrants (migrating in the late 1960s, early 1970s). The subsequent generations migrated in the context of family reunion and/or marriages or were born in the Netherlands. From a cultural-religious perspective (the Netherlands is predominantly Judeo-Christian), religion (Islam) is considered to be one of the distinguishing cultural and religious characteristics of both migrant communities, even though there are marked differences in religious identification within the communities. To capture the complexity of markers that can define group membership, we use the terms cultural and migrant minority interchangeably in this chapter. Where relevant, reference will be made to more specific defining characteristics.

Intimate partner violence (IPV) among minorities in the Netherlands: empirical data

Prevalence of IPV and the role of gender among native Dutch

In 1989, the results of the first Dutch in-depth national survey on the prevalence, nature, dynamics, social background, and consequences of domestic violence and marital rape of women were published. At that point, the limited population size of migrant communities in the Netherlands made it virtually impossible to include them in sufficient numbers in a representative population survey. This limitation was explicitly addressed when the first results were published (Römkens 1989; 1992; 1997). Results indicated that at least 21% of all Dutch women had experienced unilateral physical violence from a male partner (for almost half of them that also included rape), over 5% had been involved in mutual violence (both partners initiating and using physical violence with comparable frequency and severity) and another 3% reported having been raped without additional physical abuse.

The question of whether prevalence rates among migrant (Muslim) women were higher was a non-issue in the 1980s. The high prevalence data among native Dutch women were taken as an indication of the pervasiveness of the problem generally. As far as migrant women as victims of domestic violence were concerned, the focus was on improving support and interventions, training professionals to enhance their understanding of specific issues in migrant communities (Deug 1990; De Lima 1994). The assumption was that although the norms and values justifying gendered violence against women might differ across cultures, the prevalence or severity of the violence did not.[2] Domestic violence was considered a gendered problem that affects women equally regardless of class or race/ethnicity.

Towards the late 1990s, two related changes took place: 'wife abuse' was discursively gender neutralized on the one hand and culturalized on the other. In public, and notably Dutch policy discourse, the then common terminology of 'wife abuse' and 'marital rape' was replaced by the generic term *huiselijk geweld (*domestic violence, in *German: haüslicher Gewalt,*). The violence was increasingly analysed as a gender-neutral phenomenon, at least as far as Dutch native women were concerned. Crucial in this tendency was a second population survey on 'family domestic violence', conducted in 1997 at the request of the Justice Department, through a brief gender-neutral questionnaire. Cultural minorities were not included, again for statistical and demographic reasons. Findings on male and female victimization by an (ex-) partner were hardly segregated. The emphasis was on generic prevalence data on any kind of 'domestic violence' (lumping together partner violence, physical and sexual child abuse and elder abuse) which was reported by 43% of the respondents. For the first time the gender neutrality of the phenomenon was suggested. Intimate partner violence was presented as a gender-neutral phenomenon that affected both men and women, although it was mentioned that men's violence was somewhat more severe (Van Dijk et al. 1997; 1998).[3] The question how these results relate to the outcome of the first Dutch survey, underlining the gender-specific nature of domestic violence against women, remained unaddressed. Only secondary analysis, published

---

2 Dutch training and development institutes like Movisie (formerly Trans Act), mostly government-funded, play a pivotal role in the education and training of professionals, see <http://www.movisie.nl>.

3 Note that this survey met with severe methodological criticism (both re. the gender neutrality of its concepts and the width of operationalisations, resulting in prevalence figures with a limited validity as partner violence and childhood victimization were difficult to segregate). The study concluded that men and women were equally at risk of experiencing 'any form' of violence from a partner.

much later (2005), revealed that there actually was a substantial gender difference, indicating a lifetime over-all prevalence for both physical victimization and sexual abuse (as a child by parents, family members, and/or abuse by an ex-partner) for 16% of women and 7% of men (Wittebrood and Veldheer 2005).

Prevalence of IPV and the role of culture among minorities

Concurring with the starting gender neutralization of domestic violence during the late 1990s, there was an unrelated yet growing tendency in the Netherlands to position cultural minorities as a problem (Entzinger 2003). This then translated in the recurring question, both in the media and in political and policy debates, of whether the prevalence and severity of domestic violence among cultural minorities actually differed from the native Dutch (Roggeband and Verloo 2007). In the early 2000s, the Dutch Department of Justice commissioned a replication of the 1997 family violence survey, this time specifically focusing on minority groups. Ignoring the major methodological concerns that had been voiced about the gender biases in the 1997 survey, the same instrument was used, since it would allow a comparison of results, despite its bias. No attention was given to gender or culturally relevant questions in the questionnaire. Only interviewers from the ethnic communities were selected to conduct the face-to-face interviews.

Results regarding prevalence of 'domestic violence' (again adding up physical/sexual child abuse, psychological abuse, and intimate partner violence) turned out to be substantially *lower* for Moroccans and Turks (14% and 21%) compared to the native Dutch in the earlier survey (43%). The severity of intimate partner violence was comparable to that suffered by Dutch victims (Van Dijk et al. 2002: 28). The authors went to great lengths to explain why the prevalence data on domestic violence among ethnic minorities suffered from severe underreporting. It is safe to accept that underreporting affected these data, as it affects any study on domestic violence. What is striking is that the underreporting received selective attention: only in the study of ethnic minorities (Van Dijk et al. 2002: 61). The results of the 1997 survey among native Dutch respondents were actually presented, arguing that they were hardly affected by underreporting (Van Dijk et al. 1998).[4] It is noteworthy that the results of the 2002 prevalence study among ethnic minorities are rarely referred to in Dutch policy papers

4 However, only 3% of the respondents in the migrant study mentioned 'shame' as a reason to not disclose violence, in comparison with 18% of the native Dutch respondents.

on domestic violence. Since results were immediately presented in the context of presumed unreliability, the ongoing assumption was implicitly revealed: ethnic minorities, notably Muslims, are more violent than the native Dutch.

The growing numbers of minority women seeking help (either from the police or in shelters) have often been used to support this assumption,[5] despite the fact that the number of women seeking help can hardly be a reliable indicator of prevalence. Furthermore, the overrepresentation of minority women in shelters for domestic violence victims is an indicator of the relative lack of social resources, which severely limits migrant women's alternatives in their own social networks when in need of temporary accommodation or support. Research in the 1980s showed that, before native Dutch women turn to a shelter, virtually all had first stayed with relatives or friends, up to five times or more (Römkens 1989). Most migrants not only face relatively poor housing conditions, but have few or no relatives to turn to. High levels of social control within some migrant communities easily lead to loyalty conflicts if women seek help.

The limited qualitative Dutch studies in this area indicate that it is the social and cultural contexts in which the violence occurs that merits more attention (Wolf 2006). It is the relational dynamics and justifications for domestic violence that are particularly bound to cultural values. In-depth research among abusive Turkish and Moroccan migrants in the Netherlands revealed that, in the context of migration, traditional patriarchal gender roles that are dominant in the community of origin are under pressure. The exposure of Turkish and Moroccan women to a relatively liberal social climate is perceived by many male family members, notably husbands, as potentially weakening their dominance. For some, this results in justifying violence in culturally specific terms: feelings of loss of control over wives and daughters are perceived as a loss of masculinity and subsequently the loss of a valued social identity in their community. The researchers emphasize that (Islamic) religion is hardly ever invoked as a justification for violence by Turkish or Moroccan perpetrators (Yerden 2008).

5 Muslim migrant women, mostly coming from Turkey and Morocco, constitute about 50 to 60% of the shelter population (Wolf, 2006). With a total of about 14%, they are also slightly overrepresented among domestic violence victims calling the police for help (Ferwerda 2007). Policy makers within the Ministry of Justice immediately raised the question of whether special registration of 'ethnic origin' was required. The many hurdles of the concept 'ethnic origin' as a registration category emerged in a pilot study in two police districts. It resulted in unreliable data that led to negative advice with respect to the feasibility of registering ethnic origin (Willemsen 2007).

International context

International data on prevalence of domestic violence among minority women do not provide an unequivocal answer to the question of whether or not there is more violence among cultural minorities. Varying definitions of the category of (ethnic) minorities pose limitations for an international comparison (Sundaram et al. 2003; Garcia-Moreno et al. 2006).

In the United Kingdom, data are available with respect to fairly broad categories (distinguishing between 'white', 'black' and 'Asian' ethnicities). No significant differences in prevalence of domestic violence were reported between these groups (Walby and Allen 2004). In Germany a slightly higher prevalence of domestic violence against women of Turkish origin was reported (37% vs. 29% German women). Part of this difference is attributed by the researchers to the fact that women of Turkish origin tend to stay longer in violent relationships than women of German origin, whose divorce rate is generally higher (Schröttle et al. 2004). This finding is in line with US studies, indicating that, rather than culture or ethnicity, a complex of intersecting variables affect women's vulnerability to prolonged victimization of domestic violence, notably social isolation, residence status, and the availability of an independent income (Hampton et al. 2005; Richie et al. 2005; Malley-Morrison and Hines 2007; Grzywacz et al. 2009). Within Europe recent research indicates that the psycho-social impact of immigration is a major variable that is positively correlated to prevalence and severity of domestic violence of men against women (Echeburúa et al. 2009; Vatnar and Bjørkly 2010).

Spouse killing, honour killing and the role of 'culture' in the Netherlands

Of all spouse killings in the Netherlands between 1992 and 2006 (N=603), women were by far the majority of victims (79%). Without exception, all women were killed by a male partner. On average 33 women and seven men are killed annually by their intimate partner or ex-partner in the Netherlands (Nieuwbeerta & Leistra 2007: 66). Turkish and Moroccan minorities, and migrant women of other ethnic minorities, are slightly overrepresented among the victims. Of all female victims, 14% are Turkish or Moroccan (Liem et al. 2007: 26). How can this heightened risk of being killed by their spouse for these migrant women be explained? Against the backdrop of the growing number of non-lethal honour-based violence (usually of young women/daughters),[6] it has been suggested that the number of honour-based killings could explain the increase.

Before looking at empirical data, the concepts of spouse killing and so-called honour-based killings need to be dissected. As illustrated in the opening vignette, these concepts are regularly conflated as synonyms as soon as the victim and/or perpetrator are of Turkish or Moroccan descent. The specific meanings of the concept of honour (of the women/girl and *ipse facto* of the family) vary widely (Brenninkmeijer et al. 2009; Van Eck 2001; Bakker 2005).[7] Having said that, the pivotal common element, norms regarding women's sexuality are constitutive of what is culturally defined as appropriate i.e. 'honourable' gender behaviour. Men (i.e., brothers, fathers, husbands) acquire masculine honour through 'protecting' a woman's reputation of chastity, and are responsible for controlling and limiting their sister's (or mother's, or cousin's) social behaviour or any other behaviour that could be interpreted as 'sexual'. Women acquire feminine honour when their behaviour is perceived as chaste. In practice, this translates into a wide range of rules and prohibitions governing women's social and sexual behaviour.[8] A

---

6 Based on reports from shelter staff and the police about women who are abused or under severe threat when they do not submit to traditional gender norms re. sexuality and partner choice, honour- based violence against young women of second generation immigrants seems to be increasing. Since the early 2000s, increasing efforts have been undertaken in the area of prevention and support of victims of honour-based violence, both for police, social work and shelter facilities. The Dutch Ministry of Justice created a special link on honour-related violence on its website on 'Security' and 'Prevention' in the Netherlands, providing information on all aspects of honour-based violence and where to find help or information: <http://www.veiligheidbegintbijvoorkomen.nl/onderwerpen/Agressie_geweld/Eergerelateerd_geweld/>
The principal author is a member of the expert committee and is preparing advice for the Prosecutor General's office on national guidelines for police and prosecutors regarding honour-based violence, to be expected in 2011.

7 In the Turkish-Kurdish community, a distinction is made between two kinds of honour: *sheref*, referring to the social reputation of a man in the community, and *namus*, referring to the chastity in the sexual behaviour of women as the basis of the husband's and the family's honour, which it is the responsibility of the husband or male family members to monitor and protect and to avenge when offended. According to some experts, *namus* is a more absolute category (one has or loses *namus),* whereas *sheref* is more relative, referring to social status and prestige. The husband's *namus* is offended if the wife (or daughter, sister) is the subject of public gossip because she might be *perceived* as independently sexually active (mainly outside marriage). In the Moroccan community, honour-based violence is less common and cultural norms regarding honour are more variable. The general Arabic concept of *heshma* is used as a common denominator for honour and shame-related issues. They touch upon the sexual honour of women (*hurma*) especially girls' chastity, and women's obedience generally (*sharaf*) (Brenninkmeijer et al. 2009, 19–21; Yerden, 2008 37–38). In virtually all Muslim cultures lesbian or gay activities are unacceptable (often criminalized) and considered an offence against honour.

8 For a wife, they range from a prohibition of any outdoor activity that is unsupervised by a male relative, that could involve encounters with unrelated men, to a prohibition of extra-

spouse killing qualifies as an honour-based killing if the motive for the killing is related to the woman's sexual behaviour perceived as unchaste. The killing of an abused wife, who had no other reason to separate than the wish to escape from her partner's violence, would therefore not qualify as a so-called honour-based killing. From this perspective, the number of so-called *honour killings of wives* is not increasing in the Netherlands. Of all 603 spouse killing cases between 1992 and 2006, *not one* case was actually an honour killing (Nieuwbeerta and Leistra 2007).

However, major ethnic minorities in the Netherlands are overrepresented among perpetrators of female spouse killing. A recent study, based on the analysis of psychiatric files of suspects of spouse killing, focused on differences in motivation of native Dutch perpetrators and those from the major minorities (Liem et al. 2007).[9] It was concluded that on the level of *situational characteristics*, the 'separation after violent abuse' was the most common feature of all spouse killings with no significant difference between the subgroups. On the level of *personal motivational characteristics* a cultural difference seemed to emerge, according to the researchers. 'Hurt pride/honour', referring to sadness and anger about the loss, notably the loss of control over the wife who left (or wanted to leave), and 'grief and shame' about the perceived loss of masculine honour were more often reported about Turks (77%) and Moroccans (59%), compared to 29% of the native Dutch perpetrators. Note however, that in none of these cases sexual honour as defined above had been compromised. It was the perpetrator's failed efforts to effectively control the wife and prevent her from leaving which, across subgroups, was experienced by the men as hurting their honour and pride. The second most frequently reported personal motive was 'fear of loss/abandonment'. This motive was mentioned by almost one third of the Dutch perpetrators (29%), compared to a small minority of Turkish (8%) and Moroccan (12%) perpetrators. In conclusion, the Turkish or Moroccan perpetrators' motives were ultimately categorized by the researchers as specifically 'culturally' motivated: 'referring to an interconnected set of norms and meanings that guide people's perspective on life', in contrast to only 1% of the cases of Dutch perpetrators (Liem et al. 2007: 41, 73, 82–84). The Dutch were pre-

marital sexual activity as violations of the wife's (and her husband's) honour. For a daughter or sister, it means a prohibition of pre-marital sexual or dating activity (up to a prohibition of any social activity that might involve unsupervised encounters with non-related men).

9 The study is based on analyses of 282 psychiatric reports on male perpetrators of spouse killing: 238 native Dutch, 26 of Turkish and 17 of Moroccan descent. Since the number of Turks and Moroccans are very small, the quantitative results need to be interpreted with caution since a shift of one or two respondents translates into suggestively large percentage shifts.

sented as predominantly guided by motives of a psychological nature when killing their wives.

This conclusion deserves scrutiny. Analytically speaking we can observe a selective and biased representation of how masculine honour permeates both Muslim and Western culture. On the one hand, it reflects the conflation indicated before, where any killing of a wife by someone with a Muslim background is labelled as honour-killing, without a deeper analysis of the specifics of the case. On the other hand, it also reflects a lack of understanding of how deeply ingrained masculine honour of men is in Western patriarchal culture. Without glossing over the differences in the way masculinity is defined across cultures with respect to the concept of honour, and the public interest that is attached to honour as a family-value, it is important to recognize commonalities in the way honour and masculinity are intertwined in any patriarchal culture in order to avoid the selective culturalisation of individual motivations for perpetrators from a Muslim background. As a flipside to the selective culturalisation of motives, a selective individualisation of motives of native Dutch perpetrators is taking place. The feelings of hurt pride and offended masculinity, as obvious manifestations of traditional Western gender norms where masculinity and control over a (female) partner are closely linked, are labelled as individual psychological characteristics in the case of the Dutch perpetrators, ignoring the cultural patriarchal nature of such a motive.

The question is why cultural values and traditions regarding masculine honour and pride, which inevitably affect individual psychological motives, are primarily and selectively attributed to Muslim perpetrators and not Dutch (Western) men. In doing so, Turkish and Moroccan perpetrators are constructed as cultural dopes, inevitably and unreflectively influenced by a collective mentality, whereas the native Dutch men who killed their (ex-)wife are portrayed as reflective individuals who make choices informed by their psychological make-up (Volpp 2000).[10] Implicitly Western traditional patriarchal norms – in this case about the masculine honour implied in being in control of one's wife – are mainstreamed as part of the psychology of the individual male, and are as such no longer identified as of a cultural origin.

These selective interpretive shifts cloud the similarity between Western and Muslim cultural concepts and individual experiences with respect to hurt male pride and honour. An oppositional and biased binary of cultural differ-

10 The generalizing conclusions in this study are also problematic from a methodological perspective: the limited sample size of the minority perpetrators (respectively 9% and 6% of the sample), hardly allows any meaningful quantitative comparison given the small numbers.

ence is constructed between Muslim and Western men, which simultaneously erases the heterogeneity that might be present within the subgroups.

Role of 'culture': the need for an intersectional perspective

The fact that lethal domestic violence occurs slightly more often among migrant minorities the question is how to explain this. Available research data are limited, and indicate a tendency to emphasize the role of different cultural values in family violence between ethnic groups (the cultural deviant or culturalist perspective). Some argue that this contributes to an entrenchment of existing stereotypes (Hampton, Carrillo and Kim 2005). More research is needed to understand the complexity of underlying factors that might contribute to the heightened vulnerability of migrant women that goes beyond their culture of origin as the defining variable. Due to profound methodological problems, it has been concluded that available data on the role of race or ethnicity in US-based research on family violence are limited in quality and generalizability (Malley-Morrison and Hines 2007). Important shortcomings persist related to sampling problems (representativeness, size), the conceptual lumping together of different ethnic or cultural categories and the lack of adequate attention for possible confounding of socio-economic status and other demographic variables with race or ethnicity as main errors. Furthermore, the use of a unified concept of 'culture' leads to a comparison that often ignores within-group variability (Raj and Silverman 2002).

Findings regarding over-representation of ethnic minorities need to be contextualized in order to address the complexity of experiences and to fully understand the role of 'culture' as well as 'gender' in domestic violence and homicides (Bograd 1999; Kasturirangan et al. 2004; Sokoloff and Dupont 2005; Thiara and Gill 2010). This requires going beyond simplifying and functionalist categorical concepts like culture and taking a closer look at how the lives of immigrant and cultural minority women and men are affected in the process of migration and acculturation. Research on immigration shows the need to understand the structural forces that shape the acculturation and assimilation process of transnational migrants (Batia and Ram 2009). Acculturation and assimilation are after all the result of an interactive dynamic relation between migrants and the host country (Jasinskaja-Lahti et al. 2003). We have very limited systematic knowledge of how migration affects the perpetration or victimization of violence in intimate relationships. Race, gender, sexual orientation and class are core factors that ultimately contribute to different sets of vulnerabilities. For individuals in migrant communities, usually in disadvantaged and marginalized positions vis-à-vis mainstream society, multiple forms of prejudice and discrimination and institutionalized violence may exacerbate abusive family relationships (Richie et al. 2005).

In the current European context, the increasing Islamophobic and hostile attitudes towards Muslim (im-)migrants is another crucial variable to take into consideration (FRA 2009; 2010). Demographic categories such as (im-)-migrant group membership, ethnicity or religion are sometimes used as a proxy for culture because they allow easy categorization. These categories, often used to collect census data, refer to heterogeneous groups of people facing complex social dynamics of inclusion and exclusion. To understand the impact of those dynamics requires looking more closely at the impact of existing hegemonic structures in different nation states, societies and cultures on violence in intimate relationships.

In the Netherlands, two political-cultural dynamics seem to feed particularly into the popularity of biased narratives on Muslim women as the ultimate victim of domestic violence: the growing anti-Islam and xenophobic attitudes, on the one hand, and the tendency to gender-neutralize violence against native Dutch women, on the other. In the aftermath of the particular share of fundamentalist-jihadist violence that the Netherlands has been confronted with,[11] the issues of VAW and Islam have become particularly intertwined. With the shift towards a growing criticism of multiculturalism in the Netherlands around the turn of the millennium, migrant women were increasingly considered in policy frames to be vulnerable and suffering from oppression, which resulted in a dominant policy discourse in which migrant women and their acculturation and integration were portrayed as an outright problem (Roggeband and Verloo 2007). It was implied that Turkish and Moroccan women in general were 'oppressed' by their husbands and fathers. This has become a recurring theme in public discourse and policy developments in the Netherlands, in fact amplifying problems of integration and acculturation (Entzinger 2003).[12] The selective attribution of women's oppression to Muslim cultures, in contrast to the 'emancipation' of Dutch women, seems to feed into the attribution of more and more severe violence to Muslim men

11 Although not a large-scale terrorist attack, the murder in 2004 of Dutch film director Theo Van Gogh, a well-known critic of abuse of women in Muslim communities, by a Dutch-Moroccan fundamentalist Muslim, exacerbated the Dutch discourse on violence of Muslim minorities.

12 Just as the difference between honour-based killing and spouse killing can become blurred all too easily as soon as it happens in ethnic minorities, the distinction between forced marriage and voluntary migration-marriage is at times erased. Exemplary is the response to the launching of a Muslim dating site: *'Muslims are now able to choose whom they are forced to marry'* (www.editienl.nl; May 14, 2009). No irony or sarcasm was intended.

who abuse their wives. Domestic violence has become a vehicle to stereotypically portray the gendered oppression that Muslim women suffer, unlike Dutch (native) women.

Concurring with the tendency to selectively culturalize domestic violence, the Dutch policy framing of domestic is increasingly gender-neutralized. Building on the data of the 1997 survey, as discussed before, and leaving aside initial analyses and research data emphasizing the gendered nature of domestic violence against women, the Dutch government produced in 2002 a white paper on domestic violence[13] as a gender neutral phenomenon. In 2007, the CEDAW Committee has strongly criticized this shift towards gender neutrality in its response to the Dutch CEDAW country report. It has urged the Dutch government to develop a more gender-sensitive approach (CEDAW 2007). The CEDAW commission explicitly voices its concern that Muslim women are portrayed as essentially oppressed and Muslim culture is constructed as inherently violent towards women, whereas native Dutch women are constructed as liberated. The net result is that Dutch culture is implicitly positioned as virtually non-violent towards women.

The underlying rhetorical strategy here is very similar to the one encountered in the research on spouse killing presented above. While domestic violence among minorities is predominantly attributed to 'culturally' oppressive traditions, domestic violence against native Dutch women has become the result of the (apparently widespread) psychological problems of the perpetrator or relational troubles between the partners. In more European countries a severing of domestic violence from a context of gender inequality is taking place (e.g. Krizsan et al. 2007; Hearn and McKie 2008). More research is needed to understand the paradoxical discursive and policy development of gender-neutralization and culturalisation of domestic violence in several countries, precisely at a time when VAW more generally is actually recognized in mainstream United Nations and European politics as a major public concern deserving attention (e.g. European Parliament Resolution 2010/C 285 E/07; 26 November 2009) .

Conclusion: deconstructing violence against women and culture in Fort Europe

For an adequate understanding of why the discourse on the cultural specificity of domestic violence among Muslim communities is persistent, it must be

13 *Privé geweld, publieke zaak* [Private violence, public concern].

situated in the wider context of anti-immigrant and especially anti-Muslim attitudes that increased across Europe over the last decade (EUMC 2006; FRA 2009). The dynamics addressed here are not unique to the Netherlands. They fit in with the nativist backlash against immigrants and refugees that flourishes in many industrialized countries in the global North. Even before the more recent anti-immigration tendencies took hold, Western liberal democracies never resolved the tensions which ethnocultural diversity evoked (Kymlicka 1998). After the fundamentalist attacks of Islamic jihadists in New York, and subsequent attacks in Europe (Madrid, London), tensions revived which resonated with deeply rooted anti-Oriental sentiments (Said 1995/1978). In the late 1990s, the two topics of immigration and VAW (mostly focusing on Muslim communities) have been connected in the debate on multiculturalism (Okin 1999; for a critique see Volpp 2000; Römkens 2002). Establishing the link between VAW and Muslim culture has been contested yet holds political currency. The US Government, for example, used it when calling for military interventions in Iraq and in Afghanistan. Repeatedly reference was made to VAW as a violation of women's human rights that imposed a 'solemn duty' (…) to bring freedom and liberty to the region", according to former US president Bush (Römkens 2005). In a shifting political landscape, where the continuation of the war against terrorist threats is increasingly questioned, the ongoing abuse of women and girls in Afghanistan in 2010 is hardly a subject of any public concern any longer in political debates on what the West should or could do in Afghanistan. Against a backdrop of anti-immigration sentiments 'Fort Europe' needs its building bricks, and there the topic of VAW, positioning Muslims as particularly violent still provides politically useful currency.

The need for an intersectional analysis illuminating the structural yet diverse nature of variables underlying VAW and girls across cultures has been convincingly argued and called for repeatedly. Theoretically, the concept of intersectionality provides an important attempt to cover this complexity. However, how the simultaneous and intersecting impact of all different forms of structural disempowerment varies within and between cultures is empirically still an under-researched domain. Ultimately, the goal is to understand differences within and between social and cultural groups without essentializing them.

From an international legal and political perspective, VAW is gaining more prominence on the European agenda as a fundamental human rights violation that is in no way culturally specific. A recent ruling of the European Court of Human Rights (Opuz v. Turkey)[14] underlined once again that do-

14 *Opuz v Turkey* (Appl. No. 33401/02) ECHR 9 June 2009.

mestic violence is a violation of women's rights that is not specific to any particular culture, and which requires effective state intervention with due diligence to protect women. Preparations to construct a more transnational legal basis for a concerted European effort to prevent VAW and to better protect victims are underway, both within the Council of Europe and in the European Commission.[15] When addressing VAW in a European context, it is more urgent than ever to take the multiple inequalities that women face into consideration. With anti-migration and xenophobic resentment growing across the EU, an improved understanding of the complex impact of cultural differences on VAW is necessary in order to get beyond culturalist stereotypes.

References

Bakker, Hilde (2005): Eergerelateerd geweld in Nederland: een bronnenboek. Utrecht: Transact.

Batia, Sunil/Ram, Anjali (2009): Theorizing Identity in Transnational and Diaspora Cultures: A Critical Approach to Acculturation. In: International Journal of Intercultural Relations 33, 2, pp. 140–149.

Bograd, Michelle (1999): Strengthening domestic violence theories: Intersections of race, class, sexual orientation and gender. In: Journal of Marital and Family Therapy. 25, pp. 275–289.

Brenninkmeijer, Nicole/Geerse, Miriam/Roggebrand, Conny (2009): Eergerelateerd geweld in Nederland. Onderzoek naar de beleving en aanpak van eergerelateerd geweld. Den Haag: Sdu Uitgevers.

CEDAW (Committee on the Elimination of Discrimination Against Women) (2007): Concluding Comments of the Committee on the Elimination of Discrimination against Women: Netherlands. CEDAW/C/NLD/CO/4: 15 January–2 February 2007.

Da Lima, Julia (1994): Het klappen van de zweep. 20 jaar Blijf van m'n Lijf [Cracking the whip. Twentieth anniversary of the battered women's shelter]. Amsterdam: Jan van Arkel.

Deug, Febe (1990): Dan ben je pas echt ver van huis. Turkse en Marokkaanse vrouwen en meisjes over seksueel geweld en de hulpverlening [More than a long way from home]. Utrecht: Stichting tegen Seksueel Geweld.

15 The Council of Europe has launched a Committee that is currently in the process of preparing a Convention Against violence against women and domestic violence (CAHVIO), scheduled to finalize its work in 2011. See:<http://www.coe.int/t/dghl/standardsetting/violence/CAHVIO_2009_1%20Terms%20of %20reference.pdf>. The European Commission commissioned an EU-wide comparative analysis of on legislation in all EU countries on violence against women, children and sexual identity-based violence, aiming to address the feasibility of harmonisation of legislation in this area. See Kelly, L., C. Hagemann-White, R. Römkens, Zwamborn, M. (forthcoming), Feasibility study to assess the possibilities, opportunities and needs to standardize national legislation on violence against women, violence against children and sexual-orientation-based violence. Brussels: EC Directorate of Justice, Freedom and Security.

Echeburúa, Enrique/Fernández-Montalvo, Javier/de Corral, Paz/López-Goñi, José J. (2009): Assessing Risk Markers in Intimate Partner Femicide and Severe Violence: A New Assessment Instrument. In: Journal of Interpersonal Violence. 24, pp. 925–939.

Entzinger, Han (2003): The Rise and Fall of Multiculturalism: The Case of the Netherlands. In: Joppke, Christian/Morawska, Ewa (eds.) (2003): Toward Assimilation and Citizenship. Immigration in Liberal Nation-States. London: Palgrave Macmillan, pp. 59–86.

European Monitoring Centre on Racism and Xenophobia (2006): Muslims in the European Union: Discrimination and Islamophobia.

European Parliament Resolution on the elimination of violence against women. (26 November 2009) .2010/C 285 E/07).

Ferwerda, Henk B. (2007): Huiselijk geweld: Met de voordeur in huis. Omvang, aard en achtergronden in 2006 op basis van landelijke politiecijfers. Arnhem: Advies- en Onderzoeksgroep Beke.

FRA (Fundamental Rights Agency) (2009): European Union Minorities and Discrimination Survey. Data in focus: Report 2: Muslims. Vienna.

FRA (Fundamental Rights Agency) (2010): Experience of discrimination, social marginalisation and violence: a comparative study of Muslim and non-Muslim youth in three EU Member States. Vienna.

Garcia-Moreno, Claudia/Jansen, Henrica/Ellsberg, Mary/Heise, Lori/Watts, Charlotte H. (2006): Prevalence of Intimate Partner Violence: Findings from the WHO Multi-Country Study on Women's Health and Domestic Violence. In: Lancet 368, pp. 1260–1269.

Garssen, Joop/Van Duin, Coen (2009): Allochtonenprognose 2008–2050: naar 5 miljoen allochtonen. Bevolkingstrends 2de kwartaal 2009. Den Haag: Centraal Bureau voor de Statistiek. http://www.cbs.nl/NR/rdonlyres/2397CD68-7E21-4F38-B971-D09817635A3/0/2009k2b15p14art.pdf (Last assessed September 20, 2009).

Grzywacz, Joseph G./Rao, Pamela/Gentry, Amanda/Marín, Antonio/Arcury, Thomas A. (2009): Acculturation and Conflict in Mexican Immigrants' Intimate Partnerships: The Role of Women's Labor Force Participation. In: Violence Against Women 15, pp. 1194–1212.

Hampton, Robert L./Carrillo, Ricardo/Kim, Joan (2005): Domestic Violence in African American Communities. In: Richie, Beth/Sokoloff, Nathalie/Pratt Christina (eds.) (2005): Domestic Violence at the Margins: Readings on Race, Class, Gender, and Culture. New Brunswick, NJ: Rutgers University Press, pp. 127–141.

Hearn, J./McKie, L. (2008): Gendered policy and policy on gender: The case of domestic violence. In: Policy & Politics, 36(1), pp. 75–91.

Jasinskaja-Lahti, Inga/Liebkind, Karmela/Horenczyk, Gabriel/Schmitz, Paul (2003): The Interactive Nature of Acculturation: Perceived Discrimination, Acculturation Attitudes and Stress among Young Ethnic Repatriates in Finland, Israel and Germany. In: International Journal of Intercultural Relations 27, 1, pp. 79–97.

Kasturirangan, Aarati/Krishnan, Sandhya/Riger, Stephanie (2004): The Impact of Culture and Minority Status on Women's Experience of Domestic Violence. In: Trauma, Violence, & Abuse 5, 4, pp. 318–332.

Krizsan, A./Bustelo, M./Hadjiyanni, A./Kamoutis, F. (2007): Domestic violence: A public matter. In: Verloo, M. (Red.): Multiple meanings of gender equality. A critical frame analysis of gender policies in Europe. Budapest, New York: Central European University Press, pp. 141–184.

Kymlicka, Will (1989): Introduction: An Emerging Consensus? In: Ethical theory and moral practice 1, 2, pp. 143–157.

Liem, Marieke/Geene, Kim/Koenraadt, Frans (2007): Partnerdoding door etnische minderheden. Utrecht: Dutch University Press.

Malley-Morrison, Kathleen/Hines, Denise A. (2007): Attending to the Role of Race/Ethnicity in Family Violence Research. In: Journal of Interpersonal Violence 22, pp. 943– 972.

Mohanty, Chandra T. (1991): Under Western eyes: Feminist scholarship and colonial discourses. Bloomington: Indiana University Press.

Mohanty, Chandra T. (2004): 'Under Western eyes' revisited: Feminist Solidarity through Anticapitalist Struggles. In: Mohanty, Chandra T. (ed.) (2003): Feminism without Borders. Durham, NC: Duke University Press, pp. 221–251.

Narayan, Uma (2000): 'Essence of Culture and a Sense of History: A Feminist Critique of Cultural Essentialism'. In: Narayan, Ua/Harding, Sandra (2000): Decentering the Center. Philosophy for a Multicultural, Postcolonial, and Feminist World. Bloomington and Indianapolis: Indiana University Press, pp. 80–100.

Nieuwbeerta, Paul/Leistra, Gerlof (2003): Moord en doodslag in Nederland. Een overzicht van alle zaken in de periode 1992–2001. In: Tijdschrift voor Veiligheid en Veiligheidszorg 2, 3, pp. 36–57.

Nieuwbeerta, Paul/Leistra, Gerlof (2007): Dodelijk geweld. Moord en doodslag in Nederland [Lethal Violence. Homicide in the Netherlands]. Amsterdam: Uitgeverij Balans.

Okin, Susan M. (1999): Is Multiculturalism Bad for Women? Princeton: Princeton University Press.

Raj, A./Silverman, J. (2002): Violence against immigrant women: The roles of culture, context, and legal immigrant status on intimate partner violence. In: Violence Against Women, 8, pp. 367–398.

Richie, Beth/Sokoloff, Nathalie/Pratt Christina (eds.) (2005): Domestic Violence at the Margins: Readings on Race, Class, Gender, and Culture. New Brunswick, NJ: Rutgers University Press.

Roggeband, Conny/Verloo, Mieke (2007): Dutch Women are Liberated, Migrant Women are a Problem: The Evolution of Policy Frames on Gender and Migration in the Netherlands. In: Social Policy & Administration 41, 3, pp. 271–288.

Römkens, Renée (1989): Onder ons gezegd en gezwegen: geweld tegen vrouwen in man – vrouw relaties. Amsterdam: Ministerie van Welzijn, Volksgezondheid en Cultuur.

Römkens, Renée (1992): Gewoon geweld? Omvang, aard, gevolgen en achtergronden van geweld tegen vrouwen in heteroseksuele relaties. Amsterdam.

Römkens, Renée (1997): Prevalence of Wife Abuse in the Netherlands. Combining Quantitative and Qualitative Methods. In: Journal of Interpersonal Violence 12, 1, pp. 99–125.

Römkens, Renée (2002): Over cultuurbarbarij gesproken. Geweld tegen vrouwen en het debat over multiculturaliteit. In: Een verdrag voor alle vrouwen, Verkenning van de betekenis van het VNvrouwenverdrag voor de multiculturele samenleving, Den Haag: E-Quality.

Römkens, Renée (2005): In the Shadow of No Law. Navigating Cultural Legitimacy and Legal Protection of Women against Violence in Afghanistan. In: Wolleswinkel, Ria/ Westendorp, Ingrid (eds.) (2005): Violence in the Domestic Sphere. Antwerpen: Intersentia, pp. 71–98.

Said, Edward (1995/1978): Orientalism. London: Penguin Books.

Schröttle, Monika/Müller, Ursula (2004): Lebenssituation, Sicherheit und Gesundheit von Frauen in Deutschland. Eine Repräsentativbefragung zu Gewalt gegen Frauen in Deutschland. Federal Ministry for Family Affairs, Senior Citizens, Women and Youth.

Sokoloff, Nathalie/Dupont, Ida (2005): Domestic Violence and the Intersection of Race, Class and Gender: Challenges to Understanding Violence against Marginalized Women in Diverse Communities. In: Violence against Women 11, 38, pp. 38–63.

Sundaram, Vanita/Curtis, Tine/Helweg-Larsen, Karin/Bjerregard, Peter (2003): Can we Compare Violence Data across Countries? In: Circumpolar Health, pp. 389–396.

Thiara, Ravi K./Gill, Aisha K. (eds.) (2010): Violence Against Women in South Asian Communities: Issues for Policy and Practice. London: Jessica Kingsley Publishers.

Van Dijk, Tom/Flight, Sander/Oppenhuis, Erik/Duesmann, Brig (1997): Huiselijk geweld. Aard, omvang en hulpverlening. Den Haag: Intomart.

Van Dijk, Tom/Flight, Sander/Oppenhuis, Erik/Duesmann, Brig (1998): Domestic violence: A national study of the nature, size and effects of domestic violence in the Netherlands. In: Journal on Criminal Policy and Research 6, pp. 7–35.

Van Dijk, Tom/Oppenhuis, Erik (2002): Huiselijk geweld onder Surinamers, Antillianen en Arubanen, Marokkanen en Turken in Nederland. Aard, omvang en hulpverlening. Hilversum: Ministerie van Justitie/Wetenschappelijk Onderzoeks – en Documentatiecentrum.

Van Eck, Clementine (2001): Door bloed gezuiverd: eerwraak bij Turken in Nederland. Amsterdam: Prometheus.

Vatnar, Solveig Karin Bø/Bjørkly, Stål (2010): An Interactional Perspective on the Relationship of Immigration to Intimate Partner Violence in a Representative Sample of Help-Seeking Women. In: Journal of Interpersonal Violence. 25, pp. 1815–1835.

Verloo, Mieke (2006): Multiple Inquealities, Intersectionality and the European Union. In: European Journal of Women's Studies 13, 3, pp. 211–228.

Volpp, Leti (2000): Blaming Culture for Bad Behavior. In: Yale Journal of Law and the Humanities 12, pp. 89–116.

Walby, Sylvia/Allen, Jonathan (2004): Domestic Violence, Sexual Assault and Stalking. Findings from the British Crime Survey. Home Office Research Study 276. London: Home Office Research, Development and Statistics Directorate.

Willemsen, Frank (2007): Huiselijk geweld en herkomstland. Een verkennend onderzoek naar de incidentie van huiselijk geweld en allochtone daders en slachtoffers. Den Haag: WODC. Cahiers 2007–17.

Wittebrood, Karin/Veldheer, Vic (2005): Partnergeweld in Nederland: Een secundaire analyse van de Intomart-onderzoeken naar huiselijk geweld [Partner violence in the Netherlands: A secondary analysis of the Intomart surveys on domestic violence]. In: Tijdschrift voor Criminologie 47, 1, pp. 3–23.

Wolf, Judith (2006): Maat en baat in de vrouwenopvang. Onderzoek naar vraag en aanbod. Amsterdam: SWP.

Yerden, Ibrahim (2008): Families onder druk. Huiselijk geweld in Marokkaanse en Turkse gezinnen. Amsterdam: Van Gennep.

Immigrant Women and Domestic Violence: Intersectional Perspectives in a Biographical Context

Nadja Lehmann

This paper presents the material findings of a study submitted as a doctoral thesis with the title '*Immigrant Women in Women's Shelters. Biographical Perspectives of Domestic Violence'* at the Free University of Berlin, Department of Political and Social Science' (Lehmann 2008c). Based on biographical case reconstructions, the study examines how immigrant women seeking support in women's shelters deal with the violence they have experienced. Subsequently the discussion deals with theoretical points of reference for violence research.

Introduction

This work originated from my own professional experience as a social worker in women's shelters, the large share of immigrant women in these shelters and the lack of research in Germany done on immigrant women and domestic violence. Research on immigrant women in shelters or more generally on immigrant women and domestic violence was highlighted in Germany only in 2004 when the first large-scale representative study on violence against women 'Living situation, Safety and Health of Women in Germany' (Schröttle and Müller 2004), followed by the comparative secondary analysis on 'Health and Violence Related Situations of Women With and Without Migration Backgrounds in Germany' (Schröttle and Khelaifat 2008) was published. This explicitly included and raised the question about the extent to which immigrant women were affected by violence. However, there is still a lack of research and in-depth analyses of domestic violence.

The biographical-theoretical study presented here shows how complex biographic linkage of different dimensions of violence and oppression influence the experience of domestic violence. This paper[1] adopts intersectionality in theoretical and practical approaches to domestic violence and refers to some branches of violence research in the United States, where this theoretical perspective has become more widely utilised. The legal scholar Kimberlé Crenshaw (1994) developed the concept of 'intersectionality' based on the situation of 'women of color' affected by domestic violence. The feminist psychologist and academic in the field of violence research, Michele Bograd, explains the fundamental assumptions intersectionality[2] is based on which are relevant for domestic violence:

> … intersectionality suggests that no dimension, such as gender inequality, is privileged as an explanatory construct of domestic violence, and gender inequality itself is modified by its intersection with other systems of power and oppression.(…) While all women are vulnerable to battering, a battered woman may judge herself and be judged by others differently if she is white or black, poor or wealthy, a prostitute or housewife, a citizen or an undocumented immigrant (Bograd 2005: 27).

Domestic violence occurs in individual life stories and is experienced as a personal event. It is, however, at the same time a cultural and social product, which is affected by overlapping links between 'gender', 'ethnicity', 'social class' and other social differences (Feltey in Sokoloff and Dupont 2005: 1). The situation of a large group of immigrant women in shelters affected by violence is characterised to a high degree by the structural circumstances of their migrant status. For most immigrants with a limited residence permit, the step into a women's shelter initially means terminating the violence. At the same time, however, many new problems arise such as, for instance, a less secure residence status, no work permit, restricted opportunities in the labour market, intercultural differences, language difficulties, poor or no medical and psychological support. Migrants affected by domestic violence experience marginalisation, stigmatisation and racism within the violent relationship and through institutional discrimination and also in the shelter community (Aktaş 1993; Lehmann 2001; Glammeier, Müller and Schröttle 2004). They are required to come to terms with perceptions and stereotypes of their 'culture' which are predominant in public discourse, find their place as an individual within it and take a position. Many immigrant women have experienced violence and trauma at various levels (e.g. within the context of migration and seeking refuge), which can only be captured insufficiently by

---

1 Some extracts of the paper have been published elsewhere (cf. Lehmann 2008a, 2008b, 2006, 2004)

2 The term 'intersectional analysis' resp. 'intersectionality' is meanwhile well-established in German-speaking countries.

terms like 'gender based violence' and 'domestic violence'. These aspects substantially influence the living situations of migrants and, consequently, especially when attempting to deal with difficult stages in life. For staff in women's shelters, the focus of working in the area of counselling immigrant women has gradually shifted.[3] Frequently, there are problems which are initially far more pressing and vital to deal with than the experience of domestic violence.

Approach

Based on my professional experience in women's shelters, the research was guided by the following question: What are the effects of the manifold experiences of abused immigrant women during their lifetimes within the context of country of origin, migration and the host country Germany on how they experience domestic violence? To further examine this question it was considered important to gain insight into the subjective points of view and interpretive patterns of abused immigrant women. Thus, how do immigrant women describe their experiences and how do they place and evaluate them? In other words, how do the interviewed women deal with their experiences of violence during their lives?

Between 1999 and 2004, a total of 15 biographical narrative interviews were conducted with immigrant women, who had sought shelter from physical and emotional violence in a women's refuge. These were women who had experienced violence in their relationships with partners from their own countries of origin or with a German origin partner. The women were between 21 and 50 years of age at the time of the interview and were from a number of different geographic as well as educational backgrounds. All the interviewed women had an immigrant background and had come to a women's shelter to escape domestic violence. The analysis took the form of a biographical case reconstruction (Rosenthal 1995; Fischer-Rosenthal and Rosenthal 1997). Biographical research is the appropriate approach for questions of this kind, as here the priorities and points of view of the interviewees are material and the interlocking of social and subjective perspectives are at the centre of the analysis.

The interviews showed that all of the interviewed women discussed and experienced the violence they suffered as a subjectively formidable experi-

3 In 2001, the Intercultural Women's Shelter was opened in Berlin focussing especially on abused immigrant women and their children for conceptional improvements on experiences (Grubic and Lehmann 2003).

ence of marginalisation and oppression. The ways in which the women discussed and/or dealt with violence, however, were complex and differed among individuals, revealing three levels of engagements, which are presented here[4].

Engagement with violence takes place in a social context

The experience of violence is discussed in this case within the context of experiences of marginalisation and oppression in society, as, for instance, based on gender, ethnic origins, class or other kinds of social inequality. These can refer to either the country of origin or the host country, Germany. This can be illustrated by the case of Mirja Johannsen[5] a woman from Romania, who belongs to the Roma community.

Case study: Mirja Johannsen

At the time of the interview, Mirja Johannsen and her three children lived in a women's shelter in a big city in Germany and had an unlimited residence permit. Mirja Johannsen was born in Romania in 1961 and belongs to the Roma community. She graduated from school in Romania after year ten, and then took up a job in a factory. Her father and her bad relationship with him are predominant in her accounts of her childhood. Mirja Johannsen recounted, amongst other things, that her father beat her mother. After her marriage, she and her husband spent the first part of their married life in her parent's home. Giving birth to two daughters in quick succession, working hard at a construction site, her unhappy marriage, and a number of self-induced abortions, followed by frequent illness mark this stage in her life in her account. It becomes clear in the interview that being marginalised as Roma significantly influenced the entire family's living situation as well as Mirja Johannsen's future.

4 The resulting interpretations and subsequent hypotheses result from an intricate process of interpretation and analysis and do not exclusively refer to the respective paragraph from the interview presented here. Interpretations and analysis results came about in close exchange and interaction with many persons and groups participating throughout the course of the research process.

5 All names are anonymised.

In 1990, to escape her personal and social situation, for which she could not see a future, Mirja Johannsen and her two daughters illegally fled to Germany as asylum seekers without her family's or her husband's knowledge. She and her two daughters lived in a refugee home and in 1992, her asylum application was turned down and she was requested to leave the country. The deportation warning led her to decide to secure her residence in Germany through marriage. She met a German man and, having overcome some hurdles, they got married as her only option of remaining in Germany was to marry a 'German'. At her own request, she did not live with her husband and, due to her job, she was economically independent from him. It turned out, however, that Mirja Johannsen gradually got emotionally involved in the relationship and in January 1998 had a daughter. She commented on the birth of her daughter as follows: *'In 1998 I had her, and – and then my troubles – my problems so to speak, started, after Elisa was born'.*[6]

The comment that this is when her problems started refers to the fact that, with her emotional involvement, her problems acquired a new dimension. Even before the birth of her daughter, and in her account preceding it, there were grave problems for her as a single mum without any financial or other support that she had to deal with. Mirja had to give up her job after the birth of their daughter, took parental leave and lived on social benefit. When she and her husband went on holiday together, he took her passport off her, and, on their return to Germany, cashed in all the family's benefit, leaving her without any money to live on. Initially, she was only able to feed herself and her three children with an income from giving blood. Mirja sought help from a women's counselling organisation to prevent her benefit money from being paid to her husband. She recounts her experiences with ignorant officers at the social welfare agency in detail, who generally trusted the German husband more, and only after Mirja's repeated requests stopped paying her benefit to him. When she approached the child welfare agency to file for sole custody for her daughter, Mirja reported how he put her under pressure and blackmailed her:

> He said: 'I'll show you what I can do, I'm German. I lie and lie and everybody believes what I'm saying.' He only said that, he said: 'Yes, I'll send some foreigners to your home and then they'll knock on your neighbours' doors and they'll ask if this is where Mirja lives and everyone will say you're a whore and then you'll be off home and I'll have Elisa'.

Here the escalation of the relationship's dynamics becomes clear. The conflict of power openly breaks out over the question of custody and the hus-

---

6 The quotes have been reworked linguistically for this paper, without changing their meaning.

band plays on his claim to power as a German. He tries to offend her by stigmatising her sexual morals by way of her ethnic origins, thus referring to dominant images in the public discourse.

Tearfully she describes one weekend, he turned up with the police on her doorstep, brandishing a decision on the determination of physical custody of their daughter and took the girl away, even though she was still breastfeeding at the time. He called Mirja a 'gypsy' and 'Romanian', who neglected her child and wanted to abduct the child to Romania. Only after some days and with difficulty, she was able to obtain another decision and get her daughter back. After that, Mirja decided to seek shelter in a women's refuge with her daughters:

> Because I was scared, because I thought 'Goodness, he is German, he lies and everybody believes him', he was able to do that and then I thought 'okay then, I'll go to the shelter until there's a decision on what I can do'. Then I came here, he wrote a couple of applications, saying I was a gypsy (with a gasp) he was afraid for Elisa, because I don't take care of her; he's better, he's good; he is! (ironically) Well, now I'm here at the shelter, (drawing her breath).

Given this reality, Mirja Johannsen saw only one option for herself which was to go to the shelter in order to find support there in her dispute with her husband, which had become a legal one.

Summary

What is relevant in the analysis of the entire interview is Mirja Johannsen's perspective as a member of a minority community in her country of origin, where she's experienced a tradition of discrimination. The menace of her husband, who played on his status as a German in their relationship by making it clear that she did not stand a chance against a German, when, for instance, fighting for the custody of a child, because nobody would believe her, the 'gypsy', anyway, is predominant in her individual experience of violence and is inseparably tied to her experiences of discrimination as a Roma in her Romanian society of origin. Throughout the interview, it becomes clear what role historic ethnicised and discriminating discourses about Roma in the Romanian society of origin, as well as discourses about Romanian Roma in Germany effective at the time of her immigration, play in how she experienced violence during her relationship with a German.

Engagement within the context of experiences in the family of birth

Women in this group deal with their experiences of violence within the context of their families of birth. This social context is blanked out of their biographies and described only on further enquiry and is immaterial for the individual way of dealing with violent behaviour. The story of Nihad Amin, a woman from Iraqi Kurdistan serves as an example.

Case study Nihad Amin

At the time of the interview, Ms Amin and her two sons lived in a sheltered flat belonging to a women's refuge in a big city in Germany. Nihad Amin was born in 1972 as a family's fourth daughter and fifth child in Iraqi Kurdistan. Her relationship with her mother plays a prominent role in Nihad's later life and in the context of her violent experiences, which is why her family background is of such importance in this case. Her mother gave birth to a total of 12 children, 3 sons and 9 daughters, every one to two years up until 1983. At Nihad's birth, her mother was in her early twenties and had already given birth to seven children[7]. It is Nihad Amin's impression that her mother did not give the same amount of love to all her children. This is reflected retrospectively in the following paragraph of Nihad Amin's interview on the mother's relationship with her children:

> Because there were so many of us, that's why she couldn't give her love to all of us. She only likes my older brother and my older sister, and all the others she doesn't care about, and my little sister, she likes her, yes, and all the others are all the same to her.

Generally speaking, it is not unusual in the Iraqi Kurdish society to have twelve children. The interview with Nihad, however, shows that this social norm does not lead to her having any specific expectations of her mother. She experiences her mother's attitude towards her as indifferent and hostile, and this is an experience that materially influences her in later life. Nihad's father, a communist, was politically persecuted, something that affected the entire family. He died of cancer, having been degraded from a teacher and headmaster to work as a train conductor, subject to political arbitrariness and various imprisonments. After his death, the children and their mother lived

---

7 Two sons had already died.

together under difficult economic circumstances. The mother wanted Nihad Amin to marry and not to study or get vocational training.

> My mother, she wasn't so educated. She's from a village, she didn't know anything. She never understood what learning was and she always kept saying we must all stop learning. I've got many brothers and sisters and I just carried on. I always enjoyed learning and she kept saying that's not important. 'Getting married is more important than learning, and if you were a teacher or something, you wouldn't get good wages, so it's useless. Getting married is the best thing for women' and I wanted to finish high school. She said, no I must marry now, that is not so important. This caused many problems with my brothers and sisters and my mother. Especially, I never understood her. I don't like her at all. And sometimes, when I think about it, I hate my mother, because of this, feeling. I still want to learn, but I haven't got the opportunity. Yes, and I did graduate from high school and she said, I wasn't allowed to study and go to college.

Ms Amin got married in 1995 in Iraqi Kurdistan to a man 20 years her senior, who had been living in Germany for 18 years, had a German passport, and was of Iraqi Kurdish origins. They got engaged in 1994 when he was on a visit to Iraqi Kurdistan and after the wedding she came to Germany with him in 1995. Nihad Amin told us that she married her husband out of 'spite', because her mother was no longer willing to accept her repeated rejection of marriage candidates and also because her husband-to-be came from Europe and had promised her that once they were married she would be allowed to learn in Germany. She made it clear that she did not marry for love and that her mother had pushed her to choose a husband. Still, she held on to her original aim of 'learning'. She then described the disappointing experiences during the early years of her marriage and shows how inadequate and wrong the decision was, something which her mother had pushed her into taking. Her husband kept putting her off to start with and then rejected her desire to learn: *'And then it started so (...) that I wanted to study and so on, because he was so, he had a complex. He wants me to be only the wife, at home like my mother. He was just like my mother. And then I noticed, my husband, he is just like my mother'.*

They had two sons together, who were born in 1996 and 1997 in Germany. Ms Amin had been severely abused and raped by her husband since 1998. In 2001, with the support of the child welfare agency, she found refuge in a women's shelter with adjoining sheltered flats, where she lived in her own flat with her children.

Summary

Nihad Amin has had to deal with her violent experiences in the context of her family history. For Ms Amin, her experience of her relationship with her husband was like a re-enactment of her family history. The husband, who is supposed to love her, does not feel any love for her and wants to keep her from learning and from growing as a person. Also her mother, who should have loved her, did not do so and wanted to keep Nihad from learning and growing. Her negative experiences with her husband acquired a specific meaning through this parallel. She did not discuss her experiences of severe abuse during marriage in the 'context of gender'. She rather equated her husband's behaviour towards her with her mother's behaviour towards her by using the phrase *'My husband is like my mother'*. All other contexts, e.g. her mother's oppression as an 'uneducated' woman in her father's family or her family's situation of political persecution influencing her life in so many ways, are not seen by her in the context of her experience of violence. The evaluation of the interview shows in detail that the reason for this is to be sought in her own emotionally damaged relationship with her mother, whom she blames for her own fate.

Engagement within a biographical context as a singular experience is made

Within this group of women, the experienced violence is not presented in a way that is connected with their own biographies. Only on enquiry and within the context of the entire interview, it becomes clear that describing the experienced violence as fate and as a singular experience is an important way for the interviewees to distance themselves from it. An example of this is the third reconstructed individual case, that of Ella Noack from Poland.

Case study Ella Noack

Ella Noack was born in 1954 in Poland and immigrated to Germany in 1988 with her daughter from her first marriage to live with her German boyfriend. She married him after a few months and then lived for eleven years in Germany with her husband, daughter and stepson. After that, she spent some time in a women's refuge and afterwards in sheltered housing. By then she had received German citizenship, got a divorce and has her own flat. In her interview, Ella Noack discussed the violence she experienced at first as the central dramatic stage of her life, which is merely framed by the rest of her life. The violent experience is not set in relation to other experiences during her life, i.e., there is no biographical continuity and no connections with her family's history. Intensive questioning, however, and the evaluation of the entire interview show that there are pronounced continuities and many aggravating experiences in her life, which stand in close topical and emotional relation to the experience of violence, which I demonstrate by way of some examples.

Ella Noack was born in Poland in 1954 in a town of approximately 15,000 inhabitants. She was the first child of a newly wed couple. At the time of Ella's birth, her father was about 20 years of age and worked as an electrician for a radio station. Her mother was about 22 years old when Ella was born and worked in a clothes factory. Both parents had grown up in villages and moved to the town from different areas of Poland. Ella's parents grew up during the war and both became part of the large internal migration surge from rural areas to the towns and cities during the phase of industrialisation from 1945 to 1964. Her parents separated when Ella was two years old. From that moment onwards, Ella had no contact with her father. Ella's mother said that the reason for their separation was violence from Ella's father. Ella Noack at first did not indicate the reason for separation as 'battering' during her interview and thus avoided the perspective of her mother being victimised by her father's violent behaviour. This omission is also significant in respect to her later first hand experiences with violence perpetrated by her own husband. As becomes clear in the evaluation, she avoids looking at the parallels between her mother's life and her own. Obviously, there is the possibility that Ella Noack simply did not have the capacity to realise and reflect these relations. She does, however, prove to be able to analyse and construct relations in her family's history with regard to her mother's experiences.

After her parents' separation, Ella and her mother lived together in a small town. Ella describes her mother as a devout Catholic. Ella's mother later joined the Jehovah's Witnesses and turned away from the Catholic Church. Ella Noack tells us that her mother as an outsider had always felt a 'stranger' in the small town she had moved to and that she was isolated. Her mother suffered from depression and delusions and at times was not capable of looking after her daughter. She was hospitalised for her mental problems a number of times. According to Ella Noack, the reasons for her mother's mental illness are to be sought in her childhood. Ella's mother lost her own mother at the age of seven. Straight after the death of Ella Noack's grandmother, the war began and, according to her account in the interview, the family had to leave their farm because of the Germans. Ella Noack describes her mother's situation with empathy:

> Yes, that's difficult, that is, at seven you're a youngster, (...) so it wasn't nice for her, no, so that was no good time for my mummy (...) yeah well and, she was ill as well, she was in hospital, she needed quiet, psychological quiet she needed, you know, the events – her mother's death, probably, and the war and everything, they wore her out, I think the two sisters they were tougher than my mother, psychologically I mean, you know what I mean, my mummy is weaker, YEAA.

Ella Noack constructs biographical contexts between events that happened when her mother was growing up and the particular problems that her mother had as an adult. She, therefore, offers a biographical family perspective on her own life. It becomes clear that she has very close emotional ties with her mother. Their relationship is, however, marked by a strong ambivalence. It can be assumed that this is due to the fact that her mother had serious psychological problems. Ella Noack shows, during the interview, how she attempted to distance herself from her mother's life at different levels, without becoming disloyal.

> She was happy she had me, she had a task then, she always told me she loved me more than anything and still and she said 'I didn't want to get married then, I didn't want a man to hurt you or something', no, and I'm a little different from my mummy there (laughs) must be like my father.

Here, an aspect of Ella's conflict of loyalty becomes clear. Here as well as in other parts of the interview, there is an indication of her fear of becoming like her mother. For her, this is even more threatening, as there are many parallel developments in her life when compared to her mother's. For instance, Ella Noack's first marriage, just like her mother's, failed early on and she as well was then a single mother with a little girl. Like her mother, she remarried when her daughter was a little older and experienced domestic violence. Apart from these obvious parallels, there are also numerous differences, as Ella Noack, for instance, is far better educated and has higher vocational qualifications. On the other hand, children of mentally ill parents often are afraid of falling ill themselves and this fear can become very important in their later lives. For Ella Noack, it is a psychological way out to secretly hope that she is more like her father.

What becomes very clear is Ella Noack's strong desire to belong and to have a family, which dominates her life story and relates back to her family history. This is also how to interpret her long lasting violent relationship because of which she then had to turn to a women's refuge. Enormous personal efforts and repressing this past must have been necessary to make this relationship and a family possible at all. The relationship with her German husband-to-be was marked by disappointments and negative experiences from the outset and still she decided to give up her economically independent life in Poland. She and her daughter, for years, lived in a family situation characterised by fear and violence. Her desire to emigrate was clearly coupled with her desire for a family. This is also demonstrated by the fact that Ella Noack did not break out of her marriage even when she held a residence status of her own and even a German passport at a later point. She stayed and the more threatening and violent the situation at home became, the more desperately she fought for keeping her values and her image of a happy family life. She now accepts the reality of her failed dream. At the same time, however, she strives not to regard this as her personal failure and defeat.

Summary

Blanking out family history and biographical continuities, in Ella Noack's case, illustrates her fear of her life being predetermined by her mother's 'heritage' and her own biographical failure therefore being inevitable. Ella Noack is the daughter of a woman traumatised by her wartime experiences, shamed in her religious values by her divorce and stigmatised and isolated by her mental illness and who suffered the consequential social and communal marginalisation of post-war Poland. Avoiding a biographical perspective, therefore, can be interpreted as an important strategy for Ella Noack to deal with her violent experiences. In this way, she can develop new perspectives for her future and she fights for giving her life some positive meaning. Yet she only succeeds in this by mustering up enormous psychological strength for repressing this past. This strategy of reframing situations and applying a positive meaning to them has also led to Ella Noack remaining, for many years of her life, in a violent relationship and not being able to protect herself, her daughter and her husband's son from it.

Conclusion

A material outcome of the study is to show that the various levels of discussing the experiences of violence are related in a manifest or latent way to the biographical experience of marginalisation and oppression in the context of society and family of birth. These experiences, along with family and social discourses related with it, structure the discussion *as well as* the actual experiences of violence. The subjective points of view and interpretive patterns of the interviewed immigrant women have objective and real consequences because they substantially influence their actions and perceptions[8]. The analysis of the interviews shows that the applicable gender contexts do not necessarily become significant points of reference for dealing with the experiences of violence, notwithstanding the fact that all these women were in a women's shelter, where this point of view on domestic violence predominates. On the contrary, for the interviewed women, the injuries deriving from mother-daughter relationships or the experience of discrimination in the countries of origin or the host country play prominent roles.

The violence experiences are the point from which the presented biographical self-portraits take their structure. In the interviews, domestic violence is categorised as a severe experience of oppression and 'crisis of belonging'. This is what connects it to migration, a background experience common to all of the women. For all the interviewed immigrant women, migration is the common direct link with the history of the abusive relationships. Also migration specific circumstances such as, for instance, social isolation, residence status or experiences of racism constitute dynamics in the intimate partner relationships. Migration generally requires a redefinition of belonging. Still, this does not mean that old feelings of belonging are given up at the same time. The meaning of migration strongly depends on the context. It is a symbol of belonging, but not of the crisis itself. Consequently, migration can be constructed as a relevant but unspecific biographical context.

The discussion of the experiences of violence in this context can be classed as dealing with 'belonging' at various levels. Where does in/exclusion take place? Where does marginalisation take place? Where does oppression take place? Where is 'belonging' called into question? Where is it desired particularly strongly? What importance do the interviewed women award these types of dealing with the violence experienced? The different ways of discussing this can be termed 'biographical work' (Fischer-Rosenthal 1995), that is strategies for dealing with violence in a biographical context. Biographical narratives are a way of dealing with and working on hurtful and traumatic events. This also has an important social function. By telling stories, we create and express social belonging. As every person belongs to numerous social groups – women, migrants, Kurds, residents at a women's shelter, mothers – the question arises, what category or position is perceived in what discursive situation. These categorisations, positions and their discussions reflect power relations in society. The narrative offers an opportu-

8 This is a basis of philosophy of science for biography research and/or interpretative social studies.

nity to come to terms with negative categorisations, for example, with verbal humiliation in a violent relationship, but also with other attributions like negative stereotypes and discriminating discourses. Stereotypes can be rejected in such a way or it is possible to retroactively defend oneself against situations, where the person was wronged (Czyzewsky 1995). Such narratives about 'belonging' also show how we position ourselves in terms of differential categories like, for instance, gender, ethnicity and class (Anthias 2003: 22). For counselling and support work this would mean that focussing exclusively on gender, the migrant status or the applicable culture for defining problems of domestic violence can result in not perceiving the complexity of experiences and the subsequent problem solving strategies of women affected by violence. These, on the other hand, may be very important resources as the needs of battered women in general vary individually as do their requirements for support.

Theoretical integration and discussion

The biographical study presented here points to the relevance of social and family contexts for the experience of domestic violence. It showed that discussions and experiences of violence must not only be considered within the context of gender but that other differential power structures pervade them and they are, therefore, 'intersectionally' structured (Crenshaw 1994; Rommelspacher 2006). This means that the category 'gender' does not have an isolated effect within the biographical context but as a contextualised category. This perspective is not only relevant for abused immigrant women but it focuses on the heterogeneity and diversity of all women experiencing violence at home. It is, therefore, only consistent for the American psychologist, author and experienced violence researcher, Mary Ann Dutton (1996) to point out that violence research requires multi-dimensional models. Comprehensive context analyses need to systematically take into account social, ethnic and cultural contexts, the life story, networks and especially the individual perspectives of abused women (ibid.: 111). The results of my work are in line with a quote by Mary Ann Dutton, who summarises the requirements of future theoretical research and practical approaches to domestic violence as follows:

> The next decade of work with battered women is compelled to address the real complexity and diversity of battered women's experience – across women who vary from each other according to race, ethnicity, social class, age, sexual preference, and physical ablebodiness. Social context analysis is one tool easily accessible for the task (Dutton 1996: 123).

References

Aktaş, Gülşen (1993): Türkische Frauen sind wie Schatten – Leben und Arbeiten im Frauenhaus. In: Hügel, Ika/Lange, Chris/Ayim, May et al. (eds.): Entfernte Verbindungen. Rassismus, Antisemitismus, Klassenunterdrückung. Berlin, pp. 49–60.

Anthias, Floya (2003): Erzählungen über Zugehörigkeit. In: Apitzsch, Ursula/Jansen, Mechthild (eds.): Migration, Biographie und Geschlechterverhältnisse. Münster, pp. 20–37.

Bograd, Michele (2005): Strengthening Domestic Violence Theories: Intersections of Race, Class, Sexual Orientation, and Gender. In: Sokoloff, Natalie J./Pratt, Christina (eds.): Domestic Violence at the Margins. Readings on Race, Class, Gender, and Culture. New Brunswick; New Jersey; London, pp. 25–38.

Crenshaw, Kimberlé (1994): Mapping the Margins: Intersectionality, Identity Politics and Violence against Women of Color. In: Albertson Fineman, Martha/Mykitiuk, Roxanne (eds.): The Public Nature of Private Violence. New York/London: Routledge, pp. 93–118.

Czyzewski, Marek/Gülich, Elisabeth/Hausendorf, Heiko/Kastner, Maria (eds.): Nationale Selbst- und Fremdbilder im Gespräch. Kommunikative Prozesse nach der Wiedervereinigung Deutschlands und dem Systemwandel in Ostmitteleuropa. Opladen.

Dutton, Mary Ann (1996): Battered Women's Strategic Response to Violence. The Role of Context. In: Edleson, Jeffrey L./Eisikovits, Zvi C. (eds.): Future Interventions with Battered Women and their Families. Thousand Oaks; London; New Delhi, pp. 105–123.

Glammeier, Sandra/Müller, Ursula (2004): Unterstützungs- und Hilfebedarf aus der Sicht gewaltbetroffener Frauen. Resultate der Gruppendiskussionen. Im Auftrag des Bundesministeriums für Familie, Senioren, Frauen und Jugend. (pp. 618–731);http://www.bmfsfj.de/Kategorien/Forschungsnetz/forschungsberichte,did=20560.html (16.08.2005)

Grubič, Rada/Lehmann, Nadja (2003): Interkulturelle Arbeit im Frauenhaus. In: Ev. Konferenz für Familien- und Lebensberatung e.V. Fachverband für Psychologische Beratung und Supervision (EKFuL) (ed.): Integration gestalten – Psychosoziale Beratung und Begleitung im interkulturellen Kontext: Kriterien-Konzepte-Kompetenzen. Dokumentation der Fachtagung vom 4.–6.11.2002 in Berlin-Mitte. Meckenheim, pp. 54–68.

Fischer-Rosenthal, Wolfram (1995): Schweigen – Rechtfertigen – Umschreiben. Biographische Arbeit im Umgang mit deutschen Vergangenheiten. In: Fischer-Rosenthal, Wolfram/Alheit, Peter. (eds.) Biographien in Deutschland. Opladen; Wiesbaden, pp. 43–86.

Fischer-Rosenthal, Wolfram/Rosenthal, Gabriele (1997): Narrationsanalyse biographischer Selbstpräsentation. In: Hitzler, Ronald/Honer, Anne (eds.): Sozialwissenschaftliche Hermeneutik. Eine Einführung. Opladen, pp. 133–164.

Lehmann, Nadja (2001): Migrantinnen in Misshandlungssituationen. In: Frauenrat und Frauenbeauftragte der Alice-Salomon-Fachhochschule für Sozialarbeit/Sozialpädagogik und Pflege/Pflegemanagement (ed.): Quer – denken, lesen, schreiben. Gender/Geschlechterfragen update. Ausgabe 04/01. Berlin, pp. 10–13.

Lehmann, Nadja (2004): Auf dem Weg von Ost nach West: Kontinuitäten, Relevanzen und Verbindungen von ‚Ethnizität' und ‚Geschlecht' am Beispiel einer rumänisch-deutschen Migrationsbiographie. In: Miethe, Ingrid/Kajatin, Claudia/Pohl, Jana (eds.): Geschlechterkonstruktionen in Ost und West. Biographische Perspektiven. Münster, pp. 131–155.

Lehmann, Nadja (2006): Biographische Perspektiven und Bewältigungsstrategien gewaltbetroffener Migrantinnen – Schlussfolgerungen und Überlegungen für Theorie und Praxis. In: Landeskommission Berlin gegen Gewalt (ed.): Berliner Forum Gewaltprävention. Dokumentation einer Fachtagung in Kooperation mit der Friedrich-Ebert-Stiftung am 22.02.06. Nr. 25/2006, pp. 30–39.

Lehmann, Nadja (2008a): Migrantinnen und biografische Perspektiven auf Gewalterfahrungen. In: Borde, Theda/David, Matthias (eds.): Frauengesundheit, Migration und Kultur in einer globalisierten Welt. Frankfurt/Main: Mabuse-Verlag, pp. 249–254.

Lehmann, Nadja (2008b): Migrantinnen und häusliche Gewalt im biografischen Kontext. In: Gahleitner, Silke Birgitta/Gerull, Susanne et al.: Sozialarbeitswissenschaftliche Forschung. Einblicke in aktuelle Themen. Opladen & Farmington Hills: Budrich Unipress, pp. 59–66.

Lehmann, Nadja (2008c): Migrantinnen im Frauenhaus. Biografische Perspektiven auf Gewalterfahrungen. Reihe: Rekonstruktive Forschung in der Sozialen Arbeit. Opladen & Farmington Hills: Verlag Barbara Budrich.

Rommelspacher, Birgit (2006): Interdependenzen – Geschlecht, Klasse und Ethnizität. http://www2.gender.hu-berlin.de/geschlecht-ethnizitaet-klasse/www.geschlecht-ethnizitaet-klasse.de/index5ae0.html? set_language=de&cccpage=referat&set_z referentinnen=6

Rosenthal, Gabriele (1995): Erlebte und erzählte Lebensgeschichte. Frankfurt a.M.; New York.

Schröttle, Monika/Müller, Ursula (2004): Lebenssituation, Sicherheit und Gesundheit von Frauen in Deutschland. Eine repräsentative Untersuchung zu Gewalt gegen Frauen in Deutschland. Im Auftrag des Bundesministeriums für Familie, Senioren, Frauen und Jugend. http://www.bmfsfj.de/Kategorien/Forschungsnetz/forschungsberichte,did=20560.html.

Schröttle, Monika/Khelaifat, Nadia (2008): Gesundheit-Gewalt-Migration. Eine vergleichende Sekundäranalyse zur gesundheitlichen und Gewaltsituation von Frauen mit und ohne Migrationshintergrund in Deutschland. Kurzzusammenfassung zentraler Resultate. Im Auftrag des Bundesministeriums für Familie, Senioren, Frauen und Jugend. http://www.gendermainstreaming.net/bmfsfj/generator/Kategorien/Publikationen/Publikationen,did=108722.html

Sokoloff, Natalie J./Pratt, Christina (2005) (eds.): Domestic Violence at the Margins. Readings on Race, Class, Gender and Culture. New Brunswick, New Jersey, London.

From the Racialization of Sexism to Sexism as an Identity Marker[1]

Christelle Hamel

In recent decades, relations between the sexes among North African migrants and their French children have been regularly attracting media attention: news stories about forced marriage, honour crimes and headscarves have each in turn been given intensive coverage. With the recent focus on gang rapes, sexist behaviour patterns *'dans les quartiers'* ('on the housing estates') have once again been in the political and media spotlight. Discussion of these practices has been brought into debates about 'delinquency', 'urban violence' and 'assimilating young people of immigrant background', debates that were a marked feature of the campaigns for the municipal and presidential elections of 2001 and the parliamentary election of 2002. Following the terrorist attacks of 11 September 2001 in the United States, the question of domestic security was reformulated in France around the real or supposed threat of an extremist/fundamentalist form of Islam practiced by young people of North African immigrant background. These debates strengthened the far right vote of 21 April 2002 and led to a tightening of law and order policies.

In April 2003, at a meeting of the Union des Organizations Islamiques de France in Le Bourget, Interior Minister Nicolas Sarkozy stated that Muslim women should appear without headscarves on their ID card photographs. This launched a third 'headscarf affair' which took up the slack from the indignation triggered earlier by gang rapes on housing estates and the fear aroused by the terrorist attacks. In the media, the headscarves worn by some young women were presented as a sign that a particularly sexist and fundamentalist form of Islam was spreading, promoted by fathers and brothers to whom these young women were considered to be completely subjugated[2]. This interpretation led to the passing, on 15 March 2004, of an act of parlia-

1 This text was originally published in the journal *Migrations Sociétés* vol. 17, No.99–100 August 2006, pp. 91–104.

2 Editorial note: This text was written prior to the debate running up to and the passing of the Anti-burqua law in April 2011.

ment banning the wearing of 'religious signs' in schools. Thus male violence against women within a minority group is the prism through which political issues of a different order – migration, integration, national and international security – are perceived. The denunciation of this violence is mixed up with political issues that go far beyond the fight against sexist violence, and indeed mask that issue while manipulating it. This complicates the task of preventing such violence.

This paper examines the way in which racism manipulates the denunciation of sexism and describes the effects of such discourses on the people they target. It argues that far from reducing sexist violence, the racist logic hidden behind the anti-sexism tends to strengthen it. I use data gathered during a study on the experience of racism, sexuality and management of the risk of HIV infection conducted between 1997 and 2003 among 69 young men and women aged 18 to 25 to demonstrate my argument (Hamel 2003).

The racialization of sexist violence and rejection of the sons of immigrants

An analysis of gender relations within North African immigrant families must pay particular attention to the dynamics of the racist social relations that shape interactions between these families and people said to be of 'French extraction'. The racism they are subjected to has an impact on the way in which post-colonial migrants and their French-born children elaborate the norms and values that guide their behaviour. Their experience of relations with 'people of French extraction' is marked by a confrontation with prejudice and discrimination in access to jobs, housing, knowledge, health care, leisure, among others. Both North African emigrants and their French-born descendants are predetermined potential targets of unequal treatment on the basis of their name or appearance, though not all are affected in the same way. The best educated and qualified possess resources that reduce the negative effects of racism and are less stigmatized than those with no qualifications. And while not all 'people of French extraction' are agents of discrimination, all are liable to receive the preferential treatment that is the counterpart of discrimination against migrants and their children. Discriminatory practices divide individuals into two groups in a hierarchy: an inferiorized minority made up of those who are subject to discrimination and a dominant majority consisting of those who practice that discrimination or are its potential beneficiaries. As racial discrimination is practiced on the basis of name or skin colour, both the groups this creates have a racial connotation reflected in the commonly-used terms *Français de souche* (of French extraction), *Maghrébins* (North African), *Arabes* (Arabs).

Some members of the majority group highlight a few differentiating cultural features specific to some members of the minority group; this then serves to legitimize the racialized boundary line at the cultural level. Cultural traits that have come to be seen as differentiating characteristics even though they are not shared by all members of the minority group include honour crimes, religion and the wearing of headscarves, because these readily invite stigmatization. The media overkill casts discredit on all members of the 'racialized' group, who are suspected of approving such practices. They are thus relegated to an insuperable cultural otherness and considered 'impossible to integrate' because they are 'too different'. This process justifies the discrimination *a posteriori*, giving a cultural ratification for the idea of an otherness that is synonymous with 'obvious' or indeed 'natural' inferiority.

Today, this relegation of North African immigrants and their children to an insuperable otherness is channelled through the recurrent denunciation of sexist violence and the construction of separate representations of men and women. The norms governing relations between the sexes within this group are then constructed in response to the discrimination and the discourse. How has this racist and gender-specific rhetoric been elaborated? Since early 2001, the profusion and juxtaposition of TV broadcasts about *les banlieues* ('the suburban estates') have implied that violence against women is far more common there than in the rest of society and that its prevalence is due to the 'Arab'[3] or 'Moslem' culture of the estates' inhabitants. Through these two implied assertions, denunciation of violence has become a medium for attributing 'otherness' to the members of the minority group and a favoured ground for erecting a frontier between 'them' and 'us', making the minority group a 'foreign body' within the nation. Since sexism is assumed to be a basic archaism while sexual egalitarianism is considered proof of a 'modern' and 'civilized' mindset, sexism serves as an indicator of a social group's level of modernity and civilization.

However, the factors used to measure this sexism rule out any comparison between the discriminating majority group and the 'racialized' minority group. Since sexism takes slightly different forms in different social groups (despite a common basic pattern), the majority group can all the more fiercely censure a few particular forms of sexism found among the 'racialized' group because they, the majority group, can make a distorted comparison and claim not to be sexist themselves. Lastly, attributing only to a mi-

3 It is worth noting that for the majority group the term 'Arab' refers to a set of individuals who do not necessarily define themselves as such.

nority group sexist practices common to all groups (collective rape) enables the majority group to focus attention on the minority group rather than making a full analysis of sexism in society as a whole.

Presenting collective or 'gang' rapes on housing estates as if they were a new and growing phenomenon that demonstrates the incompatibility between 'Moslem' and 'Western' culture, the 'clash of civilizations'[4], is one example of the way sexist violence can be made an attribute of 'otherness'. The expression *jeunes de banlieue* ('youths from the estates') is used to single out the sons of post-colonial immigrants and particularly those of North African extraction without referring to them explicitly. These young men (a tiny minority of whom have committed such crimes) (Hamel 2003: 434; Jaspard et al. 2003: 370) have been accused as a body of being too attached to the 'traditional' values of their 'culture', as if their sexism could only be explained by their supposedly 'Arab' or 'Moslem' identity. The extreme male chauvinism of some of these young men and boys has been set up as revealing the essentially sexist nature of 'Arab culture', a term understood as comparable to 'archaic', 'barbarian' culture. This type of reasoning, which has reactivated the figure of the 'Arab rapist' created in the days of colonization (Zehraoui 1997), is a familiar theme on the French far right (Venner 1995), but with the media coverage of gang rapes (Hamel 2003: 124) it has spread with worrying ease through society as a whole. These young men are thus treated more than ever as 'foreigners in our midst'.

These rapes were also set up as proof that women's rights are losing ground in France, immigrants' sons being blamed for this (Guenif-Souilamas and Mace 2004: 106). The rapes are obviously unacceptable, but to legitimately speak of regression in women's rights some proof must be provided that gang rape was less common in the past and is less widespread in the majority population. Neither of these assertions is true, as we discussed in 2003 (Hamel 2003; see Debauche in this volume). The minority group being blamed for the 'regression' in women's rights, the conclusion is drawn (explicitly or implicitly) that the integration of immigrants' children 'has failed', or that it is 'impossible' and their presence on French soil not legitimate. The majority group has ignored the scale of sexist violence by men of French extraction (rape and conjugal violence occur in all social classes) (Jaspard et al. 2003) and highlighted certain cultural differences in the ways sexism is manifested (such as the will to keep women veiled) while ignoring its own particular form of sexism (reducing women to sex objects and displaying images of naked women in all kinds of circumstances). The resulting reasoning

4 Paul Amar, 'L'islam est-il soluble dans la République?', broadcast on 16 and 19 November 2002 on TV programme *On aura tout lu !*, France 5.

not only culturalizes sexist violence but also ethnicizes and 'racializes' it. Sexist violence is seen as the product of an atemporal, ahistorical and highly sexist 'Arab' or 'Moslem' culture. And any individual whose phenotype matches what is called 'Arab' culture is seen from the outset as being sexist in this way. In short, so-called 'Arab' culture is considered sexist in essence and 'Arab' men sexist by nature. This then corroborates the idea that immigrants' sons are incapable of integrating into French society. The denunciation of sexist violence on suburban housing estates has been used in this way by anti-Arab and anti-black xenophobic rhetoric. Such reasoning has enabled the authorities to justify closing borders to immigrants and has allowed members of the majority group a certain sense of legitimacy in discriminating against the male elements of the minority group.

The 'emancipated *beurette*'[5] as a figure of successful integration

In parallel with the stigmatization of 'Arab boys', the emergence of the *Ni putes ni soumises* movement ('neither tarts nor submissive'), which rightly denounced the sexist violence in the segregated poor neighbourhoods of France's big metropolitan areas, was very favourably received by the media, the authorities and the population. For society as a whole, the immigrants' daughters taking part in this movement symbolize 'successful integration', in contrast to their brothers. They embody the figure of the 'emancipated *beurette*' rejecting the submission that is assumed to be systematically imposed by parents and brothers. As this image implies, for the majority group it is only by virtue of a break with the sexist 'culture' of their parents and brothers that the girls can integrate into society. The boys, supposedly, fiercely defend 'their culture'. The girls, because they refuse to have their freedom restricted and to be treated differently, appear in the collective French imagination as wanting to 'integrate' and capable of doing so.

The majority group's manipulation of young women's desire to break free of patriarchal restrictions, thus, has the effect of dividing them from men, when men and women could otherwise unite in joint action against racism. For, although the women are less stigmatized in the rhetoric, they are no less discriminated against in practice. Of people of Algerian immigrant parentage aged 20 to 29 and possessing a vocational high-school certificate,

---

5 Translator's note: *beurette* is a feminine form derived from *beur*, a type of back-slang for *Arabe* and an identity term that youngsters of immigrant extraction have adopted for themselves. It is less clear who invented the corresponding feminine form.

39% of the men and 36% of the women are unemployed, as against 20% and 10% respectively of young women and men with French-born parents (Tribalat 1995: 76–77). Furthermore, using denunciation of sexist violence to accuse the men of 'not wanting to integrate' attributes a specific meaning to the women's revolt against sexism. That rebellion seems to validate the racist idea of male refusal to integrate, so putting the women in a position where, for the men of their group, they are implicit allies of the majority group's racism.

'Integration' and 'sexual emancipation' for the daughters of immigrants

Sexuality is also at stake in discourses according to which the girls are capable of assimilating into French society but the boys are not. Metaphorically, they lead to an eroticization of the figure of the '*beurette*: the encouragement given these young women to emancipate themselves carries a connotation of sexual emancipation. And in a context where 'Arab boys' (Guenif-Souilamas and Mace 2004) are presented as male chauvinists by nature, the call to rebel against them carries a secondary message: it invites the girls to construct their sexual and emotional lives not with a man from their own group but with a man from the majority group, supposedly more 'modern' and less sexist. Thus, sexuality is one field in which immigrants' sons are judged by comparison with men 'of French extraction'. The ethnicization and racialization of sexual and sexist violence stigmatizes and devalues young men of immigrant parentage, so making those of French parentage more desirable. Whether a minority-group girl chooses a partner in her own group or the other will be interpreted as validating or invalidating the supposed lesser desirability of 'Arab' men[6]. This message transforms every daughter of immigrants into an eroticized object of male sexual competition in which the men symbolize so-called 'ethnic' or 'racial' categories.

Those who denounce the sexism of 'Arab' culture need not say (or even think) that the one group is inferior to the other for that message to be perceived by some, if not all, young men and women of North African extrac-

6 If the reader thinks this exaggerated, here is what one young woman of North African extraction told us when this paper was presented at a research meeting in May 2004: *'It's the first time I've heard anything that made so much sense to me. It's really how I feel. And ... forgive me for saying this, but it's rare for a French person'*. She then added, *'In fact, we're really obliged to invent a new feminism, because we have to defend the men too, it's paradoxical.'*

tion. The racialization and ethnicization of sexist violence and particularly rape already convey this message. Thus majority-group discourses that favour the daughters of immigrants but denigrate the sons often stem from a racism that makes the denunciation of sexism an instrument of its domination and sexuality one of its spheres of expression. Significantly, the interlinking of racist and sexist relations of domination can explain some young women's defence of the headscarf: since it is seen as making the wearer sexually unavailable to men of the majority group, for its wearers it may embody, consciously or not, a form of resistance against a racist eroticization that is scarcely 'emancipating'.

Identity-marker sexism, a product of racism

The social control exercised by parents and brothers over young women's sexuality can be analysed from three standpoints: the ordinary sexism found in every society and social group, the injunction to immigrants' daughters to emancipate themselves, and the colonial history of France. We address the last point first, outlining the migratory trajectory of the parents and situating the sexism observable in some families today within its historical genealogy. Legislation in North African countries restricts women's rights to varying degrees, giving them an inferior status and criminalising extramarital sex. Family codes are the product of a patriarchal system that predates colonization, but their codification into 'positive' law after independence was also part of a wave of reaction against colonization (Daoud 1996). It has to be said that the French colonists had eroticized 'native' women by producing postcards with nude pictures of them, while the French army organized the prostitution of North African women to 'entertain' the troops (Taraud 2003) and rape was among the methods used to torture female members of the resistance or make their husbands talk[7].

Thus, sexuality was one area of the exercise of colonial power, particularly in Algeria. More generally, the colonizers tried to break the resistance capacity of colonized societies by gaining the complicity of the women, called upon to 'emancipate' themselves from their husbands' domination and revolt against their fatherland. Men were described as 'sadistic vampires' who treated their wives 'barbarously' (Fanon 1959; Clancy-Smith 1998). Having been the target of the colonialists' 'emancipating' discourse, women who at the time of independence were fighting to improve their legal status

7 See the testimony of Madame Ighilariz in the documentary by Patrick Rotman, *L'ennemi intime*, broadcast on 6 March 2002 on France 3.

and obtain equality were suspected of betraying their society and were accused of '*assimilationism or wanting to Westernize* (Daoud 1996: 219). Their place in the family became a focus of nationalist discourse: keeping women in their inferior status and controlling their sexuality in the name of Islam, the newly-proclaimed State religion, kept opposition to colonialism alive but also accentuated the pre-existing patriarchal thinking, incorporating it into the emerging national identity.

Among the North African women who came to France after decolonization, clearly some were leaving their country to escape the gradually hardening norms governing relations between the sexes. Equally clearly, others were steeped in that mode of thinking. Today, male immigrants are represented as 'backward' fathers, particularly sexist towards their wives and daughters. It is now the daughters who are encouraged to emancipate themselves and the sons regarded as delinquents or even rapists. This cannot but help to maintain, reactivate or activate strong social control over the daughters. While many immigrants have abandoned the plan of one day going back, some refer back to their country of origin when considering the education of their daughters; they refer to the values that are, or were, prevalent there rather than those current in France. It follows that some may see their daughters' desire for independence as a validation of racism, which in turn leads to increased surveillance. The discriminatory way in which girls are raised is not the same as the sexism found in the majority group: it can be said to be an identity marker because it is part and parcel of a process of self-defence against racism.

Identity issues in virginity and choice of spouse

Identity-marker sexism is reflected above all in the control of girls' sexuality. Girls are generally required to remain virgins, though there is almost no such requirement for boys. Since this is the case in many situations where colonization and racism are not at issue, it is not our aim here to explain the root cause, which is undeniably a patriarchal mindset. Our aim is to explain why the parents continue to give importance to their daughters' virginity once they have emigrated, whereas one might expect this notion to have lost all meaning for those who have been in France for several decades. A survey conducted on young people's sexual behaviour in 1994 showed that the girls are raised to respect the principle of virginity: of girl respondents with one or both North African parents, only 45.8% had already had sexual intercourse at the age of 18, compared to 70.3% of girls with two French parents and

79.1% of sons of North African immigrants (Lagrange and Lhomond 1997). Maintaining this norm is one reaction to the racist rhetoric described above. In a social climate where denunciation of sexist cultural traits sends the message to North African immigrants and their French sons that they should be ashamed of their culture and their being, any daughter's desire to transgress the rules can be seen as a kind of validation of the racist discourse, and hence as a rejection of their parents, their history, their 'culture', their group and their being. Zora, a 21-year-old undergraduate student of English, had to have long discussions with her parents, who worried about preserving her virginity, before they would allow her out in the evenings:

> For our parents, we're forgetting them if we want to make things change. For them, it's all a question of traditions, religion and honour. Honour above all! And they say 'We came to France, but that's no reason to behave the way they do!' In fact they don't want us to assimilate. [...] But you know, if I actually did listen to them and drop my studies they'd be disappointed too in a way. So we have to do things against their will too, and in spite of everything, they're happy, but it's tiring, because they reproach us, 'Take care! The family back there ... you have to follow the lineage'.

The parents' fear of seeing their daughters disown them is understandable when we examine the discourse that incites them to 'integrate' by making a break with their family and 'emancipating themselves' sexually with men of the majority group. This fear helps to maintain the importance placed on virginity and family honour and helps to perpetuate the social control.

The choice of spouse is another area in which daughters' sexuality is controlled. In 1992, the INED survey *Mobilité géographique et insertion sociale* (Geographical mobility and social integration) (Tribalat, Riandey and Simon 1992) revealed that among French people aged 20 to 29 born of Algerian parents, 15% of the women had a spouse whose parents were both French, compared to 50% of the boys (Tribalat 1995: 78). This imbalance shows how far girls' and boys' sexuality is treated differently in the family. Of the 27 young women interviewed, 23 said they could not consider marrying someone of French 'extraction' without risking a break with their parents, and four had an elder sister who had been *'banished from the family'* for that reason. Conversely, three said that their mothers had guaranteed them the right to choose their own husband, regardless of his so-called 'ethnic' origin.

It also emerges that those who do choose to live with a man of French extraction are often stigmatized: Seif, studying for a degree in Arabic, refused to involve himself in his sister's love life and attached no importance to the virginity of his future wife, but explained how much a 'mixed' marriage by his sister would be felt as a betrayal:

> He must be North African! A Moslem first and North African second. Even better if he is Moroccan! [laughter] If he's French that will pose a lot of problems. My parents would take it very badly. She would have to expect a break with the family and to not see certain people any more. It's a question of what you belong to: at root, belonging to the religion, the culture, everything. For my parents, we're Moroccan and that's that! We're not French. Whether we're here or there makes no difference, we're Arabs of France. Integration doesn't exist for them, doesn't mean anything. They don't want to integrate into French society. They've understood that our lives are here, but let's keep among ourselves. She couldn't possibly marry someone from outside [...]. My father, he couldn't tell his brothers, his friends back there, his family back there, that his daughter was marrying a Frenchman. If only as a matter of honour he couldn't do it. It's a matter of honour! Your daughter's married a Frenchman, so she's a tart, ain't she. She's considered a tart because she's given herself away.

To really grasp the sense of what Seif's parents feel regarding their daughter's husband and understand what is meant by the expression 'integration doesn't exist', we must take into account that they have vigorously encouraged all their sons and daughters to undertake long years of study and that they are not thinking of going back to Morocco. Seif explains this as follows: *'My father is too French in his head now: he could never go back there'*. So while this father has adopted 'French' values, he feels 'Moslem' and 'Moroccan' when it comes to his children's 'integration' or more precisely his daughter's sexuality. Seif also explained that if his sister lost her virginity, that would not dishonour her in her father's eyes as long as she married a North African. But marriage with a Frenchman would be dishonourable even if she were still a virgin.

So virginity would appear less important than the spouse's so-called 'ethnic' origin. A so-called 'mixed' marriage would mean that the daughter had validated the stigmatization aimed at the father along with all other 'Arab' men, presented as being less desirable than so-called 'French' men. Thus the term 'integration', as associated by the dominant group with a girl's 'mixed' marriage, implies relegating the father to 'racial' inferiority. It underpins society's 'dehumanization' of him and we can well imagine that this is hard to bear. Unable to react against the dominant group, he turns on his daughter. These marriages are dishonourable above all because they are perceived as a betrayal of the family's identity and a breaking of solidarity with the men of the minority group. The importance placed on the principle of virginity in the migrant community has more to do with preventing these 'mixed' marriages than with the desire to forbid the daughter any form of pre-marital sex.

Social control of girls and sexist violence

A study of media discourses and ethnographic data shows that sexuality is socially constructed by racist social relations. These racist social relations manipulate gender divisions and present women's sexual choices as either validating or invalidating racist discourse. This makes women's sexuality a particular issue for the minority group, men's social control over them tends to increase and the result is sometimes violence. It is a mistake to think that this control and violence are due to 'Moslem' or 'North African' culture, irrespective of time and place, being 'more sexist' than others. Although this 'culture' like any other is based on a hierarchy between the sexes, it cannot be said that its sexism has not changed over the centuries or that it is not liable to change. On the contrary, it can be said with certainty that the exacerbated sexism of some North African emigrant men and some of their French sons today is partly due to the racism characteristic of the current socio-historical context. By presenting North African immigrant men and their sons born in France as sexist by nature, this racism tends, as we have seen, to result in some of them behaving in accordance with this 'mythical portrait' (Memmi 2002).

References

Clancy-Smith, Julia (1998): Islam, gender, and identities in the making of French Algeria, 1830–1962. In: Clancy-Smith, Julia/Gouda, Frances (eds.): Domesticating the Empire: race, gender, and family life in French and Dutch colonialism. Charlottesville, London: University Press of Virginia.

Daoud, Zakya (1996): Féminisme et politique au Maghreb. Sept décennies de luttes, Casablanca: Eddif, 409pp.

Fanon, Franz (1959): L'Algérie se dévoile. In: Fanon, Franz: L'an V de la Révolution algérienne. Paris, Maspero, republished by La Découverte and Syros, 2001, pp. 16–50.

Guénif-Souilamas, Nacira/Macé, Éric (2004): Les féministes et le garçon arabe, La Tour d'Aigues: Éditions de l'Aube, 106pp.

Hamel, Christelle (2003a): L'intrication des rapports sociaux de sexe, de 'race', d'âge et de classe: ses effets sur la gestion des risques d'infection par le VIH chez les Français descendants de migrants du Maghreb. EHESS, Paris, doctoral thesis in anthropology, 2003, 720pp.

Hamel, Christelle (2003b): ''Faire tourner les meufs'. Les viols collectifs: discours des médias et des agresseurs'. In: Gradhiva, No.33, pp.85–92.

Jaspard, Maryse et al. (2003): Les violences envers les femmes en France. Une enquête nationale. Paris: La Documentation française, 370pp.

Lagrange, Hugues/Lhomond, Brigitte (eds.) (1997): L'entrée dans la sexualité: le comportement des jeunes dans le contexte du sida. Paris: Éd. La Découverte, 431pp.

Memmi, Albert (2002): Portrait du colonisé précédé de Portrait du colonisateur. Paris, Gallimard, 171pp. (1st edition 1957).

Mucchielli, Laurent (2005): Le scandale des 'tournantes'. Dérives médiatiques, contre-enquête sociologique. Paris: Éd. La Découverte, 124pp.

Taraud, Christelle (2003a): Mauresques. Femmes orientales dans la photographie coloniale, 1860–1910. Paris, Albin Michel, 144pp.

Taraud, Christelle (2003b): La prostitution coloniale, Algérie, Tunisie, Maroc, 1830–1962. Paris, Payot, 496pp.

Tribalat, Michèle (1995): Faire France. Une grande enquête sur les immigrés et leurs enfants. Paris: Éd. La Découverte, 231pp.

Tribalat, Michèle/Riandey, Benoît/Simon, Patrick (1992): Mobilité géographique et insertion sociale. INED survey.

Venner, Fiammetta (1995): Femmes d'extrême droite: discours et militantes. In: Dore-Audibert, Andrée/Bessis, Sophie (eds.): Femmes de Méditerranée: politique, religion, travail. Paris: Éd. Khartala, pp. 143–155.

Zehraoui, Ashène (1997): Images de l'Autre: la population d'origine maghrébine au regard de la société française. In: Migrations Société, No. 54, November-December, pp.7–20.

Part 3:
Forms and Effects of Violence Against Women

Male Violence Against Migrant Women: Denying Rights in a Racist Gender System

Sabine Masson and *Patricia Roux*

Introduction

In this paper we analyze gender-based violence from an intersectional angle, taking into account both the gender and the racial/ethnic/national group membership of women living in Switzerland. The analysis echoes other papers that show the relevance of intersectionality for understanding the meaning and impact of male violence. Male violence is an instrument in the reproduction of the gender system, but it has different effects depending on social and racial factors (Crenshaw 2005; Hooks 1984). As in many other Western countries, migrant women victims of marital violence in Switzerland do not have access to the same support as Swiss women in similar situations and do not have the same rights. This paper sets out to show that the cause of this flagrant injustice is a twofold discrimination, based on gender and nationality. Migrant women are victims of gender-based violence in the same way as other women, but they are also caught up by institutional restrictions due to their residency conditions and the racist basis of immigration laws and policies and representations of 'foreigners'[1]. Because their legal status is dependent on their marital tie, migrant women are more exposed to marital violence and risk being deported if they leave their husbands.

The context to this discrimination is one where immigration laws and policies, grounded in the gender system and racism, are being tightened. At the same time as the trend is towards denying migrant women all rights to protection, there has rarely been so much public talk of 'migrants' violence'. Violence is treated as if it were a cultural trait that radically differentiates 'foreigners' from Swiss nationals. This *'geography of sexist violence'* (Tissot and Delphy 2009: 2) demonstrates not only the way social relations are interwoven with the stigmatization of migrants and the women's exposure to male violence, but also the way in which Swiss society hides the reality of

1 Official category that includes all persons not of Swiss nationality, even if born on Swiss soil.

male violence in general. In other words, whereas migrant women are more exposed to male violence because of their residence status, ethnicization and racialization of sexist violence helps to 'euphemize' violence in general, under new strategies for legitimizing gender inequality (Romito 2006).

Our approach is based on our activist feminist position. We are white academic women; we are not speaking in the name of migrant women but on the basis of our engagement against a discriminatory system and our active solidarity with these women.

Political and legal contexts produce double discrimination against women migrants

To understand Switzerland's response to migrant women victims of marital violence, we need to examine the political and legal framework governing immigration. Standards in this regard infringe women's rights in many respects. When a woman arrives in Switzerland seeking refugee status, her reasons for fleeing her country are not properly recognized under existing laws.[2] In practice, although jurisprudence has made some progress[3], women fleeing their country for gender-related reasons find that the political nature of their persecution is denied (Schmidlin 2006; Schmidlin and Masson 2009). For women coming to Switzerland to work or to join their husbands, admission and residency rights are based on a system of a double-thinking called the 'two circles policy'.[4] Whereas for nationals of the European Union and European Free Trade Association countries the Agreement on the Free Movement of Persons gives them residence rights for the purposes of work, women from other countries have no such right. Their entry to Switzerland is governed by the Law on Foreigners (*Loi sur les étrangers*, LEtr), under which they cannot work unless they are issued the relevant residence permit (Schmidlin 2008). These permits are granted only rarely, when justified by high qualifications and a high level of integration. Although these require-

2 Gender is not included among the reasons for persecution that enter into the statutory definition of 'refugee' (Art. 3 of the Law on Asylum).

3 In 2006, the Federal appeal court acknowledged that a woman refugee was discriminated against because she was a woman. Persecution by private individuals is also more widely recognized than before, when a close link with the State had to be demonstrated (Schmidlin 2006; Schmidlin & Masson 2009).

4 The 'two circles policy' has a long history in Switzerland. It follows on from the 'three circles policy' which appeared in the 1980s and was a response both to xenophobic conceptions and the needs of the market (Mahnig 2005). At that time the Council of State set up a system of selection by nationality; today's 'two circles' policy establishes a hierarchy between two zones: the European Union and all other countries.

ments are formulated in neutral terms, they are based on gender discrimination because in most countries few women or none can reach managerial status (Baronne 2006; Baronne and Lempen 2007). And there is no provision for legal authorization to work in sales, catering or domestic work; these skills are not recognized as such.

Consequently, most women economic migrants from countries outside Europe have no legal status[5], making their working conditions even more insecure (Carreras 2007). There is also gender discrimination against women entering under family reunion provisions. In the first place, this status primarily concerns women[6]. Secondly, their right to work being extremely limited, marital immigration is often the only solution for these women. There are, however, also restrictions on residence in the case of marital reunion. While the right to a residence permit has, for many years, been closely tied to marital status, the new Law on Foreigners (LEtr) has strengthened that link with a requirement that husband and wife live together. A major consequence of this situation is that migrant women from non-European countries are exposed more than others to marital violence.

Migrant women more exposed to marital violence

Before analyzing the greater exposure of migrant women, we must point out that in Switzerland as elsewhere, figures on marital violence are hard to establish because there are no nationwide statistics or systematic institutionalized reports on domestic violence (BFEG 2007: 1). However, the only nationally representative study conducted in 1994 unveiled for the first time the extent of marital violence in Switzerland[7] (Gillioz, De Puy and Ducret 1997). More recently, a survey of homicide revealed that the family is the most murderous context of social relations and is twice as much so for women as for men.[8] This situation has led to more vigorous campaigns against domestic

5 Exploratory research shows that there are more women than men with no legal status (Valli 2003).

6 In 2005, 40% of all cases of legal immigration concerned family reunion. However, there are twice as many marriages between Swiss men and foreign women as the reverse (Barone 2006).

7 This survey interviewed 1500 women and showed that 20.7% of them had suffered physical and/or sexual violence by a partner (Gillioz, De Puy and Ducret 1997).

8 Forty-five per cent of homicides in Switzerland between 2000 and 2004 were committed in the domestic setting; 317 of the victims were women and 159 were men (Federal Office of Statistics (OFS) 2006). Another survey, of consultations at official victim assistance centres, shows that in 52.6% of cases of violence – more than half – there was a family tie between the victim and the suspected perpetrator (OFS 2008; BFEG 2007).

violence and some advances in legal provisions.[9] But there are still major obstacles that limit the effects of these essentially penal measures: the burden of proof is on the victims, there is the risk of renewed victimization during the proceedings, and the victims are exposed to their husband's threats. These procedural constraints have been noted particularly by the Federal Office for Gender Equality (BFEG), which recommends that a study be conducted of their impact *'on the scope of the civil law standard for protection against violence'* (Art. 28*b* CC) and that measures be taken (BFEG 2008: 96). Various national and international institutional and voluntary bodies are also worried by the fact that victims can now ask for provisional suspension of the penal proceedings. According to Switzerland's third report on the implementation of the Convention on the Elimination of all forms of Discrimination Against Women (CEDAW), *'the prosecution authorities tend to suspend proceedings quite quickly. The additional protection that automatic prosecution was intended to give the victims, is thus insufficient in practice'* (Switzerland's third report 2008: 48). The BFEG report (2008) also stresses the problematic nature of this measure, because women use it under pressure from their partners, relatives, friends and even judges. This loophole in protection reflects a degree of continued denial of violence in the family, since it does not apply to other automatically prosecuted breaches of penal law.

Social and legal conditions that increase migrant women's exposure to marital violence

Their insecure socio-economic situation and residence status further weakens migrant women's protection against marital violence. The legal loopholes are all the more worrying in that migrant women are particularly at risk of domestic violence (OFS 2008).[10] The reason for the probable over-representation lies in their social conditions (place of residence, lack of occupational skills and economic resources) and not nationality as such (Belser 2005).

9 In particular the fact that the Swiss Penal Code now provides for automatic prosecution for physical or sexual marital violence (Art. 189, 190 and 123, 126 CP), and the fact that the courts can order the violent partner's eviction from the family home. However, the victim can provisionally suspend proceedings in such cases (Art.55 CP) and this often leads to charges being dropped (see Mösch-Payot 2008). There is also a continuing lack of civil law provisions to protect the individual, of provision for intervention, counselling for victims and financial resources for consulting centres and battered wives' homes.

10 Although foreign women are under-represented in prevalence studies, they are over-represented in police statistics. According to the police figures, migrant women are concerned 2.5 times as often (OFS 2008; DINT 2008). However, these data must be interpreted with caution as they are certainly affected by other factors, e.g. the fact that the police intervene more readily in poorer neighbourhoods.

Other social causes such as language difficulties and a narrow social network play their part, increasing a woman's dependence on her husband. Social isolation, a factor that favours marital violence (BFEG 2008), is further increased by a residence status tied to the marriage because this limits a woman's possibilities for establishing connections outside the family. The combination of isolation and economic difficulties reduces migrant women's possibilities for independence, defence, protection and information in face of male violence.

Migrant women are made more vulnerable in face of marital violence by their insecure residence conditions. The third Swiss report on implementation of the CEDAW (2008) recognizes that the various protection and intervention measures have had 'limited effects' for migrant women because of their fear of being deported.[11] This adds to the more general obstacles described above, such as provisional suspension of prosecution proceedings. Suspension is all the more likely where the victim is exposed to the risk of losing her residence permit; husbands often make use of this danger to strengthen their hold on the victim (Hanselmann & Dürer 2008). Pressure from the authorities responsible for granting residence permits can also persuade the victim to suspend the proceedings as they may threaten to withdraw the permit or shorten its validity period if they know the couple is in crisis or has split up. In short, migrant women confronted with this situation are quite likely to see the charges against their husband dropped. If they then try to have the decision against renewal of their residence permit re-examined, the fact that they withdrew their case or suspended proceedings may be taken as lack of proof.

In the light of this situation the Federal Office for Gender Equality recommends specific research and protection and prevention measures (BFEG 2008), including an examination of the application of the provisions for *cas de rigueur* (serious cases) in the Law on Foreigners (Art. 50, para. 1b, LEtr), to see *'to what extent the Federal and canton authorities make use of the possible margin of interpretation to protect victims'* (BFEG 2008: 96). For authorities that answered various parliamentary questions on the subject[12], current legislation and practice is satisfactory thanks to the inclusion in the

11 In 2003, the Committee for the Elimination of all forms of Discrimination Against Women was already recommending that an assessment be made of the impact of revocation of the residence permit in the case of foreign women victims of violence (CEDAW 2003, recommendation No 35).

12 See the reply of the Federal Council to the question from National Councillor Francine John-Calame (http://www.parlament.ch/F/Suche/Pages/geschaefte.aspx?gesch_id=20081102#) and the report of the Council of State of the canton of Vaud at the request of deputy Fabienne Freymond Cantone (http://www.vd.ch/fr/organisation/autorites/grand-conseil/liste-des-objets-en-attente-de-traitement-par-le-grand-conseil/).

LEtr of an article explicitly referring to domestic violence[13]. However, under this law, marital violence can only be taken into account as 'major personal reasons' justifying maintenance of the residence permit if *'social reintegration in the country of origin seems to be seriously compromised'*. This condition is in addition to that of proof of the violence, a requirement of the legal proceedings for all women and which cannot be based 'simply on allegations'.[14]

Recognition of violence is thus subordinated to a major limitation, based on fuzzy or indeed arbitrary criteria[15]. For the Federal Office for Migration, a person can reintegrate in their country of origin *'as long as they are not integrated in Switzerland, (...) if they have not been long in Switzerland, if they have not established close ties with Switzerland and their reintegration in their country of origin does not pose a particular problem'* (Report of the Council of State 2009: 4). The question of reintegration in the country of origin is thus closely linked to that of integration in Switzerland, which becomes the *'essential criterion for a migrant victim of marital violence who wishes to obtain an individual residence permit'* (Dürer & Hanselmann 2008: 61). Making maintenance of the residence permit conditional on a positive assessment of integration in Switzerland reveals the false neutrality of this term and the underlying gender inequality. For women victims, the integration requirement is especially discriminatory because *'women who suffer violence do not manage to integrate, for their husbands often forbid them to go out or to take language lessons* (Report of the Council of State 2009: 1).

These legal provisions establish a hierarchy within women's universal right to physical and sexual integrity, on the basis of a social classification by nationality. This ratifies a twofold violence, administrative and gender-based, against women migrants. Administrative sanction represents a kind of 'sec-

13 Article 50 of the LEtr:
1 After the breakup of the family, the right of the spouse and children to a residence permit and the prolongation of its validity period according to Art. 42 and 43 remains in the following cases:
a. the marital union has lasted at least three years and integration has been successful;
b. continued residence in Switzerland is necessary for major personal reasons.
2 The major personal reasons referred to in para. 1b are those where the spouse is a victim of marital violence and the possibility of social reintegration in the country of origin seems to be seriously compromised.

14 Article 77 para. 6 of the ordinance on admission, residence and pursuit of an income-earning activity (Canton de Vaud) lists the indications of marital violence, mainly *a. medical certificates; b. police reports; c. penal action; d. measures under the meaning of Art. 28b of the civil code 1, or e. penal judgement pronounced in the matter.*

15 The Federal Council makes a very narrow interpretation of 'seriously compromised' regarding the possibility of reintegration in the country of origin. It only takes into account extreme cases and the post-traumatic aftermath of domestic violence does not seem to be systematically taken into account (OMCT 2009).

ond punishment' (John-Calame 2008) in addition to the violence at home. This twofold violence feeds the cycle of marital violence because dependence on residence status accentuates the husband's pressure on the victim who has denounced him or wishes to do so:

> by making the residence right of a wife entering Switzerland under family reunion provisions conditional on her living with a husband who is in work, the current law on foreigners facilitates abuse of power and violence by the husband and makes the potential victim's position insecure (Third Swiss report 2008: 56).

In practice: marital violence assessed according to the migrant woman's skill level

The press has lately reported several cases of women who had lost their residence permits because they had separated from violent husbands to protect themselves. At present there is no systematic census of such cases, partly because most women in this situation keep quiet or disappear from emergency shelters when they lose their permits or see they are at risk of doing so. Also, the application of the new LEtr law is still recent and the authorities have not organized any census. In the field, however, NGOs report that many migrant women victims are faced with a dilemma owing to the legal vacuum described above. They must choose between continuing to suffer violence and losing their residence permit.[16] These organizations are therefore fighting for an amendment to the current law.[17] One of the main problems they report is the prevalence of the integration factor in assessments of violence. In the jurisprudence (mainly established under the previous law, given that the LEtr only came into force on 1 January 2008) and in cases the associations encounter in the field, the integration criterion is used almost systematically. It is used even when the women concerned have been living in Switzerland for many years, in combination with other arguments such as lack of proof and the fact that the woman has withdrawn her legal action.[18] A negative assess-

16 In French-speaking Switzerland several activists and professionals in aid for women victims of marital violence have recently expressed their view in the press (*Le Courrier*, 17 November 2008; *Le Courrier*, 13 December 2008; *Tribune de Genève*, 29 December 2008; *Le Courrier*, 9 May 2009; *24 Heures*, 13 May 2009).

17 Particularly 'by removing the requirement to show that social reintegration in the country of origin is impossible, in order to ensure that the victims of acts of family violence receive a residence permit without any other condition than having shown plausibly that they have been victims of such acts' (OMCT 2009: 6).

18 See jurisprudence of the Canton Tribunal, Court of Administrative and Public Law of the Canton of Vaud (CDAP); *Observatoire du droit de l'asile et des étrangers* (ODAE); petition of feminist collective *Sorcières en colère* (December 2008); petition of the group *Non aux*

ment of integration is based on the absence of family ties, lack of integration in the labour market, lack of economic independence or occupational qualifications or non-recognition of diplomas awarded in the country of origin. Once poor integration has been alleged, reintegration in the country of origin is stated as possible – as it is if the victim has relatives in the country of origin. Violence is thus only one criterion among others, addressed conditionally and dependently on other factors, even when backed up by proof such as legal action, trial or specialist protection. The following example is of a Brazilian national with four years' residence in Switzerland.

> [the applicant] has been employed as a cleaner in a restaurant since 1 January 2008. The income from this work is not known, but it is reasonable to doubt that it is enough to provide financial independence for her and her three children (…). Furthermore, the applicant is not highly qualified and her work does not require special knowledge. (…) it seems from the applicant's file that her integration in the social fabric and local life of her place of residence cannot be called exceptional. (…) While it is true that the applicant has long been devoting her energy to solving the serious marital problems she was faced with and fleeing her husband's violence, it does not emerge from the file that she has demonstrated a particularly successful adaption. (Court of Administrative and Public Law, Canton of Vaud, PE.2008.0096, TA, 12.09.2008)

All in all, renewal of the residence permit depends primarily on skills or qualifications as a criterion of integration. The violence is only secondary. Migrant women victims are caught up in a chain of constraints: the racist and sexist admission system prevents them from entering the country as workers in their own right; family reunion is the main possibility open to them. This legal status makes them entirely dependent on their husbands, and when there is marital violence, the restrictive laws on residence and termination of marriage further strengthen this dependence. Prevented from protecting themselves by so many restrictions, they are all the harder hit by the cycle of violence. At the root of this situation is the patriarchal concept of residence dependent on married status, which defines women entering under family reunion provisions exclusively as wives and mothers (Minder 2005). Yet it does not recognize the skills involved in domestic labour, childcare and education, nor the social activities and paid work the women may have in Switzerland. The couple is a place where women of every social class encounter violence. To deprive one category of women of all legal independence simply strengthens patriarchal domination.

Explusions (September 2008); World Organization Against Torture (OMCT 2009); parliamentary question by National Councillor Francine John-Calame of 2/10/2008; *Amnistie! Le Magazine pour les Droits Humains* No 47/2006.

Gender violence instrumentalized by racist discourse

Two paradoxes stand out from our examination of migration policies and law governing the situation of migrant women victims of marital violence. The first is that the State worsens migrant women's exposure to their partner's sexism while simultaneously denying that violence, since in assessing their residence applications the fact of violence is subordinated to their integration in Switzerland and the possibility of their reintegration in their country of origin. The second is that this double penalization takes place in a social context where more and more measures are being adopted to deal with the problem of marital violence, which affects one woman in five in Switzerland (Gillioz, De Puy and Ducret 1997). What can explain the social acceptance of the denial of rights inflicted on migrant women victims of violence? In our view, a partial answer to this question is the racist representations and discourses that attribute male violence to 'the culture' of immigrant communities rather than to structural factors concerning Switzerland itself.

In public debate, the media and political discourses, the argument that migrants from non-European and/or Muslim countries are violent is repeatedly put forward to explain the problems they encounter in Switzerland and to show that their lifestyles, values and identities are incompatible with Swiss conceptions and practices (Roux, Gianettoni & Perrin 2006; 2007). The chain of reasoning that seems to prevail in these representations and discourses could be described as follows: (1) these migrants are different from the Swiss; (2) the proof of this is that they are violent; (3) this violence is a threat to Switzerland: it disturbs the peace and calls into question the established moral order, especially the principle of gender equality to which the country subscribes; (4) Switzerland has the right to reject this menace and protect itself by tightening conditions for the granting of residence permits. In this reasoning, which is reflected in increasingly restrictive policies towards increasingly broad categories of migrants, the women are invisible and do not count. Attention is focused on migrant men's violence and very little on the effects of this violence on migrant women. On the contrary, it even implies that they are responsible for their fate, or at least that their peers or migrant partners are, which in either case absolves Switzerland and relieves it of its duty to address the problems raised by male violence.

We think this is a process of 'racialization of sexism' (Hamel 2003), which does much to render invisible the real and specific problems migrant women may encounter. This last part of our paper attempts to decipher this process, which stems from a stigmatization of migrant communities, legitimized by acts of violence attributed only to migrants: forced marriages, genital mutilation and gang rape, to which some (both men and women) add the wearing of headscarves and demands by Muslim families that their daughters be excused from swimming at school. Political intervention in this field, from left and right, feminist and otherwise, is increasing. This might be cause for rejoicing but in fact the political strategies and discourses involved generally reinforce racial hierarchies and even gender hierarchies.

To illustrate the strengthening of racist and sexist systems, let us take the example of gang rape. When migrants are involved in such acts, the media, judges and politicians, male and female, use a common explanatory register: the rapes are due to the origin and culture of the young rapists and their parents, a culture considered barbarous, archaic and eminently patriarchal. This culturist register that 'fabricates the Other' (Delphy 2008), makes the migrant different – different from the Swiss rapist and different from the abstract figure of 'the Swiss citizen' who has other, 'modern' values. This fabrication of the Other which is used to prove 'non-ordinary' sexism and violence (Delphy 2006), specific to that culture and unrelated to the 'ordinary' sexism current in Switzerland, has its mirror image in political, media and legal discourses about gang rapes by Swiss nationals. In the latter case there is no reference to the 'patriarchal culture' of the rapists; their act is attributed to an unhappy childhood (sexual abuse, insecure living conditions etc.) or to individual deviance or pathology. This is also true in other countries; Leti Volpp, for example, has made the same observation in an analysis of cases of violence brought to court in the United States, where the dominant are seen as individual actors whose behaviour is not the product of an identity group (2006: 18). She also shows that racializing male violence – attributing it to a cultural problem foreign to the country – makes it possible to push the problem away, beyond the country's borders.

The process of racializing sexism thus discriminates against migrants and women in many ways. It is a way of stigmatizing entire migrant groups (in Switzerland Kosovars and Albanians are particularly targeted at present), or indeed the entire category of 'foreigners', who are supposed to import archaic cultural values completely different from Swiss values. The process also contributes to the underestimation of the structural strength of gender distinctions in the country, regardless of the statistics showing the wage gap between men and women, the failure to share domestic labour and the presence of marital violence in all social classes. It also has specific effects on migrant women, the social category defined by the intersection of the racial and gender hierarchies. By incriminating the migrants' 'culture' and euphemizing Swiss gender-based violence, this process makes it possible to ignore the fact that the laws in force strongly expose migrant women to the risk of male violence. As a result, all preventive or protective action is blocked (Minder 2005). But although they are over-represented in, battered wives', shelters and in police call-out statistics, this is because *'Swiss law applicable to foreigners incorporates discriminatory elements that have repercussions in situations of domestic violence'* (Minder 2005: 26) and not because of their culture of origin or their nationality.

From this analysis, we think it can justifiably be said that the denial of migrant women's rights is inherent in Switzerland's gendered immigration policies and racist culturalist discourses that instrumentalize the question of gender-based violence. This instrumentalization is used to legitimize the tightening of measures concerning migrants. More generally, racist rhetoric instrumentalizes the entire question of gender equality. This can be seen particularly in the debate on integration. For example, in a 'Guide to the application of the integration agreement' planned under the new LEtr, the Federal Office for Migration suggest that cantons organize integration classes for migrants to *'get to know Switzerland, its particularities and customs, current norms, the rights and duties of its citizens, its principle of equality between men and women, its health system', etc.* (our emphasis). In this document as in many political statements on integration, Switzerland is presented as a benchmark in matters of equality. Equality is not a goal to be attained but a way of strengthening a 'feeling of Western superiority' (Nader 2006), stigmatizing migrants, culturalizing them as barbarous, sexist and violent, and criminalizing them.

For a woman migrant confronted with a violent husband it is extremely difficult to publicly denounce their situation because they are afraid it will reinforce these stereotypes (Crenshaw 2005). They anticipate the discriminatory effects these prejudices are bound to have on all racialized men and on themselves. For the women concerned to be able to break the silence, Kimberlé Crenshaw proposes that the policies introduced to protect them from male violence be designed also to protect them from racism.

Conclusion

The violence suffered by some migrant women cannot be properly combated as long as it is seen as the product of a specific and particularly sexist culture. Nor can the combat advance until it is recognized that we live in a racist system which establishes a hierarchy between the rights of Swiss nationals and those of migrants. As we have seen, this hierarchization results in a denial of the rights of women migrants, who are more exposed to the risk of male violence because of the discriminatory conditions of their residence status. Responses to this situation need to combine the feminist and ant-racist struggles, because sexist and racist divisions jointly structure institutions, policies, social practices and everyone's daily lives. They also combine to shore up the legitimacy of a social order in which domination is the rule. In this situation the antiracist feminist struggle seems to us the only one that can really address the particular oppression of migrant women. It also opens the way to defending *all* women's rights, because the gendered construction of racism today, in which a culturalized image of violence is a major element, also casts a veil of silence over sexist discrimination as a whole.

References

Amnistie! Le magazine pour les droits humains: Violence domestique, la Suisse bouge. N° 47, novembre 2006.

Baronne, Anne-Marie/Lempen, Karine (2007): Des lois qui discriminent discrètement les femmes. In: Féminin-Masculin, mai 2007.

Baronne, Anne-Marie (2006): Femmes migrantes, femmes invisibles? LEtr: discriminations cachées, mais réelles. In: Féminin-Masculin, septembre 2006.

Bureau fédéral de l'égalité entre femmes et hommes (BFEG) (2007): Feuille d'information: La violence domestique en chiffres, Département fédéral de l'intérieur (DFI), novembre 2007.

Bureau fédéral de l'égalité entre femmes et hommes (BFEG) (2008): La violence dans les relations de couple. Ses causes et les mesures prises en Suisse. Rapport final. Berne, septembre 2008.

Belser, Katharina (2005): La violence domestique survient dans tous les milieux – mais dans certains peut-être un peu plus souvent. In: Questions au féminin, 1/2005, pp. 13–17.

Carreras, Laetitia (2007): Femmes migrantes et externalisation du travail domestique. Constats et pistes de réflexion. In: Centre Contact Suisse-Immigrés (CCSI), Genre et intégration en contexte migratoire. Actes de l'Université d'été – 25/26 août 2006. Genève: CCSI.

Comité pour l'élimination de la discrimination à l'égard des femmes (CEDEF) (2003): Examen des rapports présentés par les États parties – Suisse. Genève: Nations Unies. Vingt-huitième session du 13 au 31 janvier 2003. Centre de contact Suisse.

Comité d'action interassociatif Droits des femmes, droit au séjour (2004): Femmes et étrangères: contre la double violence. Témoignages et analyses. Paris. http://doubleviolence.free.fr

Crenshaw, Kimberlé Williams (2005): Cartographies des marges: intersectionnalité, politique de l'identité et violences contre les femmes de couleur. In: Cahiers du Genre, 39, pp. 51–82.

Delphy, Christine (2006): Antisexisme ou antiracisme? Un faux dilemme. In: Nouvelles Questions Féministes, 25/1, pp. 59–82.

Delphy, Christine (2008): Classer, dominer. Qui sont les 'autres'? Paris: La Fabrique.

Gillioz, Lucienne/De Puy, Jacqueline/Ducret, Véronique (1997): Domination et violence envers la femme dans le couple. Lausanne: Payot.

Département de l'Intérieur du Canton de Vaud (DINT) – Coordinatrice en matière d'intégration des étrangers et de prévention du racisme: Violences domestiques et populations migrantes: enjeux en matière d'intégration. Lausanne, mai 2008.

John-Calame, Francine (2008): Traitement pour les personnes étrangères victimes de violences domestiques. Interpellation déposée au Conseil National le 2/10/2008, http://www.parlament.ch/F/Suche/Pages/geschaefte.aspx?gesch_id=20081102

Jurisprudence du Tribunal Cantonal. Cour de droit administratif et public du Canton de Vaud (CDAP). http://www.vd.ch/fr/themes/etat-droit/justice/lois-et-jurisprudence/

Hamel, Christelle (2003): 'Faire tourner les Meufs': Les viols collectifs dans les discours des agresseurs et des médias. In: Gradhiva, 33, pp. 85–92.

Hanselmann, Magaly/Dürer, Sylvie (2008): Femmes migrantes et violence conjugale: plus exposées, moins protégées. In: Questions au Féminin, 2/2008, pp. 60–64.

Hooks, bell (1984): Feminist theory: from margin to center. Boston: South End Press.

Mahnig, Hans (sous la dir.) (2005): Histoire de la politique de migration, d'asile et d'intégration en Suisse depuis 1948. Zurich: Seismo.

Minder, Maja (2005): Violence doemstique et migration – Pour une approche professionnelle et objective excluant la culturalisation du problème. In: Questions au féminin, 1/2005, pp. 26–28.

Mösch-Payot, Peter (2008): La situation juridique actuelle en matière de violence domestique en Suisse: innovations, contexte, questions. Sous l'angle spécifique de la poursuite d'office et de la suspension provisoire aux termes de l'art.55a CPS. In: Questions au féminin, 2/2008, pp. 22–27.

Nader, Laura (2006): Orientalisme, occidentalisme et contrôle des femmes. In: Nouvelles Questions Féministes, 25/1, pp. 12–24.

Observatoire romand du droit de l'asile et des étrangers (ODAE): Fiches descriptives. http://stopexclusion.ch/observatoire/fichesdescriptives.html.

Office fédéral de la statistique (OFS) (2006): Criminalité et droit pénal. Enquête sur les homicides. Berne: Communiqué de presse du 12.10.2006.

Office fédéral de la statistique (OFS) (2008): Criminalité et droit pénal. Aide aux victimes d'infractions. Berne: Communiqué de presse du 12.10.2006.

Organisation mondiale contre la torture (OMCT) (2009): Mise en oeuvre du Pacte international relatif aux droits civils et politiques (PIDCP). Note d'information concernant les discriminations et les violences domestiques à l'égard des femmes ayant un statut précaire en Suisse. Pré-sesion en vue de l'examen de la Suisse par le Comité des droits de l'homme, Genève, février 2009.

Rapport du Conseil d'Etat au Grand Conseil sur le postulat Fabienne Freymond Cantone et consorts: MigrantEs victimes de violences conjugales. Quand il y a péril en la demeure. Mars 2009. http://www.vd.ch/fr/organisation/autorites/grand-conseil/liste-des-objets-en-attente-de-traitement-par-le-grand-conseil/

Romito, Patrizia (2006): Un silence de mortes. La violence masculine occultée. Paris: Syllepse.

Roux, Patricia/Gianettoni, Lavinia/Perrin, Céline (2006): Féminisme et racisme. Une recherche exploratoire sur les fondements des divergences relatives au port du foulard. In: Nouvelles Questions Féministes, 25/1, pp. 84–106.

Roux, Patricia/Gianettoni, Lavinia/Perrin, Céline (2007): L'instrumentalisation du genre: une nouvelle forme de racisme et de sexisme. In: Nouvelles Questions Féministes, 26/2, pp. 92–108.

Schmidlin, Irène/Masson, Sabine (2009): Les persécutions genrées des femmes. In: Bulletin de SOS asile, N° 90, 1er trimestre 2009, pp. 2–3.

Schmidlin, Irène (2008): Exercer en Suisse une activité lucrative: Une critique féministe des normes en matière d'autorisation de séjour. Mémoire pour le Diplôme d'études approfondies (DEA) pluriuniversitaire en 'Etudes Genre'. Genève, Lausanne.

Schmidlin, Irène (2006): Deux pas vers la reconnaissance des persécutions fondées sur le genre. In: Bulletin de SOS asile, N° 81, 4e trimestre 2006.
Troisième rapport de la Suisse sur la mise en oeuvre de la Convention sur l'élimination de toutes les formes de discrimination à l'égard des femmes (CEDEF) (2008). Berne: Confédération Suisse.
Tissot, Sylvie/Delphy, Christine (2009): Géographie du sexisme. Discours autorisés sur la violence faite aux femmes au pays de Johnny Hallyday. http://lmsi.net/spip.php?article873
Valli, *Marcelo (*2003): *Les* migrants sans permis de séjour à Lausanne. Lausanne: Ville de Lausanne.
Volpp, Leti (2006): Quand on rend la culture responsable de la mauvaise conduite. In: Nouvelles Questions Féministes, 25/3, pp. 14–31.

Articles de presse

Le Courrier, 17 novembre 2008: 'Les femmes battues sont-elles vraiment protégées par la loi?' par Pablo de Roulet.
Le Courrier, 13 décembre 2008: 'Une loi qui piège les migrantes agressées par leur époux', par Isabelle Stücki.
Le Courrier, 9 mai 2009: '1300 paraphes déposés pour Genet D.', par Arnaud Crevoisier.
Tribune de Genève, 29 décembre 2008: 'Mari violent: elle est expulsée après avoir divorcé', par Nadine Haltiner.
24 Heures, 13 mai 2009: 'Solidarité pour une migrante battue', par Martine Clerc

Violence Against Migrant Women, Health and Sexuality: Trajectories of Women from Sub-Saharan Africa Living with HIV/AIDS in France

Dolorès Pourette

Research into violence against women has shown the impact it has on their health (Jaspard et al 2003; Saurel-Cubizolles 2005). The experience of sexual violence in childhood or of intimate partner violence puts women at risk of health problems, particularly sexually transmitted diseases, as it makes women less able to negotiate safe sex or control their sexual and reproductive lives (Damant et al. 2003; Salomon and Hamelin 2008). Illness is a time of physical, physiological and social frailty. Research among people living with HIV/AIDS has shown that the diagnosis leads to isolation from family and society, marked social vulnerability and exclusion from the labour market (Pierret 2006), particularly for foreign migrants (Lot et al. 2004). For these migrants, however, illness can open the way to regularising their administrative status by means of a residence permit for medical reasons. Illness thus becomes a political issue (Fassin 2001) though these permits are becoming increasingly hard to obtain, so limiting immigrant patients' access to citizenship and employment.

Immigrant women are particularly disadvantaged. They are subject to inequality in a number of forms owing to their fragile administrative status, their gender, class and 'race', and their confinement to a limited fraction of the labour market, particularly formal or informal sector domestic service (Anderson 1997; Momsen 1999; Oso Casa 2005). The administrative exclusion of immigrants and their exclusion from the labour market are products of an institutionalised racism (Bataille 1999) which hampers their access to Europe and to social and political rights. It makes women particularly vulnerable and exposes them to multiple forms of exploitation and interpersonal violence, intimate partner violence in particular. Those suffering from a stigmatised disease for which treatment is not available in their country of origin are even more vulnerable. For these sick, destitute immigrant women, survival often involves exploitation of their bodies (Sayad 1999), through domestic labour and through sexual exploitation; women's sexuality is still subject to control and violence (Tabet 2004), particularly in situations of social insecurity. While the link between intimate partner violence and the risk of HIV infection has been demonstrated (Van der Straten et al. 1995; Maman et al. 2000; Jewkes et al. 2003; Murray et al. 2006), few have analysed the combined effects of immigrant status and HIV status on the risk of being a victim of violence.

This paper, based on the narratives of African women living with HIV in France, will highlight the different types of institutional and interpersonal violence that shape their experience of migration and illness. We will show how the different types of violence they suffer form an interconnected pattern inherent in a particular social and political context. We will describe the strategies or tactics women adopt to cope with these constraints in situations where remaining in France is a matter of survival.

Background

One feature of the AIDS epidemic in Western Europe is the large number of foreigners among those living with HIV/AIDS. Most of these people are from Sub-Saharan Africa and many of them are women (O'Farrell et al. 1995; Del Amo et al. 1996; Low et al. 1996; Hamers and Downs 2004; Staehelin et al. 2004; Dieleman 2008). In 2009, approximately 4,000 new HIV infections were diagnosed in persons infected through heterosexual contact: around 1,600 women and 1,100 men born abroad, mainly in Sub-Saharan Africa (InVS 2010). The high proportion of Sub-Saharan Africans among HIV/AIDS patients in Europe is due to the severity of the epidemic in African countries[1], the lack of access to treatment in the countries of origin and the migration flows between European countries and their former colonies. The high proportion of women among the immigrant patients is due to the fact that in those countries HIV is transmitted primarily through heterosexual intercourse[2].

---

1 On UNAIDS estimates, of the 39 million people living with HIV in the world nearly 25 million live in Sub-Saharan Africa (UNAIDS 2006).

2 In Sub-Saharan Africa approximately 60% of HIV-positive individuals are women (UNAIDS 2006).

Residence rights increasingly hard to obtain

Research on immigrants living with HIV/AIDS in France, conducted in the late 1990s and early 2000s, highlighted the extent to which recognition of a person's HIV-positive status could be a condition for obtaining residence rights (Fassin 2004). HIV-positive foreigners living in France can apply for a temporary residence permit[3] for medical reasons[4]. This permit is intended for foreigners living in France and suffering from a serious illness that cannot be treated in their country of origin[5]. Since 2002, however, legal residence has become increasingly difficult to obtain and the conditions for the issue of permits increasingly restrictive (Sopena 2006); immigration policy now aims to restrict the number of residence permits issued for medical reasons. This has led to numerous malfunctions in the application of the law in this respect. The Observatoire du Droit à la Santé des Étrangers Malades (ODSE) has denounced the appalling reception conditions in the prefectures; the fact that applicants are asked to produce documents not required by law; demands for undue fees; failure to respect medical confidentiality; long processing delays, amongst others (ODSE 2008). As a result, since 2003 there has been a sharp drop in the application acceptance rate in *départements* (local authority areas) where demand is high (Veisse 2006). Every year since 2007 has seen an increase in the numbers of refusals to renew medically-based residence permits for people whose state of health has by no means improved, with more applicants detained and more sick foreigners deported. A study of local practice in processing applications for *Aide Médicale de l'État* (AME, the health coverage for undocumented foreign residents who are waiting permits shows how administrative practice and managerial organisation slow down the ap-

3 There are three types of residence permit in France: a provisional residence permit (*autorisation provisoire de séjour*), variable in length but rarely exceeding 6 months; the temporary residence permit (*carte de séjour temporaire*) valid for a year, and the ten-year permit (*carte de résident*).

4 'Unless his/her presence constitutes a threat to public order, the *carte de séjour temporaire* marked 'private and family life' is delivered as of right (...) to a foreigner living habitually in France and whose state of health requires medical care lack of which would have exceptionally serious consequences, provided he/she cannot in reality obtain appropriate treatment in their country of origin. The decision to issue a *carte de séjour* is taken by the prefect or, in Paris, by the chief of police, on the advice of a doctor, either the public health inspector from the health and social services office of the *département* where the applicant lives or, in Paris, the head of the police prefecture's medical service. The doctor in question can call in the applicant for medical examination before a regional medical commission whose composition is decided by the Council of State, by decree. The permit issued under the present clause gives the holder the right to work."

5 Based on a full medical report issued by a hospital doctor or other authorised doctor, a public health medical inspector pronounces on the severity of the illness and the necessity of having it treated in France. The prefect has the final decision, however.

plication process and so hamper access to care (Gabarro 2009; Carde 2006; 2007).

Discrimination in the labour market

Foreigners in France cannot legally work without a residence permit. The difficulty of acquiring one makes them vulnerable in the labour market. Neither a receipt for application for a residence permit, nor a provisional permit, nor refugee status gives the holder the right to work legally. Even the one-year *carte de séjour* does not necessarily bestow the right to work (the ten-year *carte de résident* does so). Nor do employment policies favour the inclusion of immigrants and foreigners in the labour market: foreign diplomas are not necessarily recognised by the French system. And access to vocational training is subject to highly restrictive conditions: one must be registered as a job seeker with the national employment agency, and to be so registered one must have at least a one-year residence permit marked 'salaried employee' (Langlet 2005).

As regards foreign and immigrant women specifically, even those with legal residency documents face discrimination in the labour market. As many studies of gender and international migration have shown, migrant women are to a very large extent confined to domestic work connected with the reproductive sphere (Anderson 1997; Momsen 1999; Oso Casas 2005). The main obstacle to finding work is the fact that most of these women have no qualifications, or at least are considered unqualified, having little professional experience in France and being marked out for discrimination by their physical appearance[6]. Social constructs also represent 'black' women as tougher and stronger than 'white' women and better able to endure difficult working conditions (Ferreira de Macêdo 2003). Further, migrant women's attempts to form businesses or open shops are by no means encouraged by the authorities. Such initiatives are rarely granted start-up subsidies and are restricted to 'traditionally' female occupations in the service industries, where sales volumes and wages are relatively low (Morokvasic Muller 1987).

---

6 In France, the 'rate of employment of women born in Sub-Saharan Africa (...) remains lower than the rate for economically active women as a whole' (Roulleau Berger and Lanquetin 2004: 21).

The survey

This paper is based on anthropological research conducted in 2005–2006 among women from Sub-Saharan Africa living with HIV/AIDS in France[7]. Thirty-two women were interviewed in anonymous, individual, semi-structured interviews. They were recruited in several hospitals in the Paris region and two community associations helping people living with HIV.[8] [9] The women interviewed were aged between 22 and 51, with an average age of 35. They came from eleven Sub-Saharan African countries, the main ones being Cameroon, Côte d'Ivoire, Democratic Republic of the Congo and Republic of the Congo (Congo-Brazzaville). Their personal, social, migratory and family trajectories varied widely. Although they often had several reasons for emigrating (Morokvasic 1983; Kofman, Phizacklea, Raghuram and Sales 2000), analysis of their migration trajectories brought to light three main profiles (Pourette 2008a).

The first profile was that of *migration for health reasons.* These women had discovered they were HIV-positive in Africa and had adopted the strategy of coming to Europe for treatment. They were between 28 and 34 years old at the time of the interview and had migrated alone, with the help of family or associations. They had arrived in France between 2000 and 2005. On arrival all had been, or were, in situations of extreme insecurity, living on the street or emergency hostels, without papers. Most were from middle class backgrounds. Five were without work, three were working full time and one part time. Two were married, one was cohabiting with a partner, four were in living-apart relationships and two were single. Only one woman said her papers were not in order. Four had one-year *cartes de séjour*, three had provisional permits and one a full *carte de résidente.*

A second profile was that of *economic migration.* These women had adopted a strategy of migrating to obtain work, education or training. Most were young women who had come to France on their own. They had learned of

7 This was post-doctoral research conducted at Inserm-INED research unit 569, and was funded by Sidaction and the Fondation de France (see also Pourette 2006, 2008a, 2008b).

8 The recruitment criteria were as follows: over 18 years of age, born in a country of Sub-Saharan Africa, having been living in France for at least a year and having been diagnosed as HIV-positive at least a year before the date of the survey. In the hospitals, the doctors were responsible for presenting the study to eligible patients and asking for their agreement to take part. The same principle was applied in the associations. The choice of location for the interview (at the hospital, in the association's premises or in my office) was left to the interviewee. Each interview lasted one to three hours and was recorded with the respondent's agreement. The interviews were transcribed and analysed using a biographical approach and a cross-thematic approach.

9 For the purposes of comparison, interviews were also conducted with ten men from Sub-Saharan Africa, under the same conditions as the interviews with women.

their HIV status after arriving in France (after 2000), and this had led them to redefine their initial migration project. They too had been in very insecure situations on arrival (including those from privileged backgrounds). They were between 22 and 45 years old at the time of the interviews. Most of these women were single and out of work at the time of the survey. Only one of them had a full time job (as an accountant). Four were working part time in the domestic service sector. They were from a variety of social backgrounds: six were working class, six were middle class and three were upper class. Most of these women's applications for work permits were being processed at the time of the survey; for the rest, four had three-month provisional permits and four had one-year *carte de séjour*. Only one woman said she had no papers.

A third profile was that of *family migration*. These women had come to France in the 1980s and 1990s through the family reunification procedure. They had discovered they were HIV-positive while living in a couple and had already been settled in France for over ten years. They had been tested for HIV in the 1990s and were between 30 and 51 years old at the time of the interview. All were or had been married (three were divorced). Their access to residence had come either under the rules for family reunification or in the context of marriage with a French national. Their social situations were varied. One was working full time, three part time, and four were not in work. Two of them had French nationality. Three had the full ten-year residence permit; three had one-year permits.

Institutional and interpersonal violence

Analysis of the interviews shows that the tougher legislation, migrants' insecure situations and their weak position in the labour market are forms of institutional violence that increase their vulnerability and make their experience of migration especially distressing when, as is often the case, they are very isolated. Their trajectories highlight the impact of this institutional violence on their lack of security and their living conditions as migrants. Although several women had been temporarily housed by acquaintances on arrival, most had to sleep in emergency shelters or even in the street, or were housed by associations for people living with HIV. In this type of collective accommodation, they found themselves with homeless or sick people and felt they were seen as belonging to these stigmatised categories. The women also deplored the fact that they could not bring their children to France[10] which

10 Ten of the 32 women interviewed had left one or more children in their home country.

reinforced their sense of isolation. As regards resources and employment, those without the right to work legally had to turn to the informal sector – unofficial domestic work (housework, childminding etc.) or prostitution – to survive (Moujoud and Pourette 2005). For those who had obtained a residence permit that allowed them to work, domestic work, often part time, was still the main job opportunity whatever qualifications they may have (one woman in the survey had a postgraduate diploma in history, another had begun medical studies). These jobs involved a certain amount of physical exertion, which these women could not always supply because of their state of health. Of the 32 women interviewed, only five had full time jobs; eight were working part time and 19 were not in paid work.

Discrimination and institutional violence against migrant women, and the resulting social, economic and administrative insecurity, made them particularly vulnerable when confronted with interpersonal violence.

Interpersonal violence

Exploitation and discrimination

The women's narratives show how their exclusion from the labour market exposes them to numerous forms of exploitation by unscrupulous people (men and women). Many of the women had suffered forms of violence from their informal 'employers'. One such was Ella:

> Ella is 22 years old, from Ghana. She came to Europe clandestinely, reaching Italy by boat, in the hope of finding work. Arriving in a French coastal town in December 2003, Ella slept in the open until she was taken in by a Ghanaian who offered her lodging in exchange for domestic services. But he also forced her to have sex with him. It was her first sexual experience. She managed to escape from him, stealing €30 to take the train to Paris. In the capital, she again slept in the street until a Ghanaian woman took her in. Ella had not only to do all the housework but also to work without respite in the woman's fabric shop. After a few months, feeling ill, with no papers and no medical insurance, she went to a hospital. The doctor who agreed to examine her found she was six months pregnant. A few days later she was told she had the AIDS virus. At the time of the interview, Ella was living in a maternity hostel with her six-month-old daughter, who was in good health.

This example is a classic case of exploitation of migrants by migrant men or women, sometimes from the same country. In addition, while these forms of violence are not directly related to health status, the way the women were seen by others (apart from medical staff and family who, when informed, generally provided considerable support), the malicious gossip and the discrimination against HIV-positive people, constitute moral violence and were felt to be such by the women concerned. To avoid discrimination on account of their illness, the women did all in their power to keep it secret. But sometimes the truth came out. The consequences were often painful for the women concerned, as 45-year old Nayah from Cameroon explained:

> A woman with HIV is not happy. I'll tell you a story. My husband insulted me in front of a neighbour and the neighbour heard that I had AIDS. As I'm a home help and he knows the elderly family I work for, he went to see them and told them 'The lady who does your housework, she's got AIDS'. They asked me if it was true and I said no. But since then I feel ... shaken. I feel uncomfortable. I feel weird when I go to their place. You feel the rejection. As AIDS is not a disease like ... cancer... You can't tell people you have AIDS. They see you differently...

It is within the couple relationship that the women are particularly exposed to violence of various kinds.

Violence in the couple

Several studies have shown the links between intimate partner violence and HIV. In the first place, violence in the couple is an obstacle to taking preventive measures and is associated with a higher risk of infection (Van der Straten et al. 1995; Maman et al. 2000; Jewkes et al. 2003; Murray et al. 2006). Secondly, studies in African countries among women living with HIV/AIDS have shown that they are more often victims of violence than are uninfected women (Gielen et al. 1997; Gielen et al. 2000; Maman et al. 2002; McDonnell et al. 2003). The accounts of the women we met in this research highlight the different forms of violence involved. Nayah's account, though not exhaustive, illustrates the link between HIV infection and conjugal violence.

> Nayah is 45 and comes from Cameroon, where she lived until 2001. She has had no children but is raising her sister's daughter, whom she regards as her own. The child was 14 at the time of the interview. She had several couple relationships before coming to France. The last of these was a four-year relationship with a married man to whom she was much attached. Although Nayah was, in her own terms, his 'mistress', she knew his family and it was a firmly established relationship. Nayah had several HIV tests performed while undergoing medical examinations for her sterility. These were negative when the relationship began. Looking back she says she did not dare ask him to take a test because he was married and of a certain 'social rank'. When he ended the relationship (Nayah explains the breakup as being due to her failure to give him a child), she was very depressed and thought she would have more luck with an 'expat'[11]. She met the man who

11 As used by Nayah, the term 'expat' means a French person living in France (and who may never have lived anywhere else).

was to become her husband via the Internet. The first virtual contact was in November 2000; he went to meet her in Cameroon in February 2001; in June 2001 she came to France with her daughter and they were married. Their first sexual relations were protected. They both had tests carried out before the marriage, but the future husband did not want to wait for the results before marrying; he said the test results would not change his decision to marry her. The test proved negative for him and positive for her. At first, Nayah's husband was supportive and considerate, but then his attitude changed radically:

'The man who accepted me as I was has turned against me very badly. That really hurts ... And I was grateful to him because it's thanks to him that I'm alive, it's thanks to him that I found out ... He used to say 'If I hadn't been there you'd already be buried in your village!' ... He forced me to work. I didn't have the right to have a cheque book or a credit card (...). He even forbade me to come and see the psychologist here'.

A victim of psychological violence, Nayah also suffered physical and sexual violence: her husband beat her, forced her to have sex and did not always use a condom, so that Nayah feared he would be infected by her. This situation lasted for three years until he forced her to leave their home. The divorce proceedings were under way at the time of the interview. After the separation the moral hurts continued: her husband told her daughter her mother had AIDS and also betrayed the secret to his family:

'But I had kept my health status secret because he himself kept it secret for three years. He'd introduced me to his whole family. I was welcomed. The whole family liked me. He said that if I told them [that he beat me] he would tell them about my state of health ... I think he has told them now. Because I have no more news from anyone.'.

Nayah's narrative shows how a conjugal relationship based on unequal social and administrative integration in the host country and inequality in HIV status (serodifference) favours violence in the couple. Although the violence did not begin at the time of the positive test result (as it did for two other interviewees), the husband based his domination on the secret of his wife's HIV status. In immigrant situations, this is often a secret shared only with the spouse. The threat of revealing the facts to family, friends and neighbours is a particularly effective way to force submission in a social and administrative setting where immigrant women have few alternatives for working and surviving, and hence little freedom to denounce a violent husband's acts.

Nayah's narrative echoes several experiences of violence related by other interviewees in serodifferent couples (couples where one partner is HIV-positive, the other HIV-negative): threats to reveal HIV status; carrying out that threat after the separation; moral, physical and sexual violence; refusal to routinely use a condom; imposing on the partner a form of sexuality she describes as unwanted and distressing. Some women in seroconcordant couples (where both partners were HIV positive), or where the woman did not know whether her spouse was or not, told of other forms of violence. Several women learned that their spouse was infected, and knew it, when they discovered that they themselves were HIV-positive. Their spouse had not told them and had not practised safe sex. One such case was Clémence: only when she wanted to leave the man who had been her partner for a year did he tell her he was 'ill'. Tissina, who was tested for HIV when she was pregnant, supposed that her spouse already knew he was infected because he showed no surprise when she told him the positive test results. Further, couples who are both HIV-positive are advised to use condoms to avoid superinfection, but it seems this advice is rarely followed. The women interviewed told us how hard they found it to negotiate condom use with their partners. Though some spouses take risks with their own health this way, their refusal to wear condoms also puts their partner's health at risk, which can be regarded as a form of violence.

Denial of the wife's illness (leading to unprotected sex) can also be experienced as abuse. Sonia, aged 30 and from Senegal, had been married for two years when, following a high fever, she discovered she was HIV positive. She was then 24 years old. She tried to talk to her husband about it but he denied the illness, saying that *'it's something the whites invented, it doesn't exist'*. Since her positive test in 1999, Sonia had never managed to establish a dialogue with her husband about the illness, their sexual and reproductive life or the fact that he too might be infected. She did not know whether he had had himself tested. This denial of the illness goes hand in hand with physical and sexual violence in the couple, which had worsened since the diagnosis. Physical, psychological and sexual violence are not limited to the couple's life together; several of the life histories reveal violence by ex-spouses. After their divorce, Barbara's ex-husband harassed her by telephone until the police put a stop to it. He told his friends and neighbours she had HIV and he refused to pay maintenance for their two children. When Anne ended her relationship with a man after discovering that he was married, she learned from a friend that her ex-partner was telling people she 'killed people'.

For immigrant women living with HIV, institutional and interpersonal violence are often linked. It is because they are socially and administratively excluded that they enter into highly unequal relationships that nonetheless enable them to stay in France (as they must if they are to survive), or are subjected to some form of domestic or sexual exploitation. It is because they are socially and administratively excluded that they cannot denounce the violence they suffer or leave a violent husband.

Women confronted with violence

Having come to France to find work, better living conditions or treatment, all the women interviewed had adopted migration strategies to leave home for Europe, sometimes with the help of their families. Once in France, they were confronted with a set of structural forces that kept them in highly unequal relations of class, gender and 'race' and subjected them to institutional and interpersonal violence and exploitation. In view of the necessity of staying in France to receive treatment they developed 'strategies' or 'tactics' (de Certeau 1980) according to the resources available to them and the constraints placed on them. A clear example of such strategies is the decision to marry, marriage being the main legal way to acquire residence papers (Pourette 2008a). But as we have seen, this strategy can lead women into relationships of extreme domination and violence.

The other strategy women use to stay in France is to proclaim their illness and make it a 'profession' (Herzlich 1989). This means acknowledging themselves as people with HIV and establishing that identity in other people's eyes in a situation where HIV-positive people are stigmatised. They then make HIV their main preoccupation, joining AIDS prevention associations or HIV victims support associations. Three of the women interviewed had become health mediators in community associations helping patients (two were working part time, one full time). It was thanks to these associations that they had obtained residence permits giving them the right to vocational training and then the right to work in France. For these women the fight against their illness became the central focus of their lives, a profession and the basis of a particular but lasting form of social integration (Herzlich 1989).

Conclusion

In the current French political context, immigrants find it increasingly hard to acquire social rights, citizenship and medical treatment, while the women experience gender inequality in addition to the inequalities of 'race' and class. In this context, the fact of being infected with a sexually transmitted disease, a virus with strongly negative social connotations and for which the treatment is unavailable in many Southern countries, accentuates these women's isolation and confines them to the privacy of the marital home. And we know how seriously abusive a place that can be. Needing to live in France to receive treatment and survive, they are faced with painful choices: to stay among their family and friends but as a sick person with a shorter lifespan, or leave them to go far away to survive for an indefinite time. These women's narratives show the strategies they adopted for leaving home and surviving as immigrants. But the situations they describe highlight the need for immigrant women to have access to official work contracts and financial independence so that they will not be forced into intimate partner relationships that often prove highly unequal, or so that they can leave a violent spouse or end an unsatisfactory relationship.

References

Anderson, Bridget (1997): Servants and Slaves: Europe's Domestic Workers. Race and Class 39,1, pp. 37–49.

Bataille, Philippe (1999): Racisme institutionnel, racisme culturel et discriminations. In: Dewitte, P. (1999): Immigration et intégration. L'état des savoirs. Paris: La Découverte, pp. 285–293.

Carde, Estelle (2006): On ne laisse mourir personne. Les discriminations dans l'accès aux soins. In: Travailler 6, pp. 57–80.

Carde, Estelle (2007): Les discriminations selon l'origine dans l'accès aux soins. In: Santé Publique 2, pp. 99–110.

Damant, Dominique/Trottier, Germain/Paré, Ginette/Binet, Lise/Noël, Linda/Lindsay, Jocelyn/Langevin, Marie-Ève (2003): Femmes, violence, ITS/VIH-SIDA. Rapport de recherche, Montréal, Centre de recherche interdisciplinaire sur la violence familiale et la violence faite aux femmes, 99 p.

De Certeau, Michel (1980): L'invention du quotidien. 1. Arts de faire, Paris, Gallimard.

Dieleman, Myriam (2008): Migrantes subsahariennes et VIH. Trajectoires et vulnérabilités. Bruxelles: Observatoire du Sida et des sexualités (FUSL).

Fassin, Didier (2001): Une double peine. La condition sociale des immigrés malades du sida. In: L'Homme 160, pp. 137–162.

Fassin, Didier (2004): Le corps exposé. Essai d'économie morale de l'illégitimité. In: Fassin, Didier/Memmi, Dominique (2004): Le gouvernement des corps. Paris: Editions de l'EHESS, pp. 237–266.

Ferreira de Macêdo, Maria Bernardete (2003): Femmes de ménage et veilleurs de nuit: une approche sexuée du travail précaire dans un hôtel en France. Cahiers du Genre 35, pp. 189–208.

Gabarro, Céline (2009): Instruction des demandes d'Aide Médicale de l'Etat: comment les pratiques managériales et administratives de l'Assurance maladie accroissent les difficultés d'obtention de cette prestation. Colloque « Migrations humaines et circulations des ressources. La santé en temps de mondialisation », Université Paris Diderot, 24–25 septembre 2009.

Gielen, A.C./O'Campo, P./Faden, R.R. et al. (1997): Women's disclosure of HIV status: experiences of mistreatment and violence in an urban setting. Women Health 25, 3, pp. 19–31.

Gielen, A.C./McDonnell, K.A./Burke, J.G. et al. (2000): Women's lives after an HIV-positive diagnosis: disclosure and violence. In: Matern Child Health J. 4, 2, pp. 111–20.

Hamers, Françoise F./Downs, Angela M. (2004): The Changing Face of the HIV Epidemic in Western Europe: What are the Implications for Public Health Policies? In: Lancet 364,3, pp. 83–94.

Herzlich, Claudine (1989/1992/2005): Santé et maladie, analyse d'une représentation sociale. Paris: Editions de l'EHESS.

InVS (Institut de Veille Sanitaire) (2010): Surveillance de l'infection à VIH-sida en France, 2009. Bulletin Epidémiologique Hebdomadaire 45–46, pp. 467–472.

Jaspard, Maryse/Brown, Elizabeth/Condon, Stéphanie/Fougeyrollas-Schwebel, Dominique/Houel, Annik/Lhomond, Brigitte/Maillochon, Florence/Saurel-Cubizolles, Marie-Josèphe/Schiltz, Marie-Ange (2003): Les violences envers les femmes en France. Une enquête nationale. Paris: La Documentation française.

Jewkes, R.K./Levin, J.B./Loveday, A. et al. (2003): Gender inequalities, intimate partner violence and HIV preventive practices: findings of a South African cross-sectional study. In: Soc Sci Med 56, pp. 125–134.

Kofman, Eleonore/Phizacklea, Annie/Raghuram, Parvati/Sales, Rosemary (2000): Gender and International Migration in Europe. Employment, welfare and politics. London, New York: Routledge.

Langlet, Marianne (2005): Accès à l'emploi: mirage inaccessible pour des étrangers malades? In: Journal du sida 181, pp. 21–2.

Lot, Florence/Larsen, Christine/Valin, Nadia/Gouëzel, Pascal/Blanchon, Thierry/Laporte, Anne (2004): Parcours sociomédical des personnes originaires d'Afrique subsaharienne atteintes par le VIH, prises en charge dans les hôpitaux d'Ile-de-France, 2002. In: Bulletin Epidémiologique Hebdomadaire 5, pp. 17–20.

Low, N./Paine, K./Clark, R./Mahalingam, M./Pozniak, A.L. (1996): AIDS Survival and Progression in Black Africans Living in South London, 1986–1994. In: Genitourinary Medicine 72, 1, pp. 12–16.

Maman, S./Campbell, J./Sweat, M.D. et al. (2000): The intersections of HIV and violence: directions for future research and interventions. In: Soc Sci Med 50, 4, pp. 459–478.

Maman, S./Mbwambo, J.K./Hogan, N.M. et al. (2002): HIV-positive women report more lifetime partner violence: findings from a voluntary counseling and testing clinic in Dar es Salaam, Tanzania. In: Am J Public Health 92, 8, pp. 1331–1337.

McDonnell, K.A./Gielen, A.C./O'Campo, P. (2003): Does HIV status make a difference in the experience of lifetime abuse? Descriptions of lifetime abuse and its context among low-income urban women. In: J Urban Health. 80, 3, pp. 494–509.

Momsen, Janet (1999): Gender, Migration and Domestic Service. London: Routledge.

Morokvasic, Mirjana. (1983): Women in migration. In: Phizacklea, Annie (ed.) (1983): One Way Ticket. London: Routledge, pp. 13–31.

Morokvasic Muller, M. (1987): Entreprendre au féminin en Europe: Cas des immigrées et des minorités en France, en Grande-Bretagne, en Italie, au Portugal et en République fédérale d'Allemagne: motivations, situations et recommandations pour action. Bruxelles: Commission des Communautés européennes.

Moujoud, Nasima/Pourette, Dolorès (2005): 'Traite' de femmes migrantes, domesticité et prostitution. À propos de migrations interne et externe. Cahiers d'Etudes Africaines 179–180, pp. 1093–1121.

Murray, L.K./Haworth, A./Semrau, K. et al. (2006): Violence and abuse among HIV-infected women and their children in Zambia: a qualitative study. In: J Nerv Ment Dis, 194, 8, pp. 610–615.

O'Farrell, Nigel/Lau, R./Yoganathan, Kathir/Bradbeer, C.S./Griffin, G.E./Pozniak, Anton (1995): AIDS in Africans Living in London. In: Genitourinary Medicine 71, 6, pp. 358–362.

Observatoire du droit à la santé des étrangers (ODSE) (2008): La régularisation pour raison médicale en France. Un bilan de santé alarmant. Rapport de l'ODSE (unpubl.).

Oso Casas, Laura (2005): Femmes, actrices des mouvements migratoires. In: Verschuur, Christine/Fenneke, Reysoo (2005): Genre, nouvelle division internationale du travail et migrations. Paris: L'Harmattan pp. 35–54.

Pierret, Janine (2006): Vivre avec le VIH. Enquête de longue durée auprès des personnes infectées. Paris: PUF.

Pourette, Dolorès (2006): Le couple migrant confronté au VIH. In: Hommes et migrations 1262, pp. 88–97.

Pourette, Dolorès (2008a): Migratory Paths, Experiences of AIDS and Sexuality: African Women living with HIV/Aids in France. In: Feminist Economics 14, 4, pp. 149–181.

Pourette, Dolorès (2008b): Couple et sexualité des femmes d'Afrique subsaharienne vivant avec le VIH/sida en France. In: Médecine/Sciences. Numéro spécial: Les femmes et le sida en France. Enjeux sociaux et de santé publique 24, 2, pp. 184–192.

Roulleau Berger, Laurence/Lanquetin, Marie-Thérèse (2004): Femmes d'origine étrangère. Travail, accès à l'emploi, discriminations de genre. Paris: La Documentation française.

Salomon, Christine/Hamelin, Christine (2008): Normes de genre, violences sexuelles et vulnérabilité au VIH/sida en Nouvelle-Calédonie. In: Médecine/Sciences. Numéro spécial: Les femmes et le sida en France. Enjeux sociaux et de santé publique 24, 2, pp. 103–110.

Saurel-Cubizolles, Marie-Josèphe (2005): Violences envers les femmes et état de santé mentale: résultats de l'enquête Enveff 2000. In: Bulletin Epidémiologique Hebdomadaire 9–10, pp. 36–37.

Sayad, Abdelmayek (1999): La double absence. Paris: Seuil.

Sopena, Antonin (2006): Nouvelle stratégie contre les malades étrangers. In: Plein Droit 71, pp. 26–29.

Staehelin, Cornelia/Egloff, Niklaus/Rickenbach, Martin/Kopp, Christine/Furrer, Hansjakob (2004): Migrants from Sub-Saharan Africa in the Swiss HIV Cohort Study: a Single Center Study of Epidemiologic Migration-specific and Clinical Features. In: AIDS Patient Care STDS 18, 11, pp. 665–75.

Tabet, Paola (2004): La grande arnaque. Sexualité des femmes et échange économico-sexuel. Paris: L'Harmattan.

Van der Straten, A./King, R./Grinstead, O. et al. (1995): Couple communication, sexual coercion and HIV risk reduction in Kigali, Rwanda. In: AIDS 9, 8, pp. 935–944.

Veïsse, Arnaud (2006): Le médecin, la santé et le séjour des étrangers. In: Plein Droit 69, pp. 32–35.

Violence Against Women and the Social, Ethnic and Sexual Division of Labour: Continuity and Disparity Between Community Care Workers' Experiences

Emmanuelle Lada and Ghislaine Doniol-Shaw

Introduction

Compared to the academia in Anglo-Saxon countries, the question of violence against women, including violence in the workplace, has long been a poor relation in feminist and gender research in France (Corrin 1997; Romito 1997). That should not be taken to mean that the issue has not been addressed. There have been feminist analyses of this context of violence since the late 1970s. Various publications reflect this, such as the first issue of *Questions Féministes* in 1977 with a translation of Jalna Hanmer's article 'Women, Violence and Social Control', and the journal published by the AVFT (*Association contre les Violences faites aux Femmes au Travail*) from 1985 to 1996 (Louis 2009), which focused more on workplace violence. The 1990s and early 2000s marked a turning point, with the issue in the limelight again as a research issue in women's studies and beyond, and also in public debate (Jaspard et al. 2003). In the current period 'gender violence in the workplace' has been viewed from a new angle. While sexual harassment and the effects of the sexual division of labour are still the aspects most commonly addressed (AVFT 1990; Rogerat 2001; Jaspard et al. 2003), special attention has been paid to the gendered organization of labour and working conditions, and here the concept of violence is understood in a broad sense. A book of papers by women researchers and women working in occupational medicine (Semat 2000), a ground-breaking piece of work in the French context, analysed the different forms taken by workplace violence against women, particularly according to age and seniority in the labour market (Doniol-Shaw, Renou-Parent and Machefer 2000). One strand of the ENVEFF survey, the first large-scale nationwide survey on violence against women (Jaspard et al., 2003), gave a quantitative overview of violence in the workplace while moral harassment from a gender perspective was analyzed (Rogerat 2001).

All these studies focused on women as such and added to knowledge of the forms and underpinnings of the sexual division of workplace violence.

But very few addressed the effects of the ethnic/racialized and social division of labour in the construction of workplace gender violence. However, research on migrant, exiled and/or racialized women, though not directly addressing the question of violence, has shown the extent to which these women are faced with violence connected with migrants' legal status, European countries' restrictive migration policies (Freedman and Valluy 2007; Falquet et al. 2010), racism in the workplace and racialized forms of violence (Crenshaw 1991; Sassen 2003), within and beyond the diversity of this group. Studies of this kind are absolutely essential for building up knowledge about workplace violence, but they leave aside another important question: focused solely on racialized women, and sometimes only one such group, they provide no basis for understanding the pattern of workplace violence in situations involving working-class women of different origin and status. That is the question this paper addresses.

One issue for feminist and gender research today is to continue building up knowledge and fully incorporating the experience of migrant and/or racialized women in our theoretical and empirical understanding of 'workplace gender violence'. This in particular means understanding the different forms it takes, depending on a person's position in the social and gender division of labour. In this paper, we address the workplace violence encountered in France by women wage earners in home care for the elderly and fragile. Home care is a field in which employment is insecure and the great majority of workers are women from working-class backgrounds, including some immigrants. As in other European and North American countries, it is a fast-growing sector. We take a broad definition of the notion of workplace violence (Jaspard et al. 2003) and argue for the need to link employment conditions with working conditions to analyse work situations (Lada 2005). Focusing on women wage-earners in the non-profit sector we consider the 'ordinary violence' (Sémat 2000) that is a daily occurrence in the working lives of these women at the bottom of the occupational ladder.

We will show how this violence is not only profoundly gendered (which means that we have to consider gender relations to describe it) but also how the perspective must be broadened to take into consideration ethnic, racial and class relations. The gendered organization of labour (Acker 1990) must be considered in its interactions with the social and ethnicized organization of labour. We were able to compare the position of women in a minority group (racialized women) with that of mainstream-group women in the same type of working situation. It became clear that the former suffer forms of workplace violence that the latter do not, or to which they are exposed in a different way. We posited that the risk of being faced with violence is greater for those who are placed in an inferior position by ethnic social relations.

However, some forms of violence are suffered by all these women alike. Constructed by the gendered organization of labour, this violence is a constant, an experience shared by all these women. These are the hypotheses we present here.

Context of the analysis

Home care for the elderly in the non-profit sector

We shall look at the form of home care most common in France, at least in the formal sector (Marquier 2010): home care for the elderly performed by women employed by non-profit bodies specialising in this field. The home care sector is typified by insecure employment where employees work in isolation from each other and working conditions and workers' rights are often below the legal minimum. Non-profit associations working in this sector are distinguished by their commitment to improving working conditions. It, therefore, seemed interesting to start from the progress made and report on its effects and weaknesses. This seemed to us especially useful because while it is an established fact that domiciliary care is structured by the social, gendered and ethnic division of labour, little was known about what became of immigrants and racialized women once they have escaped from the forms of violence and arbitrary treatment associated with illegal work and isolated working conditions.

The position of migrant and/or racialized women wage-earners in the division of jobs and modes of care provision within the home care sector

This approach requires some preliminaries. First, the idea that in France domiciliary care for the elderly and those in fragile health is a sector made up overwhelmingly of recent immigrants must be put aside. That belief seems to have become established after research into internationalization, the commodification of care and the increase in the proportion of women among immigrants. It has been refuted by various research results. A quantitative survey (Marquier 2010) shows that 97% of women working in formal sector domiciliary care for elderly dependants are French and were born in France. While nationality is not a sufficient criterion for analysing the dynamics of discrimination, the Marquier survey supports our thesis that 'global care chain' theories cannot fully account for the overall organization of mixed care systems (Simonazzi 2008). This is especially true if we add in the ethnic and social division of labour as well as the gendered. In rural areas, moreover, where there has been little post-colonial immigration, women with no personal or family migration history still make up the great majority of home carers owing to the lack of other job prospects.

These findings do not invalidate the idea that this gendered and class-based occupational sector is also shaped by an ethnic division of labour. In this regard it seems to us that to account for the position of this social category of women in the social, economic and political organization of domiciliary care we must address two hypotheses. One is that migrant and/or racialized women are relegated to the margins of domiciliary care; the other is that women's working conditions vary according to their position in the social and ethnic division of labour. All these data suggest that we should employ the notion of supposed or imputed origin. It is in the light of this marker that the violence to which they are subjected should be understood. Skin colour is a factor for attributing origin, and those categorized as 'black', 'Arab', 'gypsy' etc. are subjected to racism and discrimination that engender workplace violence.

A survey among experienced employees

This paper is based on a qualitative survey conducted between 2006 and 2007 in six domiciliary care associations in both rural and urban areas (Doniol-Shaw, Lada and Dussuet 2007). Fifty-five recorded life course interviews (of about three hours each) were conducted with home carers of various ages having more than five years' cumulated experience as home carers (three years for those aged under 30). Twenty-two per cent of the interviewees had migrated to France as children or young adults from North Africa, Sub-Saharan Africa, southern Europe or Eastern Europe, or were children of migrants. The data gathering was completed with a systematic record of their weekly time schedule. It was in this context that reports of violence at work emerged. In addition, thirteen semi-structured interviews were conducted with care association managers and staff of institutions.

Institutional and organizational underpinnings of workplace violence encountered by all women

The violence suffered at work by these wage-earning home carers was not only the result of isolated individual behaviour in interpersonal relations (Dejours 2007). It was first of all the product of institutional and organizational dynamics that incorporate gender relations (Molinier 1999), interwoven with class and ethnic relations.

Gender as fertile ground for workplace violence

The purpose of domiciliary care is to enable people made fragile by age, illness or life events to live at home for as long as possible by providing help with day-to-day activities. Care of the caree's home, their living conditions and their body are all part of the home carer's work

Working in another person's home

One particular feature of home care is that the place of work is another person's home. This is an important factor because a person's home is outside the scope of the inspectorates responsible for working conditions and compliance with labour law. Although there are various levers for improving working conditions (booklets for new staff, a trade union agreement for home care which covers the French non-profit home care sector, a labour code applicable to all wage earners), it is hard to use these to put pressure on the caree owing to the legal status of an individual's home. The home is therefore particularly fertile ground for workplace violence, not only fostering such violence but also making it easy to keep it hidden and making it difficult to punish the perpetrator. This is worsened by the care associations' role in defining the tasks and the organization of the work. The *real* organization of the home carer's work takes shape at the junction between the association's instructions as employer, the nurses' instuctions, the statutory bodies that pay all or part of the home care allowances, and the caree.

While an analysis of home carers' practices is needed to complete the picture, this configuration has an impact on the violence the home carers encounter, exacerbated by the fact that the workplace is a person's home. It blurs the real organization and conditions of the work and allows carees to assume special rights, especially higher-income carees, who may have to pay most of the cost of the service. The workplace violence reported was concentrated around housework issues. If the caree or their family consider the carer's housework tasks to go beyond what is needed to preserve the caree's autonomy, the door is open for putting the carer in a position of servitude which in turn encourages violence.

> Last time she wanted me to clean the cellar. I didn't want to. She said she was going to tell the association. I warned them about it. They said I shouldn't let myself be pushed around. But I'm stuck really. Threatening me like that. Afterwards, not so long ago, she had me clean the outside walls. She got angry. (...) Well I did it, because I didn't want a fuss. (aged 30, 10 years' experience)

The carers most often faced with these situations are those in the most vulnerable positions, either because they only recently joined the labour force, or due to their (actual or imputed) ethnic origin, or because they are replacing a colleague and cannot contest a task presented as being a usual part of the work. Also vulnerable are carers working for associations that have little concern for issues of work organization or which are in a difficult financial situation and therefore have to be more indulgent towards their carees' demands.

Isolated work situations

Home carers are also finding themselves increasingly isolated in their work. This is a result of the way work is organized by the associations but also a direct or indirect result of public actions, particularly the reorganization of public funding for home care (Doniol-Shaw and Lada, forthcoming publication). For example, formal group meetings where carers can share experiences or analyse their practice are being increasingly phased out. But when carers are subjected to violence in the homes where they work, such meetings enable them to discuss with their colleagues and supervisors, within working hours, to find ways to put an end to it. As the survey showed, this type of forum also allows carers to depersonalise the experience of violence. For example, it was through such exchanges that carers learned that in people with Alzheimer's disease, violence can be one of the symptoms and not the result of problems in the personal relationship; they were then able to act accordingly, particularly by asking for specific training.

Ordinary violence

The initiation ordeal

Almost all the carers interviewed had encountered violence at work from their first days in the job. They started work alone and as a rule with no particular information about their carees, any illnesses they might have, or the tasks to be performed. Starting the job in this way, they were faced with verbal violence and interactions that directly called into question their skills and knowledge.

This violence is compounded by the fact that newcomers to an association (whether or not they have experience as carers elsewhere) are confronted with 'extreme cases' well known to the supervisors. Analysis of the event histories showed that they often started out with carees for whom other staff were unprepared to work. Their first experiences were often of insanitary homes and violent, sometimes alcoholic, carees who refused to be washed or groomed. Later on, carers may find meaning in their work through such extreme situations because they can use their experience and knowledge to restore the person's dignity and independence (Doniol-Shaw 2009). But at the beginning they are merely an ordeal, painful to remember even years later. This observation led us to formulate the hypothesis that newcomers to the job are deliberately 'put to the test' by confronting them with extreme situations in the very first days. As part of a staff management approach, this would be a kind of training policy. Associations in difficult financial circumstances, working in a sector where staff turnover is high, might put newcomers to the test and only offer training to those who stay on after such confrontations. But it might be thought, on the contrary, that such practices are among the reasons for high staff turnover.

> Q. Did you have an interview for the job?
>
> No. (...) But the first job I was given was a difficult one. When I told her, she (the caree) said she was testing me. It was an old woman, I had to go to her place from Monday to Sunday, feed her (…) She wanted to test me by shouting orders at me, she was bad-tempered. I told her I was leaving. I'm like that. (…) She wanted me to clean her sculptures with a toothbrush, and the table legs. I did it once a week and said nothing. She was always after me. (…) I worked for that lady for three weeks; a three-week ordeal. (aged 38, 5 years in a retirement home, 6 years working for the association)

Sexual harassment and expectations of sexual availability

Doing menial work in a person's home is a situation where sexual harassment or sexual approaches are more invisible than in other places of work. While employers seem rarely to discuss this, it emerged spontaneously from a number of interviews. Such incidents were too often reported to be dismissed as anecdotal; they are characteristic of home care situations. Care workers told us how, when they worked for men living alone or able-bodied husbands of disabled wives, these carees or clients expected their services to extend to making their bodies available.

> When you go to handicapped men... If you're a woman, if you go to those gentlemen, they have sexual needs and sometimes they hang around the person who's been sent to help them.
>
> Q. Has this happened to you?
>
> Yes. It was a gentleman. He tried proposition me, he hung around me. I told the manager and said I didn't want to go there any more. And that they ought to talk to him about the proper distance to keep. But there was no need because he was waiting for a place in a convalescent home.
>
> Q. And your colleagues, do you often talk to your colleagues?
>
> Yes. Clients made declarations of love to them, said they were in love with them. After that it was difficult to reframe the situation.
>
> I can wash their faces, yes, but not the shower, I wouldn't dare. Feet and hands: yes. But sure, if she wees, I wash her with a face-cloth; you can't leave people in that state. Mind you some old men are proper sadists. I knew one, he did it on purpose; I said I wasn't there to play with his thing and he stopped after that.

Interviews were also studded with accounts of the tactics adopted to keep their bodies from male eyes, with particular attention to dress. Bare arms, skirts and low necklines were avoided. Individual tactics like these, adopted without prompting by the employer, sometimes matched the employer's expectations. Some employers freely criticised care workers for their choice of clothing if they thought it was not sufficiently discreet.

Associations whose care workers had suffered sexual harassment rarely terminated their contract with the client or helped the worker report it to the police. They usually responded by sending a different care worker to that home, at the risk that they would be subjected to the same pressure and aggression.

Humiliation at work: the servant-employer relationship

While sexual violence came almost exclusively from men, the humiliations the care workers described having suffered in their subordinate position as home carers usually involved women. It was usually a woman who organized the housework, whether they were the caree (state of health permitting), the caree's spouse or both partners. It was when care workers were required to do housework despite their skills as carers that the work became humiliating. In such cases violence was inflicted by women who, on their own or as part of a couple, tried to transform the caring relationship into one of employer and servant through repeated criticism and other humiliating remarks.

In this context, workplace violence is also constructed by the class relations between care worker and the caree. The following interview extract provides a telling example.

> A lady, where I replaced a colleague: Very chic, 'chignon' and all. (...) She showed me what had to be done. It was hot, and I was thirsty. I asked if I couldn't have a glass of water. I said, Excuse me but I won't be able to carry on, I had nothing more to drink in my bag. And she said 'Oh but I can't give you anything to drink!' I said why not, and she said 'But in my fine crystal glasses!' I swear it! I didn't do anything, I didn't say anything, I told her 'Here's your duster, I'm leaving. If we don't have the same values I'm sorry, you'd better call the association to get someone else.' I phoned the association myself first. (...) Now, I always have something to drink in my bag. That way if they don't want to give me anything to drink I can drink even so. I took a resolution on it!

It is not possible to draw up a typology of ways to resist or confront workplace violence, singly or, more rarely, collectively. The forms it takes vary too widely, less according to the educational or social capital of the care worker as of their position in the association, their or their own family's position in the local labour market and the supervisors' or managers' ability to address the issue. But for all these women we saw how such experiences shape their approach to other carees.

Gender violence in the light of the social and ethnic division of labour

All the care workers, whether racialized or not, suffered the forms of violence described so far. But racialized women also suffered racialized forms of violence constructed by and within the ethnic division of labour combined with the social and sexual division of labour, racism and discrimination. And as we have seen in the analysis of gender violence, reducing or ending such violence depends on the organization of the work, the practices of the legal employer and the sector as a whole, as well as the mobilization of the workers themselves.

Occupational and social downgrading plus a chaotic life course are fertile ground for ethnicization of gender violence and ethnicization as a form of violence

The most highly qualified racialized women faced with occupational downgrading

Although our sample was too small to allow generalization, research results crossed with other field data suggest some altogether serious avenues for understanding the ethnicization of gender violence and its underpinnings. It is important to note that taking work as a home carer, whether in the formal or informal sector, represents a decline in occupational and social status for the better qualified racialized women migrants. Unlike the other women, who were all from working class backgrounds, these women came from the dominant classes in their home countries. Joining the French labour market involved a drop in job status and a decline in their place in the social division of labour and in life. For these women, taking work in the formal or informal home care sectors was a further step in this objective downgrading, though it is important to note that joining the non-profit branch of the home care business represented an upturn in their careers.

Erasing of inter-generational differences as a sign of discrimination

This experience of social downgrading tends to continue once these women join an association's workforce. The dynamic of their career in home care is similar to that of their less skilled elders and of all racialized women. This suggests that, for racialized women, the difference between the forms in which the different generations join this sector have erased. By contrast, these differences seem to be increasing for non-racialized women, assuming that the policy of increasing skill levels in these jobs (by introducing diploma courses in the school system) will constitute a standardized entry route to home care for new, young entrants.

Thus while all the women in our sample were confronted with increasingly insecure employment, this was especially true of the racialized women. Their careers had been more fragmented and they had had greater difficulty in finding a stable place in the labour market (Chaib 2001) and gaining access to training. In this regard, unlike their colleagues they tended to acquire training through intermediaries in the labour market. This suggests that the agencies/associations they work for enable racialized women to bypass the effects of the discriminatory dynamics encountered in the labour market.

Jobs at the bottom of the heap and difficulty in acquiring qualifications

These women's confinement to the bottom of the skills ladder points the same way. Looking at their careers in the non-profit sector, the great majority of these women are at the bottom of the qualifications ladder. Most associations keep few data on their staff and such statistics as exist are difficult to compare. This prevents us from putting this observation into perspective with the socio-demographic characteristics of the A-grade women. However, this point deserves consideration as the finding matches analyses of the labour market position of migrant women and female descendents of migrants.

These observations support the hypothesis that this situation is a product and expression of the discrimination encountered by these women throughout their careers because of their origin and gender. In other words, what we see in practice and over the long term is the combined effects of gender and ethnic discrimination and the vulnerable position of working class women in the labour market (Lada, forthcoming publication).

How the question of origin arises and how racism is expressed in home care

Analysis of the interviews raises the question of racism in the hiring process and on the job. This is not always experienced as such by those who are subjected to it, and it is not always put into words (Poli 2004), especially as denial and silence on the subject are defensive strategies that enable people to 'bear up' (Gaignard 2006). Our respondents' words can be understood in this light. For example: Ms N. (age 25, A-grade, 5 years' seniority), born in Sub-Saharan Africa. When she was looking for work in the home care sector, employers she telephoned would call her in for an interview once she had outlined her career path and told them her age. But when she met the employer, despite the promising telephone discussion, she received a negative response even before the interview began and before she even had time to describe her career path again.

The recurrent accounts of such situations matched the talks we had with association managers, who explained how often (depending on place and branch of work) they met with explicitly discriminatory requests from client families, to which they had to respond, always finding an ad-hoc solution for the case in hand. They might be asked quite explicitly not to send a 'black woman', 'an Arab' or 'any gypsies': '*Someone phoned today, a first contact. (...) She didn't want a black care worker. (...) People say it straight out. They make no bones about it. The last time it was someone who didn't want a gypsy'* (Supervisor). While the managers we met all said they gave no credit to such requests, it may be supposed that like other employers and employment agencies (Damant et al. 2003), some associations complied with such demands, less by conviction than for fear of losing a customer.

Ordinary workplace racism is, if not frequent, at least sufficiently common to amount to another form of violence at work. Sometimes women keep this experience to themselves, sometimes the women discuss it. They meet 'ordinary racism' from the first time they visit a caree. The welcome they receive from the carees hints at their employing association's policy on this issue.

> I arrived, I said hello, I introduced myself, just as my friend had explained to me. She said 'Yes, they told me it would be a coloured person'. Because there are people who won't accept that, you see. They always tell the person in advance. Anyway now she knew I was coloured. (aged 54, 6 years' seniority)

> Q: You mentioned colour in your interview. It's a recurring theme. Is that because of your experience?

> There. Let's talk about it. We're the ones who get the jobs where you have to walk for two, three hours and go up and down stairs. But if it's a normal job … (she shakes her head). But I say it. (…) because there are people in residential homes and they have carers too, you see? Why don't they give us jobs like that? (…) For us no, it's two hours here, an hour there. They send us here, then there. You see how that upsets my life: I can't look for another job or anything! (…) We talk about it together. The others don't get many hours either. We can see compared to the other women. (age 54, 6 years' seniority)

> Some people don't mind Arabs. They're old people; they were used to it over there, in Algeria or wherever, having people work for them. Rod of iron, you know. They tell me they make them wash walls and floors. (Field notebook, home care worker)

It may also be supposed that the difficulties some women routinely encounter when replacing a colleague are also due to this mechanism. With time, mistrust often gives way to trust. That said ordinary racism does not completely disappear from the work relationship. Some contexts or social events are particularly likely to put the question of origins back on the agenda.

> They ask me about my residency permit. They pass remarks, they say: you're one of those foreigners that come and take our money. Then I say, No, I work. Old people have their ways of thinking. Otherwise, all in all, it goes smoothly. I don't take everything to heart or I'd already have left. They say, You know, blacks like you, they do this, they do that. I laugh and say I'm brown, not black. They ask me if this is my real hair because they think black people have frizzy hair. (aged 30, 4 years' seniority)

> Mrs. X, she doesn't like foreigners. She always says to me 'But what have they all come here for? They should go back home, there's nothing but blacks and Arabs here. (…) I don't know if she forgets I'm Tunisian or if she does it on purpose.' (Ms L. age 54, A-grade, 18 years' seniority)

Only one woman made the link between origin and hours of work. The rest were silent on that point. Nor did they say anything about the toughness of the work. But what some of their colleagues had to say about the attitudes of some families was particularly striking. It shows how workplace racism can generate mental and physical suffering in addition to having to undergo the experience of violence at work (Lada 2009).

Conclusion

It is in situations of servitude that workplace violence is constructed and takes form. Though neither servitude nor violence is an everyday occurrence and not all service users are concerned, the organization of work and the place of work provide a space where they can arise. So much so that they seem to be constituent elements in the careers of *all* the home care workers interviewed and some had suffered the experience several times. Such experiences leave their mark and shape the care workers' behaviour and how they approach their carees, even several years later. The danger is always there, especially as they start a new job, based on testing the worker, which reactivates the possibility of abuse and puts workers in exploitative situations that are sometimes intolerable. The workers do not call this violence by that name. It arises through their day-to-day work and is smothered beneath an 'organizational' silence. It seems to us specific to home care in that the 'organizational' approach puts workers in positions of servitude and exploitation and makes that servitude an integral part of their daily situation at work. Sexual violence, essentially by men in the home setting, is part of this dynamic. Racialized workers are especially subject to such violence because they are more often forced into a position of servitude owing to stereotypes that render gendered, ethnicized and class-ridden forms of unpleasantness at work invisible.

This empirical conclusion also calls for some theorization. One issue for feminist and gender studies thinking and intersectionality approaches is to take into account power relations between women as well as between the sexes in analysing the oppression of women. This perspective, taking into consideration the divisions among women as much as the antagonistic relations between men and women is not in itself a subject of debate. What is still under debate seems to us (in agreement with Galerand 2007) to relate more to the best way to incorporate all these realities into an analysis. To contribute in a very practical way to the discussion, we have attempted here to show how the fact of occupying different positions in the gendered division of labour, particularly owing to social/racial relations, does not dilute the effects this gendered division of labour and therefore the effects of gender relations.

The gendered division of labour and its consequences by no means disappear beneath the ethnic division of labour, as we have attempted to show in our earlier studies. More precisely, the construction of a survey that allowed us to make comparisons between women shows how the different divisions of labour mutually construct each other and together construct workplace violence. In that regard, the decision not to posit a hierarchy of social relations as reference frame at the outset seems to provide a heuristic way of understanding the social world in general and the problem of workplace violence in particular. It gave us the means to consider how, in practice and over time, social relations interconnect and fabricate different positions in the sexual division of labour. This position does not mean altogether abandoning a theoretical framework in face of the complexity of the real world. On the contrary, it means taking very seriously the co-construction of social relations, as does Danièle Kergoat (Kergoat 2005). This leads us to identify not only the contradictions and the things that divide women, but also the strong lines of continuity between women.

References

Acker, J. (1990): Hierarchies, Jobs, Bodies: A Theory of Gendered Organization. In: Gender and Society, vol. 4, n°2, Juin, pp.139–158.

Association européenne contre les violences faites aux femmes au travail (AVTF) (1990): De l'abus de pouvoir sexuel. Le harcèlement sexuel au travail. Paris, Montréal, La Découverte/Boréal.

Chaib, S. (2001): Facteurs d'insertion et d'exclusion des femmes immigrantes dans le marché du travail en France: quel état des connaissances? Rapport à la CFDT.

Corrin, C. (1997): La violence masculine contre les femmes: résistantes et recherches féministes. In: Nouvelles Questions Féministes, vol.18, n° 3–4.

Crenshaw, K. (1991): Mapping the Margins: Intersectionality, Identity Politics, and Violence Against Women of Color. In: Stanford Law Review, 43, pp. 12–41.

Dejours, C. (2007): Conjurer la violence – Travail, violence et santé. Payot.

Doniol-Shaw, G. (2009): L'engagement paradoxal des aides à domicile dans les situations repoussantes. In: Travailler, 22, pp. 27–42.

Doniol-Shaw, G./Lada, E./Dussuet, A. (2007): Les parcours professionnels des femmes dans les métiers de l'aide à la personne. Leviers et freins à la qualification et à la promotion, Rapport de recherche. http://www.35h.travail.gouv.fr/IMG/pdf/Latts_rapport_definitif_21_mars_2008-2.pdf

Doniol-Shaw, D./Lada, E.: 'Work schedules of home care workers for the elderly in France: fragmented work, deteriorating quality of care, detrimental health impact', *Work*, (forthcoming publication)

Doniol-Shaw, G./Renou-Parent, D./Machefer, J. (2000): Analyser la violence et les formes de résistance. In: Semat, E.: Femmes au travail, violences vécues. Paris, La Découverte, Syros, pp. 164–182.

Hanmer, J. (1977): Violence et contrôle social des femmes. In: Questions féministes, n° 1.

Jaspard, M./Brown, E./Condon, S./Firdion, J-M./Fougeyrollas-Schwebel, D./Houel, A./ Schiltz, M-A. (2003): Les violences envers les femmes en France. Une enquête nationale. Paris, la documentation française.

Falquet, J./Hirata, H./Kergoat, D./Labari, B./Le Feuvre, N./Sow, F. (2010): Le sexe de la mondialisation. Genre, classe, race et nouvelle division du travail. Paris: Presses de Sciences Po.

Freedman J./Valluy J. (dir) (2007): Persécutions des femmes: savoirs mobilisations et protections. Paris: Editions du Croquant.

Galerand, E. (2007): Les rapports sociaux de sexe et leur (dé)matérialisation. Retour sur le corpus revendicatif de la Marche mondiale des femmes de 2000, Thèse de doctorat, UQAM/Versailles Saint-Quentin.

Kergoat, D.: Rapports sociaux et division du travail entre les sexes. In: Maruani, M.: Femmes, genre et sociétés. L'état des savoirs, pp. 94–101.

Lada, E. (2009): Division du travail et précarisation de la santé dans le secteur hôtelier en France: de l'action des rapports sociaux de sexe et autres rapports de pouvoir. In: Travailler, n° 22.

Lada, E. (2005): Quand les marges deviennent centre. Mise au travail, jeunesses populaires et rapports sociaux (de sexe) dans le secteur public et associatif. Thèse de sociologie, Université Versailles Saint Quentin en Yvelines.

Louis, M-V.: À propos des publications de l'AVFT. 1985–1996. http://www.marievictoirelouis.net/document.php?id=967&themeid=352

Marquier, R. (2010): Les intervenantes au domicile des personnes fragilisées en 2008. In: Etudes et Résultats, n° 728.

Molinier, P. (1999): Prévenir la violence: l'invisibilité du travail des femmes. In: Travailler, 3, pp. 73–86.

Poli, A. (2004): Le renouvellement de l'action publique contre le racisme en France. Le dispositif 114/CODAC. In: Cossée, C./Lada, E./Rigoni, E. (dir.): Faire figure d'étranger. Regards croisés sur la production de l'altérité. Paris, A. Colin, pp. 211–225.

Rogerat, C. (2001): Harcèlement et violence: les maux du travail. In: Travail, Genre et Sociétés, n° 5.

Romito, P. (1997): Epistémologie, méthodologie et évolution sociale des études sur la santé des femmes. In: Nouvelles Questions Féministes, vol.18, n° 2.

Sassen, Saskia (2003): Global cities and survival circuits. In: Ehrenreich, B./Russel, A. (eds): Global Woman. Nannies, Maids and Sex Workers in the New Economy. London: Granta Books, pp. 254–274.

Semat, E. (2000): Femmes au travail, violences vécues. Paris, La Découverte, Syros.

Simonazzi, A-M. (2008): Care regimes and national employment models. In: Cambridge journal of economics,(10), pp. 1–22.

Ethnicities in the Aftermaths of Sexualised Coercion – Common Issues and Diverse Personal Meanings

Bodil Pedersen

Introduction

In Denmark, except concerning communities that are over-generalised as 'Muslim' minorities, the notion that gender equality is already a fact is widespread. Yet statistics show that from 2000 to 2006 the Centre for Victims of Sexual Assault in Copenhagen was contacted by only 27 men. In the same period, however, 1764 women contacted the Centre (Madsen/Nielsen 2006: 5). From 2000 to 2004, slightly exceeding their representation in the general population, 14% of the women were from non-western ethnic minorities (Årsrapport 2004: 10).

In this article, as its title indicates, I use the broad concept of sexualised coercion. It encompasses the psychologically not clearly distinguishable but related practices of rape, attempted rape and other forms of sexualised subjection (Sidenius/Pedersen 2004). Although not an exact reflection of the frequency of sexualised coercion, the figures above do indicate that notions of gender equality in Denmark must be questioned. Nevertheless meanings of sexualised coercion are customarily understood in traumatology terms that neutralise gender, ethnicity and culture (Elklit et al. 2003; Foa/Rothbaum 1998; Van der Kolk 1996). Consequently personal meanings of sexualised coercion are frequently conceptualised and analysed regardless of person, place and time (Marecek 1999; Pedersen 2004; Ronkainen 2001). When gender and ethnicity are included, as in national surveys and in other statistical reports (Elklit 2002; Helweg-Larsen/Kruse 2003; Helweg-Larsen/Kruse 2004), they are conceptualised as separate entities. It is a conceptualisation that does not fully grasp the intersections of their meanings with other aspects of the personal conduct of life. One reason is that personal meanings of participation in social practices are rarely researched from first-person perspectives (Danziger 1990), as it is the aim of the study of which this article is a part (Sidenius/Pedersen 2004; Pedersen 2008c).

The study draws on 40 series of consultations with women subjected to sexualised coercion, supplemented by 15 interviews. Meanings of ethnicities, gender as well as of sexualised coercion and other life events (Clemans 2005; Salkvist/Pedersen 2008) are seen as constituted and re-constituted through processes of personal participation in the diverse contexts of everyday life (Dreier 2008). One implication is that personal and societal meanings of ethnified and gendered social relations are changed over time and place in diverse intersecting social practices. The first-person perspectives of the participants in the study are therefore discussed as having been developed in and through participation in such practices. In them, gendered and ethnified participation takes on forms that are habitual but changing.

In everyday life, ethnicities are not lived in essentially unified cultural and religious forms. There are no clear lines of demarcation between the conduct of lives of persons of diverse ethnic groups. Rather their lives are creolised (Eriksen 1994; Hannerz 1992): They are lived as socially positioned personal hybrids of perspectives and practices in dealing with intersecting aspects of life conditions. Social positions may themselves be composed of multiple, sometimes intermingled and untraceable elements in ongoing and situated 'culture'.

'Cultures' must then be understood as part of a continual historical process of change e.g. of creolisations. They *seem* unique and stable in our reifying categorisations (Baumann 1996; Hall 1992). But they, and the ways they are personally lived change as they engage in common and diverse local/societal practices. Such changes are related to forms of participation in a diversity of contexts constituted by changeable social relations and practical goals. This conceptualisation of creolisation is developed by drawing on Eriksen's and other anthropologists' discussions of the concept and related phenomena (1994), combined with a critical psychological approach to subjectivity (Dreier 2008; Holzkamp 1995; Nissen 2005). Accordingly, when analysing meanings of ethnified and gendered lives exclusively from the perspectives one ethnic group, one risks over-emphasising similarities within the group, as well as differences in comparisons with other groups (Haavind 2000).

A transversalist multi-ethnic approach

In 2001 the Centre for Victims of Sexual Assault made a statistical analysis of the ethnic/national origin of the women it attended to that year. 19 out of 212 women, 9%, were first or second generation migrants from non-western countries. In comparison their overall percentage of the population of Denmark was 3.7. But the Centre exclusively receives women from the Copenhagen area. Here they constituted 6.2%. The representation of women from non-western countries thus slightly exceeded their representation in the area (Rapport 2001: 24–25), which may be linked to their expectations of severe difficulties in talking to families and friends, expectations that may sometimes be exaggerated (Rapport 2001: 29–30).

Since research on ethnified gender has often focused on one specific minority, it has produced descriptions of what apparently constitutes the development of specific ethnified meanings (Abu-Ras 2007; Huisman 1997; Goodenow/Espin 1993; Methora 1999). It may raise our awareness of restrictions in the lives of minority women, co-determined by what is conceptualised as 'heritage', as well as of limitations imposed by social marginalisation. It may also, however, imply turning a blind eye on issues common in and across the conduct of diverse minority lives as well as majority ones.

Moreover, excluding majorities from studies implicitly constructs reductive and static dualisations of majorities versus minorities, western versus non-western, and migrants versus non-migrants (Quin 2004). The following remarks by minority women participating in this study underscore the need to overcome such dualisations. They point to the complex constellations of changing meanings of sexualised coercion in the conduct ethnified lives (Salkvist/Pedersen 2008). Zarah stated: *'It* (the meanings of revealing experienced events of sexualised coercion) *depends on how the families think, how far they have gotten with their lives....'*. Jasmin added: *'It depends on what family you come from; just because it's a foreign family, it's not just one way* […]. *Actually it is so different, even though they all have the same religion, but for example they have different traditions.'* But, the study showed that most majority women, exempting the mention of religion, would have acquiesced to such reflections. Many described their families as central to the meanings they delegated to having been subjected to sexualised coercion. Also, and in contrast to majority conceptions of the crucial meanings of religion for non-western minorities, the only woman who referred to religious practices as a specific difficulty was from the majority. While being underdetermined in studies of majorities, the meanings of ethnicities, cultures and/or religions are often over-determined in studies of minorities.

Strategies of action by majority and minority persons are answers to a multitude of similar and often contradictory processes in the *same* societies. Multiple meanings of ethnified and de-ethnified participation are situated and creolised in these processes. What may sometimes be termed (re)traditionalisation is intimately entwined with late-modern globalised conditions for the conduct of lives (Giddens 1991). Diverse processes of ethnic minorisation intersect with other forms of social and economical marginalisation. In some cases they seem to provoke diverse forms of retrenchments into 'tradition' imposed on, and/or chosen by, ethnic minority women (Goodenow/Espin

1993). But this is also the case in diverse aspects of the lives of majority women. Moreover, for minorities as well as majorities marginalisation may simultaneously enhance processes of 'modernisation'.

In fact both tendencies, and the personal ways in which they are performed, intersect with equally situated versions of other societal processes. Personal possibilities are always engendered as well as restricted by ethnicities, gender, and other relations of power. Participation is disconnected from unequivocal 'traditions', and is more or less open to negotiation (Staunæs 2005). Closing in on situated personal dilemmas without naïvely equating their situation, recent research illustrates how persons from majorities as well as minorities may face similar issues and difficulties. They may consequently develop comparable and similar strategies of action otherwise understood as specifically 'ethnic' (Staunæs 2005; Pedersen 2007).

In consideration of this I have chosen a multi-ethnic and transversalist approach to the meanings of sexualised coercion. It is one that crosses ethnic categorisations and includes gender. It explores common issues without ignoring the diverse positions of those to whom universalities supposedly apply (Yuval-Davis 1997: 125).

Critical issues and personal concerns

When personal meanings of ethnicities and gender are excluded from research, tendencies to overlook personal concerns related to critical issues connected to sexualised coercion are reinforced. As in Nina's proposition, they may be especially precarious:

> I think, to start with… you loose control during coercion. And then when you don't have control over what is going to happen, because other people are making the decisions on what is going to happen, then it feels like you don't have control over your own situation.

She highlights how crucial loss of agency is. Loss of agency, during the events and their aftermaths were equally *the* critical issue described by all women regardless of ethnicities (Salkvist/Pedersen 2008). In order to explore the meanings of loss of agency an agency-oriented research approach is needed (Dreier 2008; Quin 2004). The proposed analysis therefore focuses on *personal concerns and strategies of action.* Consequently discussions are structured around personal perspectives on crucial issues. One result of the study on which the article draws was that in its aftermaths sexualised coercion was attributed and reattributed changing meanings. Hence the following paragraphs do not focus on isolated meanings of events of sexualised coercion.

Accounts chosen

The vast majority of women who contacted the Centre for Victims of Sexual Assault in the period of the study were between 15 and 25 years old (Statusrapport 2000–2004). Consequently accounts by 5 *young* minority women and 5 from the majority, were strategically selected. According to the case method, and in order to construct the foundation for a knowledge-generating analysis, the goal of selection was to create as rich a material as possible (Flyvbjerg 2001). When the number of participants is limited, a strategic selection may maximise the access to relevant information, and strengthen the analysis. Accounts of participants were therefore chosen on the basis of their informative value. They are each and together the most saturated in relation to the subject of the article. As extreme, deviant or critical cases are criteria that enable a critical questioning of dominant perspectives, they also represent a maximum of variation. Hence accounts were selected in consideration of similarities *and* diversities.

Jasmin (22), Leyla (25), Zarah (23), and Madiha (20)[1] come from diverse ethnic minorities from the Middle East. Jessica's (18) mother is from a Far Eastern country and her father from the ethnic majority. Anna (19), Catrine (18), Jennifer (17), Jette (23) and Nina (23) are from the ethnic majority. The few times these pseudonyms are not used, the quotes are chosen from the main study in order to boost discussions.

Lives of young women

The young women participating in the study were in the process of developing new strategies of action. While seeking to extend and establish new contexts of action, they sought through these to change and limit their participation in, and dependence on, those co-determined by their parents. Furthermore, the necessity of dealing in an individualised manner with changes and choices in and between diverse courses of action is generally intensified in late modernity (Giddens 1991). So when having been subjected to sexualised coercion, many of the women's reflections concerned contradictions between receiving help and support from parents, while developing or at least maintaining acquired aspects of agency. But when daughters had been subjected to sexualised coercion parents often worried more, and their attempts at control escalated.

1 Madiha was interviewed by Karin Sten Madsen (Rapport 2001: 32–33).

One young woman from the ethnic majority wanted to distance herself from her parents who tried to keep track of her whereabouts through frequent calls to her cell-phone. After the event she said: *'I feel as if I have been put in a playpen. They constantly want to know where I am'*. Fearing her parents would increase what she experienced as their 'interference', she did not want them to know how upset she actually was. Jasmin, who had been living with the perpetrator, feared him as he stalked and threatened her, and was afraid of living alone. Her parents were informed and wanted her to move back in with them. Her brother and sister also encouraged her to do so. Feeling *'claustrophobic'* at the mere thought, she adamantly refused. In addition, and like other women, she wanted to protect her parents from the possible aftermaths of the events of coercion. Then instead, and in order to avoid what she saw as their attempts at controlling her life, she shared a single room belonging to a girlfriend. After the event Catherine lived with her parents, but, against their wish, spent most of her time at her boyfriend's. Describing staying with her parents she said: *'My mum always asks me how I am. It is almost too much... My dad doesn't ask anything. He just looks worried... I don't want to talk to him about it either'*. Like many of the women, she primarily turned to peers for support. Another young woman described getting help from girlfriends as: *'Yes, the girls! We have gotten together many times, sat down, cooked a good dinner, and then things were talked about.'*

Most informants had limited experiences in dealing with crisis-like situations without the support of their parents. In the aftermaths of sexualised coercion they found developing agency a project fraught with contradictions and personal ambivalences. When they experienced anxiety and felt at risk of further events of coercion, dependency on their parents increased. Both minority and majority women frequently experienced parental involvement, in what they also referred to as their *private* lives, as potential threats to their agency. Even when having moved out of their parents' homes, their relations with them were full of dilemmas. Nina, who had been living on her own for quite a while, briefly moved back in with her parents. She said:

> For example my parents, they wanted to help. It was nice when they were at home. But they weren't supposed to talk too much about it, and they weren't supposed to sit in the same room as me, and not to look too much at me. But I did not want them to be indifferent either.

As in her statement above, loss of agency was inherent to the experience of sexualised coercion. She, like several of the women, needed support and a safe place to live. But moving back in with parents could be experienced as just another loss of agency.

Individualisation of blame and guilt

Theory frequently connects events categorised as traumatic with feelings of guilt (Herman 1992). In what may seem an illustration of this Jasmin explained:

> Yes, well it is not my responsibility *(that I was raped)*. But when it is someone that I have had a relationship with, then maybe I think the thought that: Oh no, could it be my own fault?' She added: 'Even if it isn't... then I might sit and argue with myself: Oh no, maybe I did something wrong, something or other, right?'

In most cases registered by the Centre for Victims of Sexual Assault, women were acquainted with their perpetrators (Rapport 2001). Knowing the perpetrator contributed to wondering about responsibility for the event. Additionally, and pointing to the sociality of the meanings of events (Refby 2001), both majority and minority women spoke of sexualised coercion as something they may be blamed for. Jennifer (17), who was twice subjected to sexualised coercion, had been drinking. She described her parents' perspective: *'They were very angry with me and told me off, and said that surely now I would stop drinking so much. Yes... they thought it was my own fault'*. She was in despair over their attribution of guilt, and, like Jasmin, it made her worry about questions of responsibility and reflect on them.

Ascriptions of guilt sometimes contradicted what may otherwise have been considered normal and appropriate. Parents of minority women, for example, may be proud of their daughter's self-determined lives, and majority parents may accept the consumption of alcohol as an integral part of being young. But when it became associated with sexualised coercion, it was connected to notions of responsibility, if not guilt, and took the form of woman blaming (Pedersen and Stormhøj 2006; Roche and Wood 2005). Persons from the majority as well as minorities were apt to associate events of coercion with personal ways of conducting life. Especially, but not exclusively, in the case of the young majority women, an implicit late-modern individualisation of responsibility for one's life seemed connected to this. Thus Anna stated: *'I don't like telling my parents about it* (sexualised coercion). *They have taken such good care of me. It is as if I haven't taken proper care of the freedom they have given me'*. 'Woman blaming' and other individualisations like this one mask connections between victimisation and aspects of gendered conditions for lives (Ronkainen 2001; Pedersen 2009).

Reflections on agency and feelings of responsibility in the study suggested that 'feelings of guilt' are not natural, universal reactions to sexualised coercion, as assumed in much theory and 'trauma talk' (Marecek 1999; Helliwell 2000). They were evidently related to blame assigned by others. Jasmin reflected in the following in a way that was reminiscent of most of the young women: *'I think it is much easier if... if I had been assaulted on the street* (instead of by someone she knew), *and then raped. Then perhaps it was not* (seen as) *my responsibility'*. She connected her remark to assumptions about responses by 'her' ethnic community. Meanwhile, and most importantly women's consequent (re)evaluations of their actions concerned personal agency. They were attempts of subjects at (re)constructing personal perspectives on agency in the aftermaths of subjection to coercion (Salkvist and Pedersen 2008).

Mainstream concepts of culture over-determine differences in ethnic minorities. Jasmin and the other minority women connected their dilemmas to their ethnic backgrounds. On the other hand, taking their own perspectives for granted, majority women did not reflect on their experiences as ethnically related. But obviously reflections made by minorities as well as by majorities must be understood as ethnically/culturally informed attempts at understanding events and their aftermaths.

Sexualisation and sexuality

In late-modern Scandinavia, serial monogamy or having multiple sexual partners is widely practiced by ethnic majority youngsters (Byriel and Rasmussen 2002; Johansson 2007). While not necessarily on a basis of gender equality, sexual relations are negotiated and regulated by the participants themselves (Giddens 1995). Young women customarily view such relationships as 'natural' explorations of sexuality and social relations. In this study sexuality was generally a discussable topic in conversations with women friends. However, and despite an extensive sexualisation of the public sphere (Nordisk Ministerråd 2006), struggling with the sexualised aspect of coercion, which made it especially difficult to speak to her father, Nina said: *'It was difficult to tell my mum and dad... it is also embarrassing... We never talked about sexuality in the family'*. When associated with sexuality, sexualised coercion seemed to be a sensitive, and in some contexts, 'private' subject.

Yet Jette explained that the sexualised aspects of coercion were *not* the most difficult for her. Reminiscent of other informants, she compared the experience to waking up next to a man after a night on the town thinking: *'What am I doing here?'* She did not feel that it reflected on her reputation, nor on her experience of her sexuality. Nor did she, as it is often assumed, experience sexual problems in the aftermaths of the event (Hilden and Sidenius 2002). But as she understood sexualised coercion as an offence against her right to self-determination, it made her very angry. Even subsequently experiencing many problems, another young woman pointed out: *'He had nothing to do with my relationship to sexuality, sensuality and that kind of thing. He was not a part of my sex life as such. So I don't think my relationship to sex has changed much.'* Similarly, Nina reflected: *'When you use the word sex you immediately think of something nice. Something two people have together. So when you use the word sex in association with the concept of rape, then it doesn't seem quite right, right?'*

Although young women from non-western countries seem to be the least sexually active youngsters in Denmark, many embrace sexual practices (Byriel and Rasmussen 2002). Jasmin told her friends that she had been subjected to sexualised coercion. But the sexualised aspect was not her main concern, being stalked and threatened by the perpetrator was. Again, the critical issues do not seem to pertain to 'sex' as much as to agency and self-determination.

Issues and dilemmas for minority women

Minority informant's lives did not correspond to Danish stereotypes. They were not married, and did not live with their parents. All had secondary educations and were employed. Yet they reported that their parents expected them to protect their virginity until marriage. But conducting their lives in creolised ways, they had sexual relationships while pretending abstinence.

In host countries minorities' traditionalisations of the regulation of daughters' lives may be co-determined by marginalisation, and acquire diverse meanings (Goodenow and Espin 1993; Mørck 2002; Yuval-Davis 1992). In host countries like Denmark men may experience discrimination as disempowering and emasculating. This may encourage (re)constructions of traditional(ised) gendered strategies of action (Yuval-Davis 1997: 67). Woman-blaming practices may be aspects of such strategies. Madiha said: *'When you are raised not to be out late at night or go clubbing... not to do this and not to do that, then of course it is the woman's fault* (that you experience sexualised coercion)... *The hardest thing was to think about telling my father. Fathers react very, very strongly'*. The risk of being blamed for events appears to be enhanced by (re)traditionalisations. Despite their very different relations to their families, both Zarah and Madiha referred to their experiences as potentially soiling family honour. Madiha explained: *'It is also hard for the family to go through all that...* (instead) *do something ... the family can be proud of.*' Such dilemmas may mistakenly be understood as static expressions of religions or traditions, instead of as answers to overarching aspects of contemporary social relations or to relations between majority and minority (Baumann 1999). Besides, in diverse family contexts, young majority women like Anna also kept silent about the events. They were equally worried about feelings and actions of family members, sometimes especially about those of fathers and brothers.

All the same the young minority women seemed especially concerned about perspectives of families and communities, including the sanctions or rejections of potential future husbands. Minority boys and men were ascribed stances similar to those of the parental generation. So concerning their possibilities of marrying someone from 'their' ethnic communities, public knowledge of their 'loss of virginity' became a real worry. This may make the women refrain from reporting sexualised coercion to the police. Furthermore, Jasmin described how she was accosted in the street by men instructing her to behave in accordance with 'tradition'. It was also suggested that she marry the perpetrator, and she included it in her reflections on how she may again be fully recognised as a member of 'her' community. Most majority women made sharp distinctions between the meanings of self-initiated sexual relationships and sexualised coercion. To minority women this distinction did not seem so clear. Jasmin said:

> There it is again that thing, that you *(majority women)* don't have to be a virgin when you get married. But we do. If I was Danish, and had Danish parents, of course I would tell them *(about being subjected to coercion)*, but not when my parents are foreigners.

The creolisation of their lives seemed to contribute to complicate their relations to their parents and to others. They reflected on how to keep events secret, as they simultaneously wanted to participate in aspects of traditionalised life as well as in the multiethnic life of youths. Thus (re-)traditionalisation of perspectives on sexuality, with an emphasis on virginity, was described by minority informants as occasioning interconnected dilemmas. Zarah said: *'If they* (her parents) *said that there was nothing wrong with it, that it wasn't a problem with virginity, then of course you would tell them quietly and easily'*. She continued: *'I live alone. Of course it wasn't* (OK) *in the start. But I fought until the end, so now I have moved.'* She stated this as an argument against telling her parents about coercion, and added that physicians have to get permissions from parents when you are under 18 and in need of an abortion. Since both self-initiated sexuality and experiences of coercion were associated with restrictions of (re)traditionalisation, some minority women experienced particular ambivalences in attempts at developing connected aspects of their agency.

Jessica's mother was from the Far East and a practicing Catholic. For support Jessica turned to her father and her sister-in-law, who both came from the ethnic majority. Discussing her reasons for not wanting to talk with her mother about her problems she, like Jasmin, explained that she considered her mother to be too 'old fashioned'. The conflicts and ambivalences the young women experienced were evidently mediated through their participation in contradictory practices of diverse and interconnected majority and minority contexts. Keeping secrets and working out who to tell and what to tell them became a constant necessity. In their trajectories across contexts, they had grown critical of (re)traditionalisations of women's sexuality and thus risked conflicts with, and exclusion from, facets of their life in minority communities. It meant risking deprivation of possibilities of participating in constitutive parts of their current life. In the aftermaths of sexualised coercion, social isolation and marginalisation was an issue for all informants (Salkvist 2006). But for minority women 'belonging' to minority communities it seemed to accentuate the risk of isolation.

Modifying the conduct of minority lives

Linked to participation in diverse contexts over time and place, personal stances and strategies of action are intentionally and continuously re-flected on and transformed (Dreier 2008). Regarding gender, the conduct of life of the minority women seemed specifically conflict-ridden. Perhaps therefore gendered and generational modifications of stances seemed most conspicuous in their accounts. Speaking about relations to a possible future daughter Zarah said: '... *I'd rather that she'd come and tell me* (about being subjected to sexualised coercion)'. Jasmin argued: *'But that is double standards. You want your daughter to come and tell you, but you won't tell your own parents'*. Zarah replied: *'Yes, I know, but that's because our parents are much more eh... a little more old fashioned'*. Jasmin wanted to protect her parents from knowledge that she expected they did not to want. Experiencing their own stances as far more negotiable (Giddens 1991; Søndergaard 1996), Jasmin's and Zarah's exchange referred to conflicts with (re)traditionalised ones as necessitating specific strategies. Zarah emphasised it saying: *'I wouldn't tell my parents... Perhaps later on I'll tell my siblings'*. Evocative of majority women, when in need of support concerning gendered and sexualised experiences, they regularly turned to girlfriends.

Nonetheless, summing up a discussion about disclosing events of sexualised coercion, Leyla stated: *'I think it is more sort of personal... how you want it yourself... how you judge it'*. Acquiescing in this description of their choices as being personal, the young women were actively modifying and creolising aspects of their stances so as to resemble individualising 'majority discourses'. These young women, wanting more self-determination than they experienced was possible in parts of the minorities, developed kaleidoscopic ways of conducting their lives. Accordingly conflicts and modifications were more clearly voiced by them than by majority women. Despite of this, reflections on and modifications of perspectives and stances were central for all participants. In its aftermaths, subjection to sexualised coercion made each one of them re-evaluate and/or modify her perspective on the gendered conduct of daily life (Pedersen 2008b).

Concluding remarks

The conduct of lives of the minority informants constituted rather advanced and sophisticated forms of creolisation. It is difficult to determine how accounts and analyses would have evolved if women with more (re)traditionalised conduct of lives had participated. Furthermore, the informants do not speak for all young women who have been subjected to sexualised coercion (Pedersen 2003). Meanwhile, the issues they deal with are not just individual psychological issues. Although they may present themselves in different ways and be attributed diverse personal meanings, they are issues of daily life that many women have to deal with. They are issues embedded in societal praxis.

The article examines the meanings of issues connected to ethnified minorities and majority. Ethnification of daily life intersects with gendering and (re)traditionalisation as well as with individualisation. The impression of ethnic differences in their interwowen personal meanings is boosted by analytical categorisations into majority and minorities. It is also strengthened by the explicitness of ethnicity in accounts by minority participants versus its implicitness in accounts by majority participants. These dynamics are linked to the current Danish discursive over-determination of gender-trouble in the lives of minority women, and to its corresponding under-determination in the lives of majority women. Masking aspects of diverse gendered relations of power inherent in practices of sexualised coercion, both over- and under-determination may be understood as symbolic violence (Pedersen 2009; Bourdieu 1998). In countries in which women have obtained legislative equality this form of violence may even be basic to practices of gendered inequality (Krais 1993).

With an analytical focus on personal meanings of ethnicities as well as on the social, intersecting and changing character of the conduct of lives, some issues stand out. In this study, diverse forms of symbolic violence were seen to inhibit young women's efforts at dealing with central issues concerning the meanings of the aftermaths of sexualised coercion. Minority women did not conceive their problems to be similar to those of majority women, nor linked to issues common to *young* women in general. They formulated them within a gendered discourse of 'them and us', and consequently over-generalised minority women as having essentially different problems. In contrast, majority women rarely voiced sexualised coercion as forms of violence against *women*. In a Danish context, linking sexualised coercion to gender may appear to be a negation of the proclaimed gender equality, and may have seemed unfounded. Thus, when subjected to individualising and woman-blaming discourses, they did not recognise them as such. Consequently, both minority and majority women had difficulties unravelling the complex agency-related intersecting meanings of ethnicities, gender and sexualised coercion. Yet they did not seem to feel guilt as often and automatically as trauma-literature may lead us to expect. Rather their feelings and reflections were concretely linked to social and gendered ascriptions of meanings. As minority as well as majority women are released from tradition-orientated regulations of sexuality and other aspects of their lives, they are ascriptions that are undergoing change.

Living the lives of young women had consequences for agency in general, and for relations to families in particular. Some were more secretive about the events of coercion than others. Some, especially some minority women were more experienced in leading secret lives. Meanwhile, some experienced specific dilemmas relating to their parents and other members of the ethnic communities. Expectations regarding virginity restricted them in confiding in, and getting support from parents. Public knowledge of the events entailed specific risks of exclusion. Generally, the more constrained and contradictory the lives of the young women were, the more they were troubled in their struggles to (re)gain agency. At times creolisation of their conduct of lives contributed to this. Other major struggles were, however, apparent in the lives of some majority women. Besides, as supported by the study on which this article draws, the events of sexualised coercion as such did not determine the meanings ascribed to them (Pedersen 2008c). In their aftermaths, regardless of ethnicity, they were social and situated, hereby contributing to their diverse and changing meanings. Ascribed meanings were connected across diverse contexts of the informants' pasts, presents and envisaged futures, each informant having her own unique and personal trajectory. Thus, the study as a whole suggests that research should focus more on the contextualisation and re-contextualisation of the personal meanings of the aftermaths of sexualised coercion.

Research must unmask the symbolic violence inherent in dualisations of universalist versus relativist approaches, in conceptualisations of majority versus minority, in practices individualising gendered violence, and in the gender blindness of certain versions of multiculturalism. They should be replaced by approaches that encompass agency in its connectedness to the complex and intersecting social relations in which we conduct our lives. Wishing to avoid further victimisation of already victimised women, gender-informed transversalist research that includes first-person perspectives is necessary for prevention and support practices.

References

Abu-Ras, Wahiba (2007): Cultural Beliefs and Service Utilization by Battered Arab Immigrant Women. In: Violence Against Women, 13, 10, pp. 1002–1028.

Baumann, Gerd (1996): Contesting Culture. Discourses of identity in multi-ethnic London. Cambridge: Cambridge University Press.

Baumann, Gerd (1999): The Multicultural Riddle. Rethinking National, Ethnic, and Religious Identities. London: Routledge.

Bourdieu, Pierre (1998): Practical Reason. Cambridge: Polity Press.

Byriel, Lene/Rasmussen, Bjarne (2002): Ung 99: En seksuel profil. Rapport 1, 2, 3, og 4: Unge med anden etnisk baggrund end dansk. Copenhagen: Foreningen Sex og Samfund.

Clemans, Shanti E. (2005): A Feminist Group for Women Survivors. In: Social Work with Groups, 28, 2, pp. 59–75.

Danziger, Kurt (1990): Constructing the Subject. Cambridge: Cambridge University Press.

Dreier, Ole (2008): Psychotherapy in Everyday Life. Cambridge: Cambridge University Press.

Elklit, Ask (2002): Forholdet mellem køn og vold i en empirisk psykologisk kontekst. In: Gender and Violence in the Nordic Countries – Rapport från en konferens i Køge, Danmark. Copenhagen: Nordisk Ministerråd, pp. 71–95.

Elklit, Ask et al (2003): Efter en voldtægt. Psykolog Nyt 17, pp. 4–9.

Eriksen, Tomas H. (1994): Kulturelle veikryss. Essays om kreolisering. Oslo: Universitets Forlaget.

Flyvbjerg, Bent (2001): Making Social Science Matter. Cambridge: Cambridge University Press.

Foa, Edna B./Rothbaum, Barbara O. (1998): Treating the Trauma of Rape. Cognitive Behavioral Therapy for PTSD. New York: The Guilford Press.

Giddens, Anthony (1991): Modernity and Self-Identity. Cambridge: Polity Press.

Giddens, Anthony (1995): The Transformation of Intimacy. Cambridge: Polity Press.

Goodenow, Carol/Espin, Olive M. (1993): Identity Choices in Immigrant Adolescent Females. In: Adolescence 28, 109, pp. 175–184.

Haavind, Hanne (2000): Analytiske retningslinier ved empiriske studier av kjønnede betydninger. In: Hanne Haavind (red.): Kjønn og fortolkende metode. Oslo: Gyldendal Norsk Forlag.

Hall, Stuart (1992): 'New Ethnicities'. In: Donald, James/Ratansi Ali (eds.): Race, Culture and Difference. London: Sage, pp. 252–259.

Hannerz, Ulf (1992): Cultural Complexity. New York: Columbia University Press.

Helweg-Larsen, Karin/Kruse, Marie (2003): Violence against women and consequent health problems. A register based study. In: Scand. J. of Public Health, 31, pp. 51–57.

Helweg-Larsen, Karin/Kruse, Marie (2004): Mænds vold mod kvinder – omfang, karakter og indsats mod vold. Copenhagen: Statens Institut for Folkesundhed.

Johansson, Thomas (2007): The Transformation of Sexuality: Gender and Identity in Contemporary Youth Culture. United Kingdom: Ashgate.

Hilden, Malene/Sidenius, Katrine (2002): Seksuel dysfunction efter voldtægt. In: Ugeskrift for Læger, 164, 41, pp. 4801–4802.

Helliwell, Christine (2000): 'It's Only a Penis': Rape, Feminism and Difference. In: Signs: Journal of Women in Culture and Society, 25, 3, pp. 709–816.

Herman, Judith L. (1992): Trauma and Recovery: From domestic abuse to political terror. London: Pandora.

Huisman, Kimberly A. (1997): Studying Violence Against Women of Colour – Problems Faced by a White Woman. In: Schwartz, Martin D. (ed.): Researching Sexual Violence against Women: Methodological and Personal Perspectives. London: Sage Publications, pp. 179–208.

Krais, Beate (1993): Female Oppression in the Light of Pierre Bourdieu's Theory of Social Practice. In: Kalhoun, Craig/Lipuma, Edward/Postone, Moishe (eds.): Bourdieu Critical Perspectives. Cambridge: Polity Press, pp.154–177.

Holzkamp, Klaus (1995): Alltägliche Lebensführung als subjektwissenschaftliches Grundkonzept. In: Das Argument, 37, 6, 212, pp. 817–846.

Madsen, Karin S./Nielsen, Hanne (eds.) (2006): Årsrapport 2006 – Center for Voldtægtsofre. København: H.S. Rigshospitalet.

Marecek, Jeanne (1999): Trauma Talk in Feminist Clinical Practice. In: Lamb, Sharon (ed.): New Versions of Victims – Feminists Struggle with the Concept (1999). New York: New York University Press, pp.158–182.

Methora, Meeta (1999): The social Construction of Wife Abuse – Experiences of Asian Indian Women in the United States. In: Violence Against Women, 5, 6, pp. 619–640.

Mørck, Yvonne (2002): Multiculturalismens kønsblinde øje – Mangfoldigheds-udfordringer og kønsligestilling. In: Dansk Sociologi, 3, 13, pp. 7–25.

Nissen, Morten (2005): The subjectivity of participation. In: International Journal of Critical Psychology, 15, pp. 151–179.

Nordisk Ministerrråd (2006): Unge, køn og pornografi I Norden: Slutrapport, Kvalitative studier, Kvantitative studier, Medierapport. Denmark: Nordisk Ministerrråd.

Pedersen, Bodil/Stormhøj, Christel (2006): Køn, 'onde cirkler' og (dis)empowerment – Om samfundsmæssige og personlige betydninger af voldtægt. Psyke og Logos, 27, pp. 432–465.

Pedersen, Bodil (2011): Rape, Trauma and Social Relations – A Conduct of Daily Life Approach. Roskilde: University of Roskilde.

Pedersen, Bodil (2009): Victimisation and Relations of Symbolic Violence. http://www.inter-disciplinary.net/wp-content/uploads/2009/04/vch8pedersen.pdf

Pedersen, Bodil (2008a): 'Vi kan jo ikke gå hen og voldtage en mand vel?' – Om køn, intimitet, selvopfattelse og seksualitet. In: Kvinder, Køn og Forskning 17, 3, pp. 9–18.

Pedersen, Bodil (2007): 'My mother would worry every single time I went out...' – Meanings of ethnicities and sexualised coercion. In: Annual Review of Critical Psychology 6, www.discourseunit.com/arcp/6.htm, pp. 1–26.

Pedersen, Bodil (2004): Perspektiver på Voldtægt. In: Psyke og Logos 1, 25, pp. 311–337.
Pedersen, Bodil (2003): Et socialpsykologisk perspektiv på betydningerne af voldtægt. In: Psykologisk Set, 20, 52, pp. 14–25.
Rapport (2001): Rapport fra Center for Voldtægtsofre. Copenhagen: HS Rigshospitalet.
Refby, Miriam H. (2001): En ny kontekstualitet: Hvem ejer symptomerne – individet eller fællesskabet? In: Psyke og Logos, 22, 1, pp. 60–71.
Roche, Susanne E./Wood, Gale G. (2005): A Narrative Principle for Feminist Social Work with Survivors of Male Violence. In: AFFILIA, 20, 4, pp. 465–475.
Ronkainen, Suvi (2001): Gendered Violence and Genderless Gender. A Finnish Perspective. In: Kvinder, Køn og Forskning, 10, 2, pp. 45–57.
Salkvist, Rikke (2006): Når det utænkelige sker – om sociale følger af voldtægt og voldtægtsforsøg. In: Psykologisk Set, 23, 62, pp. 20–30.
Salkvist, Rikke S./Pedersen, Bodil (2008): Subject Subjected– Sexualised Coercion, Agency and the Reformulations and Reorganisation of Life Strategies. In: Critical Social Studies – Outlines, 10, 2, pp. 70–89.
Sidenius, Katrine/Pedersen, Bodil (2004): Prevention of traumatization following sexual assaults. In: NORA – Nordic Journal of Women's Studies, 12, 1, pp. 48–57.
Staunæs, Dorthe (2005): From Culturally Avant-garde to Sexually Promiscuous: Troubling Subjectivities and Intersection in the Social Transition from Childhood into Youth. In: Feminism and Psychology, 15, 2, pp. 149–167.
Søndergaard, Dorte Marie (1996): Tegnet på kroppen. Copenhagen: Museum Tusculanums Forlag.
Van der Kolk, Bessel. A. et al. (1996): The Effects and Overwhelming Experience on Mind, Body and Society. New York: Guilford Press.
Quin, Dongxiao (2004): Toward a Critical Feminist Perspective of Culture and Self. In: Feminism and Psychology, 14, 2, pp. 297–312.
Yuval-Davies, Nira (1992): Fundamentalism, multiculturalism and women in Britain. In: Donald, James/Rattansi, Ali. (eds.): Race, culture and difference. London: Sage, pp. 278–293.
Yuval-Davies, Nira (1997): Gender and Nation. London: Sage.
Årsrapport (2001): Center for Voldtægtsofre. København: H.S. Rigshospitalet.
Årsrapport (2004): Statusrapport (2000–2004). Center for Voldtægtsofre: København: H.S. Rigshospitalet.

Correlates of Partner Violence and Health among Migrant Women in Germany: Results of Comparable Analyses of Quantitative Survey Data

Monika Schröttle and *Nadia Khelaifat*

Introduction

Although partner violence[1] has elicited studies world-wide, relatively few have examined partner violence among migrants and their descendants or specific risk factors in such violence (see chapter by Condon/Lesné/Schröttle in this Reader). Furthermore, whilst violence and its health impacts have been a focus for research in many countries (also through the DHS survey programme, see Hindin/Kishor/Ansara 2008), there has been little national level research on such relationships in Europe (Martinez, Schröttle et al. 2006a). There is thus substantial knowledge internationally about the relevant *risk factors/correlates*[2], but, given the lack of quantitative survey data allowing such analysis, the potential differences between population groups have as yet received little attention (Schröttle and Khelaifat 2008; see chapter by Romito et al. in this volume). This article is based on the results and secondary analyses of the first national representative survey on violence against women in Germany (Schröttle and Müller 2004). It examines correlates of partner violence of i) Turkish origin women and ii) women from the former Soviet Union who have migrated to Germany, and compares the data to that of indigenous German women.[3] It partly distinguishes Turkish migrant women of the first and second migrant generation, and, furthermore, it dis-

1 We use the term 'partner violence' here interchangeably with domestic violence and abuse.

2 Risk factors and correlates will be used interchangeably: a risk factor or correlate is here interpreted as something that is associated with, or correlates with, a woman's exposure to violence.

3 For this chapter the terms migrant women, Turkish origin and women from the former SU are used instead of the term 'ethnic minority women' as neither the women from Turkey are related to (only) one ethnic group nor do the women who have migrated from the former SU to Germany; many of the latter have German origins related to their ancestors but were socialized in the countries of the former SU. The term 'migration background' (Migrationshintergrund in German) is a defining criterion of German official statistics to describe a population composed of migrants and their descendants since 1950 and is used here, because it widens the perspective from men/women who have migrated themselves to their descendants and next generations.

tinguishes different forms, levels and patterns of violence. This type of information is crucial for a better understanding of the specific risks of partner violence for migrant and ethnic minority women.

Migrants born in Turkey or in countries of the former Soviet Union constitute the largest migrant groups in Germany. While the Turkish migration flow began under the 'Gastarbeiter' (guest worker) scheme in the 1950s, the flow from the former Soviet Union and other Eastern European countries, often repatriates of German descent, began much later, in the 1990s (Münz and Ulrich 2000; Krobisch and Heckmann 2008). There is now a substantial population of people born in Germany whose parents or grandparents were born in Turkey. These, and their migrant parents, whose values and customs are often labelled as 'non German', have been in the spotlight in widespread debate on issues linked to integration. Such debate is shaped by aggressive anti-Islamic rhetoric against Turkish migrants, who are accused of not being willing to integrate into German society. Assumptions about 'traditional' gender relationships as well as violence against women (and girls) in these communities are being used for anti-immigration-politics. Yet this debate lacks attention to internal differences, thereby contributing to a collective prejudice against all Turkish migrants and to all migrants associated with Muslim religions.

The examination of quantitative data, despite several limitations (see Condon/Lesné/Schröttle in this Reader), can contribute to more detailed identification and differentiation of women affected by violence and thus make suggestions for appropriate intervention, support and prevention programmes tailored to the migrant women's specific needs. Although higher rates and more serious levels of partner violence particularly against Turkish origin women were found in the German VAW prevalence survey, it is important not to stigmatise the whole (Turkish) migrant community as being more oppressive towards women, since partner violence is also a major problem among the German origin majority and other migrant groups.

Data used for the study

The following results are based on secondary analyses of the first large-scale representative study on violence against women in Germany. The original study was conducted in 2003 on behalf of the Federal Ministry for Family Affairs, Senior Citizens, Women and Youth and was published under the title '*Life situation, safety and health of women in Germany*' (Schröttle and Müller 2004). It included survey data of more than 10,000 randomly selected women aged between 16 and 85 who were living in German households and had different ethnic origins. While in the main study women were interviewed in German, in additional samples, randomly selected women with a migration background, not fluently speaking German, were interviewed in both Turkish and Russian.[4] The samples for all age groups included 501 interviews with women who migrated from former countries of the Soviet Union, 371 interviews with women of Turkish origin and 8,699 interviews with indigenous German women. The ethnic origin of the interviewees was determined by the country of birth of both parents, and, as a subordinate criterion, by the citizenship of the interviewee. Therefore, migrants of first and second generations were included and third generation migrants only when they did not (yet) hold German citizenships. All interviewees were chosen from a representative community sample, which guarantees high quality and representativeness of the sample. Overall, the original study found that one in four women of the entire study population had experienced at least one case of physical and/or sexual assault by their current and/or former partners. Most violence was found to be domestic violence perpetrated by current or former intimate partners in their own homes (Schröttle and Müller 2004).

The study *'Health – violence – migration'* (Schröttle and Khelaifat 2008) was a secondary analysis of the data from the national prevalence study and examined the connections between health, migration background, and violence. It aimed at finding out i) whether, and to what extent there was a difference in the current health of women with and without migration backgrounds, ii) what factors could cause difference, and iii) how violence, discrimination and social imbalances may have an influence on women's health. The initial study analyses of the data had found increased prevalence rates of partner violence among women with a Turkish migration background in particular; furthermore, research findings of the German and other national prevalence data show a general relationship between violence and negative health consequences (Martinez, Schröttle et al. 2006b). This secondary analysis included: interviews with 8,023 indigenous German women, 368 women of Turkish origin and 475 women from former Soviet countries, aged between 16 and 75 years.[5] This analysis was supplemented by a further study

4 The Turkish and Russian interviews were conducted using translated questionnaires and face-to-face-interviews with additional (written) self-completion questionnaires on childhood and partner violence. All interviewers were female, intensively trained for the interviews and most of them had a migration background themselves and could conduct the interviews in their mother tongue. That was an important precondition for reaching more migrant women to make them feel comfortable and confidence.

5 The case numbers/sample sizes differ slightly between individual secondary analyses/ studies, because either different age groups or only subsamples of women with current or previous partner were included; furthermore definitions of "migration background" differed.

into the levels of severity, patterns, risk factors and consequences of partner violence (Schröttle and Ansorge 2009), which concentrated on the entire survey population and included a few additional analyses on migrant women.

The correlates of partner violence among Turkish women were examined in another secondary analysis within a Masters Thesis (Khelaifat 2007).[6] A distinction was made between first and second migrant generations. Here, the overall objective was to explore correlates of partner lifetime violence among Turkish origin women to find out "high risk groups" and investigate possible differences between the first and second generation. It was based on 310 Turkish women under the age of 60 years who had been identified to have been in at least one partnership, 78% of whom were of the first migrant generation.

Prevalence, severity levels and patterns of partner violence

Although the majority of (severely) abused women in Germany do not have a migration background, in the German study, migrant women of Turkish origin, by comparison, reported violence at the hands of their partners more often, and it was more severe and more frequent than violence reported by women of German origin and women from the former Soviet Union (Schröttle and Ansorge 2009). Turkish origin women in this study were affected most frequently and most seriously by physical and/or sexual partner violence.

Table 1 shows that with respect to *current and/or former partners,* women of Turkish origin reported slightly higher rates of physical and/or sexual violence, but with respect to the *current* partner, there was twice the rate of at least one act of physical and/or sexual violence (see Table 1).

6 The data analysis included a sample description at the bivariate level using chi-square tests. Furthermore crude and stratified odds ratios were calculated. In the study, different from the other studies, migrant status was used. The migrant status was based on two variables: 'country of birth' and 'country, where a woman had mostly grown up until the age of 16'. Ergo when a woman was born in Germany and had also grown up in Germany she was considered to belong to the second generation, while women who were born in Turkey and had either grown up in Turkey, Germany, or another country were considered to belong to the first generation.

Table 1: Prevalence of partner violence in the sample groups by comparison based on women below 75 years of age

	Origin of respondents		
	German Origin	**Turkish Origin**	**Former USSR**
Partner violence			
At least one act of physical and/or sexual violence by current and/or *previous* partners*	26%	37%	27%
At least one act of physical and/or sexual violence by *current* partner**	13%	29%	16%
Sexual abuse by current partner **	1%	5%	3%
More severe forms of *psychological* abuse by current partner (with and without other forms of violence)**	16%	39%	30%
Patterns of *severe* forms of *psychological* violence without physical/sexual violence	10%	21%	20%
Patterns of *severe* domestic *physical/ sexual/psycholgical abuse* by current partner (more frequent acts and regularly in combination with severe psychological violence)	5%	18%	9%

* Related to women who have a current and/or former relationship
** Related to women who have a current partner

(sources: Schröttle and Khelaifat 2008; Schröttle and Ansorge 2009)

The detailed analysis of physical, sexual and psychological partner violence prevalence highlighted that women of Turkish origin are not only more frequently but also more severely affected by physical, sexual and psychological abuse by their current partner. One in six Turkish origin women (18%) had reported patterns of severe physical, psychological and partly sexual violence by the current partner in comparison with 5–9% of women from the other groups. Furthermore, both groups of migrant women had reported levels of severe *psychological* violence through current partners which were twice as high as those reported by women of German origin (see Table 1). This suggests that, as far as psychological abuse is concerned, not ethnicity but the consequences of migration and the accompanying social tensions and strains on gender roles may have an important role in amplifying the risk of violence.

With respect to violence experienced through different perpetrator groups, including violence *inside and outside* the domestic context, women from former Soviet countries – irrespective of victim-perpetrator relationships – more frequently encountered sexual abuse (18% vs. 12–13% in the other groups, see Table 2, second line). Contrary to this, indigenous German women reported sexual harassment more frequently than women with a migration background (61% vs. 51–54% of migrant women; see Table 2). Psychological and physical violence in various areas of life, committed inside and outside the main partner relationship, had been experienced by all groups to the same extent, or with no significant (or distinctive) differences. However, both migrant groups had faced significantly higher rates of *discrimination* from their social environment than German origin women. More than one in five women with a migration background stated that they had experienced disadvantage or mistreatment due to their sex, age or ethnic origin, compared with less than one in ten women of German origin (see Table 2).

Table 2: Prevalence of violence through all perpetrators in the sample groups by comparison based on women below 75 years of age

	Origin of respondents		
	German Origin	**Turkish Origin**	**Former USSR**
Violence – all perpetrators			
Physical abuse – irrespective of victim-perpetrator relationship	38%	45%	40%
Sexual abuse (only criminal offences)	13%	12%	18%
Sexual harassment	61%	51%	54%
Psychological abuse – irrespective of victim-perpetrator relationship	42%	44%	45%
Discrimination based on sex, age or ethnic background	9%	23%	21%

(sources: Schröttle and Khelaifat 2008; Schröttle and Ansorge 2009)

It is important to include data of the different types, severity levels and patterns of violence within and outside the domestic context for a better understanding of the lived situation of migrant and ethnic minority women (within national and social contexts). The German data shows a very high prevalence of psychological violence through partners of both migrant women groups. Women of Turkish origin, in particular, experienced patterns of severe abuse (physical, psychological and sexual violence) by their current partners to a significantly higher extent than other groups in this study. Yet the study also shows that the majority of women with and without migration background *were not* affected by any form of violence through partners. Thus, simplified stigmatisation of specific groups of ethnic minority women due to abusive partner relationships cannot be confirmed by the existing empirical data. The results demonstrate that violence against migrant women is not only found in the domestic context but also in other life settings, and social discrimination also contributes to the victimisation of these women. Some migrant women were victimised through specific forms of violence (e.g. sexual violence) outside the domestic context, and this could be due to vulnerable working conditions and isolation which might lead to higher risks. The analyses highlight that the victimisation of migrant women and German origin women might differ considerably.

Correlates and risk factors for partner violence

Understanding the causes of partner violence is crucial for its prevention. Partner violence is considered to be 'entirely a product of its social context' (Jewkes 2002: 1423). Partner violence is understood to be the result of 'interplay of personal, situational and cultural factors…' (Krug et al. 2002: 97; Schröttle 1999). However, systematic research on risk and protective factors in partner violence is limited; most studies are of cross-sectional design and only examine a restricted number of predictive factors. There is not enough evidence in these studies to indicate i) which factors are the most important, and ii) how the direction and interplay of multiple risk factors with victimisation can be identified (Krug et al. 2002). With most 'risk factors' or correlates, the causal relationship cannot be established. Risk factors or correlates, which have been found so far, thus should be treated cautiously and cannot be assumed to be complete (ibid.).

Which factors are correlated with the increased violence experienced by migrant women, particularly in relation to the increased violence affecting different generations of Turkish migrant women? Is this primarily a case of increased risks resulting from difficult social and economic conditions, and discrimination experienced/faced by migrants in Germany? To what extent are gender-specific power-relations and gender-equal task-sharing within the partner relationship relevant? These questions were examined in the multivariate analyses. Overall, it was found that the migrant women more often had disadvantaged social situations; they frequently lacked educational and financial resources, had limited knowledge of the German language, held in some cases more traditional values, but also lacked awareness of support facilities. This, in turn, all complicates women's attempts at breaking out of a violent and abusive relationship and increases the risk of severe violence. Most of all, violence experienced by women in their families of origin, especially violence between parents, was an important factor for the victimisation of women in later adult life.

Socioeconomic and educational resources

Although suggested in some studies, no simple educational and social class correlation with regard to domestic violence was found for the whole population in either the initial or further analyses of the 2004 German prevalence study. With respect to the severity levels and patterns of violence, women with lower levels of education and income are not generally more affected by severe abuse than women with higher education or a privileged social situation. However, analyses of risk factors for migrant and ethnic minority women affected by severe partner violence showed that a higher level of education and socio-economic status, having an independent income and occupation appear to be protective factors for migrant women.

Education

More highly educated Turkish origin women experienced significantly lower rates of severe physical and sexual partner violence than less educated Turkish women. For highly educated women, the rates of partner violence are comparable to German women. Yet, almost all women of Turkish origin who reported physical or sexual violence by their current partner had no accredited professional training or higher education. The role of education cannot be disregarded: while in itself it cannot protect women from partner violence, it is vital for empowering women to leave violent relationships because it helps them to gather and understand information about violence and support institutions, and consequently gain control over their world (Kishor 2000 as cited by Kishor and Johnson 2004: 31).

Employment and professional status

Employment and occupational status were relevant protective factors especially for women of Turkish origin with respect to severe grades and patterns of partner violence. Employed women of Turkish origin were, in contrast to migrant women from the former SU, less frequently affected by psychological, physical and sexual violence and severe patterns of abuse by intimate partners than unemployed women of Turkish origin. A low professional status heightened the risk for Turkish women of severe forms of current partner violence, while women from the former SU were at higher risk when they had a middle or high professional status. Thus, these results partly support previous studies which showed that working women might be at increased risk of partner violence under certain circumstances (Yilmaz and Battegay 1997; Kishor and Johnson 2004). For women from the former Soviet Union (SU) countries, whose men were often unemployed in the migration context, the women's employment status might be perceived as a threat or a loss of power, often accompanied by higher alcohol consumption and to some extent by violence towards the partner. But for Turkish women the results rather confirm studies which have found a correlation between unemployment of women and partner violence (Coker et al. 2000; Richardson et al. 2002; Vest et al. 2002; Walby and Allen 2004).

Male status, occupational/economic resources and the related dynamics within the couple relationship, varied depending on the (sub)cultural, social and ethnic backgrounds and were found to affect domestic violence in different ways. In the German majority population similar contradictory mechanisms were found as the two groups who were most affected by partner violence were women under 35 with no education and no social resources on the one hand, and women over 45 with higher incomes, higher education and higher occupational status on the other hand. Unemployment of male partners was discovered to be a factor that heightened the risk for violence against women, independently of their cultural or ethnic background: here the prevalence rates were equally high in all examined groups and no group differences emerged. As Jewkes (2002) has pointed out, 'Violence is frequently used to resolve a crisis of male identity' (ibid.: 1423). Although this underlines male unemployment as being a violence-promoting factor, it cannot be the single causal factor because the majority of violent male partners of women from the German survey were not unemployed nor did they hold subordinate job positions.

Income and social position

Low household net income (or when partly or fully dependent on state benefits) and a marginal household or personal income was highly correlated with domestic violence but only for *migrant* women within the survey. Low monthly household net income was found to increase the risk of partner violence, particularly among younger second generation migrant women of Turkish origin. This finding confirms previous studies which have also found a similar association (Bureau of Justice Statistics 1994; McCauley et al. 1995; Dearwater et al. 1998; Coker et al. 2000; Sahin and Sahin 2003; Malcoe et al. 2004; Walby and Allen 2004) but it must be stressed that these correlations are not significant for the whole survey sample.

The direction of causality between violence and income is not clear: it is possible that poverty precedes partner violence or vice versa, since divorce or separation often means that women become poorer (Kishor and Johnson 2004: 27). As maintained by İllkkaracan (1996: 5–6), Turkish women who had faced partner violence were often quick to give up legal procedures involving the payment of alimony to avoid future threats and pressures or because they did not know their rights due to language problems. This can also contribute to the lower socio-economic status of women affected by intimate partner violence.

Traditional gender relations/gender relationships and male dominance

Male dominance in the relationship increased the risk of (severe) partner violence for all women irrespective of their origin. However, women of Turkish origin more often described their current partners as very dominant, though migrant women from the former SU also reported this. Male dominance in relationships was found to be a relevant factor in all population groups but is especially significant for partners of migrant women; yet most partners of migrant women (independently of their country of origin) do not display male dominance within relationships. Male dominance in intimate relationships is found to be a risk factor, but also a consequence of violence in intimate relationships, thus the direction of causality cannot be determined due to lack of longitudinal studies.

Divorce and separation

As observed in social work and police practice for many years, the post-separation and divorce situation pose a high risk for all women with regard to severe violence by the current or former partner. This was also confirmed in the findings of the German survey: being divorced or separated was found to be significantly correlated with the experience of lifetime partner violence. Separated/divorced women of the whole sample population (with and without migration background) were three to five times more likely to have experienced partner violence than women who were not divorced/separated. This result is also in line with several studies and national prevalence surveys, which have identified being divorced or separated to be highly associated with partner violence (Martinez and Schröttle et al. 2006b; Bureau of Justice Statistics 1994; McCauley et al. 1995; Coker et al. 2000; Richardson et al. 2002; Vest et al. 2002; Walby and Allen 2004; Watson and Parsons 2005; Hyman et al. 2006).

Although separation is correlated with violence for all women, for women with a Turkish migration background this risk is considerably higher: separated/divorced women of Turkish origin were more than six times more likely to have experienced partner violence when compared to married women, and more than four times more likely than single/widowed women (Khelaifat 2007). When stratified by age, it was ascertained that women under 35 of Turkish origin had an almost fifteen-fold risk of partner violence when compared to their married counterparts, and an almost tenfold risk when compared to their single/widowed counterparts.[7] When these women separated from their partners, they stated significantly more frequently than other respondent groups having experienced threatening or violent (stalking) acts and, furthermore, having been exposed to higher rates of violence and threats regarding the joint custody of children. Overall, the data shows that about one third of the women with a Turkish migration background were eminently at risk of becoming a victim of violence by their previous partners during separation or divorce. This applies to one in seven women from former SU countries, and one in ten women of German origin (Schröttle and Ansorge 2008). This increased risk of encountering violence makes separation for some groups of migrants even more hazardous.

Language skills, duration of stay in Germany and social integration of the women

Poor German language skills in both migrant groups were found to correlate with physical and sexual assaults by partners. For migrant women who had lived less than ten years in Germany, the duration of stay was not related to violence by current partners. Additionally, there was no significant correlation between German born and other migrant women. Fewer social contacts, or not feeling socially integrated, were correlated with partner violence for all women irrespective of their origin. Both groups of migrants were significantly less embedded in social relations than women of German origin. About one quarter of migrants of both populations were socially integrated to a low degree compared to 7% of women of German origin in current partner relationships. Twice as many women of German origin as women with a migration background were highly socially integrated (41% vs. 19–20%). Nevertheless, compared to the other respondents groups, Turkish migrants experienced extensive occurrences of violence, and this was found even when there was increased social integration. There is speculation that stronger involvement in traditional family structures might hinder some migrant women leaving violent partners and this may also be a related factor.

---

7 However, this result should be treated cautiously as the sample size was very small.

The causality of the association between low social contacts and partner violence cannot be established here. It is possible that low levels of social contacts make Turkish and other migrant women more vulnerable to partner violence. Nevertheless, partner violence has also been found to decrease social contacts because abusive partners may restrict and control women's social interactions to prevent detection, and women might withdraw from sources of help and support due to feelings of shame (Smith, Tessaro and Earp 1995: 173–174). However, without social contacts, abused women are trapped in their relationships because they lack much needed support, advice and help to leave. Social contacts in migrant communities might not be helpful *per se*. Some migrant communities pressure women to remain silent when they encounter partner violence (Bhuyan and Senturia 2005: 897). In these communities, violence is excused on grounds of tradition, love or honour, and the group norms are considered to be superior to a woman's individual needs. In addition, when women do not adhere to group norms, pressure, isolation and even violence can be sanctioned (İllkkaracan 1996: 5).

Violence in childhood and youth

Childhood experiences of violence seem to be the most powerful risk factor for violence against women in couple relationships according to this study and several other national surveys worldwide (Schröttle and Ansorge 2009; Martinez and Schröttle et al. 2006: 30f; Straus and Yodanis 1996; Coker et al. 2000; Jewkes et al. 2002; Kishor and Johnson 2004; Watson and Parsons 2005). Women who had experienced violence during childhood and adolescence in the German study had, independently of migration/national background, a two to threefold risk of suffering partner violence in later life; women, who had been sexually abused before their 15th birthday, had a fourfold risk of suffering sexual abuse in adult life. Three quarters of women affected by patterns of severe violence in current relationships had experienced physical, sexual and/or psychological assaults during childhood or adolescence. This has an immense impact on their psychological and physical health, which calls for continuing support (beyond an acute violent situation) for women (and their children) independently of their social and migration background.

When not confronted with violence during their childhood and youth, women with and without a migration background experienced physical/sexual violence and severe patterns of violence by intimate partners less often. In comparison, migrant women in the German survey had not reported significantly higher rates of violence during their childhood and youth with respect to parental physical and mental violence, as well as sexual assaults during childhood and youth. The only difference was found with respect to witnessing violence between parents which was reported by women of Turkish origin significantly more often. Witnessing violence between parents was significantly correlated with physical/sexual intimate partner violence. If no violence between parents was witnessed by women, no significant differences emerged any more between the different groups of women with and without migration background. Overall, the above results emphasise the vital role for raising awareness of the intergenerational transmission of violence within prevention programmes directed at all women and men regardless of their ethnic origin.

Health factors, violence and migration background

Indicators for the negative health consequences of VAW have been established in several national and international studies since the 1990s[8]. In the German survey, as in other European prevalence surveys on VAW, two sources were used in order to examine health impact on VAW: on the one hand questions on the current physical and psychological health status were included and results correlated with different forms of victimisation through violence (here confounding factors for the current health status like age, social and economic situation are controlled); on the other hand the direct impact of violence perceived by the women were investigated (Martinez and Schröttle et al. 2007). The results from the German survey, in line with other studies, found strong correlations of VAW with psychosomatic health complaints such as: head and stomach aches, gastro-intestinal complaints, cerebral problems, dizziness, respiratory complaints, circulatory problems, skin conditions, abdominal pains, menstrual problems and other gynaecological complaints. Several psychological problems were also quoted significantly more frequently by those affected by violence, especially stress symptoms, sleeping disturbances, feeling low, depression, suicidal thoughts, anxiety and panic attacks, reduced working performance and eating disorders (Schröttle/Hornberg/Bohne et al. 2008; Schröttle and Khelaifat 2008). Furthermore, victims of violence had nearly twice as many complications during pregnancy or childbirth.

8 For an overview of international results, see Schröttle, Hornberg and Bohne et al. 2008 and for methodological considerations, Martinez and Schröttle et al. 2006 b, 2007, see also Krug et al. 2002

Interestingly, the German study found in parallel that not only a less positive self-assessment of current health was particularly evident especially among Turkish migrants above 45 years, but also that several of the above stated health and psychological complaints were reported more often by migrants, especially by Turkish origin migrants of the elder generation (e.g. headaches or stomach aches, gastrointestinal complaints, stress symptoms, cerebral problems gynaecological symptoms, anxiety, panic attacks, sleep disturbance and suicidal thoughts). Thus, as violent assaults, as well as health problems, were identified to be more frequent in women of Turkish origin, the hypothesis was tested by multivariate statistical analysis, whether and to what extent the worse health situation of specific groups of women migrants was related to their experiences of violence.

It was found that the greater health burden of Turkish origin migrant women was not solely or predominantly due to their increased affectedness of violence, but was also linked to variables of their present life situations. The poor health situation reported by a proportion of women migrants, in particular women of Turkish origin in Germany, was mainly linked to the women's difficult social situation: here indirect influences are highly relevant such as the interconnected factors of education, income and social integration. Low educational and income status, a lack of social contacts, low social integration, and insecure or poor working conditions were found to be the main factors influencing Turkish migrant womens' health status. Thus, the health situation of these women is compromised not only by a higher prevalence of violence, but to high extent by additional social and economic factors, including social discrimination. Vice versa, the problematic health and social situations of relevant groups of women migrants may increase their vulnerability to intimate partner violence, consequently making it more difficult to leave violent (couple or family) relationships.

Discussion of the results with respect to intervention, support and prevention

A considerable proportion of migrant women in Germany are affected by violence and health problems and find it difficult to leave abusive situations because they are undermined and impaired by social as well as psychological and interpersonal discrimination in German society. The findings associated with risk factors of violence, in this study, show that the violence faced by some of the migrant women living in Germany is similar in terms of violence-promoting conditions faced by women without a migration background. Yet, these conditions seem to be more frequent and more severely prevalent within certain migrant populations. Vocational and social support for women with or without a background of migration, particularly before and during the phase of starting a family, is a crucial precondition for improving women's health status and reducing the prevalence of violence. Economic and work security, plus psychosocial support in the context of separation and divorce are also vital in this context. This provides a direct and indirect positive influence on the health and violence situation of women, children and subsequent generations.

Several issues require further and parallel attention. Migrant women and men should be given specific and individual support regarding their professional and educational needs, factors of discrimination must be actively addressed, whilst raising awareness of gender equality in intimate relationships may be an additional important objective for family and partner relationships. However, it should be pointed out that discrimination of women and equality differences between genders continue to exist in wider German society, and the reduction of these problems should be a common project for all women and men, with and without a migration background. Improving social support in a way that addresses concrete needs and expectations is a key factor in preventing violence against migrant women. Thiara (2005: 4) asserts that migrant women 'require higher levels of support over a longer period of time' since they often face 'extreme isolation and also feelings of guilt due to thinking that they have failed both their families and their community'. She found that migrant women felt much more comfortable and positive about services when they were able to talk to women who had similar backgrounds and spoke their languages. Women from similar cultural backgrounds, in turn, could relate much better to the pressures and contradictions faced by abused migrant women and thus were in a better position to counter-act traditional views (Thiara 2005: 4). The provision of culture-sensitive support for Turkish migrant women could consequently facilitate the development of trustful working relationships, which would in turn help abused women to make informed choices (Thiara 2005: 4). Hence women with a background of migration require multilingual and culturally sensitive services for protection and support. This support must not only be built up for, but also, by women with a migration background.

24 hour telephone hotlines regarding partner violence offered in Turkish on a national basis within a national helpline that is just starting in Germany might be a further valuable intervention. To reach first generation women, or women aged 35 years and older with low social integration, it may be effective to design national strategies with Turkish immigrant communities as well as trans-national cooperation with Turkey (the government and Turkish

women's rights organisations). Among Turkish migrant communities in Germany, using the Turkish Television/broadcasting network and printed media might also be influential in addressing the issue of partner violence. Providing mother-tongue therapeutic and long-term offers of psychosocial support (e.g. continuing support after staying in a women's refuge) is urgently required due to the distinctive difficulties and stresses faced by migrant groups. This has not been sufficiently addressed, and the provision of a broad-range of services for traumatised women, including comprehensive support, crisis intervention and trauma therapy, is sparse. The study found that Turkish women seldom use support through therapy. This may be a language problem because therapy is not regularly available in different languages in Germany, but also a fear of stigmatisation as Turkish women are often not used to these kinds of services. When considering the serious adverse affects on physical and psychological wellbeing caused when violence was experienced or observed during childhood and adolescence, it is crucial to initiate longer term processes of stabilisation and recovery for affected women and their children. Serious action is required to terminate destructive cycles of violence and prevent transmission to future generations. Early prevention and intervention and a range of high quality support for women and children with and without migration background affected by violence are not a social 'luxury' for economically prosperous times. They are a social necessity when considering the human misery and resulting economic costs.

Specific support and safety measures for all affected groups, during and after separation, are required. Thus, violence prevention and intervention should be tailored to the needs of migrant women during and after separation and divorce. Furthermore, legal advocacy and assistance is probably essential according to İllkkaracan (1996: 4–5). Turkish origin women are faced with more problems when seeking their legal rights because i) they often do not know the German legislative system, ii) they often have problems understanding the language and iii) they have nowhere to stay after separation (İllkkaracan 1996). Moreover, they fear they will lose their children. In addition, some migrant women might still be dependent on their husbands regarding their residence permit. The current residence act in Germany, similar to that in other European countries, in forcing many women migrants to stay in violent relationships for several years, has to be criticised intensely and changed fundamentally in order to better protect women and their children. There are national (Lehmann 2002; Hagemann-White, Katenbrink and Rabe 2006: 24) and international (Bhuyan and Senturia 2005; Hague et al. 2006; Raj et al. 2004) recommendations to inform migrant women about their rights.

Nevertheless, discussions about violence against women should not only focus on the social problems of the abused migrant women and their situations at large, as these situations may vary greatly in reality as we can see from this and other studies presented in this Reader. Further studies with larger migrant populations are required to gain more insight into the occurrence and correlates of partner violence, whilst distinguishing between different groups of migrants. In addition, gender relations in mainstream German society (particularly in the middle and upper middle classes, where the German study found either high rates of violence that were hidden more easily) should be examined. The prevention of domestic violence and support of victims of violence is essential irrespective of their social or ethnic backgrounds whilst acknowledgment must be given to the different needs of women affected. Reducing violence in society, at the same time as increasing gender equality in education, the professions and economic life more generally, requires interlinked strategies, which address the interdependencies of gender, power, health and violence. This must be studied urgently and in greater detail, given the continued displacement of traditional gender roles affecting all women and men irrespective of their origin.

References

Bhuyan, Rupaleem/Senturia, Kirsten (2005): Understanding domestic violence resource utilization and survivor solutions among immigrant and refugee women: introduction to the special issue. In: Journal of Interpersonal Violence, 20, 8, pp. 895–901.

Bureau of Justice Statistics (1994): Violence between intimates: domestic violence. NCJ-149259, pp. 1–10.

Coker, Ann L./Smith, Paige H./Bethea, Lesa/King, Melissa R./McKeown, Robert E. (2000): Physical health consequences of physical and psychological intimate partner violence. In: Archives of Family Medicine, 9, 5, pp. 451–457.

Hagemann-White, Carol/Katenbrink, Judith/Rabe, Heike (2006): Combating violence against women. Stock-taking study on the measures and actions taken in Council of Europe member States. Strasbourg.

Hague, Gill/Gangoli, Geetanjali/Joseph, Helen/Alphonse, Mary (2006): Domestic violence, marriage and immigration: if you are immigrating into the UK to marry, what you might need to know. The Violence Against Women Research Group, University of Bristol, Bristol.

Hindin, Michelle J./Sunita, Kishor/Donna, L. Ansara (2008): Intimate Partner Violence among Couples in 10 DHS Countries: Predictors and Health Outcomes. DHS Analytical Studies No. 18. Calverton, Maryland, USA: Macro International Inc.

Hyman, Illene/Forte, Tonia/Du Mont, Janice/Romans, Sarah/Cohen, Marsha M. (2006): The association between length of stay in Canada and intimate partner violence among immigrant women. In: Amercian Journal of Public Health, 96, 4, pp. 654–659.

İllkkaracan, Pinar (1996): Domestic violence and family life as experienced by Turkish immigrant women in Germany. Women for Women's Human Rights Report No. 3, Istanbul, Turkey.

Jewkes, Rachel (2002): Intimate partner violence: causes and prevention. In: The Lancet, 359, April 20, pp. 1423–1429.

Jewkes, Rachel/Levin, Jonathan/Penn-Kekana, Loveday (2002): Risk factors for domestic violence: findings from a South African cross-sectional study. In: Social Sciences and Medicine, 55, 2002, pp. 1603–1617.

Khelaifat, Nadia (2007): Correlates of Partner Violence among Turkish Migrant Women: A Cross-Generational Comparison. Master's Thesis. Bielefeld: University of Bielefeld/Department of Public Health (unpubl.).

Kishor, Sunita (2000): Empowerment of women in Egypt and links to the survival and health of their infants. In: H.B. Presser, and G. Sen (eds.), Women's empowerment and demographic processes: Moving beyond Cairo. New York: Oxford University Press.

Kishor, Sunita/Johnson, Kiersten (2004): Profiling Domestic Violence – A Multi-Country Study. Calverton, Maryland: ORC Macro.

Krobisch, Verena/Heckmann, Friedrich (2008): Dokumentation: Migration und Integration in Deutschland – Chronologie der Ereignisse und Debatten. In: Krüger-Potratz, Marianne/Bommes, Michael: Migrationsreport 2008, pp. 239–318. Frankfurth a.M.

Krug, Etienne G./Dahlberg, Linda L./Mercy, James A./Zwi, Anthony B./Lozano, Rafael (2002): World report on violence and health. Geneva: World Health Organization.

Lehmann, Nadja (2002): Migrantinnen im Frauenhaus = Interkulturelles Frauenhaus? Presentation, 3.5.2002 in Münster, Katholische Fachhochschule Nordrhein-Westfalen.

Malcoe, Lorraine H./Duran, Bonnie M./Montgomery, Juliann M. (2004): Socioeconomic disparities in intimate partner violence against Native American women: a cross-sectional study. In: BMC Medicine 2004, pp. 2:20 http://www.biomedcentral.com/1741-7015/2/20 (Accessed 12.6.2009).

Martinez, Manuela/Schröttle, Monika et al. (2006a): State of European research on the prevalence of interpersonal violence and its impact on health and human rights. CAHRV – Report 2006. Co-ordination Action on Human Rights Violations funded through the European Commission, 6th Framework Programme, Project No. 506348. Internet: www.cahrv.uni-osnabrueck.de/reddot/190.htm (01.05.2011)

Martinez, Manuela/Schröttle, Monika et al. (2006b): Comparative reanalysis of prevalence of violence against women and health impact data in Europe – obstacles and possible solutions. Testing a comparative approach on selected studies. CAHRV – Report 2006. Co-ordination Action on Human Rights Violations funded through the European Commission, 6th Framework Programme, Project No. 506348. Internet: www.cahrv.uni-osnabrueck.de/reddot/190.htm (01.05.2011)

Martinez, Manuela/Schröttle, Monika et al. (2007): Perspectives and standards for good practice in data collection on interpersonal violence at European level. CAHRV – Report 2007. Co-ordination Action on Human Rights Violations funded through the European Commission, 6th Framework Programme, Project No. 506348. Internet: www.cahrv.uni-osnabrueck.de/reddot/190.htm (01.05.2011)

McCauley, Jeanne/Kern, David E./Kolodner, Ken/Dill, Laurie/Schroeder, Arthur F./ DeChant, Hallie K./Ryden, Janice/Bass, Eric B./Derogatis, Len R. (1995): The 'battering syndrome': prevalence and clinical characteristics of domestic violence in primary care internal medicine practices. In: Annals of Internal Medicine, 123, 10, pp. 737–746.

Münz, Rainer/Ulrich, Ralf E. (2000): Migration und zukünftige Bevölkerungsentwicklung in Deutschland. In: Migrationsreport 2000, pp. 23–57, Bundeszentrale für Politische Bildung, Bonn.

Raj, Anita/Silverman, Jay G. (2003): Immigrant South Asian women at greater risk for injury from intimate partner violence. In: American Journal of Public Health, 93, 3, pp. 435–437.

Richardson, Jo/Coid, Jeremy/Petruckevitch, Ann/Chung, Wai S./Moorey, Stirling/Feder, Gene (2002): Identifying domestic violence: cross sectional study in primary care. In: British Medical Journal, 2, pp. 224–274.

Sahin, Huseyin A./Sahin, H. Güler (2003): An unaddressed issue: domestic violence and unplanned pregnancies among pregnant women in Turkey. In: The European Journal of Contraception and Reproductive Health Care, 8, pp. 93–98.

Smith, Paige H./Tessaro Irene/Earp, Jo A. L. (1995): Women's experiences with battering: A conceptualization from qualitative research. In: Women's Health Issues, 5, 4, pp. 173–182.

Schröttle, Monika (1999): Politik und Gewalt im Geschlechterverhältnis. Eine empirische Untersuchung über Ausmaß, Ursachen und Hintergründe von Gewalt gegen Frauen in ostdeutschen Paarbeziehungen vor und nach der deutsch-deutschen Vereinigung. Bielefeld.

Schröttle, Monika/Müller, Ursula (2004): Lebenssituation, Sicherheit und Gesundheit von Frauen in Deutschland. Eine repräsentative Untersuchung zu Gewalt gegen Frauen in Deutschland. [Health, well-being and personal safety of women in Germany. A representative study on violence against women in Germany]. Berlin: Bundesministerium für Familie, Senioren, Frauen und Jugend, [Federal Ministry for Family Affairs, Senior Citizens, Women and Youth].

Schröttle, Monika/Khelaifat, Nadia (2008): Gesundheit – Gewalt – Migration: Eine vergleichende Sekundäranalyse zur gesundheitlichen und Gewaltsituation von Frauen mit und ohne Migrationshintergrund in Deutschland [Health – Violence – Migration: A comparative secondary analysis of the health and violence situation of women with and without a migration background in Germany.] Berlin: Bundesministerium für Familie, Senioren, Frauen und Jugend [Federal Ministry of Family Affairs, Senior Citizens, Women and Youth].

Schröttle, Monika/Hornberg, Claudia/Bohne, Sabine/Khelaifat, Nadia/Pauli, Andrea (2008) Gesundheitliche Folgen von Gewalt: Unter besonderer Berücksichtigung von häuslicher Gewalt gegen Frauen [Health consequences of violence with special reference to domestic violence against women], Gesundheitsberichterstattung des Bundes [Federal Health Monitoring System], 42, Berlin: Robert Koch Institut. Also avalaible at: http://edoc.rki.de/documents/rki_fv/ren4T3cctjHcA/PDF/26Herxag1MT4M_27.pdf (Accessed: 20 May 2011)

Schröttle, Monika/Ansorge, Nicole (2009): Gewalt gegen Frauen in Paarbeziehungen – eine sekundäranalytische Auswertung zur Differenzierung von Schweregraden, Mustern, Risikofaktoren und Unterstützung nach erlebter Gewalt [Violence against women in couple relationships – a secondary analyses on levels of severity, patterns, risk factors and support]. Berlin: Bundesministerium für Familie, Senioren, Frauen und Jugend [Federal Ministry of Family Affairs, Senior Citizens, Women and Youth].

Straus, Murray A./Yodanis, Carrie L. (1996): Corporal punishment in adolescence and physical assault on spouses in later life: what accounts for the link? In: Journal of marriage and family, 58, 4, pp. 825–841.

Thiara, Ravi (2005): Strengthening diversity: responses from BME women experiencing domestic violence in the UK. CAHRV European conference on interpersonal violence, 26–28 September, Paris.

Vest, Jushua R./Catlin, Tengan K./Chen, John J./Brownson, Ross C. (2002): Multistate analysis of factors associated with intimate partner violence. In: American Journal of Preventive Medicine 22, 3, pp. 156–164.

Walby, Sylvia/Allen, Jonathan (2004): Domestic Violence, sexual assault and stalking: findings from the British Crime Survey. Home Office Research Study 276. London: Home Office.

Watson, Dorothy/Parsons, Sara (2005): Domestic abuse of women and men in Ireland: report on the national study of domestic abuse. Dublin: Stationery Office.

Yilmaz, Ali T./Battegay, Raymond (1997): Gewalt in der Partnerschaft bei Immigrantinnen aus der Türkei. In: Der Nervenarzt, 68, 1997, pp. 884–887.

Racism, Violence and Health: The Living Experience of Immigrant Women In An Italian City

Patrizia Romito, Giuditta Creazzo, Daniela Paci and Emanuela Pipitone

Introduction: gendering the 'immigrants, racism and health' question

Migration, especially economic migration, is characterized by the selection of populations that are young, healthy, as well as capable of and motivated to join the workforce. Notwithstanding this 'healthy migrant' effect, after some time in the host country, in most cases immigrant people present a prevalence of health problems higher than natives. Historically, this excess of bad health has been attributed either to genetic causes or to 'cultural differences', such as eating, hygiene or sexual practices. These explanations still persist, despite the lack of scientific evidence and more than a century of research exposing their limits (see Atkin and Chattoo 2006).

More recently, a number of studies have shown that not only social disadvantage, but also discrimination and racism, circumstances all linked to being an immigrant or a 'visible minority', are associated with an increased risk of mental and physical bad health (Krieger 2000; Nazroo 2006). The associations with health problems are observed using self-reported measures of discrimination or objective measures, such as difficulties in obtaining a bank loan (Gee et al. 2002; Harris et al. 2006; Velig et al. 2007). Unfortunately, the scope of most of these studies is limited by their lack of a gender perspective (Llacer et al. 2007). Generally 'sex' is not considered as an important, explicative variable, being instead only statistically treated as an 'effect modifier variable', missing the opportunity of exploring gender differences in the migrants' experiences, or in the associations between risk factors and health. Even when only women are studied, the risk factors considered do not include sexual harassment in the work place, sexual violence or intimate partner violence (Schultz et al. 2002), despite this violence being tragically common in women's lives. This omission is particularly striking, as this violence is likely to be even more frequent among women who are socially vulnerable: immigrant, and especially undocumented migrants, and minority, racialized women (Krieger et al. 2006). While the studies on racism and health tend to assume a gender-neutral approach, neglecting women's specific social position and experiences, the studies focusing exclusively on migrant women's health tend to reduce them only to two traditional feminine personifications: the mother and the prostitute. For instance, a traditional field in public health concerns migrant/minority women's reproductive life and functions, an important yet specific topic (Rash et al. 2007; Wolff et al. 2008; Lyons et al. 2008). More recently, a number of studies have focused on the health effects of being a trafficked woman, another important but hyper-specific issue (Zimmerman et al. 2008).

Interpersonal and institutional racism, discrimination and violence

There are different ways to conceptualize and measure racially motivated discrimination and violence. Most authors distinguish between interpersonal discrimination, which refers to discriminatory interactions between individuals, which usually can be directly perceived, and institutional discrimination, which refers to discriminatory policies or practices embedded in organisational structures, that tends to be more invisible (Karlson and Nazroo 2002). A Canadian document (CRIAV 2002) makes a distinction between overt and covert/subtle/polite racism: the first refers to explicit acts (or omissions), such as calling people names, attacking them physically, or excluding them on the basis of race or ethnicity; the second, to the various ways of letting people know that they are different, or that their only or most salient characteristic is race. In addition, racism may be 'structural', being so deeply embedded in every aspect of society, that most people 'do' it almost unconsciously (CRIAV 2002). Racist discrimination can be found in access to jobs and income, and is usually coupled with gender discrimination[1]. In Italy, among nurses, immigrants from outside the EU are paid 20–40% less than Italians; unfortunately, the data are not analyzed by gender (Bencini, Cerretelli and Di Pasquale 2008).

Other discrimination concerns housing: immigrants and minorities are concentrated in poorer and often segregated geographic areas and in poorer quality and overcrowded accommodation, and have more difficulties in obtaining a bank mortgage to buy a house (Nazroo 2006; Bencini, Cerretelli and Di Pasquale 2008). Still other discriminations can be observed in access

1 For instance, in Canada, in 1995–96, the average annual income for all Canadian men was 31,117 dollars; for 'visible minority men', it was 23,600 dollars; for all Canadian women, 19,200; for aboriginal men, 18,200; for 'visible minority women', 16,600, and for aboriginal women, it was 13,300 dollars (CRIAV 2002).

to health care and to justice. This latter aspect is particularly relevant for the issue of women and violence. In some countries, because of the racism of police forces, criminal justice system and prisons in the host country, immigrant and racialized women appear to be reluctant to call the police in cases of domestic violence out of loyalty to their family and community, not wishing to fuel racist stereotypes (CRIAV 2002; Thiara and Gill 2010; for a different picture, see the Italian data in the Creazzo et al. chapter in this volume).

Thus, interpersonal discrimination and violence are common in the lives of immigrant or minority people. In the UK, according to the Fourth National Survey of Ethnic Minorities, 13% of ethnic minorities reported experiencing racially motivated physical or verbal attacks in the previous 12 months (Karlson and Nazroo 2002). Similar figures were observed for Maori and Asian peoples in New Zealand (Harris et al. 2006). High discrimination in the workplace was observed among UK ethnic minority groups, with 19% of ethnic minorities reporting being refused a job in the previous 12 months, both for perceived religious and ethnic reasons (Modood et al. 1997). In these articles, figures are not presented separately by gender. Most of these studies consider the relationships between racist discrimination, violence and health for 'visible minorities', people who are citizens with, at least in theory, all citizenships rights. But immigrant people must struggle also with other difficulties: restrictive immigrant laws, abrupt changes in laws or policies, bureaucratic delays and harassment. Few studies have considered the effects of being an undocumented migrant on migrant women's health. A study in Geneva (Wolff et al. 2008), on medical care in pregnancy, showed that undocumented migrants have more unintended pregnancies, delay prenatal care, use fewer preventive measures, and are exposed to more partner violence during pregnancy. Authors conclude that not having a legal residence permit leads to a greater vulnerability for pregnant women.

Women' immigration in Trieste and Italian immigration laws

According to official data, in 2005 around 2.5 million immigrants lived in Italy, of which more than half (55.8%) were women. Internationally, Italy ranks 16 among the 20 top destination countries for international migrants (UNDP 2006). However, official statistics only count regular immigrants while many immigrant women and men are in Italy illegally, without the necessary documents. For instance, the Italian Catholic Unions (ACLI) estimate that, in 2008, there were 500,000/600,000 illegal immigrant women working as nannies or house helpers[2] (around the same number was working legally). Available data show that, in the last ten years, the number of immigrants in Italy rose steadily: in the Friuli-Venezia Giulia Region (this study was carried out in its administrative centre, Trieste), from 1991 to 2001, their number has tripled. At the time of the study, 40,985 foreigners[3] (around 3.3% of the Region population) lived in Friuli-Venezia Giulia; 48% of them were women (Caritas 2002). More specifically, according to the files of the Trieste Register office, in 2002, 108,447 Italian women and 4,558 foreign women, mostly from countries of ex-Yugoslavia and Eastern Europe, were living in the city.

Notwithstanding the historical experience of millions of Italians as migrants, Italy seems ill prepared to become an immigration country. Immigration laws have been traditionally restrictive, considering immigrant people only as work-force, and treating them as a security, 'law and order' issue (Scevi 2004). At the time of the study, the law in operation was the 'L.189/ 2002', also called 'Bossi-Fini', from the names of two right-wing male Ministers who had drafted it. According to the estimated needs of the labour market, a fixed number of immigrants were accepted each year. Immigrants could enter Italy only if they already had a regular job, with the employer signing a 'contract of residence for work', an accommodation guarantee and the commitment to pay the return journey of the worker to the country of origin. With the 'residence contract', the immigrant could request a 'residence permit', lasting two years. An immigrant found without the 'residency permit' had to be expelled. The 'Bossi-Fini' was a tough immigration law: the residence status of immigrants was rendered precarious and totally dependent on the employer, with a heightened risk of blackmail and abuse; family reunification was deeply restricted; immediate repatriation of the ones who do not leave Italy after being ordered expulsion; and the crime of not compliance with the order of leaving Italy were also introduced. The process was made even harder by the gap between the law and its application. Due to the inefficiency of the Italian bureaucracy or to the racism of its officials, or both, even when the immigrant worker and her/his employer presented all the necessary documents, there were very long, and anxiety generating, delays: in the summer of 2009, many of the applications regularly presented in 2007 were still unanswered[4]. Sadly, in July 2009, the right-wing Italian government promulgated a new immigration law, which was even more restrictive,

2 '600,000 le badanti irregolari', La Repubblica, July 7, 2009, p.16.
3 Not all the foreigners are classed as 'immigrants'. In this case, 13% of foreigners were the US soldiers and their families, at the Aviano US Army base.
4 'I ritardi: Flussi bloccati e 311,000 domande respinte'. La Repubblica, July 6, 2009, p.9.

within which, among other measures, being an illegal immigrant became a penal crime.

On the other hand, Italian health policies concerning immigrant people have been more respectful of human rights. Between 1995 and 2000, and until now, several laws and measures have been promulgated, asserting that health is a right for every person living in Italy, independently from her/his status. Immigrants, regular or irregular, have the right to medical care, including prevention and rehabilitative measures. Those with a regular residence permit have the same rights to access the National Health System (NHS) as Italian citizens, while those without the permit to stay can be provided with a 'Regional card' by the Health Regional Agencies, which gives access to emergency care and to 'essential' care. As for Italians, all medical care concerning women's reproductive and childrens health, and the prevention of infectious diseases is totally free within the NHS. Health operators are forbidden to inform the authorities of irregular immigrants. In a first draft of the new law, the Italian government tried to cancel the forbiddance, but, in the face of a strong opposition from health professionals' associations, the measure was dropped, and, until 2011, irregular immigrants could still safely access health services.

The study aims and methods

The data presented in this chapter are drawn from a multi-method study on *'Health and health care of immigrant women in Trieste'*[5], a city of 210,000 inhabitants located in North-eastern Italy. The study, carried out between 2003 and 2006, comprised different parts: a secondary statistical analysis of the files of immigrant women's access to reproductive health services; a qualitative study, with interviews with women and 'key informants'; and a quantitative survey, with questionnaires to a sample of the women. In this chapter, we present only the results of the questionnaire survey.

The aims of the study were to analyze the health and health care of immigrant women, in order to facilitate their access to health facilities and to implement specific information and preventive measures. To meet these objectives, the study had to involve also those women who are often excluded both

5 The study was promoted by the Office for Women and Migrants policies, directed by Dr. Daniela Gerin of the Agency for Social and Health Services of Trieste (ASS n.1) and was funded by the Health Department of the Regione Friuli Venezia Giulia. Giuditta Creazzo was the principal investigator; Daniela Paci, the study coordinator; Emanuela Pipitone, the data manager and statistician: Patrizia Romito, the scientific advisor. The working group also included: Donatella Barbina, Iris Tekovich, and Imma Tromba.

from surveys and from health care: women who are undocumented immigrants, illiterate, or do not speak Italian. Constructing the sample and interviewing the women represented the main difficulty of the study, and was possible only with the involvement of twelve female cultural mediators working within the Trieste health services. They come from eleven countries[6], and were trusted by the women of their communities. They collaborated in the different parts of the study, contributing to defining the aims and constructing the interview guide and the questionnaire; translating the questionnaire or checking its translation; contacting the women to be interviewed; and helping the women, when necessary, in filling in the questionnaire.

The quantitative survey: sample, instrument and procedure

Overall, 465 immigrant women participated in the survey. We wanted to involve women living in different situations: legal and illegal/undocumented migrants, whether they spoke Italian or not, and whether or not they used the health service. Moreover, in constructing the sample, we wanted to respect, as far as possible, the estimated proportion of nationalities of immigrant women in the city. Most women were approached by the cultural mediators, among those contacting health services, NGOs, cultural or religious associations; others were recruited by the women themselves via a 'snowball sampling' technique. Mediators explained the study to the women (its aims, anonymity of the questionnaires and confidentiality of the answers), stressing that they were free to participate or not to do so, and that declining to participate was not going to affect in any way their health care. Informed, spoken consent was requested and, when obtained, an appointment for filling in the questionnaire was set; in some cases, and with the women's agreement, a group appointment was set up in a location chosen by the women.

The questionnaire was inspired by national and international literature, and by the content of the interviews carried out in the qualitative part of the study. It comprises 115 questions, including: socio-demographic information; migration history; physical and mental health; reproductive history; experiences of violence and discrimination; knowledge of rights; access to health services and experiences with health professionals; family and social relationships; comments and suggestions. An earlier version of the questionnaire

6 Albania, Romania, Serbia, Croatia, Hungary, Iran, Morocco, Senegal, Kenya, Venezuela, and Colombia.

was tested with a different sample of 50 women, and revised according to their suggestions. The revised version was translated by the Mediators, with the researchers' assistance, into 6 languages: Spanish, Serbian/Croatian, Albanian, Rumanian, French, and English. The questionnaire was intended to be self-administered. The Mediator explained to the women its content, and stayed nearby, available for help. In 43% of the cases, due to women's illiteracy, or bad sight or difficulties in understanding some questions, the mediators administered the questionnaire or helped the women filling in the answers; 73% of women answered the questionnaires in their mother tongue; 23% in Italian; and 4% in another language they knew.

Measures of women's health and experience of discrimination and violence

In the questionnaire, we asked questions about several indicators of physical and mental health: symptoms of common problems, symptoms of panic attacks, depression (measured with the General Health Questionnaire, Goldberg, 1972), medicine consumption. In this chapter, we present only the results concerning one indicator of mental health – that of panic attacks. Women were asked if, in the last year, they had experienced anxiety or panic attacks, described, according to the DSM-IV (1994) as occurrences of intense fear or discomfort, that might include rapid heart beats, feelings of suffocation, nausea, fear of losing control or dying. Answers were: no; yes, one or twice; yes, more often, and were re-coded dichotomously: no and yes.

Different types of indicator of discrimination and violence were used. Firstly, the indicators of institutional/structural discrimination were: having or not having a legal residence permit and, among those who had it, how much time they had to wait to obtain it; the partner having or not a legal residence permit; the fact that the children, or some of them, were living in the woman's home country; being insured, regularly or with a temporary card, or not to the National Health Services; subjective evaluation of income; characteristics of housing. Secondly, a number of questions were designed to produce indicators of interpersonal, ethnically based, harassment/discrimination. The woman was asked if, in the last year, someone did or said something against her as a foreigner, that hurt, offended, humiliated or deeply irritated her. A list of perpetrators was provided, including employers, colleagues, acquaintances, family members, or unknown people. Answers were: no; once; 2/3 times; more often. In the analyses, answers were re-coded dichotomously: no and yes. Women were considered as having suffered from ethnically motivated discrimination if they reported at least one occurrence of discrimination from one perpetrator. In addition, the woman was asked if, in the last year, a health professional did or said something against her as a foreigner that hurt, offended, humiliated or irritated her. Among the women who had contacts with health services, answers were: no; once; 2/3 times; more often; and were recoded dichotomously: no and yes. Thirdly, two questions were put on the topic of interpersonal violence, on psychological violence and on physical/sexual violence. Women were asked if, in the last year, they had experienced psychological violence (defined as being offended, insulted, followed, controlled, impeded to do something or to see someone, having their belongings destroyed). In another question, they were asked if they had experienced physical or sexual violence (being physically attacked or beaten up, or being obliged or pressurized to have sexual contacts against their will). A list of possible perpetrators was provided, including a husband/fiancé or ex husband/fiancé, a family member, an employer, a colleague, acquaintances, and unknown people. Answers were: no; once; 2/3 times; more often. In the analyses, answers were re-coded dichotomously: no and yes. Women were considered as having suffered from violence if they reported at least one occurrence of violence from one perpetrator.

Strategy of analysis

After a description of the demographic and social characteristics of the women interviewed, we calculated the frequency of the different types of discrimination and violence suffered by them, and the bi-variate relationships between discrimination and violence and symptoms of panic attacks in the last year. We then carried out the Cochran-Mantel-Haenszel test to calculate the Odds ratios of experiencing a panic attack in presence of each type of discrimination and violence, controlling for age and ethnicity, as both may have an influence on discrimination/violence and on panic attacks. Migrant groups were categorized as: Europe, Central/South America, Africa and Asia. Preliminary analyses (not presented here) have shown that perceived income was strongly associated with all the health indicators. We, therefore, also calculated the Odds ratios of a panic attack, controlling for age, ethnic group and perceived income.

Demographic, health and social characteristics of the women interviewed

Among the 465 women who answered the questionnaires, 59% born were in Europe (36% in ex-Yugoslavia, 22% in Central-Eastern European countries, and 1% in other countries); 18% were born in Central and South America, 18% in Africa and 5% in Asia. Women's geographical origins correspond to the origins of foreign women in Trieste (although Asian women were slightly underrepresented in the sample). Most women came to Italy independently, to study (10%), work (33%), or financially help their families (25%); 16% migrated with their husband for a better life; 23% followed their husbands who were already in Italy; 9% said they were escaping war or social disorders; and 2% were escaping a violent partner or ex-partner (more than one answer was possible).

The women's ages ranged from 18 to 64 years, with most women being between 18 and 44 years old. Most were married or cohabiting (66%), and had children (68%). Educational levels of the sample varied widely: 18% of the women attended school or University for 15 years or more; 46% for 9–14 years; 28% for 6–8 years; only a minority (7%) was illiterate or with few years of schooling. As regards occupation, 41% had a regular job, 17% were working illegally, 11% were unemployed, 24% did not have paid work and 7% were students or in other situations. Among those who were employed, 87% had a blue collar or service job. Their knowledge of the Italian language varied: 38% said they speak and understand 'well', 30% 'fairly well', 24% knew only a few words, and 8% did not speak or understand at all. This means that the study had a broad coverage of education levels, Italian language proficiency, occupational status and family circumstances. Concerning women's mental health: in the previous month, 14% of them had experienced depression symptoms and 11.5% was taking psychotropic drugs. In the last year, 25.6% had experienced one or more panic attacks

Analysis of the frequency of discrimination and violence

Table 1 presents the frequency of institutional/structural and interpersonal discrimination and violence as reported by the women. At the structural level, 24% of women, and 17% of their partners, had an illegal immigrant status, as they lacked the residence permit; among those women who had the permit, 13.8% had to wait more than 1 year to obtain it. Among those who had children, in 38.3% of cases the children, or some of them, were living away, mostly with other relatives in the country of origin. While most women (89%) had access to the NHS, 11% did not have this possibility, because they were not registered through the Regional card. As for social disadvantage, 38.8% evaluated their income as scarce or not adequate, and 16% were living in temporary accommodation: with friends, in the house where they were working as live-in nannies or house helpers, or in collective accommodation.

At the interpersonal level, sixty-two women (13.3%) had suffered racist harassment in the last year, in most cases (76%) more than once. Perpetrators were mostly unknown people (31%), otherwise employers and colleagues (34%). Among the 321 women who had some contact with health services in the last year, 9% reported occurrences of racist attitudes towards them or discrimination by the health personnel; the corresponding figure in the whole sample was 6%. In addition, 78 women (16.8%) reported occurrences of psychological violence in the last year, in 79% of cases more than once. The most frequent perpetrator was a partner or ex-partner, followed by another family member, then an acquaintance, an employer or a colleague; only in a minority of cases was the person unknown. In the same period, 30 women (6.5%) had experienced acts of physical or sexual violence, occurring, in 61% of cases, more than once. The most frequent perpetrator was a partner or ex partner, followed by an unknown person, and then by a family member. To have an estimate of Intimate Partner Violence (IPV), we considered the sub-sample of 303 women who were married/cohabiting with a partner or who were in the process of leaving him: 10% had suffered psychological violence, and 5% physical or sexual violence by a partner or ex-partner in the past year.

Relationships between institutional discrimination, interpersonal violence and panic attacks

Results of bi-variate analyses show that both structural/institutional discrimination and interpersonal violence negatively affected women's mental health (Table 2A). Not having the residency permit or having had to wait for a long time before obtaining one, living in temporary accommodation, and describing her own income as irregular or inadequate, were all strongly associated with the occurrence of a panic attack. There were no significant associations between the partner not having the residency permit, a child/children living away, the woman's working status, and not being insured at the National Health System and panic (data not shown), hence these variables were not analyzed in the multivariate analyses. At the interpersonal level, having suffered racist harassment or discrimination, including during contacts with the health services, psychological violence, and physical/sexual violence were all strongly associated with panic attacks.

The multivariate analyses confirm most of the bi-variate results. Controlling for age and ethnicity (Table 2B), women without a residence permit or having had to wait for a long time were 2.3 times more likely to have a panic attack, and those with a scarce/inadequate income were 2.8 times more likely to experience panic than women who were not exposed to these factors. Living in a temporary accommodation almost doubled the probability of a panic attack ($p<0.05$). The impact of interpersonal, racially based discrimination on mental health was strong. Women exposed to racist harassment presented an odds ratio of having a panic attack almost three times higher than those who were not exposed. A similar trend was observed for women reporting racist discrimination in health services. The impact of interpersonal violence was even more powerful. Women exposed to psychological violence were approximately seven times more likely to have a panic attack, and those exposed to physical/sexual violence were 5.7 times more likely to experience panic than women who were not exposed.

Introducing income into the models reduced partially the strength of the associations between discrimination or violence and panic attacks (Table 2C). Controlling for age, ethnicity and income, being without a residence permit/having waited for one for a long time, living in temporary accommodation, and reporting racist discrimination in the health services were no longer statistically associated with panic attacks. On the contrary, racist harassment, psychological violence and physical/sexual violence all increased significantly the probability of a panic attack. More particularly, women exposed to psychological violence were just over four times as likely to have a panic attack. Women exposed to physical/sexual violence were more than five times as likely to have a panic attack; the impact of physical/sexual violence on panic attacks was reduced only very slightly by introducing income into the model.

Discussion

The immigrant women interviewed in this Italian city had experienced various types of discrimination and violence, both at the institutional/structural and at the interpersonal level. As women, they suffered psychological, physical and sexual violence, mostly perpetrated by a partner or another family member. As immigrants, they were subjected to several instances of racist harassment and discrimination and to severe institutional/structural violence. Almost a quarter of the women were without a residence permit, a frightening situation to have to endure. Among those who had the permit, many had to wait more than one year to obtain one, a period filled with financial hardship and anxiety. Eleven percent had no national health insurance, unaware that, even if they were living illegally in Italy, they had the right to the Regional health card, without any risk. Thirty-eight percent of those who had children, their offspring had remained in their country of origin. Around 40% had an inadequate income, and 16% lived in poor, often shared, accommodation. While many had a good level of education, 87% of those who were employed had a manual job, often in the service sector. Several qualitative studies have described these experiences and the suffering they may entail (Macioti 2000; Ehrenreich and Hochshield 2004). A full analysis of the links between these various types of violence and discrimination is beyond the scope of this chapter. However, these figures illustrate how the situation of an immigrant, or minority, woman can best be understood through the lens of intersectionality, a key methodological tool allowing us to read the deep connections between various systems of domination – gender, race/ethnicity and social class/poverty – in the lives of many women and their effects on health (Crenshaw 1994).

In the bi-variate analyses, all types of discrimination and violence were significantly associated with having panic attacks. More than one third of the women without the residency permit, living in temporary accommodation, or having a poor income, reported the occurrence of panic attacks, compared with 18–23% of respondents without these institutional discriminations. The impact of interpersonal violence was even stronger: when exposed to racist harassment, also in health services, half of the women had panic attacks, as against 23–28% of those not exposed. Other studies have shown the same trend (Gee et al. 2002; Schultz et al. 2006; Williams, Neighbors and Jackson 2003). In the New Zealand Health Survey (Harris et al. 2006), experiencing any type of racial attack or discrimination by a health professional, in the workplace or when searching for housing, was associated with poor or fair self-rated health, lower physical functioning, poorer mental health, smoking, and cardiovascular disease. Not surprisingly, the impact of violence was even stronger than the impact of discrimination. Among women reporting psychological or physical/sexual violence, respectively 59.2% and 67.8% suffered panic attacks, compared with 18.8%–22.8% among the not exposed women, a trend confirmed by previous studies of this relationship (Campbell 2002; Golding 1999; Romito, Molzan Turan and De Marchi 2005).

In multivariate analyses, the strength of some of these associations was reduced. The association between housing conditions and panic was non-significant when controlling for age and ethnicity (OR 1.88, CI 0.97–3.62), and was slightly lessened adjusting also for income. The associations between the 'residence permit' variable and panic attacks was significant when controlling only for the demographic factors (age and ethnicity; see Table 2B), but become non-significant when adjusting also for income (Table 2C). This suggests that its impact on health lies in the intersection of institutional discrimination – and the additional inequities and anxiety that it generates – and financial difficulties. However, it is possible that with a larger sample, these associations would have been significant.

Interestingly, the associations between the indicators of interpersonal violence and panic were only slightly reduced after adjusting on age, ethnic groups and income (except for racism in health services that becomes not significant). Women exposed to racist harassment were 2.3 times more likely to suffer from panic attacks than those not exposed. Those exposed to psychological violence, mostly by family members and by partners, and to physical/sexual violence, mostly by a partner or ex-partner, had even higher OR (respectively of 4.53 and 5.44) of a panic attack than women not exposed. Notably, the impact of physical/sexual violence was almost unmodified after adjusting also on income.

Having a child or children living in the woman's country of origin was not associated to experiencing panic attacks. This was a common situation for the women in this study, concerning the 38.3% of those who had children, a proportion similar to that found among immigrant domestic workers interviewed in California: 40% of mothers had at least one child 'back home', usually in the care of relatives (Hondagneu-Sotelo and Avila 2005). These authors stress that 'being a transnational mother means more than being the mother to children raised in another country. It means forsaking deeply felt beliefs that biological mothers should raise their own children and replacing this belief with new definitions of motherhood' (p. 312). Other authors have described the suffering of the children, often separated from their mothers for many years (Salazar Parrenas 2004). However, there are different models and different experiences of motherhood. From the qualitative data of the Trieste study, it appears that many women were deeply aware of their crucial role in providing for the whole family and were proud of it, even if this meant being temporarily separated from their children. This could explain why this factor was not associated with worse mental health.

There are multiple theories explaining how racism may affect health. These include differential exposure to determinants of health (e.g. socioeconomic, professional, environmental and behavioural), differential access to health services, and the direct effects of racism such as trauma and stress (Karlsen and Nazroo 2002). Krieger (2003) identified five key pathways:

economic and social deprivation; exposure to environmental hazards; socially-inflicted trauma; targeted marketing of harmful products such as tobacco and alcohol; and poor health care. While these theories are good in grasping the main factors that affect minority people health, they do not fully consider the effects – direct and indirect – of being an undocumented immigrant, a 'risk factor' also for the health of male immigrants. Nor do they consider the risk factors attached to being a woman, such as psychological, physical and sexual violence, mostly inflicted by partners and family members.

Our sample was reasonably heterogeneous and, differently from other published studies, it included also undocumented women immigrants. Also for these reasons, comparing our results to those of other studies is risky, as the methods, the sample composition and the social context vary. We cannot assume that similar results mean that similar facts or experiences have been measured, nor that different figures imply a different reality. Still, and with this precaution in mind, if our results are in the same range of those of others, we can be at least partly reassured on the validity of our data. Among the women interviewed in Trieste, 13% reported racist harassment in the last year, the same percentage reported by ethnic minorities in Great Britain (Karlson and Nazroo 2002) and in New Zealand (Harris et al. 2006). In these studies, figures are not presented separately by gender, although in both cases the authors state that these attacks were more common in young males. In our study, 9% of the women who had contacts with health professionals in the last year (6% in the whole sample) reported being discriminated against within the health care system because of their ethnic origin. This is higher than the 2% of Maori and Pacific peoples and 1.3% of Asians who reported unfair treatment by a health professional because of their ethnicity in New Zealand (Harris et al. 2006). Even if Harris et al. calculated the percentage of discriminated people on the whole sample, women in Trieste reported more occurrences of bad treatment. One explanation could be that minority people in New Zealand were citizens with all the citizenship rights, while the women interviewed in Trieste were immigrants, and in same cases irregular immigrants.

Studies in Europe have shown that immigrant women report more IPV than natives (Condon and Schrottle 2007), also around pregnancy (Saurel-Cubizolles and Lelong 2005; Romito, Molzan Turan, Lucchetta and Scrimin 2007). In the present study, 10% of the interviewed women reported psychological and 5% physical/sexual IPV in the last 12 months: these figures are almost identical to those found in two studies involving Italian women of similar age and using similar questions on IPV (Romito 1998; Romito, Molzan Turan and De Marchi 2005). It is possible that immigrant women in this study had underreported violence, especially when they filled in the questionnaire with the mediator's help. However, as regards their national and cultural origins, they were a highly heterogeneous group, sharing only the status of immigrant women: there is no reason to expect a homogenous experience concerning IPV. With regard to mental health, the rate of depression reported by migrant women in Trieste (15%) was the same as that found in two other studies, involving Italian women in the same age range, and using the same instrument (the General Health Questionnaire) (Romito 1998; Romito, Molzan Turan and De Marchi 2005).

The main limit of this study lies in the fact that ours is a convenience sample. However, a representative sample of immigrant women in Trieste, including also illegal immigrant was – and is – impossible to achieve. Moreover, the sample was rather small, precluding the possibility of doing more complex analyses. Strengths of the study, however, lie in the inclusion of women who were illegal, illiterate and not speaking Italian, and in its gender perspective, allowing us to describe the living experiences of the respondents as immigrants and as women. In addition, this study is the first in Italy, and one of the few internationally, to show that racism and discrimination are bad for women's psychological health. Further studies, with larger samples, will make it possible to analyse more thoroughly the intersections of the different systems of gender, class and ethnicity, and their impact on women's health. We feel that such an approach will be useful also in order to gain a better understanding of the experiences and health of male immigrants.

After this study was completed, a new, harsher, immigration law was passed in Italy, which considers being an irregular migrant as a penal crime, making the life of migrant people even more difficult. The right-wing government, and especially one political party, the Lega, support anti-immigrant policies also at the local level, and foster a violent racist ideology (Volpato, Durante, Gabbiadini, Andrighetto and Mari 2010). Unfortunately, most Italian media seem to follow this stream (Morcellini 2009). International surveys report that contemporary Italy ranks high among EU countries for hostility and racism against immigrants (EU-MIDIS 2009; Horowitz 2010). In 2009, the day before the new Italian immigration law come into force, a young Moroccan women, Fatima Aitcardi, killed herself. According to her family, she was terrified and depressed because she had not been able to obtain a residence permit[7]. This tragedy reminds us that the health impact of racism is not only a scientific topic nor a theoretical human right issue: for many women and men it is truly a question of life or death, their life or death.

7 La Repubblica, August 7, 2009.

Acknowledgements

We wish to record our thanks to the Cultural Mediators who collaborated in the study and to the women who participated in it.

Table 1: Discrimination and violence experienced by the women

At the institutional/structural level		(N)	%
Has a residence permit			
Yes, waited 1 year or less		(280)	62,2
Yes, waited more than 1 year		(62)	13,8
	No	(108)	24,0
Partner has a residence permit*			
	Yes	(209)	83,0
	No	(42)	17,0
Children living abroad**			
	No	(190)	61,7
	Yes	(118)	38,3
Insured at the NHS			
Regularly insured		(325)	72,3
With a Regional card		(75)	16,7
Not insured		(49)	11,0
Income			
Good/adequate		(279)	61,2
Poor/not inadequate		(175)	38,8
Housing			
Owned accommodation		(107)	23,3
Rented accommodation		(278)	60,7
Temporary accommodation		(73)	16,0
At the interpersonal level, in the last 12 months		(N)	%
Racist harassment			
	No	(403)	86,7
	Yes	(62)	13,3
Racist discrimination in Health			
Services***	No	(292)	91,0
	Yes	(29)	9,0
Psychological violence			
	No	(387)	83,2
	Yes	(78)	16,8
Physical/sexual violence			
	No	(435)	93,5
	Yes	(30)	6,5

* Among those who have a non-Italian partner
** Among those who have children
*** Among those who had contacts with the health services

Table 2: Discrimination and violence at the institutional and interpersonal level and symptoms of panic attacks in the last year

	A) % of women with panic attacks		B) Odds Ratios** (95% CI) of panic attacks adjusted for age and ethnicity		C) Odds Ratios (95% CI)** of panic attacks adjusted for age, ethnicity, income	
At the institutional level	%	(n)	OR	(95% CI)	OR	(95% CI)
Residency permit						
– Yes, no waiting*	19.3	(52)	1		1	
– Long wait, no permit	37.1	(59)	2.32	(1.46–3.67)	1.57	(0.94–2.63)
	p < 0.001		p < 0.05		ns	
Housing						
– Owned or rented*	23.1	(86)	1		1	
– Temporary accommodation	37.3	(28)	1.88	(0.97–3.62)	1.86	(0.91–3.77)
	p < 0.05		p < 0.05		ns	
Income						
– Good/adequate*	18.0	(49)	1		/	/
– Scarce/not adequate	37.3	(63)	2.78	(1.70–4.54)	/	/
	p < 0.001		p < 0.001			
At the interpersonal level, in the last 12 months						
Racist harassment						
No*	22.6	(91)	1		1	
Yes	50.0	(25)	2.99	(1.53–5.82)	2.32	(1.16–4.66)
	p < 0.001			p < 0.05		p < 0.05
Racist discrimination in health services°						
No*	28.3	(81)	1		1	
Yes	50.0	(14)	2.63	(1.10–6.27)	2.21	(0.92–5.31)
	p < 0.05			p < 0.05		ns
Psychological violence						
No*	18.8	(71)	1		1	
Yes	59.2	(45)	6.95	(2.62–18.40)	4.53	(1.89–10.82)
	p < 0.001			p < 0.001		p < 0.001
Physical/sexual violence						
No*	22.8	(97)	1		1	
Yes	67.8	(19)	5.72	(3.20–10.21)	5.44	(2.61–10.17)
	p < 0.001		p < 0.001		p < 0.001	

* Reference category. ° Among women who had attended health services.
** logit estimates (Woolf, 1955; Haldane, 1955).

References

Atkin, Karl/Chattoo, Sangeeta (2006): Approaches to conducting qualitative research in ethnically diverse populations. In: Nazroo, James (ed.): Health and social research in multiethnic societies. London: Routledge, pp. 95–115.

Bencini, Camilla/Cerretelli, Sara/Di Pasquale Laura (2008): ENAR Shadow Report 2008: Racism in Italy. Cooperazione per lo Sviluppo dei Paesi Emergenti (COSPE). http://www.enar-eu.org/Page.asp?docid=15825&langue=EN

Campbell, Jaqueline (2002): Health consequences of intimate partner violence. In: Lancet, 359, pp. 1331–1336.

Caritas (2002): Rapporto sull'esclusione 2002. Diocesi di Trieste, Trieste, Unpublished.

Condon, Stéphanie/Schrottle, Monica (2007): Ethnicité et violences: Regards croisés entre l'Allemagne et la France. In: Condon, Stéphanie/Jaspard, Maryse (eds.): Nommer et compter les violences envers les femmes en Europe. Paris: IDUP, pp. 147–156.

Crenshaw, Kimberlé W. (1994): Mapping the margins: intersectionality, identity politics, and violence against women of color. In: Fineman Albertson, Martha/Mykitiuk, Roxanne (eds.): The public nature of private violence. New York: Routledge, pp. 93–118.

CRIAV (Canadian Research Institute for the Advancement of Women) (2002): Factsheet. Women's Experience of racism: How race and gender interact. htpp://www.criaw-icref.ca/factsheet/race%20and%20Gender/race, May 28, 2009.

DSM-IV. (1994): Diagnostic and statistical manual of mental disorders. Fourth revision. American Psychiatric Association.

Ehrenreich, Barbara/Hochschild, Arlie R. (eds.) (2003): Global Women. Nannies, Maids and Sex Workers in the New Economy. New York: Henry Holt & C.

EU-MIDIS. European Union Agency for Fundamental Rights (2009): European Union Minorities and Discrimination Survey. http://www.fra.europa.eu/fraWebsite/eu-midis/index_en.htm

Gee, Gilbert et al. (2002): A multilevel analysis of the relationship between institutional and individual racial discrimination and health status. In: American Journal of Public Health, 92(4), pp. 615–623.

Goldberg, David (1972): The detection of psychiatric illness by questionnaire: A technique for the identification and assessment of non-psychotic psychiatric illness. Oxford, England: Oxford University Press.

Golding, Jean (1999): Intimate partner violence as a risk factor for mental disorders: a meta-analysis. In:;Journal of Family Violence, 14 (2), pp. 99–132.

Haldane, J.B.S. (1955): The estimation and significance of the logarithm of a ratio of frequencies. In: Annals of Human Genetics, 20, pp. 309–311.

Harris, Ricci/Tobias, Martin/Jeffreys, Mona/Waldegrave, Kiri/Karlsen, Saffron/Nazroo, James (2006): Racism and health: The relationship between experience of racial discrimination and health in New Zealand. In: Social Science & Medicine 63, pp. 1428–1441.

Hondagneu-Sotelo, Pierrette/Avila, Ernestine (2005): 'I'am here, but I'm there'. The meanings of Latina Transantional Motherhood. In: Baca Zinn, Maxine/Hondagneu-Sotelo, Pierrette/Messner, Michael (eds.): Gender through the Prism of Difference. Oxford: Oxford University Press, pp. 308–322.

Horowitz, Juliana Menasce (2010): Widespread Anti-Immigrant Sentiment in Italy. PewResearchCenter Publications. http://pewresearch.org/pubs/1461/italy-widespread-anti-immigrant-sentiment

Karlsen, Saffron/Nazroo, James (2002): Relation between racial discrimination, social class, and health among ethnic minority group. In: American Journal of Public Health, 92(4), pp. 624–631.

Krieger, Nancy (2000): Discrimination and health. In: Berkman, L./Kawachi, I. (eds.): Social epidemiology. New York: Oxford University Press, pp. 36–75.

Krieger, Nancy (2003): Does racism harm health? Did child abuse exist before 1962? On explicit questions critical science and current controversies: An ecosocial perspective. In: American Journal of Public Health, 93(2), pp. 194–199.

Krieger, Nancy/Waterman, Pamela D./Hartman, Cathy/Bates, Lisa M./Stoddard, Anne M./Quinn, Margaret M./Sorensen, Gloria/Barbeau, Elizabeth M. (2006): Social hazards on the job: workplace abuse, sexual harassment, and racial discrimination. A study of black, latino, and white low-income women and men workers in the United States. In: International Journal of Health Services, 36, pp. 51–85.

Llacer, Alicia/Zunzunegui, Maria V./del Amo, Julia/Mazarrasa, Lucia/Bolumar, Francisco (2007): The contribution of a gender perspective to the understanding of migrant's health. In: Journal of Epidemiology and Community Health, 61(supp.II), pp. ii4–ii10.

Lyons, Suzi/O'Keeffe, Frances/Clarke, Anna/Staines, Anthony (2008): Cultural diversity in the Dublin maternity services: the experiences of maternity service providers when caring for ethnic minority women. In: Ethnicity & Health, 13(3), pp. 261–276.

Macioti, Maria (2000): La solitudine e il coraggio. Milano: Guerini.

Modood, T./Berthoud, R./Lakey, J./Nazroo, J./Smith, P./Virdee, S. et al. (1997): Ethnic minorities in Britain: Diversity and disadvantage. London: Policy Studies Institute.

Morcellini, Mario (ed.) (2009): Ricerca nazionale su immigrazione e asilo nei media italiani. Facoltà di Scienze della camunicazione, Università la Sapienza, Roma.;www.comunicazione.uniroma1.it.cattivenotizie.wordpress.com

Nazroo, James (ed.) (2006): Health and social research in multiethnic societies. London and New York: Routledge, Taylor & Francis Group.

Rash Vibeke/Gammeltoft, Tine/Kudsen, Lisbeth/Tobiassen, Charlotte/Ginzel, Annelie/Kempf, Lillan (2007): Induced abortion in Denmark: effects of socio-economic situation and country birth. In: European Journal of Public Health. http://eurpub.oxfordjournals.org. (Accessed June 2008)

Romito, P./Molzan Turan, J./Lucchetta, C./Scrimin, F. (2007): Violences envers les femmes autour d'une naissance: Une étude dans une ville italienne, In: Condon, S./Jaspard, M. (eds.): Nommer et compter les violences envers les femmes en Europe. Actes du colloque scientifique de La Sorbonne – 26 septembre 2005, dir Cahrv-Idup-Ined, ed. La Sorbonne, Paris 2007.

Romito, Patrizia (1998): Benessere psicologico delle donne e servizi sul territorio: Un'indagine a Muggia. Research report, unpublished. Trieste, 1998.

Romito, Patrizia/Molzan Turan, Janet/De Marchi, Margherita (2005): The impact of current and past violence on women's mental health. In: Social Science & Medicine, 60, pp. 1717–1727.

Salazar, Parrenas Rachel (2004): The care crisis in the Philippines: Children and transational families in the New Global Economy. In: Ehrenreich, Barbara/Hochschild, Arlie R.: Global Women. Nannies, Maids and Sex Workers in the New Economy. New York: Metropolitan Books, pp. 39–54.

Saurel-Cubizolles, Marie Josèphe/Lelong, Nathalie (2005): Violences familiales pendant la grossesse. In: J Gynecol Obstet Biol Reprod. 34 (Suppl.1), pp. 2S47–2S53.

Scevi, Paola (2004): La condizione giuridica dello straniero in Italia dopo la nuova legge sull'immigrazione. In: Studi Emigrazione/Migration Studies XXXIX[148], pp. 907–920.

Schulz, Amy et al. (2006): Discrimination, symptoms of depression, and self-rated health among African American Women in Detroit: Results from a longitudinal analysis. In: American Journal of Public Health, 96(7), pp. 1265–1270.

Thiara, Ravi/Gill, Aisha (eds.) (2010): Violence against women in South Asian communities. London: Jessica Kingsley Pub.

UNDP (United Nations Development Programme) (2006): Report on Human Development. http://undp.org/hdr2006/report.cfm

Velig, Wim et al. (2007): Discrimination and the incidence of psychotic disorders among ethnic minorities in The Netherlands. In: International Journal of Epidemiology, 36(4), pp. 761–768.

Volpato, Chiara/Durante, Federica/Gabbiadini, Alessandro/Andrighetto, Luca/Mari, Silvia (2010): Picturing the other: targets of delegitimization across time. In: International Journal of Conflicts and Violence, 4 (2), pp. 269–287.

WHO (2005): WHO Multi-country Study on Women's Health and Domestic Violence. Geneva.

Williams, David/Neighborsm, Harold/Jackson, James (2003): Racial/Ethnic discrimination and health: Findings from community studies. In: American Journal of Public Health, 93(2), pp. 200–208.

Wolff, Hans et al. (2008): Undocumented migrants lack of access to pregnancy care and prevention. In: BMC Public Health.

Woolf, B. (1955): On estimating the relationship between blood group and disease. In: *An*nals of Human Genetics, 19, pp. 251–253.

Zimmerman, Cathy/Hossain, Mazeda/Yun, Katherine/Gajdadziev, Vasil/Guzun, Natalia/Tchomarova, Maria/Ciarrocchi, Rosa Angela/Johansson, Anna/Kefurtova, Anna/Scodanibbio, Stefania/Nenette Motus, Maria/Roche, Brenda/Morison, Linda/Watts, Charlotte (2008): The Health of Trafficked Women: A Survey of Women Entering Posttrafficking Services in Europe. In: American Journal of Public Health, 98(1), pp. 55–59.

'Hard, Feisty Women'-'Coping on Your Own': African-Caribbean Women and Domestic Violence

Ravi K. Thiara

Introduction

Intersectionality as a conceptual tool, which gives primacy to women's multiple social dis/location and subjectivities that result from intersecting forms of oppression, has increasingly begun to be used by researchers to examine violence against women (VAW). However, while there has been a great deal of debate since the late 1980s about the concept of intersectionality and its utility in explaining 'difference' between women, it is still a relatively underdeveloped area within much VAW theory and practice. Indeed, research on issues for minority ethnic women affected by intimate violence and abuse has been fairly uneven. In the UK, the growing body of research on minority ethnic women and VAW has generally tended to focus on particular groups, mainly South Asian women, and on particular issues, mainly domestic violence and culturally specific forms of harm, such as forced marriage, honour based violence and female genital mutilation (Batsleer et al. 2002; Thiara and Gill 2010). It has also highlighted specific pressures (community, family and individual) and social barriers (racism and discrimination) that shape responses to women in such situations. Despite a long history of settlement in the UK, the experiences of African-Caribbean (AC)[1] women affected by domestic violence have largely been absent from or marginal within the debates about VAW and minority ethnic women. It is the aim of this chapter, by

1 African-Caribbean women here includes those women who have 'origins' in the islands of the Caribbean as well as subsequent generations of women classified as 'Mixed Black and White', that is women who may have one parent who is 'Black Caribbean' and the other who is 'White'. Many African-Caribbean women were recruited into industry, catering and public services in the post-war boom, with this migration flow perpetuated by family networks. Women have historically worked long hours in the lowest echelons of the labour market (Byron and Condon 2008). In the UK, the numbers of Caribbean born women recorded as living in the UK by the 2001 census were 137,637; 565,876 people classified themselves in the category 'Black Caribbean', these being a combination of Caribbean born and descendants of the migrant generation.

drawing on research conducted by the author in the UK[2], to address this omission and present some key issues highlighted about professional responses to AC women as well as women's experiences of violence in their lives[3]. In particular, it argues that the essentialist racialised construction of AC women as 'strong' and as lacking 'cultural needs' has served to reinforce their inequality and discrimination and to ultimately leave them unprotected from violence and abuse.

Limited knowledge

Clearly, an important aspect of examining AC women's experiences of intimate violence through the intersectional lens is to recognize the added forms of 'violence' and control that racialised women are subjected to by state agencies, including the police and social services (Mama 1989; Razack 1998; Thiara and Gill 2010). There is also, of course, the symbolic violence, of absence and marginality, within much feminist and race/ethnic studies discourse as well as feminist activism. The particularity of AC women's experiences of violence has also tended to be obscured by assertions of the universality of the VAW experience for women, dubbed the construction of a 'collective victimhood' by some (Thiara 2008; Thiara and Gill 2010). While it is indisputable that there are key commonalities in the experiences and impact of intimate abuse on all women, such assertions have, in fact, failed to provide any specific focus on the nature and impact of violence on AC women.

While research remains extremely limited, the first ever study of domestic violence in black communities – African, African-Caribbean and Asian – highlighted the 'brutalisation' of women at the hands of men and statutory organizations, pointing to women's experience of racism shared with black men but the additional violence of men in women's personal lives (Mama 1989; see also Batsleer et al. 2002; Thiara 2006; Thiara and Turner 1998). In looking at the prevailing political conditions which force black women to tolerate high levels of abuse in their personal lives, Mama argued that:

2 The qualitative research was conducted in two localities with a high percentage of African-Caribbean groups in the West Midlands, UK with the aim of exploring women's experiences, professional responses and improving services. A total of 26 professional interviews and 22 interviews with women were analysed for this chapter. The range of professionals interviewed included domestic violence support workers, community workers, family support workers, police officers and health professionals. Around a third of those interviewed were AC professionals. Women were aged between 21–54 and had separated from abusive men at the time of interview.

3 All of the AC women interviewed had been in relationships with AC men and it is these experiences they spoke about in the interviews.

> In the case of black women, male violence in the home is compounded by general societal racism and state repression, to create a situation of multiple oppression and further punishment for those bravely struggling to establish lives for themselves and their children, away from violent men (Mama 1989: xiii).

In the U.S., Richie, in critiquing notions of 'universal risk', has also argued that VAW of 'color' is embedded in issues of structural racism and poverty and made calls for a more complex and contextualized analysis of gender violence which takes account of both historical and contemporary social processes that differentially affect black women (2005: 54). She argues that social disenfranchisement frequently combines with gender inequality to 'lure' black women into seeking respect and 'success' in a socially constructed 'ideal' nuclear family, only to be subjected to men's violence. Moreover, while explanations of this are highly contested, US research shows that both lethal and severe forms of domestic violence are disproportionately high in African-American communities This is seen, by some, to be the result of socio-economic factors and racialised inequalities within African-American communities – such as poverty related structural conditions, racial and economic isolation, chronic unemployment, social disorganization, lack of involvement in social networks, population and housing density, and family disruption – rather than 'race' (Hampton, Carrillo and Kim 2005: 127).

Following from Mama's earlier research, in relation to VAW in the UK, research on AC women has revealed that they continue to under-utilise mainstream and statutory services, partly for fear of racism and insensitive responses. The limited use of domestic violence services also results from the continuing lack of information about services, negative perceptions about their appropriateness for AC women, and concerns about sharing facilities such as bathrooms and kitchens, which underpin women's concerns about hygiene and privacy (Thiara 2006). When seeking help, AC women are more likely to self-refer and less likely to want a refuge space though stigma and shame particularly prevent older AC women from seeking help for domestic violence (Rai and Thiara 1997; Thiara and Turner 1998). In particular, older women rarely report abuse to the police (Cook et al. 2003). Indeed, the small size and close-knit nature of many AC communities can also influence women's choices in situations of domestic violence. The role of family and friends is also significant as they are likely to be a major source of support for AC women and children, who emphasize resolving their own problems (Thiara 2006).

Responses to AC women – construction shapes protection options

The ways in which AC women, and indeed their communities, are constructed shapes the responses they receive from professionals and agencies when seeking to protect themselves and their children from men's violence. Two factors have been particularly potent in shaping professional responses. First, the normalization of violence, as part of the wider criminalization of black groups, in black communities acts as a barrier to undermine women's attempts to ensure protection against male violence. This normalization of violence appears to lead to a greater tolerance of VAW by agencies and professionals and shapes their responses to women, which are frequently marked by a reluctance to interfere. As a result of inadequate professional responses, AC women have often been left to 'wage a hidden and individualized struggle' against intimate violence (Mama 1989: xvi). Second, the notion of the strong black woman who is 'hard' and 'feisty' has often left women to negotiate services and separation from men without any support being provided. Indeed, the form of the black family has been under research and public scrutiny for decades with attention focused on female headed families and male absence (Reynolds 1997: 97)[4]. This has resulted, according to Reynolds, in two oppositional discourses, that of the lazy, irresponsible and unreliable black man, on the one hand, and of the strong, single and independent 'superwoman' (1997: 97), on the other. While critiqued by many, the construction of the black 'superwoman' is a fiction which has been made popular by the media and supported by academic research on AC's women's role in the labour force, and has significantly affected professional and academic discourse on AC women role and family life. Given its positive connotations, the importance of the image of the strong black woman to AC women's subjectivity has also created contradictions for many women, as discussed in the second part of the chapter.

Although rooted in essentialist and biological explanations, the 'superwoman' stereotype/construction – suggesting that there is something in black women's genetic makeup that predisposes them to be naturally resilient and able to survive and succeed against adversity (Reynolds 1997: 98) – affects the way in which professional responses to AC women are made in the context of VAW. It is often assumed by professionals that AC women are strong, 'give as good as they get' and can thus 'cope' with men's violence, as elaborated further below.

4 This discourse was already constructed in the Caribbean, see Christine Barrow, cited in Byron and Condon (2008) pp.170–174.

Failure to provide protection

> It's like if I go to the police they're going to come in and they're going to label me, he's this, she's that and I bet they've done drugs and that. And all the stereotypes and all the historical experiences connecting black people with any outside agency immediately come into play in somebody's head so hence they don't contact them. Because they just think rather than you judge me I'll go to a friend because I know they won't judge me. Whereas they think a police officer will be looking for cannabis and not looking at the fact that I've just been beaten up. (AC professional)

Research has shown that it can take black women much longer to get their needs met by statutory agencies (Mama 1989). This is particularly the case where women are attempting to ensure protection without any support, a situation which is evidently common for AC women who are frequently left to negotiate access to services on their own. For instance, when women are left to navigate the legal process alone, taking legal action can be experienced as an unfamiliar, unsupportive and extremely difficult process – *'you're in a zone that you don't know about, its unfamiliar territory...and what's thrown at you, its quite embarrassing and frightening especially when you're a private person but its something that you have to do'*. While the lack of knowledge and support through legal processes is an issue for many women, this takes on a greater significance for AC women for whom the decision to involve criminal justice agencies, widely perceived to be racist, in 'punishing' black men is an extremely difficult one.

Police responses

> I was at my mum's one night, I was at my nan's the next night, my friends the next night. I was sitting outside my friend's house thinking where the hell am I going to go tonight? I phone the police and say I've seen him you haven't made an arrest yet. I was crying and everything and the policeman turned round to me and says *'...I don't think you're as vulnerable as you think you are'*. (AC woman)

> The first time it happened I rang the police they said to me it's not enough for us to do anything. And he done it again, I phoned them up and they said all they can do is give me another log number...This third time I rang them again, they came out and I didn't hear nothing from them for about two months so I phoned to see what was happening and a few days later somebody rang me back to say we want another statement off you. After that he phoned me to say [partner] been charged with assault and your court date is such and such a date. When I went to the court

> it was bank holiday. The court was locked. After that I rang him I could not get through to him for about a month…eventually when I went to court it was all messy. First of all the statement they gave me wasn't the statement that I'd done, on a computer like they'd typed it over and taken out what they wanted to take out and put in what they want to put in. And my solicitor went round the court trying to chase a hand written one which was more appropriate though bits were still missing… (AC woman)

Police responses to AC women have been identified as particularly problematic and rather than being protective of women have been widely experienced by them as punitive. At best, they are marked by police inaction and, at worst, they construct AC women as 'undeserving victims' as the above words of a woman illustrate. Both serve to compromise the protection of women as violence against AC women is seen as 'less serious' or they are seen to be 'less affected by it'. This acts as an example of how racism and sexism combine to undermine the safety of women and result in differential impacts on AC women.

Professionals who were interviewed considered police responses to AC women as greatly concerning, stating that they 'are not dealt with properly and their situation not taken seriously resulting in a lack of protection for women and women losing faith in the system'. It was further commented that the unequal treatment of AC women 'is so obvious it is unbelievable'. Although the reluctance of AC women to use external services has been widely noted, women experienced negative response from many statutory agencies when they did attempt to use them. This was especially so with the police who, even when contacted by women for help, tended to respond on the basis of stereotypical assumptions and in ways which left women feeling let down. Consequently, the fear of racism and judgement prevented many AC women from seeking subsequent help.

Women tended to use the police at a point of crisis and had clear expectations about the action they wanted taken – *'I wanted him arrested, removed and kept in but they took a statement and let him go'*. However, those women who had contacted the police as their first and only port of call related very negative experiences. Officers were frequently *'very casual and unsympathetic'*, failing to contact women for days and weeks. On telephoning the police after her violent partner turned up at her workplace, a woman was told *'can't you get your family?'* The police sometimes took four to six hours to attend an incident after a report had been made and sometimes women were not contacted by officers for weeks following reports. A statement had not been taken for two weeks after a report of a serious incident. Additionally, women were not allocated an officer and had to constantly chase things to get information. They were not referred to other support services or given such information, and not asked by officers if they were safe or had concerns about their safety. Given that women's fears about their safety increased after they contacted the police, the ineffective response from the police made them more vulnerable and hence created greater danger – *'every day I was waking up thinking have they done it yet and because I didn't know if they would keep him in or he'd be out on bail I was thinking he'd get me again'*.

Although making the decision to involve the police (and the criminal justice system) had been a difficult one for many women, especially those concerned about 'betraying' black men and the repercussions of this for them and their children, the police attitude resulted in women dropping charges. Many stated they had not been heard and lost faith and could *'see why women don't go through with it'*. This creates a contradiction for AC women who, recognizing the historical surveillance of their communities and the disproportionate arrests/sanctions against black people, are less willing to use the criminal justice system (CJS) as an initial way for protecting themselves. Fear of being disloyal and not wanting to get their partners into trouble with a CJS that already discriminates against black people was a strong factor shaping women's reluctance to go to the police and *'doing things themselves to protect themselves rather than get him into trouble'*. Thus, AC women carry the responsibility for not colluding with a racist state to incarcerate/criminalize black men, despite men's violence towards them. If they do so, it is often a last resort. To be faced by racist and inadequate responses from the police, then, leave women unprotected from intimate violence. In any case, the over-reliance on the CJS as a primary response to domestic violence and to ensuring women's safety has to be reconsidered for black women as it creates concern for such women about state power or 'authorities' encroaching into personal lives (Richie 2005: 50). Indeed, only women with very severe cases tend to pursue action through the CJS and generally regarded the system as *'white, racist and middle class'*.

Greater punitive approaches also by welfare agencies, such as Social Services, to black families have been highlighted by other research (Mama 1989; Quereshi et al. 2000). In relation to Social Services, none of the women in Mama's study who had contact with them reported this as a positive experience, describing their encounters and interventions as more coercive, punitive, and threatening rather than supportive (1989: 96). Housing agencies were also reported to 'pass the buck', and to be insensitive and hostile in their responses, where black women not only had to wait a long time but were frequently offered inferior housing in undesirable areas – *'they always seem to give you the nasty houses'*. This is supported by support services assisting black women who frequently lament the response of housing, not only offering sub standard housing to vulnerable women and children but also in racist areas which makes racist victimization a high probability. This makes the finding that housing is frequently the main reason for women staying in abusive relationships even more significant for AC women. Moreover, women's reluctance to involve the police, or police inaction, can disadvantage their attempts to get housing if they require evidence of violence.

Assumption about 'lack of cultural needs'

> I think there's assumptions made and particularly about black women that the cultural differences aren't there so don't need to be taken on board. With the Asian community we understand that if somebody needs to come into the hostel and if they have religious beliefs and we're not providing for that that's going to be a barrier. I don't think black women are understood in the same way. (Professional interview)

The lack of insight and commitment to AC women's issues on the part of services and professionals, resulting from the assumption that they can cope or that their needs can be responded to through more general responses, was considered to be widespread – *'they don't understand their particular needs and their culture...I remember the word dysfunctional families being used a short while ago'*. The focus on cultural differences and diversity at the expense of racism and equality by service providers particularly tends to disadvantage AC women who are considered not to have 'cultural needs'. This is in contrast, for instance, to South Asian women who are viewed to be dominated by their cultures. This leads to a disregard by service providers of their particular requirements and cultural contexts and results in AC women viewing support services as being inappropriate and something to only be accessed as a last resort. Part of the reason for AC women's cultural needs being overlooked is because they are not as obvious as those of South Asian women, as the following shows:

> Not being able to do their own little bit of cooking... because on a Sunday it's such a traditional thing that you have like a punch that's made. But it's made with alcohol. And we had to say well you can't do that because it's a dry project and you can't... it's their tradition and in every black home if you go on a Sunday that's what they've got. They've got rice and peas and your punch. *And it was difficult for them not to do that.*

Part of the reason for this is the crude reduction of 'cultural needs' to language barriers by service providers and thus the assumption that AC women who speak English have no any specific needs. This focus on language and to some extent religious differences often obscures AC women's requirements, which can frequently be viewed by professionals as *'a weird habit'*.

> For a lot of black women that I come across hygiene is a big big issue. There's a different way of doing things from washing clothes to washing dishes to cooking…hygiene has always been something that women come to the office and say I can't cope because of the kitchen, because of the bathroom. (Professional interview)

Moreover, differing ways of expressing and dealing with issues often got misinterpreted or stereotyped by workers without the insight into AC women's 'norms':

> If they said something or did something or made a gesture we wouldn't take it to heart because we know that. That's just because of the moment, the heat of the thing, whereas it can be quite intimidating…If you're speaking to a white worker and you raise your voice…aggressive. She's going to want you to back out of the office and come back when you've calmed down. But it might not have meant that she wanted calming down. That's just how she is. But if you've not got an understanding of that then it becomes difficult. (AC professional)

Added to this is the importance placed on the 'unspoken' (gesturing, hissing etc.) as a form of communication for AC people, something again that gets misinterpreted by professionals rather than being seen as a form of cultural expression:

> You can go in a room and there are grunts and some moans and some body language that another person from a similar background will understand and somebody else quite easily misinterpret. (AC professional)

Women's responses to their situations – 'strong black woman' protecting her 'race'

> What needs to be broken down within the black community is this sense that black women are seen to be strong women and they're expected to be strong women…and there must be a greater sense of failure to admit that you need to go into a refuge or get help…that somehow they have failed because they should be able to deal with these problems on their own. (AC professional)

Clearly, VAW challenges the stereotype of the 'strong' or 'castrating' black woman (Mama 1989: 88). However, the construction of the strong black woman coupled with negative responses from agencies when accessed by AC women, shapes women's reactions to their situations. This coincides with wider pressures on women to minimize the surveillance of men in black communities, and acts in accordance with men's pressure on women not to disclose their violence and maintain the secrecy of abuse for the sake of the 'race'. All of this serves to constrict women's options and forces them to deal with their situations on their own, further reinforcing the stereotype of the strong black woman whilst normalizing the absence of black men.

As noted earlier, the construction of the strong black woman is central to AC woman's identity and subjectivity and viewed to have great potency, underlined as it is by powerful historical legacies and complex psychological processes. Although the ways in which this plays out in practice are varied, contradictory, and contested, two aspects are examined here. Firstly, as already noted, the myth of the strong black woman results in pressure for AC women to protect their 'race' by not exposing men and their violence to outside agencies and to avoid reinforcing stereotypes. Secondly, it forces women into dealing with intimate violence by themselves or through their networks to show men that they will not be 'ground down' and beaten.

Protecting the 'race'

Just as some South Asian men are asserted to invoke 'tradition', religion or 'culture' to justify and rationalize VAW, some AC men were reported to use 'race' and the history of racism to do so. This places pressure on women to tolerate men's violence, which is explained as resulting from black men's oppression and draws on reductionist accounts of struggle which *'attribute existing black family structures and familial/gender relations to slavery [and] inadvertently portray black people as objects rather than subjects of their cultural development'* (Reynolds 1997: 100). Consequently, VAW remains a 'buried phenomenon' and leads to a 'collusive silence' which protects the abuser and prevents women from accessing help (Mama 1989: 84). Thus, high levels of violence to women are tolerated by their communities and by statutory agencies. In the US, West speaks of a self imposed rule of silence in the name of solidarity within black communities as *'to speak out on violence in families of color too often invited excessive state surveillance and the stigma of community betrayal, not safety'* (West 2005: 157). This is clearly of significance to AC women in the UK as a 'gag order' imposed by women to protect themselves from stereotypes and oppressive social policies equates to community and male pressure to suppress information about domestic violence and leads to women not disclosing their abuse. Despite receiving greater attention, domestic violence still remains something that is generally not spoken about within AC communities as women *'try to keep things secret'* often because of the stigma attached to disclosing abuse.

The ways in which black people are treated in society and the institutional racism they are subjected to is a common thread in woman's narratives. Since *'black people get stereotyped a lot'*, this made women reluctant to put themselves in situations where this could happen to them – *'when people know about it they stereotype you as coming from a broken family'*. Not wanting to reinforce stereotypes of black families and black men also led to the view that *'as black people they had dealt with it in their own way'*. Certainly the emphasis by women on independence and sorting things out in their own way is easy to understand when the history of exclusion and racism is considered. Racism and stereotyping are major factors explaining the reluctance of AC people generally and women experiencing abuse in particular to seek help from agencies perceived to be white and discriminatory. However, simply assuming that AC women do not seek outside help because of racism is also too simplistic as there are clearly a range of complex personal and social reasons for women not doing so.

Moreover, the stereotype of female headed families where men are largely absent and where black children, particularly boys, are growing up without fathers, can lead AC women to remain in abusive relationships to ensure their children have fathers, something that is commonly used by abusive men. However, in their attempts to ensure fathers in children's lives and challenge stereotypes, AC women endure years of post-separation abuse from men who make demands over contact with children but use this to continue their violence against women (Thiara and Gill 2011).

Shame

> If you're already told that your black men are criminals, are drug pushers, are this and that, then you're actually having to come and say he is, you're reluctant to do it. (AC woman)

Shame is a significant factor for AC women in both naming their abuse and taking steps to deal with it. In particular, the fear of shaming the family and the 'race' was a large issue and this was especially seen to be the case for women when deciding whether to press charges. Taking action against black men was considered to bring shame on black people while pressing charges or going through the courts or exposing abuse within the community was seen to be shameful for the family – *'she didn't want to bring shame on the family and her mum who was alive at the time but she did go to court and she did press charges once her mother passed away'*.

Responses to men's violence by younger women were considered to be different from those of older women, a generational effect and not an effect of age as this generation settled in Britain with the model of bourgeois family as the norm (Byron and Condon 2008: 188–192). Younger women were seen as being more willing to take steps to tackle domestic violence. Shame was seen to be a bigger factor for older women:

> It's like how did I let this man do this to me at my time of life. And how did I get myself into this situation. And how can I face my church members. Because if they're church goers it's very difficult for them to walk into church and they know that you're not living with your husband. You know your church is where you go and meet your friends and where you talk about things. But you don't want people talking about you because that's a shame thing. (AC professional)

Thus, the many dilemmas for AC women centre around the extent to which they compound the construction of their communities (men) as criminals and families as dysfunctional by being vocal about their experiences of domestic violence. This was an argument used by many men to keep women in situations of abuse by asserting that *'she will bring shame on black people'*.

Doing it their own way/coping on your own

> Sometimes women aren't even aware, they wouldn't class it as that because people's perception and understanding and definition of domestic violence in different communities is different and some people will feel that unless men have physically assaulted them, it's not domestic violence, that it's just life, it's just pressure and that's just how men are. (AC professional)

Because they saw themselves as strong women to whom such things did not happen, many women remained in denial about their experiences of intimate abuse. When this was asserted by some women, this had the effect of silencing other women who feared being judged as weak if they disclosed abuse.

For women already reluctant or not at a stage of being able to name abuse, this especially resulted in an obscuring of their experiences with many believing they were not experiencing domestic violence. Sometimes women equated domestic violence with *'a black eye'* and did not immediately recognize their own experiences of verbal and emotional abuse as domestic violence. It was stated that *'perhaps its cultural differences…black women don't see being told that you can't go out or financial abuse as domestic violence….so its about whether you believe it yourself'*.

An associated idea, that of 'being a good woman' can also have much currency in some AC communities, where putting up with abuse signaled that a woman should be praised for being strong enough to live with these hardships, as captured in the following:

> Something I hear banded around a lot in the black community is what a good woman is. And I've certainly heard people saying that I know I'm a good woman because I have put up with the violence... There seems to be some credibility that goes with that, that you might have had it hard and you might not have been in a good relationship but if you're coping that's a sign of how strong you are and how good you are. (AC professional)

In relation to AC men and their violence, *'being a strong woman and not letting them take all your dignity away from you'* was a pervasive belief among AC women. This sometimes resulted in women tolerating high levels of violence from men to show them that they would not be *'beaten down by men'*.

Relying on family and friends

> I think women feel that they should be able to sort things out for themselves, that their family should support them. They don't like to go into a kind of institution where they have to obey the rules and regulations and structures. It's also a bit of a stigma.

A consequence of 'dealing with it in their own way', being a strong black woman, and experiences of racism from service providers was the reliance by AC women on family and friends to assist them with men's violence.

Unlike some women who cannot turn to their family and friends for support, AC women commonly used their families:

> Within the Afro-Caribbean community there's always a sense of family, so that if you have a problem you can go to some part of your family because you could expect for someone to put you up for a few nights or whatever or as long as it takes for you to get yourself straightened out. (AC professional)

Only when they were unable to rely on their family and friends was it considered likely that AC women would access outside help. In part, concerns about privacy and that AC women *'don't like a lot of people knowing about their business'* led to women making decisions about seeking external help. This sense of privacy was also bound up with a deep rooted suspicion of statutory services with the following being a common comment made: *'They're very private in that sense and they're very suspicious of services like social services, the police and they're very fearful that all those things [information about abuse] are going to be passed over'*.

Conclusion

Women's location within intersecting systems of oppression and intersectional discrimination determines their experiences of violence, societal perceptions of the deserving 'victim' and women's access to help, protection and justice. This chapter has argued that the construction of AC women as 'strong' and 'hard' by key professionals such as the police contradicts the stereotype of a victim, leading to them being viewed as less deserving of protection and less severely affected by the violence. This serves to undermine their attempts at protecting themselves and their children from male violence in their intimate relationships. It has also been argued that although AC women are reluctant to involve external agencies when they do seek assistance, often at a point of crisis or as a last resort, they are faced with insensitive and discriminatory responses. This has to be understood, in part, in the context of the historically oppressive relations of the British state to black women. The construction of the strong black woman not only shapes professional responses but is central to women's own, where they are likely to maintain the secrecy of abuse as a way of protecting black men, the 'race' and their own identity as a strong woman who will not be beaten down by men's violence. Despite these numerous pressures, AC women are not helpless to their abuse but build protective factors and seek help in a range of ways. Clearly, some contact support organizations and even the police while others draw on support from within their own family and friendship networks to resolve issues. What is clear is that although it is widely assumed that AC women are choosing to cope on their own, some were doing so because of the inappropriate and often negative responses they received from agencies they approached for help, something that has to be considered in future responses to AC women dealing with men's violence in their lives.

References

Batsleer, E./Burman, Erica/Chantler, Khatidja/McIntosh, H.S. (2002): Domestic Violence and Minoritisation: Supporting Women to Independence. Manchester: Women's Studies Research Centre, Manchester Metropolitan University.

Byron, Margaret/Condon, Stephanie (2008): Migration in Comparative Perspective. Caribbean Communities in Britain and France. London/New York: Routledge.

Cooke, Veronica/Davis, S./Wilson, Amrit (2003): Domestic Violence Service provision: Black Women's Perspectives. Luton: Race and Gender Research Unit, Luton University.

Hampton, Robert/Carrillo, Ricardo/Kim, Joan (2005): Domestic Violence in African American Communities. In: Sokoloff, Natalie J./Pratt, Christina (eds.) (2005): Domestic Violence at the Margins: Readings on Race, Class, Gender and Culture. New Brunswick: Rutgers University Press, pp.127–141.

Mama, Amina (1989): The Hidden Struggle: Statutory and voluntary sector responses to violence against women in the home. London: London Race and Housing Research Unit.

Mama, Amina (1997): Black women, the economic crisis and the British state. In: Mirza, Heidi Safia (ed.) (1997): Black British Feminism: A Reader. London and New York: Routledge, pp. 36–41.

Quereshi, Tarek/Berridge, David/Wenman, Helen (2000): Where to Turn? Family support for South Asian communities – A case study. London: National Children's Bureau.

Rai, Dhanwant/Thiara, Ravi (1997): Re-defining Spaces: The Needs of Black Women and Children in Refuge Services and Black Workers within Women's Aid. Bristol: Women's Aid Federation England, 82pp.

Razack, Sherene (1998): What is to be gained by looking white people in the eye? Race in Sexual Violence cases. In: Razack, Sherene (ed.) (1998): Looking White People in the Eye: Gender, Race and Culture in Courtrooms and Classrooms. Toronto: University of Toronto Press.

Reynolds, Tracey (1997): (Mis)representing the black (super)woman. In: Mirza, Heidi Safia (1997) (ed.): Black British Feminism: A Reader. London and New York: Routledge, pp. 97–112.

Richie, Beth (2005): A Black Feminst Reflection on the Antiviolence Movement. In: Sokoloff, Natalie J./Pratt, Christina (eds.) (2005): Domestic Violence at the Margins: Readings on Race, Class, Gender and Culture. New Brunswick: Rutgers University Press, pp. 50–55.

Thiara, Ravi K. (2006): African-Caribbean Women affected by domestic violence in Wolverhampton: A research report. Wolverhampton: The Haven.

Thiara, Ravi K. (2008): Building Good Practice in Responses to Black and Minority Ethnic Women Affected by Domestic Violence: Issues from the UK. Conference presentation, Ten Years of Austrian Ant-Violence Legislation. Vienna.

Thiara, Ravi K./Turner, Atuki (1998): Research into the Needs of African-Caribbean Women and Children Experiencing Domestic Violence. Coventry.

Thiara, Ravi K./Gill, Aisha K. (eds.) (2010): Violence Against Women in South Asian Communities: Issues for Policy and Practice. London: Jessica Kingsley Publishers.

Thiara, Ravi K./Gill, Aisha K. (2011): Domestic Violence, Child Contact, Post-Separation Violence: Issues for South Asian and African-Caribbean Women and Children. London: NSPCC.

West, Carolyn M. (2005): Domestic Violence in Ethnically and Racially Diverse Families: The 'Political Gag Order' Has Been Lifted. In: Sokoloff, Natalie J./Pratt, Christina (eds.) (2005): Domestic Violence at the Margins: Readings on Race, Class, Gender and Culture. New Brunswick: Rutgers University Press, pp. 157–173.

Forced Marriages: Between Social Construction and Experience of Family Enforcement

Beate Collet and Emmanuelle Santelli

The question of what are called 'forced' marriages has been highlighted in French politics and news media for several years now and has produced the ambiguities that often arise with issues involving immigrants and their descendents. Voluntary bodies[1] and the authorities[2] have acted to raise public awareness of the problem and find adequate ways to care for victims. However, the way in which public opinion has responded to the issue, declarations by certain political figures[3] and legal measures under the government's immigration policy, impact on representations of immigrants and their descendents. As a result, media coverage of 'forced marriages' tends to accentuate the differentiation between a civilized 'us' and an archaic 'them', so helping to maintain a monolithic vision of cultures.

The polemic over how many forced marriages there are illustrates the ambiguity. A figure of 70,000 forced marriages in France was circulated in the early 2000s. On analysis, this figure proved to be an estimate of the number of young women originating from certain countries and likely to be faced with a forced marriage. But in statements by politicians reported in the media, it had been transformed into actual cases of forced marriage per year (Dittgen 2005;

---

1 Voluntary bodies involved include *Mouvement français du Planning familial* (French family planning movement); *Ni putes, ni soumises* ('not tarts, not submissive'); *Femmes contre les Intégrismes* (women against integrism) in Lyon; *Femmes informations juridiques internationales Rhône-Alpes*, Lyon, which provides legal information for women; *ELELE – Migrations et cultures de Turquie,* Paris, which helps Turkish migrants integrate; *GAMS – Groupe femmes pour l'abolition des mutilations sexuelles* (women's group for the abolition of genital mutilation) in Paris; *Voix de femmes*, (activist group in Cergy-Pontoise) and many others.

2 Eg. Seine-Saint-Denis department *Conseil Général*, Paris municipality and the Ministry of Education.

3 Philippe de Villiers, presidential candidate, in a television broadcast on TF1, 12 February 2007.

Gresh 2007; Hamel 2008). In 2003, GAMS[4] used the same figure to appeal for better provision for victims coming to the association for help. The *Haut Conseil à l'Intégration* (consultative body on immigrant integration) cited it in its 2003 annual report[5], so making it more official, more statistical and thus scientifically grounded, whereas its purpose was in fact essentially political (see Collet, Philippe and Santelli 2008 for a more detailed analysis of how the issue of forced marriage broke into the public arena). The question is: how can unacceptable practices causing physical or mental injury or breaching the principle of equality between men and women be denounced while avoiding any confusion between arranged marriage and forced marriage? Failure to avoid that confusion only helps to cast suspicion on minority groups simply because their cultural practices do not exactly match those promoted in Westernized cultures of the early twenty-first century.

It is important to know whether there is a resurgence of forced marriages in the context of immigration today, in France particularly but also more broadly in Europe. It does not seem possible to measure the scale of the phenomenon precisely. The mere fact of bringing the issue out of the private family sphere into the public arena through discussion within various sectors of society (albeit polemical) and awareness campaigns organized by non-profit bodies increases the number of reported cases. Until there is public denunciation of these marriages they cannot be counted. The forced marriage issue is an excellent sociological example of how a social reality comes into existence once it is socially, politically and publicly constructed. Without public denunciation and the introduction of social and legal assistance (Clark and Richards 2008)[6], forced marriage would remain cloistered in the private sphere and those subjected to it would not know that they can find help to oppose it. Apart from making it possible to measure the phenomenon, denunciation of such practices enables young women to realize that this is violence and that it is possible to escape it. However, the way the issue is handled politically is not driven solely by a desire to protect women against violence. It can also involve political issues connected with controlling immigration and monitoring minorities regarded as politically sensitive, such as Muslim minorities (Wilson 2007)[7].

---

4 *GAMS, Groupe femmes pour l'abolition des mutilations sexuelles* (women's group for the abolition of genital mutilation).

5 Haut Conseil à l'Intégration (2003): *Le contrat et l'intégration* Annual report. Paris: Rapport remis au premier ministre, accessible sur internet.

6 In recent years political debate on the issue has developed in a number of European countries, together with institutional measures to prevent or ban forced marriages.

7 Wilson shows how in the United Kingdom the fight against forced marriages, and particularly the drafting of the recent act of parliament, have pursued the goals of controlling immigration and countering Islamic fundamentalist terrorism.

Forced marriage as a sociological construction

Uncertainty about the scale of the phenomenon and its polemical nature make it difficult to construct 'forced marriage' as a sociological object. A study of 'non-consent'[8] provided the opportunity to reflect on the social emergence of the 'forced marriage' phenomenon and on the sociological approaches that seek to understand it by analyzing gender relations and the multicultural realities of our society.

'Forced marriages' seem to lie at a junction between value systems: individualistic values based on love and free choice versus more holistic values that focus on marriage alliances as the basis of inheritance and symbolic transmission. Examined more closely, however, this comparison is not so simple. An apparently individual, free choice of spouse is also shaped by socially constructed, interiorized social mechanisms, while families arranging a marriage generally seek the consent of the future spouses. It should also be borne in mind that neither the so-called traditional or customary cultural practices nor the religious framework (Islam in this case) advocates the use of constraint or violence to establish a marriage. Nonetheless, the way things are presented suggests that 'forced marriage' emerges from the confrontation between value systems setting two generations in a family against each other. But this confrontation is not only intergenerational; it has become intercultural because the younger generation uses a different frame of reference to their parents' with respect to marriage preferences and practices (Neyrand, Hammouche and Mekboul 2008).[9]

The testimony of young women confronted with forced marriage (whether in preparation or already accomplished) shows the undeniably violent and sometimes altogether sordid nature of the practice. A forced marriage involves relations of domination of men over women and elders over the young. Because whether the marriage is religious or civil, we speak of 'forced marriage' once it involves violence: one of the spouses has refused

---

8 The study's title is *Entre consentement et imposition, les modes d'entrée dans la conjugalité à l'intersection du genre, de l'ethnicité et des rapports entre générations* (Between consent and enforcement: modes of entry to conjugal life at the junction between gender, ethnicity and relations between generations). It was conducted in 2006–2008 by a team of seven researchers from different institutions: Rim Ben Hassine (student), Beate Collet (sociologist, Paris-Sorbonne), Pascale Donati (senior researcher, Paris), Christelle Hamel (sociologist, INED), Claudine Philippe (sociologist, INSERM, IRIS), Saïda Ousmaal (teacher), Emmanuelle Santelli (sociologist, CNRS, MoDys Lyon). The research was based at INED and financed by INED, ISH Lyon and MSH Paris-Nord. It produced a feature in the journal *Migrations & Société*, coordinated by Emmanuelle Santelli and Beate Collet (2008).

9 This book, the first about forced marriages in France, focuses its analysis on intercultural confrontation. This is an essential dimension, but must be seen in the light of intergenerational and gender relations.

the marriage or at least has not given their free and enlightened agreement, or their consent is forced from them by psychological, moral or physical pressure. This social reality implies that forced marriage is part of a wider problem of family violence and even more broadly of gender relations.

Violence in the family is not exclusively a feature of foreign and/or immigrant families (i.e. from cultures different to that of the majority group) and patriarchal mindsets have by no means died out in France (Maruani 2005; Blöss 2001)[10]. The nationwide survey on violence against women in France (ENVEFF) shows this clearly (Jaspard et al. 2003): women of all social and cultural backgrounds suffer physical, psychological and sexual violence in some form or other. In the case of forced marriage, family violence arises in connection with marriage because in the country of origin it was traditionally the parents who controlled marriage alliances: maintaining this prerogative in the country of arrival is *'a way of asserting membership of the identity group'* (Neyrand, Hammouche and Mekboul 2008). So family tensions can be extreme if the parents are still operating in a register in which male pre-eminence and authoritarianism prevail in relations between parents and children, men and women (Kateb 2009), while the children have adopted the values current in French society. They can crystallize around marriage and lead to imposing a marriage partner by force. For the woman, to be married against her will is the expression of both intergenerational and sexist violence. The men also seem to be subjected to pressure, but on the whole have greater scope for breaking free of parental enforcement.

As well as the confrontation between value systems, there is also a confrontation between systems of sociological explanation. The debate is sometimes conducted as if recognition of minority cultural particularities were in total contradiction to the defence of women's rights. Researchers in the UK and North America, where these issues have been studied for many years, describe a tension between feminism and multiculturalism (Moller Okin 1998; Guenif-Souilamas and Mace 2004). How can the two approaches be combined? Is it possible to argue that minority populations' cultural practices must be respected while condemning violence against women and the excessively patriarchal ways of certain social milieus (of whatever cultural composition) in the name of gender equality and non-violent interpersonal relations? Anne Phillips thinks it is, provided we reject the stereotyping of other

10 Proof of this is the violence against women in the public and private domains (sexual harassment, insults, rape), but also discrimination in the labour market (the 'glass ceiling' and wage differentials) and politics (under-representation of women despite a deliberate policy of parity). See Maruani (2005) and Blöss (2001) to grasp the extent to which access to the higher echelons of power are still eminently problematic for women.

cultures and recognize that the cultural practices of any minority population will include variation and diversity (2007)[11].

For the 'forced marriage' phenomenon to exist socially, it is important that it be constructed in legal terms. Without international recognition of the principle of gender equality and the gradual elaboration of legal protection for women and children against violence[12], a social reality such as forced marriage would not be visible. National and international law recognize the principle of free consent to marriage as a fundamental principle, and any legal action to determine the forced nature of a marriage is based on the concept of consent between marriage partners. However, not all countries have written the principle of gender equality into their legislation to the same extent (Mekboul 2008). Sociologically speaking, there are still two major obstacles.

One is the divergence between international legal principles and the persistence of ancestral or customary traditions. Any social reality, anywhere in the world, is marked by such discrepancies. Simply, societies differ in the degree to which they have advanced towards recognizing such legal principles, though none has realized them fully. In France, the first thorough legal and anthropological study of 'forced marriage' was conducted by Edwige Rude-Antoine for the Council of Europe in 2005[13].

The second obstacle concerns the question of consent. The notion of consent seems to be the key to identifying forced marriage in legal terms, but it is still sociologically problematic (for a more philosophical discussion, see Fraisse 2007). But male domination of women works in many subtle ways so it is not always easy to assess the violence involved in obtaining consent. Socialized from childhood to conform to the role and place of women in a patriarchal society, women confronted with a plan for an arranged marriage may succumb to the decision rather than consent[14]. They do not always have the necessary independence to refuse such plans, especially given their emotional tie with their parents (Deveaux 2006). This raises the question whether there can be consent in a relation of domination, or more broadly in an unequal relationship. As the meaning of consent cannot be clearly defined, a more sociological definition of 'forced marriage' is difficult to establish and

11 Anne Phillips argues for going beyond controversy-based interpretations with a more flexible view of culture as being always socially and sexually constructed.

12 Attested in the various supra-regional and national versions of the Universal Declaration of Human Rights, the many International Charters and the International Covenant on Civil and Political Rights (Office of the United Nations High Commissioner for Human Rights).

13 Edwige Rude-Antoine (2005) has been comparing anthropological and legal systems regarding immigration for many years; see also an earlier book published in 1997.

14 Following Nicole-Claude Mathieu's much-quoted expression '*céder n'est pas consentir*" (1991).

the role of sociology is to deconstruct this social reality and arrive at a better understanding of the phenomenon through a more nuanced view.

These analyses also raise the question of defining the concepts of 'domination' and 'violence'. There are three different conceptions of domination depending on the sociologists' theoretical position. For sociologists working from a feminist perspective, a woman's submission to or acceptance of even the institution of marriage as such reflects a relation of domination. Seen in this way, marriage is always imposed, regardless of social or cultural milieu, since a woman's condition very rarely allows her to freely consent to sexual intercourse. In a gender-based theoretical framework, in which equality is the central issue, forced marriage is an abuse of a dominant position in a patriarchal system whose legitimacy is today called into question. The culturalist analysis, on the other hand, seeks to understand forced marriage within a specific cultural system; free consent and equality, as values, reveal the forced nature of a marriage but in so doing reveal the imposition of Western values. It is not easy to find an analytical approach that will make the junction between all these preoccupations.

The concept of violence poses the same theoretical problems. Once a relationship of domination is recognized, violence is its corollary, though taking many different forms (real or symbolic, direct or indirect, physical or psychological). It is not easy to draw a line between a tolerable social constraint (integration into a social circle, wanting to please the parents etc.) and an intolerable one (psychological pressure or physical violence). For these reasons, in our study, the only possible empirical benchmark for identifying a marriage as forced was the discourse of the women concerned. They had to have signaled that they had suffered violence, either at the time of the marriage plan or after the wedding.

Studying non-consent

To address the issue of immigrants' descendants' conjugal and family decisions, we and our colleagues conducted a study entitled *Étude sur le non-consentement* (non-consent study), expressly addressing the dual problem of gender relations and the confrontation between value systems (Collet and Philippe 2008; Santelli and Collet 2003). It was a theoretical and empirical study which began by deconstructing the emergence of the 'forced marriage' issue in the public arena before exploring the experience of victims of forced marriages and the institutional provisions made for them. From the start the study took a dual approach, both political-institutional and based on biographical experience, with the idea that this complex phenomenon could be better grasped by alternating between these two spheres. Interviews were conducted with associations, social workers, organizations and institutions responsible for finding solutions for women confronted with the problem, whether concerned specifically with violence against the women or with women's situations more generally. Carried out in Montpellier and the Paris and Lyon areas, the interviews provided the opportunity to ascertain available facilities, partnerships and changing methods of intervention. They laid the basis for analyzing the emergence of the recognition of the phenomenon while highlighting the difficulties and limitations of such methods of social intervention.

Twenty interviews were held with women confronted with the reality of an imposed or forced marriage, to gain some understanding of the process of enforcement within the family and the courses of action open to the women to deal with the situation. They were interviewed in women's shelters, the encounters being mediated by voluntary bodies or through personal contacts of members of the team[15]. The women made up a very varied population but could not be called a representative sample. Most of them were immigrants, others were young women born of immigrant parents and either born or brought up in France. Some had been exposed to the threat of a forced marriage; others had been unable to avoid it or had only denounced it some years later. Our specific mode of access to the population concerned reflects the construction of the research object. All the interviewees said they had been compelled to marry or had openly refused to obey parental orders. It was not possible to reach women living in a forced marriage, unable to express their refusal or disagreement, and who live among us without us knowing the reality of their private lives.

The analysis set out below focuses on the experiences of victims of forced marriage from an event history standpoint. How is the process of enforcing a marriage within a family to be reconstructed from these women's accounts? Forced marriage is a multifaceted phenomenon, given the different forms of violence and domination and the difficulty of defining consent between spouses. By looking more specifically at these young women's experiences we can gain a better idea of the phenomenon and its variety.

15 We would like to thank these young women for having trusted us as they did. Thanks also to Rim Ben Hassine, Pascale Donati and Saïda Ousmaal for conducting the interviews and to the various associations who enabled us to meet the women.

Women's attitudes to marriages imposed on them by their parents

Including women who had been married by force and also those who were under threat of it made it possible to describe how the process of imposing a marriage unfolds in a family and the means available to these women to oppose it. Four different attitudes for dealing with parental pressure stood out. Each reveals relations between generations, the spiral of violence and the roles of the various protagonists (mother, father, broader kin group, brothers and sisters, friends, neighbours, social services) and sheds light on the social roots of the enforcement process. The possibility of resisting this violence varies according to a woman's personal characteristics and background (nationality, the country she grew up in, how long she has been in France, her level of education, social network etc.). There are various family configurations, but all fall within a patriarchal pattern of family relations which seems to be amplified in a situation of residential segregation and closing of borders.

Refusal on principle

Some women reject their parents' plans to marry them *on principle* and from the outset, regardless of what the potential spouse is like or the motives put forward. They assert their wish to choose the man they will live with because they have developed a conception of the couple in which the partners' feelings for each other and their shared plans for their life together are essential factors. These young women have internalized the values of romantic love that predominate in Western society. These are women born in France and socialized to the values of French society. They are better educated than the rest (baccalauréat or higher). They have a diverse network of friendships (friends from different cultural backgrounds and social milieus) and have formed their reference universe through this process of socialization. This has distanced them from the values and social practices of their family and community of origin.

When they become aware of their parents' plans for a forced marriage (having already rejected all their parents' proposals) they usually flee from home, helped by friends and intermediaries such as teachers, social workers or voluntary bodies they have turned to. These are the women best able to cut family ties because they are fully aware of the incomprehension between their world of values and their parents'. By leaving home when forced marriage threatens they are often also escaping violence both in the family (illegal confinement, beatings) and in the marriage (beatings, rape). But some had been deliberately deceived by their parents (father and/or mother): on a trip to the country of origin they were deprived of their identity papers. Without access to their mutual help network they could hardly escape the marriage and its consummation (which can only be described as rape). Those that manage to escape the situation and the family circle are then able to express their aspirations and how they mean to live their lives. Very often, they make a radical break with the world in which they grew up. Their parents' marriage plan has revealed a deeper level of incomprehension than was evident before.

Circumstantial refusal

Circumstantial refusal is when women accept the principle of marrying according to their parents' proposals but reject the marriage actually proposed for circumstantial reasons. These women have internalized endogamy as a norm more than those who object on principle. They validate their parents' values, including the idea that it is legitimate for parents to organize matrimonial alliances. But they reject the particular suitor proposed because they think the time is not right (they have not completed their studies or think they are too young) or the suitor does not match their criteria (e.g. too old, not to their taste in looks). In this respect, they share with the first group the aspiration to individual choice and the project of living according to the ideal of romantic love.

While these women, like the first group, are from immigrant backgrounds, they are generally less well educated. Above all, they are less able to imagine a life without the support and comfort of their family of origin. Their family socialization has been clearly gender-specific: girls' activities outside the home were controlled, they had to do all the housework, were at the service of the men of the household and emphasis was on the prime importance of family roles for girls. More generally, they have not questioned the legitimacy of arranged marriage; it was only the circumstances they did not agree with. They might accept one arranged marriage to avoid another. When women of this group refuse, they do not imagine what the reaction will be. Their attitude crystallizes their parents' anger and disapproval. They now discover that their parents are prepared to go further and intend to maintain their authority uncontested. The arranged marriage proves to be non-negotiable. Often these women find themselves drawn into an increasingly violent spiral: insults, threats, blows, confinement, confiscation of mobile phones and ID papers. Often there had already been violence in these families; patriarchal order reigned, with the mother subjected to male authority as much as the girls. But the marriage refusal issue amplifies this violence and other family members may join in, particularly the mother, but also brothers and sisters.

These women do not have the same kind of mutual support network as the first group. They think they will be able to come to an arrangement with their parents. Their social network does not give them the same access to a world of different norms with which to contest their parents' decision. Nor does it provide the means to escape before the marriage takes place. Some may manage, usually with the help of a relative (an aunt or an elder sister), social services or the non-profit sector, but there is a marked reticence to criticize their parents and to denounce them. Despite their refusal to give in, they are not questioning the legitimacy of their parents' actions. They remain ambivalent and do not always opt for the solutions the welfare associations propose. Because of the difficulty of breaking their ties with their families, several of them had in the end been forced to marry under pressure of violence. Often it was only later, this time in the face of conjugal violence, that they decided to leave and took steps to divorce or have the marriage annulled.

Refusal after the event

A third group of women did not refuse to marry but expressed their rejection *after the event*. They had accepted the principle that it was their parents' role to choose their husband. Only afterwards, immersed in a particularly violent situation (ill-treated by the family-in-law, beaten by the husband) did they decide to flee and declare the marriage a forced one. Enduring a situation unacceptable to them, they retrospectively define their marriage as forced. We can imagine that if their marital life had been a smooth one they would never have wished to break it off. Many are so vulnerable and isolated in their family situation that they long delay before making a denunciation.

Thus, these women ultimately denounce their marriage as forced when they face marital violence, extreme subordination or humiliation: a violent husband, unjust in-laws or ill-treatment at their hands, problems such as illness, handicap or a drug problem that were not revealed before the marriage. Calling it a forced marriage is a way of de-legitimizing it and highlighting the violence used against them. Most women in this group are immigrants who came to France after their marriage and have no support network of family or friends. Some had accepted the marriage without conviction, as a means to emigrate and escape their own family. This is different from cases where family strategy on both sides is aimed at allowing a man residency in

France by right of marriage with a French citizen. Rather, it is a more common situation that these women face: a marriage alliance that serves to maintain family and community relations. In this exchange logic, and in the face of an increasingly restrictive immigration policy, women are still the prime victims in a milieu that maintains the tradition of using women as bargaining chips. The survey found many such examples: a man who offers his daughter to his friend or an orphaned woman married off so that the husband's family will take charge of her.

Some of the situations encountered were particularly sordid and can rightly be called modern slavery[16]. Deprived of their freedom, some women were forced to do all the domestic work for the husband's family. Such illegal confinement is accompanied by various kinds of ill-treatment ranging from insults to confiscation of belongings, sexual harassment or even rape by male family members (total subjection and confinement of the woman)[17]. They are so severely damaged psychologically they have difficulty taking the smallest initiative. They are not culturally prepared to rebel, just as they were not able to refuse the marriage. They have very low self-esteem, badly undermined by the violence they have suffered. Once out of their 'prison', they need help from several institutional structures to be able to cope. Most, having no qualifications or working experience, have difficulty achieving financial independence – and if their children are still with the family-in-law, their prospects are grim.

Accepted forced marriages

A fourth type of attitude is that of women who recognize the forced nature of their marriage but do not denounce it at the time and have in some way *adapted to it*. Like the women of the second and third types, these women are convinced of the legitimacy of parental authority in matrimonial matters and have not dared to oppose the project. They accept the marriage as their fate, having internalized the fact that they have no individual freedom in this sphere. The marriage can, therefore, be imposed on them without too much violence. Some of these women are immigrants, others of immigrant parent-

16 The *Comité contre l'esclavage moderne* (Committee against modern slavery, CCEM) denounces all forms of modern slavery: forced labour, debt servitude, forced marriage, illegal workshops and sexual exploitation of women and children. See 2006 CCEM annual report at http://www.esclavagemoderne.org/ img_doc/2006_bilan_site.pdf.

17 As with other types of modern slavery, there may be many women are living in these conditions without the neighbours realising or raising the alarm. A survey of this kind cannot cover these situations.

age. Their family socialization has been strongly gender-specific, based on the individual's absolute dependence on the family group. They could not envisage a personal choice, let alone a refusal. In their view, their parents are in a position to suggest the matrimonial alliance that is in their best interests, so they give way. They are ready to give up a love relationship to marry the man their parents have chosen according to their lineage tradition. Although most of these women have little education, some have had secondary education or more. Once they reach the age of 25, they are afraid of not finding a husband and, above all, of not having children, so they allow the choice of a husband to be imposed on them.

This situation is much like that of immigrants' daughters in the 1960s and 1970s whose parents imposed a husband on them. Women of this type have one thing in common: having absorbed a traditional conception of gender relations, they are aware that marriage is not a free choice but have accepted theirs and seem to accept their fate. They also clearly say that though they do not love their husband, they have learnt to tolerate him because he offers them a decent relationship. They also maintain the relationship out of respect for their families and/or their children. Despite all the drawbacks of the relationship, they accept what with hindsight they can see as a violence done to them, in the name of a certain family order that must be respected. This behaviour pattern demonstrates the difficulty of drawing a line between consent and refusal. It seems a very thin line because even if these women expressed their reticence, they did not persistently refuse and at some point they said 'yes'.

These four different ways of refusing or denouncing a forced marriage reveal the two concomitant factors that define a marriage as forced: a refusal expressed more or less assertively at some point and the parents' persistence in wishing to enforce the marriage at all costs. The question of consent is necessary but not sufficient for comprehending the process of forced marriage. Consideration must also be given to the different forms of violence used to force a woman to comply with a matrimonial system that defines a system of social relations. Our typology has also shown that some women (the second and third types above) are more exposed to violence in the family when they express ambivalence towards their parents' value system. This violence may be physical or psychological, but in all cases it exposes individuals to a patriarchal domination light years away from the values of equality and freedom. Women may find it more or less easy to escape from this depending on how far they adhere to their parents' value system.

Tighter adherence to patriarchal conceptions in the context of immigration

To conclude, it is important to highlight the particularity of some family situations. There is not the space here to discuss the social causes in terms of immigrants' situation on arrival (with conditions for legal immigration becoming increasingly restrictive) and after (with increasing segregation in the suburban housing estates). However, it seems that certain family circumstances are more likely to produce a forced marriage. These are families where the parents' attitudes have not changed; on the contrary, in the new country, they seem to have hardened, perhaps into an even more rigid conception of patriarchal control than in the home country.

A feature of all the situations encountered is that social and interpersonal relations within the family are ruled by a patriarchal logic. Young women are faced with *a traditional conception of matrimonial alliances* in which a marriage strengthens family and clan ties, helps to amass assets or supply a 'service', with women as bargaining chips. From this perspective, the women even more than the men in the family are subjected to the infallible logic of the group which, in turn, provides protection, assistance and resources for each member. Family ties are ties of dependence, not freely chosen, and are based on a strict organization in which men dominate women and elders dominate the young.

Anne-Catherine Wagner (2008) has shown that among the French aristocracy and high bourgeoisie, both men and women are subject to family imperatives based on the same idea of marriage with 'one of our own sort'. The difference lies in the way the family's matrimonial choice is imposed on the young: one punishes misalliance by disowning or banishing the couple or denying them privileges, the other has a conception of mandatory family ties and will impose family marriage alliances by violence if need be. While it is important to bear in mind that forced marriage seems to concern a very small minority, it is clearly part of a system of violent relations towards women. It is a type of restrictive and violent behaviour in the family arena which deserves censure, but it is not to be confused with customary practices in other cultural contexts. This violence against women becomes a system in itself, over and above the reference culture. While there may be conjugal violence in Western societies, here it takes on a particular resonance at the intergenerational level. What is at stake is the possibility for women to freely choose the man they will marry, but in both cases, the women remain objects of male domination.

However, it is because identities become racialized that the stigmatization is liable to be extended to the entire Muslim immigrant population, for whom, overall, practices are further removed than most from the new Western sexual order. It is by making clear that these practices are a minority phenomenon, by denouncing the social conditions that produce them and by providing suitable assistance for women seeking a way out that family values, here and elsewhere, can be transformed.

References

Blöss, Thierry (dir.) (2001): La dialectique des rapports hommes-femmes. Paris: Presses universitaires de France.

Clark, Brigitte/Richards, Claudina (2008): The Prevention and Prohibition of Forced Marriages – A Comparative Approach. In: International and Comparative Law Quarterly, vol 57, pp. 501–528.

Collet, Beate/Philippe, Claudine (dir.) (2008): MixitéS. Variations autour d'une notion transversale. Paris: L'Harmattan.

Collet, Beate/Santelli, Emmanuelle (2008): La mixité au-delà des différences culturelles. Les choix conjugaux des descendants d'immigrés maghrébins. In: Collet, B./Philippe, C. (dir.): MixitéS. Variations autour d'une notion transversale. Paris: L'Harmattan, pp. 69–94.

Collet, Beate/Philippe, Claudine/Santelli, Emmanuelle (2008): Emergence de la question du 'mariage forcé' dans l'espace public en France. In: Revue électronique Asylon(s), n° 5. http://terra.rezo.net/rubrique146.html.

Deveaux, Monique (2006): Gender and Justice in Multicultural Liberal States. Oxford: University Press.

Dittgen, Alfred (2005): Stock et Flux, les mariages ou les chiffres forcés. In: Pénombre, numéro 41.

Fraisse, Geneviève (2007): Du consentement. Paris, Le Seuil.

Gresh, Alain (2007): Mensonges sur les mariages forcés. In: Le Monde diplomatique, février.

Hamel, Christelle (2008): Mesurer les mariages forcés: l'appréhension du consentement dans deux enquêtes quantitatives. In: Migrations-Société, Vol. 20, n° 119, pp. 59–81.

Haut Conseil à l'Intégration (2003): Le contrat et l'intégration. Annual report. Paris: Rapport remis au premier ministre, accessible sur internet.

Jaspard, Maryse/Brown, Elizabeth/Condon, Stéphanie/Fougeyrollas-Schwebel, Dominique/Houel, Annik/Lhomond, Brigitte/Maillochon, Florence/Saurel-Cubizolles, Marie-Josèphe/Schiltz, Marie-Ange (2003): Les violences envers les femmes en France. Une enquête nationale, La Documentation française, Collection 'Droits des Femmes', Paris.

Kateb, Kamel (2009): Du mariage précoce au mariage tardif: Un nouveau système matrimonial dans les pays du Maghreb? In: Antoine, P./Marcoux, R. (eds.): Le mariage en Afrique. Pluralité des formes et des modèles matrimoniaux, Paris, Khartala (à paraître).

Maruani, Margaret (dir.) (2005): Femmes, genre et sociétés. L'état des savoirs. Paris: La Découverte.

Mathieu, Nicole-Claude (1991): Quand céder n'est pas consentir. In: Mathieu, Nicole-Claude: L'Anatomie politique. Catégorisations et idéologies du sexe. Paris: Côté-Femmes Editions.

Mekboul, Sahra (2008): Le mariage forcé: réponses du droit et enjeux juridiques. Législation française et européenne. In: Migrations-Société, Vol. 20, n° 119, pp. 83–98.

Moller Okin, Susan (1998): Feminism and multiculturalism: some tensions. In: Ethics, n° 108, pp. 661–684.

Neyrand, Gérard/Hammouche, Abdelhafid/Mekboul, Sahra (2008): Les mariages forcés. Conflits culturels et réponses sociales. Paris: La Découverte.

Phillips, Anne (2007): Multiculturalisme without culture. Princeton: Princeton University Press.

Rude-Antoine Edwige (2005) Les mariages forcés dans les Etats membres du Conseil de l'Europe – Législation comparée et actions politiques, CDEG, Direction générale des droits de l'Homme, Strasbourg.

Rude-Antoine, Edwige (1997): Des vies et des familles. Les immigrés, la loi et la coutume. Paris, Odile Jacob.

Santelli, Emmanuelle/Collet, Beate (2003): Comment repenser les mixités conjugales aujourd'hui. Modes de formation des couples et dynamiques conjugales d'une population française d'origine maghrébine. In: Revue Européenne des Migrations Internationales, vol. 19, n° 1, pp. 51–79.

Santelli Emmanuelle, Collet Beate (2008): Coordination du numéro Entre consentement et imposition. Réalités politiques et sociales des mariages dits 'forcés', 'Refuser un 'mariage forcés' ou comment les femmes réagissent-elles face à l'imposition parentale', Vol. 20, n° 119, pp. 209–227.

Wagner, Anne-Catherine (2008): Mariages assortis et logiques de l'entre-soi dans l'aristocratie et dans la haute bourgeoisie. In: Migrations-Société, Vol. 20, n° 119, pp. 229–242.

Wilson, Amrit (2007): 'The forced marriage debate and the British state'. In: Race Class, vol. 49 (1), pp. 25–38.

Part 4:
Responses to Violence against Minority Ethnic Women

Standing in the Same Dream: Black and Minority Women's Struggles Against Gender-Based Violence and for Equality in the UK

Pragna Patel and Hannana Siddiqui

Through the perspective of Southall Black Sisters (SBS), this article charts the journey that black and minority women in the UK have made since the 1970s in resisting racism and violence against women. We touch on early struggles against the backdrop of racism and multiculturalism and bring it up to date by examining these struggles in the context of the 'War on Terror'. The State's pre-occupation with counter terrorism coupled with its assimilationist policies on 'cohesion' has replaced multiculturalism as the dominant framework for managing race relations. More recently the new coalition government's agenda for the 'Big Society' also threatens to undermine further the gains that minority women have made both by cutting vital services and by devolving power into the hands of local religious groups. Our main argument is that the 'War on Terror' coupled with an anti-welfare state agenda consolidates the power and role of faith based groups in delivering policy and services which, in turn, has the effect of communalising the secular, progressive spaces that black and minority women in particular, have carved out for themselves since the late 1970s. A regressive politics of identity based on religion is playing an increasing role in shaping South Asian women's lives in the UK and this has profound implications for our collective struggle against gender-based violence and equality. The struggle for equality and for the human rights of minority women in the UK is now inextricably linked to the struggle for secular spaces.

'Washing our dirty linen in public'

SBS is now over 30 years old. It was founded in 1979 in the heat of anti-racist activity in Southall, West London. The late 1970s was a period of mass community (secular) mobilisations against racism and often involved all sections of black and minority communities. Many in the anti-racist movement mobilised under a 'black' political identity which signified unity against common experiences of colonialism and racism. The defining moment for SBS came during the uprisings of 1979 when anti-racists organised a mass demonstration to prevent a fascist organisation, the National Front, from marching through Southall, an area with a high South Asian population. The protests led to mass arrests and assaults by the police on Asian and African-Caribbean male youths and to the murder of a white anti-racist activist, Blair Peach, who was killed by police officers from specialist militarised police units. In the course of the anti-racist struggle, SBS was born.

Although anti-racist struggles throughout the UK involved black (Asian and African-Caribbean) women, by the late 1970s, many black women felt the need to establish autonomous black feminist groups to counter the effects of both racism in the wider society and gender inequality within their communities. The earlier struggles by black women focused largely on the need to create unity amongst different groups of minority women. It was a fragile unity but nevertheless vital in enabling black women to forge a feminist identity. However, in reality, much of the early activism by black and minority women was dominated by struggles against racism manifested in protests against immigration policies and practices and racial and police harassment.

SBS broke this mould. Having set up the first black women's service centre in West London in 1982, our struggles and campaigns, out of necessity, drew on the routine experiences of the many women who came to us with stories of violence, persecution and imprisonment in their homes and with it related issues of poverty, racism, immigration problems and homelessness. Our stance had to take account of experiences of violence and abuse in the family and was the main reason why we broke with the myth of community 'unity' since we sought to wage simultaneous struggles against both violence against women and racism. For example, in the late 1970's, we challenged the notorious practice of the virginity testing of South Asian brides entering the UK on the basis of marriage, for being both racist and sexist. Wider protests against this practice focused on the racial stereotyping of Asian women but failed to emphasise the fact that it was also a sexist practice in that it denied Asian women their right to bodily integrity.

SBS broke the silence on domestic violence in the early 1980s with protests against the murder of Mrs. Dhillon and three of her five daughters by her husband who set them alight because she had failed to give birth to a son. Unlike the mobilisations in Southall born out of anger and indignation against fascist and racist provocation in 1979, the same community responded to this atrocity with silence. When we raised concerns about domestic violence and the oppression of women more generally, we were accused of 'washing our dirty linen in public, not only by conservative elements in our communities who felt threatened by our challenge to patriarchal family values but also more disturbingly, by the anti-racist left who were concerned that by campaigning publicly we were fuelling racism against the community, thus creating further negative stereotypes of our cultures as 'backward' and 'barbaric'. Our response to such accusations was to argue that we could not prioritise the anti-racist struggle at the expense of the feminist cause or political expediency. We argued that black women's realities are as much shaped by gender inequality as by racism and that by subscribing to the view that there is a hierarchy of oppression we would be colluding in our own oppression. We argued for the need to address the family as a site of female inequality whilst also acknowledging that it could also be a 'bulwark' against oppressive state intrusion and racism manifested in, for example, harsh anti-family re-unification measures in immigration law (Joshi 2003).

Our campaigning created a backlash in the community which threatened the very existence of SBS. In the mid 1980s, SBS faced closure when local community leaders organised a petition calling for the withdrawal of our funding from Ealing Council, which funded the domestic violence services we provided. We were accused of being 'home-wreckers' and of conspiring to destroy the very fabric of 'Asian culture'. By portraying SBS as 'westernised', they attempted to use their power to de-legitimise us as if we did not belong to the community. The threat of closure was averted when many of the users of SBS mobilised and protested, arguing that without SBS, women would have no safety net when escaping violence and abuse.

As the 1980s progressed, we focussed more and more on the role of the state and its failure to protect minority women against domestic violence. The challenge was to make the state more accountable to women's need for protection in a context where domestic violence was largely regarded as a private matter and where the state took no responsibility for the violent actions of non-state actors. The situation was compounded in the case of black and minority women by the existence of racism and the politics of multiculturalism which encouraged 'cultural sensitivity', which in practice translated into non-interference into the family affairs of minority communities.

Multiculturalism and 'mature multiculturalism'

Throughout the 1990s, much of our activism was clearly focused on challenging state policy and practice towards South Asian women in particular. There were two reasons for this. Firstly, the end of the decade and the election of the new Labour government in 1997, provided more opportunities for us to influence social and welfare policies and secondly, some of the worst aspects of the policy and practice of multiculturalism had to be confronted head on for their devastating impact on minority women's rights.

Since the 1970s, multiculturalism has been the dominant social policy approach to race relations between the State and minority communities in the UK. First introduced in education, it was quickly accepted as a tool of national policy across a range of issues at the local and national levels (Anthias and Yuval Davis 1992; SBS 1989). Prior to the 1970s, the initial focus of British race relations policies was on assimilation into a 'British way of life' based on the notion that 'good' race relations can only be achieved if minority communities shed all aspects of their religious and cultural identity. This slowly gave way to a form of multiculturalism which valued the need for difference and to that extent was useful in the fight against racism. However, the problem with this notion of multiculturalism is that recognition of diversity was seen as an end in itself – a way of simply 'tolerating' difference. The difficulty with the multicultural approach was that in practice it was stripped of its more progressive elements, which were and still are necessary in the fight against racism.

SBS and other minority feminists have been critical of the multicultural model for constructing minority communities as homogeneous and for providing the space for unelected community representatives, usually male and from religious groups and the business classes, to determine the needs of the community. They act as mediators between the community and the State but in reality they have rarely recognised, let alone represented, the individual rights of women or other powerless sub-groups within the community, even though such interests are often articulated in the name of anti-racism or even human rights. In the process, the struggle for community representation at the political level becomes highly contested, but it has largely been won by predominantly fundamentalist and conservative male dominated groups who usually have exclusionary and conservative if not extremist political agendas.

Our starting point in tracing the impact and development of multiculturalism as it affects minority women, especially South Asian women, were the daily experiences of South Asian women who were denied protection in the face of domestic violence and forced marriage. Often the response from the police and social services was one of indifference and non-intervention, even when it was couched in the language of multiculturalism and anti-racism. The approach was deemed to be progressive but was simply reduced to the need to 'respect' cultural and religious differences. The struggle for female autonomy within minority communities was therefore inextricably linked to the development of multiculturalism since the approach lent itself to collusion with patriarchal systems of control of female sexuality and laid the foundation for a cultural relativist approach to women's rights. The approach often left SBS with no option but to resort to the law to challenge multicultural policies for their unintentional but often intentional effect in reinforcing rather than challenging abusive practices.

By the late 1990s and early 2000s, as a result of incessant campaigning arising from a series of cases involving forced marriage and the murder of women who failed to conform to cultural and religious values, we saw a dramatic change in State policy. In 1999, a working group on forced marriage set up by the Home Office, of which SBS was a member, produced one of those seminal moments in the history of struggles by Asian and other minority women to compel the State to take account of our needs. The then junior Home Office Minister, Mike O'Brien, made an announcement which went unnoticed in the wider society, but which was of immense significance to Asian and other minority women. He stated that 'multicultural sensitivities are no excuse for moral blindness' (Home Office 2000: 10; Hansard 1999) and advocated a 'mature' multicultural approach, which allowed for the recognition of gender-based violence and harmful traditional practices within minority communities as an abuse of women's human rights. This was a historical and potentially liberating announcement for South Asian women who had struggled for over two decades for the State to intervene in its protective capacity into the family affairs of minority communities.

Divergent views

These developments also highlighted some divisions or differences within black and minority women's organisations. Whilst many argued for greater State intervention there were divisions over the strategies needed for change. For example, some women supported the proposal to make forced marriage a criminal offence but SBS and others feared it was an empty gesture. We pointed out that criminalisation would drive the problem further underground as women and girls would be highly reluctant to seek protection through the prosecution of their parents. Instead, we argued for better implementation of current criminal laws and more specialist support services to combat the problem. SBS focused on the creation of civil remedies such as the Forced Marriage (Civil Protection) Act 2007 and robust statutory guidelines for schools, police and social and health services to ensure prevention and protection.

There were also differences between women's groups on the related issue of so called 'honour' killings' and 'honour'-based violence (HBV) which continues to receive considerable media and State attention. In 2002, Heshu Yonis, a 16 year old Iraqi Kurdish young woman, was murdered by her father for having a Christian Lebanese boyfriend, and the case was widely reported by the media, for the first time in the UK, as a so called 'honour killing'. There were divisions between South Asian women's groups like SBS and Middle Eastern women's organisations on how to conceptualise and therefore address HBV. The Middle Eastern groups wanted to see specific focus on HBV on the grounds that it is different from domestic violence because it involves the collusion of and harassment from the wider community. However, for SBS, the focus was very much on framing the issue within a wider policy framework of domestic and gender-related violence. We argued that the concept of 'honour' and the collusion of members of the extended family and the wider community has always been a part and parcel of the dynamics of domestic violence within minority communities. We emphasised the need to de-'exoticise'[1] the issue of domestic violence since it led to the creation of a false distinction between this form of gender-related violence from other forms of violence that are also rooted in patriarchal structures of power and control.

Since the Heshu Yonis case, the police and other criminal justice bodies, have made more concerted efforts to address 'honour' based violence[2], but there is still a systematic failure to protect women from the more routine cases of domestic violence. Neither does the focus on 'honour killings' deal with another equally tragic problem – the disproportionate rate of suicide and self harm amongst South Asian women (Siddiqui and Patel 2010a). These deaths are rarely interrogated by the State, although all too often, the same cultural and religious values which underpin 'honour killings' also drive women to commit suicide.

---

1 These divisions were also reflected in the State's response to HBV. For example, while some within the police and the Crown Prosecution Service (CPS) wanted to locate HBV within the domestic violence framework, others insisted that it was 'different' and therefore regarded 'culture' or 'race' as the basis of the abuse experienced by black and minority women. This ignored the common underlying patriarchal power relations, and cultural and religious values systems that legitimise such practices, for example, the notion of women as the property of men which is also the justification of violence against women in the wider society.

2 There have been a number of high profile cases including that of Surjit Atwal who was murdered in a so called 'honour killing' by her husband and mother-in-law in 1998 while on a trip to India because she wanted a divorce. The suspects were not convicted until 2007 and her body has never been found.

Multiculturalism and the rise of religious fundamentalism

By the late 1980s, the politics of multiculturalism provided space for the growth of religious fundamentalism and this had an immediate impact on women's rights as well as providing a fertile breeding ground for the rise of communalism[3] in minority communities in the UK. Religious leaders became more confident in policing dissent and in imposing patriarchal and rigid religious values on the most vulnerable within the communities that they claimed to represent.

In 1989, SBS and Women Against Fundamentalism (WAF)[4] organised a counter demonstration against the mass Muslim mobilisations calling for the banning of Salman Rushdie's book, the *Satanic Verses*. Despite criticism from the anti-racist left, SBS and WAF supported Rushdie because we recognised that the right to doubt and dissent is also an inextricable part of the feminist armoury since feminism is about challenging all forms of orthodoxies and traditions that deny women the right to freedom of self expression and equality. As women, we did not want to be silenced and censored by our communities for questioning religious and cultural values which justified violence, sexual oppression and inequality.

The Rushdie Affair became both a symbol and a catalyst for the growth of conservative religious identities in all communities, but particularly amongst Muslim young men. The anti-Rushdie protests in general created the conditions for the emergence of a culture of intolerance, fear and censorship in all religions which remains with us in heightened and incendiary forms. For example, since the 1990s, we have witnessed with alarming frequency, fundamentalist and authoritarian protests to any form of dissent from an imposed religious identity, much of which has centred directly and indirectly on the control of women's sexuality. Nor are such protests confined to Muslims only. Hindus, Sikhs, and Christians in the majority community have also sought to impose strict religious identity on followers by clamping down on

3 Communalism is a term and concept that is specific to the Indian sub-continent. It refers to the construction of a community solely around religious identity and religious conflict. Communal politics is the politics of such a religious community posing as a monolithic bloc in opposition to those who do not belong and are therefore constructed as the 'other'.

4 Women Against Fundamentalism is a feminist organisation consisting of women of many ethnic and religious backgrounds. It was established in London in 1989, at the height of the 'Rushdie affair' to counter the rise of religious fundamentalism in all religions and the racism that surrounded the affair. By fundamentalism we mean modern political movements which use religion to gain or consolidate power and control especially over women. We do not mean religious observance, which we see as a matter of individual choice.

dissent[5]. It would seem that orthodox leaders in all religions are vying for control over the representation of their communities. In the process, what is made transparent is the re-invention of essentialist notions of religion as a framework for highlighting inequalities and demanding recognition (Yuval-Davis 1992).

As minority women in the UK have no effective political representation and no power to challenge the hegemony of the religious establishment, they, along with other sub-groups, have the most to loose. Women have only their voices of dissent as a tool by which to demand more freedom. The suppression of dissent is, therefore, not just a question of freedom of expression but literally a matter of life and death for many.

Contradictions in state response[6]

Despite the rise of religious fundamentalism, black and minority women began 2000 on an optimistic note. There was the possibility of developing a 'mature multicultural' outlook and there were signs of a softening of State attitude towards the problem of women trapped in violent and abusive marriages by their insecure immigration status. However, at the same time, other powerful contradictory social trends – the 'mainstreaming' of gender and race equality, an increasingly anti-immigration agenda in other respects and a growing emphasis on a 'faith-based' approach to race relations severely disrupted and threatened the progressive changes that were achieved. These challenges also brought to the fore questions of survival and unity across ethnic and religious boundaries amongst South Asian and other minority women in particular and South Asian communities generally.

---

5 Over the years there have been a number of protests within minority populations that reflect growing intolerance of dissent from within. The Muslim fundamentalist protests against Rushdie in 1989 are only one of a growing line of protests against any form of dissent. In 2006, Hindu fundamentalists attempted to use the language of human rights to stop an exhibition of paintings in London by the renowned Indian painter MF Hussain. They argued that the naked depiction of female deities offended 'Hindu' religious sensibilities – although who exactly they claimed to represent was never established. Of course, dissent is not confined to minorities as demonstrated by the furore surrounding the broadcast of the Jerry Springer show in December 2004 by the BBC.

6 Large parts of this section borrows largely from an earlier article by the same authors, see Patel and Siddiqui (2010b).

Forced marriage and the anti-immigration agenda

The most immediate and recurrent problem that we encountered was the explicit linking of violence against minority women with an anti-immigration agenda. Hand in hand with the acknowledgement of specific harmful cultural practices as abuses of women's human rights, the State has also implemented restrictive immigration controls as a 'solution' to the problem. Although there is greater recognition that some minority women experience intersecting discrimination on the basis of race, gender and the lack of immigration status that makes them vulnerable to abuse or exploitation, a national (and European-wide) obsession with the control of immigration overrides any such recognition. Challenging culturally specific forms of abuse has become a convenient cover for limiting and controlling immigration, especially from South Asian countries, which has the effect of compounding minority women's experiences of discrimination in other areas. For example, by introducing highly restrictive immigration policies to supposedly deal with the problem of forced marriage, the State has also denied genuine migrant families their right to family re-unification.

Recent changes to the immigration rules on marriage to overseas partners in the UK, have also strengthened the discriminatory and racist nature of the immigration system (Home Office and UK Border Agency 2008)[7]. Notwithstanding the fact that forced marriage is an abuse of women's fundamental human rights, the State's focus on immigration controls as a legitimate form of protection is highly problematic. SBS has consistently pointed out that black and minority women need to be afforded safety and protection in the face of domestic violence in the same way that women are protected in the wider community. Rather than pursue yet more draconian immigration controls, the most effective measures of protection from forced marriage involve a series of legal, welfare and educational initiatives including the need for more specialist resources (refuges and advice centres) for black and minority women. Issues of violence against minority women should, therefore, be addressed within a policy framework on violence against women which takes account of the impact of immigration controls rather than through an immigration control framework which justifies further restrictive practices in the name of protecting black and minority women

7 Since 2000 onwards, the government has introduced a number of legal and policy measures, including raising the age to 21 at which an overseas spouse can join his/her British spouse. Under the pretext of 'strengthening safeguards against forced marriage'(Home Office and UK Border Agency 2008) and to prevent bogus marriages, the government proposed a series of highly questionable solutions which will have a profound impact on the settlement rights of minority communities, particularly those from the Indian Sub-Continent.

from domestic violence. It is essential to de-link the question of protection of minority women from the question of immigration control. Paradoxically, our view is that it is the relaxation of the immigration controls which will help to address problems of forced marriage, since marriage will not be seen as a route to gaining entry to the UK.

Social cohesion and the rise of the 'faith- based' approach

In 2001, we were witness to civil unrest in towns and cities in the north of England, followed by the 9/11 atrocity and the 7/7 London bombings. These events, coupled with a growing lack of State funding and a general backlash against feminism, has led to a crisis in the provision of women only, especially black and minority women's services. In place of autonomous black and minority women's organisations, we have seen the so-called 'mainstreaming' of race and gender equality issues which has resulted in corporate statutory bodies and religious organisations providing services that would once have been provided by black and minority women's organisations but without the pro-equality and feminist ethos which underpins such services. At the same time, the labour government began to oversee a shift away from the marginally more progressive framework of multiculturalism to 'cohesion' and multi-faithism, which emphasised the need for cohesion through assimilation and the adoption of 'British values'. Yet at the same time, in a somewhat contradictory fashion, the government also encouraged religion to play a greater role in public life. The result is that within minority communities, religion is regarded as the main basis for civic engagement. The increasing use of religion as the basis of identity (euphemistically referred to as 'faith') began in the late 1980s and early 1990s with the Rushdie Affair but gathered momentum throughout the 2000 decade and now poses a significant threat to the autonomy and fundamental freedoms of minority women in the UK.

The cohesion and faith-based agenda represents the 'softer face' of the State's counter-terrorism measures. It is an approach aimed solely at managing the threat of Muslim fundamentalism. All race equality initiatives have to a large extent, been reduced to achieving the State's overarching aim – to ensure Muslim and minority compliance with 'British values'. However, it would be a fundamental mistake to ignore the underlying economic imperatives which also drive the cohesion and faith-based agenda. It is an approach that neatly fits into a wider neo-conservative agenda involving the privatisation of vital state functions and reducing the public sector. The demise of the welfare state cannot be underestimated since the breach that is created has allowed religion to step in advantaged as it is over secular groups by its vast networks of membership and resources. It is this aspect that the new coalition government, in particular, is appealing to when selling its idea of the 'Big Society'. The shifting of accountability for such services onto religious institutions is a dangerous development for women in particular because it delivers them back into the hands of powerful religious leaders.

In 2007/8, SBS was forced to confront these contradictions in State policies towards minority communities head on when faced with funding cuts by our local authority (Ealing Council.) If left unchallenged, such a move would have resulted in the demise of organisations like ours set up not only to counter racism but also to provide minority women with real alternatives to community (religious and cultural based) mechanisms for dealing with disputes, including violence within the family. We felt that such a development would, in turn, set back the advances that we had made to compel the State to recognise that the human rights of minority women are non-negotiable and that they cannot be subject to differential standards when seeking protection from gender-based violence.

Ealing Council sought to justify its decision on the grounds of 'equality', 'cohesion' and 'diversity'. It argued that the very existence of groups like SBS – the name and constitution – was unlawful under the Race Relations Act because it excluded white women and was therefore discriminatory and divisive! Yet at the same time, somewhat ironically, the Council also sought to encourage and fund the creation of a wide variety of Muslim conferences, networks and organisations to discuss scholarly interpretations of Islam, Muslim mentoring schemes, Muslim volunteer schemes for hospitals, schools and the police, and to set up Muslim women's groups as part of its 'cohesion' strategy (London Borough of Ealing 2007). These initiatives were pursued regardless of the fact that they undermined progressive secular struggles led by Muslim and non-Muslims which demanded a more progressive equality and human rights framework as the basis for civic engagement. On 18th July 2008, we won our challenge against Ealing Council and in doing so created an important legal precedent on the approach that public bodies must adopt to the funding of specialist organisations under the Race Relations Act and the Race Equality Duty. However, while successful in forcing the Council to withdraw its decision and to re-think its policy on domestic violence services in Ealing, our case also sounded a warning bell to secular progressive groups.

Although critical of old style multiculturalism for fostering segregation, the new coalition government has not rejected the notion of 'social cohesion' outright. Instead, through the idea of the 'Big Society', it is continuing the previous government's policy of squeezing secular spaces out of minority communities by giving religion centre stage in controlling local resources.[8] The 'Big Society' and 'localism' agenda is perceived as a radical and dramatic redistribution of power and control from the State to the individual by encouraging greater volunteering and philanthropy at the local level. The project includes building volunteering programmes so that community groups can take over the delivery of a range of local services.[9] Whilst the plan appears laudable, one of the main problems is that it is encouraging faith based projects and leaders to play a key role in shaping policy and service delivery on a range of issues at the local level, irrespective of their highly discriminatory agenda.[10] Elsewhere, the government has condemned 'rising secularism' in the UK and has somewhat ironically stated that a Conservative government will need to *'reverse the damage done by the results of Labour pursuing a secular agenda since 1997.'*[11]

De-secularisation and its implications for women's rights

The State's new multi-faith approach has opened up the space for a reactionary politics of identity based on religion to flourish. Building on the Labour government's 'faith-based' cohesion agenda, fundamentalist and religious right forces have made significant inroads in consolidating their power and control over minority communities and resources. Demands for legal tolerance, cultural rights and access to public resources evident in, for example, campaigns to extend the blasphemy law, funding for religious schools, dress codes and the right to apply customary (religious) laws instead of civil law in the governance of family affairs are growing. These demands are led by Muslim right wing forces, but if accommodated, will inevitably lead to other

---

8 Speech delivered by the Prime Minister, David Cameron in Liverpool. July 19 2010. See http://www.number10.gov.uk/news/speeches-and-transcripts/2010/07/big-society-speech-53572

9 The idea of the 'Big Society' has met with considerable scepticism from a number of quarters, including trade unionists, social analysts and commentators across the political spectrum. The most voiced criticism is that it is seen as a convenient cover for spending cuts, particularly as the government's overarching aim is to implement massive cuts in public sector services. It is also seen as a return to Thatcherite anti-state populism, even though the idea is articulated in the language of people empowerment and community engagement. The notion of the 'Big Society' remains silent on how questions of poverty and the social exclusion of the most marginalised and vulnerable (perhaps the greatest obstacle to civic participation) in our society will be tackled.

10 See for example the speech given by Baroness Warsi the Minister without Portfolio in the Cabinet Office, at a dinner organised by the international charity 'Muslim Hands' on 23 June 2010 in which she declares religious organisations as central to delivering basic public services.

11 Speech delivered by Baroness Warsi at the Conservative Party conference in Manchester. 5 October 2009.

minority groups, predominately Hindus and Sikhs, making similar demands. Such demands deliberately use the language of human rights, anti-discrimination and even anti-racism whilst subverting these very principles. It is in this economic and political context that we argue that the struggle for equality and for the human rights of minority women in the UK is now inextricably linked to the struggle for secular spaces.

The feminist and human rights scholar Karima Bennoune has stated that the struggle to keep religion and human rights law separate is one of the most urgent struggles now taking place globally. She adds that 'the emphasis on freedom of religion has overshadowed the importance of 'freedom from religion' (2007). This is clearly evident in recent debates and developments in the UK in respect of demands made by some Muslim organisations to incorporate aspects of Sharia law in relation to the family within the English legal system, a move which is also encouraged by leading establishment figures in the judiciary and the Church itself.[12] However, in the process, what we are witness to is the subversion of the secular human rights framework and the principles of equality, universality and the indivisibility of human rights – principles which are not 'alien' or 'western' to minority women as is evident in our struggles in the UK and in our countries of origin.

The attempt by religious leaderships to erode the essentially secular legal foundations of the law is occurring in two ways: first, by demands by religious leaderships for communities to be governed by their own personal religious laws and, secondly, by demands for the courts to be more sensitive to religious sentiments in the civil and criminal legal system itself. In other words, they demand greater 'religious literacy' which has resulted in the increasing accommodation of religious identity so that religion becomes the primary lens through which matters pertaining to the family, such as marriage, divorce, custody of children and property settlements are resolved. Both these developments are interrelated since success in one area strengthens success in the other.

In both civil and even criminal courts, we are now witness to frequent contestations between minority women demanding gender equality and even the so called 'moderate' religious leaders demanding the absolute right to manifest religion. It is a contestation in which the State has shown itself to be contradictory in its stance. For example, on the one hand, the State has begun to assert more clearly that harmful cultural practices such as honour crimes and forced marriages are an abuse of women's human rights and actively seeks to intervene in families (the legacy of 'mature multiculturalism'). On

12 See for example the lecture '*Civil and Religious Law in England: A Religious Perspective.*' delivered by the Archbishop of Canterbury at the Royal Courts of Justice on 7 February 2008.

the other hand, in the face of the power of religious claims, the State fails to acknowledge the lack of ability and the absence of social 'permission' for the more vulnerable in minority communities to exercise choice in determining their cultural affiliations, practices and identity. The primacy given to the right to manifest religious beliefs brings with it a number of problems linked to questions of 'validity' and 'authenticity'. Questions about which identities and demands are valid and whose opinion constitutes the 'authentic voice' are all issues that arise in the battles that are taking place.

The recent creation of the Muslim Arbitration Tribunal (MAT) in the UK which is set up and managed in accordance with the Arbitration Act 1996 for alternative dispute resolution in civil law cases, is an example of how religion is encroaching upon the secular legal system (Muslim Arbitration Tribunal 2008; Taher 2008). The MAT will enable arbitration (mediation by another name) of amongst others, family disputes, to take place in accordance with 'Islamic sacred law[13]'. By existing within the framework of the Arbitration Act 1996, the MAT attempts to ensure that its determinations can be enforced by the English courts in cases where both parties have agreed to be bound by the outcome.

Groups like SBS and WAF have challenged developments like the MAT by arguing that the demand for religious personal laws will become the main means by which the absolute control of minority women is maintained. There is considerable evidence that these tribunals discriminate against women and are arbitrating in domestic violence and forced marriage cases solely for the purposes of keeping the family intact. The forum seeks to reconcile women with violent and abusive partners or families without any reference to risk assessments or the law and statutory guidelines which warn against mediation and reconciliation in cases of domestic violence and forced marriage.

The incorporation of religious personal laws within the legal system formalises gender discrimination and a culturally relativist approach to family cases, adding to the immense community pressures that minority women already face to agree to mediation based on their religious identity. Moreover, when combined with the wider gender inequality that persists in society more generally, women will find it difficult to obtain a hearing on equal terms. Such acceptance of tribunals also signals the view that it is legitimate for minority

13 The Muslim Arbitration Tribunals announce themselves on their website in the following way 'The Muslim Arbitration Tribunal (MAT) was established in 2007 to provide a viable alternative for the Muslim community seeking to resolve disputes in accordance with Islamic Sacred Law and without having to resort to costly and time consuming litigation. The establishment of MAT is an important and significant step towards providing the Muslim community with a real opportunity to self determine disputes in accordance with Islamic Sacred Law.'

communities to operate a second-rate justice system based on unaccountable and partial mechanisms of conflict resolution! This is in itself a racist response to demands for equality and justice, especially in view of the fact that even in countries where state-sanctioned religious laws operate, there are substantial movements, often led by women and human rights activists, for their repeal on the grounds that they are not compatible with universal human rights principles.

By allowing religious arbitration tribunals to adjudicate in family disputes, the State will in effect, be sponsoring the most dominant, patriarchal, homophobic and authoritarian, if not fundamentalist, interpretations of religions in minority communities. It is also acting in direct contravention of the UK's obligations under domestic and international human rights law which is to protect women and children from acts of violence committed in public or private spaces. The duty to exercise due diligence, in order to prevent, investigate and punish acts of violence against women including those carried out by non-State actors is a necessary function of a democratic state and the democratic principle. For the sake of economic and political expediency, this duty is clearly being subverted.

It is arguable that the need to reflect 'Muslim identity' and 'Muslim experiences' within social and political institutions and policy development verges on a form of fetishism, particularly as it results in absurd outcomes in the context of the collective needs of South Asian women. The strategy of isolating Muslim women's needs and presenting them as somehow 'different' from those of other South Asian women with whom they share a common culture is dangerous and divisive. It plays into the fundamentalist segregationist agenda and denies the overwhelming success of the inclusive and secular nature of our organisations that are now facing closure. The approach strongly undermines the solidarity that has been forged across ethnic and religious lines within and outside of our communities. It also encourages groups to compete for resources and separate provision based solely around religious identity rather than need.

More significantly, the reality of black and minority women's lives does not support the view that most black and minority women choose their identity according to their 'faith' or want 'faith-based' organisations to govern their family and private lives. In a 2009 study carried out by SBS on the impact of the 'cohesion' and 'faith based' agenda on women, the majority expressed very strong negative sentiments of mistrust and alienation from faith-based leaderships. Of the 21 women interviewed (Patel and Sen 2010),[14] all

14 The respondents were all South Asian or African-Caribbean women aged between 25 and 60 years old and reflected the main minority religions- Sikhism, Christianity, Islam and Hinduism.

except one professed to some form of religious belief. Most were practising believers but all viewed religion as a matter of personal choice or belief, rather than the basis of a social identity. They did not express any sense of belonging to a 'faith-based' community. In fact their reality showed that they adopt fluid identities which often straddle different traditions and cultures.

Women were adamant that they did not want religious authority to arbitrate on family matters. Reasons for this included memories of religious divisions back home; fear of breaches of confidentiality; fear of sexual exploitation and abuse; vulnerability to coercion and social compulsion to stay in the family; fear of not being listened to and lack of trust – corruption and factionalism and struggles for power within religious institutions – in other words they did not see religious institutions as just religious institutions but as political entities with different groups vying for power. Yet the support reserved for faith based organisations assumes that those who have no access to or interaction with broader society identify with their particular faith based communities.

Conclusion

Black and minority women have been in the forefront of important battles for equality and freedom in the UK. From the 1970s onwards, we asserted ourselves on the political landscape by waging struggles for gender and racial equality simultaneously and in the process illuminated how power is exercised to the detriment of women's equality in the family, community and the State. Our need to be visible was overriding at a time when State and community politics, including anti-racist and wider feminist struggles, conspired to silence our voices. From virginity testing to violence against women and more recently anti-fundamentalist campaigns, crucial questions have been posed about the politics of representation within and outside our communities. Along the way, some important milestones have been achieved in compelling the State to account for its indifference to the experiences of minority women, including specific forms of abuses such as honour crimes and forced marriage perpetrated in the name of religion and culture. At the same time, these issues have been hijacked by the State to justify racism, including anti-Muslim racism and inhumane anti-immigration policies and practices and to deal with questions of terrorism and national security. At the same time, the bodies of black and minority women have also been instrumentalised by right wing religious and fundamentalist forces seeking to gain control over communities and resources.

It can safely be said that the struggles of minority women have reached a crucial political juncture. The imposition of policies on 'cohesion', religion and now the 'Big Society' means that black and minority women are once again in the spotlight as we struggle to remain visible and to retain our secular feminist spaces – a necessary pre-condition for the creation of a democratic, tolerant and more equal society. As we struggle in search of answers, we ask ourselves whether we will be allowed to stand in the same dream as our feminist counterparts in the wider society.

References

Anthias, F./Yuval-Davies, N. (eds.) (1992): Racialized Boundaries: Race, Nation, Gender, Colour and Class and the Anti-Racist Struggle. London: Routledge.

Bennoune, K. (2007): Secularism and Human Rights: A Contextual Analysis of Headscarves, Religious Expression, and Women's Equality Under International Law. Columbia Journal of Transnational Law.

Home Office and UK Border Agency (2008): Marriage Visas: The Way Forward. London: UK Border Agency.

Joshi, Poonam (2003): 'Jumping through hoops: immigration and domestic violence'. In: Gupta, Rahila (2003) (ed.): From Homebreakers to Jailbreakers: Southall Black Sisters. London: Zed Books.

London Borough of Ealing (2007): Ealing's Shared Future Integration and Community Cohesion Strategy 2007- 2011. London: London Borough of Ealing.

Muslim Arbitration Tribunal (2008): Report – Liberation from Forced Marriages. London: Muslim Arbitration Tribunal www.matribunal.com

Patel, Pragna/Sen, Uditi (2010): Cohesion, Faith and Gender. London: Southall Black Sisters.

Patel, Pragna/Siddiqui, Hannana (2010): 'Shrinking Secular Spaces: Asian Women at the Intersect of Race, religion and Gender'. In: Thiara, Ravi K./Gill, Aisha, K. (2010) (eds.): Violence Against Women in South Asian Communities: Issues for Policy and Practice. London: Jessica Kinglsley Publishers.

Siddiqui, Hannana/Patel, Meena (2010): Safe and Sane: A Model of Intervention on Domestic Violence and Mental Health, Suicide and Self-harm Amongst Black and Minority Ethnic Women. London: Southall Black Sisters.

Southall Black Sisters (ed.) (1989): Against the Grain. London: Southall Black Sisters.

Hansard Adjournment Debate on Human Rights (Women). London: House of Commons 325, 8th February 1999–16th February 1999.

Taher, A. (2008): Revealed: UK's First Official Sharia Courts. 14 September, Times Online: http://www.timesonline.co.uk/tol/news/uk/crime/article4749183.ece (18.11.2008)

The Thin Line Between Protection, Care and Control: Violence Against Ethnic Minority Women in Denmark

Yvonne Mørck, Bo Wagner Sørensen, Sofie Danneskiold-Samsøe and Henriette Højberg

Since the first women's shelters were founded in Denmark about thirty years ago women from ethnic minority backgrounds have constituted a significant proportion of women fleeing violent men or families.[1] According to recent figures, 45 percent of women in Danish shelters were born outside Denmark, while even more defined themselves as ethnic minorities. Although they come from different countries – as many as 86 in 2008 (Barlach 2009)[2] – most of the women in shelters represented the larger non-Western immigrant groups from Turkey, Iraq, Bosnia, Thailand, Lebanon and Iran. The history of immigration to Denmark varies among these groups, with the largest group of immigrants and descendants being from Turkey. Immigrants and descendants total 9.5% of the entire population in Denmark, with the proportion from non-Western countries being 6.4% (Petersen et al. 2009).[3] Because of the high numbers of ethnic minority women in the shelters, and because violence against ethnic minority women in Denmark is under-researched, a Danish shelter, Danner shelter, invited researchers to examine the possible relationship between violence and culture. Danner shelter was interested in knowing what kind of violence ethnic minority women flee, but also what the

1 According to the first statistics 17.5% of women at Danner shelter had ethnic minority background in 1984. During the next twelve years their share increased gradually to 50% in 1996. The same year the national average was 38% (Jensen and Behrens 1997).

2 Women who do not have Danish citizenship represent about 28 percent of the total number of women in the shelters. About half the women without Danish citizenship are marriage migrants (Barlach 2009). The figures are based on information from 1,476 women who, in 2008, lived in one of the 36 Danish shelters organised under LOKK, the Danish National Organisation of Shelters.

3 Population statistics distinguish between foreigners of Western and non-Western origin. Bosnia is categorized as non-Western. The term foreigners is used as a common designation of immigrants and descendants. Descendants are defined as persons born in Denmark by parents born outside Denmark (Petersen et al. 2009). Such persons are often called second generation immigrants in the academic literature.

shelters currently have to offer these women and whether it is sufficient.[4] This chapter is based on the initial results of this study.

Researchers dealing with violence seem to agree that inter-personal violence, wherever it takes place, is contested, and that it implies the use of force – or its threat – as a pre-emptive means to control and maintain dominance over others (Riches 1986a; Abbink 2000; Schröder & Schmidt 2001). From the perpetrator's perspective it is neither meaningless nor senseless. Jenkins (1997) suggests that violence to others may be the ultimate form of categorization: people are put in their (right) place. Or, in Lundgren's (1995) gendered perspective, women are confined and put in their place as part of a larger process of gender construction. At the same time, many ethnographic cross-cultural studies show that the extent and use of violence varies, and that explanations of violence differ at local levels. Studies also show how different social and cultural backgrounds are likely to frame violence in different ways and give rise to specific experiences (Riches 1986b; Harvey & Gow 1994; Counts, Brown and Campbell 1999; Sørensen 1998, 2001; Aijmer & Abbink 2000; Schmidt & Schröder 2001). This chapter focuses on both general and specific aspects of violence.

Danner shelter

Danner shelter is located in Copenhagen and it is one of the first shelters in Denmark. It is well known among the public and intimately associated with the women's movement.[5] Lessons from Danner shelter show that the consequences of violence may be more devastating and prolonged for women from an ethnic minority background, not necessarily because of the nature of the violence but because of social and cultural circumstances. According to professionals at the shelter, many of these women are not only victims of violence, but also experience language barriers, lack of social networks, lack of knowledge and awareness of social and legal rights, and lack of employment

4 The project title is 'Violence in Ethnic Minority Families – a Qualitative Study with a Focus on Future Efforts'. The project has been conceived by Danner shelter and financed by the private foundation TrygFonden. Part of the project consists of a mapping of current offers to the women during and after their stay in the shelters. There is a special focus on the importance of aftercare as part of the shelter package.

5 Danner shelter has a long history. Originally, the Countess Danner, who was married to King Frederik VII, built the house in 1775. The purpose was to house single working class women. In 1960 the admission of women stopped and the Foundation Board let the house decay. The women's movement occupied the house in 1979 and turned the house into a shelter for battered women.

and education.[6] These are the barriers that ethnic minority women face when they try to make an autonomous life without violence (Nielsen 2005). There are also significant differences among the women and thus their need for assistance; these include young women taking refuge from violence from their families and/or threat of forced marriage and foreign women married to husbands in Denmark.

Methodology

Our chapter is based on interviews with 13 ethnic minority women, aged 21–47, who agreed to share their stories of violence. Some were born in Denmark; others came to live with their husbands as so-called family reunified persons[7] or they came as refugees with their parents. Women of Iraqi and Turkish descent present the largest group of interviewees.[8] Most of the women were recruited through a number of shelters. Some were living at the shelter at the time of the interview while others had left the shelter and were interviewed in their own homes or elsewhere.

The women had been exposed to different kinds of violence for varying periods of time from parents, brothers, husbands, sons, or in-laws. Men were the common perpetrators and usually the more feared ones, whereas women tended to act as either accomplices to men or as substitutes for male heads of the family or household. Our data invited a broad definition of VAW such as the one adopted in 1993 by the UN General Assembly, which includes any act of gender-based violence that results in physical, sexual or psychological harm or suffering to women, including threats of such acts, coercion or arbitrary deprivations of liberty, whether occurring in public or private life. Economic deprivation is another aspect worth mentioning. A narrow definition is not able to encompass the many aspects of violence and it tends to overlook that VAW is a structural and processual phenomenon.

The chapter focuses on three themes that emerged from the interviews: how cultural belonging and loyalty make it difficult to speak out about violence; how family honour and the ideal of protection gloss over actual control and violence; and how suffering and care intertwine with power and legitimize violence.

6 Crenshaw (1994) talks about structural intersectionality and how it shapes the experiences of many women of colour; or in our case, ethnic minority women.

7 Family reunification is a legal term that covers marriage migration among others.

8 The interviewed women originate from the following countries: 4 from Iraq, 3 from Turkey, 2 from Sri Lanka, 1 from Morocco, 1 from Iran, 1 from Ukraine, 1 from Lithuania. All the interviewees' names have been changed.

Cultural loyalty and the problem of speaking out

Our material shows that gender-based violence is a big taboo in ethnic minority families. Several of the women believed VAW to be widespread both in the country of origin and in the ethnic minority community in Denmark. However, since divorce is disapproved of, few women dared to take that step and gossip is often used as a weapon of social control. People spoke badly about women like Divani, a Tamil women who has lived in Denmark most of her adult life, who chose to leave her husband after many years of mental and physical violence: *'You have no life when you have thrown your husband out. Then you are alone. You can do nothing'*.

There are two main reasons why the interviewed women had concealed the violence, namely loyalty to the family and threats of (more and more severe) violence. A recurrent theme in the women's narratives is the importance of not disclosing the violence to outsiders, including others in their community[9] and Danes, such as teachers and social workers, who represent the public system. According to the women interviewed, the family (either their own and/or their family-in-law) perceived reporting the violence to authorities as a betrayal: one fails one's family by telling someone outside the family what is happening in the private sphere. This may play a major role in explaining why very few women reported the perpetrators to the police. Interviewees had put up with extremely severe violence for many years before they finally broke with the culturally based attitudes and spoke out about it.

The women, however, also concealed the violence from family members. Women hiding violence committed by a partner from their families is one variation of this concealment. This involved women who had engaged in premarital sexual relationships or who had entered a Muslim marriage without parental consent. In such cases, the 'secret' partner made threats of revealing their relationship to her family to make the woman stay in the relationship and/or to behave as he demanded (e.g. to have an abortion). Yet another form of this concealment is seen in Divani's story. For many years, she disguised her husband's violence from her relatives for fear of upsetting them, even though they lived in Denmark. When she finally left her husband, she still

---

9 All ethnic communities are heterogeneous regarding e.g. gender, class, age, religious and political belonging. They are also filled with contradictions and contestations in relation to issues concerning gender and sexuality. However, the interviewees have not experienced much support from neither relatives nor other members of what they refer to as 'their' ethnic community. Baumann (1996) writes that it makes a difference whether one postulates communities defined by some ethnic culture or one discerns different cultures within a community.

found it difficult to reveal the violence, especially to her parents, because she had concealed the truth from them for so long. Thus, even if the abused woman has family members in Denmark, with whom she has a good relationship, there is no guarantee that she will seek their assistance.

Such reasons for concealing the violence can be conceptualized as 'cultural loyalty' where the central question is: How can one be loyal to one's culture and religious background, while simultaneously adopting a critical position against inequality and oppression (Ahmed 1984; Mørck 1998), such as violence against women and children? Cultural loyalty is important for understanding why women did not leave the violence much earlier.[10] The potential harm to the family's reputation, honour and image resulting from disclosure can be a key reason for women maintaining secrecy (Gill 2009). Several of the young women reported that their parents feared that if their daughters destroyed the family's reputation, the parents would not be able to function socially in their communities. Their brothers, however, could do what they wanted.

The interviewees talked about gender perceptions, a collective perception of personhood and religious understandings that are used in their families' countries of origin and in the ethnic minority communities as 'arguments' for others to control their life, body and sexuality (Mørck 2000). Perpetrators concealed the violence from the majority society by emphasizing the cultural and/or religious identity of women. In doing so they constructed a dichotomy of 'us' and 'them', which they used to keep the daughter or woman in 'her right place'. In several cases, parents had described Danes in negative terms throughout their daughters' childhood. Nada, who had been abused by her mother, related how her mother constantly stressed that the family is Muslim when she and her siblings started in a Danish school. They were told to keep away from the Danes: *'We should not talk with them. We should keep ourselves from white people. We should not eat their food because it is pork. There were many things we should be careful about. We should not talk to guys'*. Her mother had been very concerned with, and from the age of 10 had monitored, Nada's body, for love bites and searched her schoolbag and mobile phone to see if she had contact with boys. Nada was not allowed by her mother to have Danish friends: *'My mom could see that I preferred the Danish culture and not where I came from'*. This can be interpreted both as a

10 In their analysis of domestic violence services for minoritized women in England, Burman, Smailes & Chantler (2004) propose the term 'cultural privacy' for a parallel phenomenon, namely how organizations, including the police, do not get involved out of respect for the women's culture and the fear of being labelled as racist. The result is that violence is silenced.

strategy to keep the violence hidden and to prevent Nada from embracing Danish norms and lifestyles.

Several of the women reflected on whether they had done the right thing by going to a shelter, as for most of them this choice had meant not only a break up with their parents but with the whole family. Punida, who had been subjected to violence from her parents, wondered if she should have resigned herself to a life of violence and submitted to the rules of her parents, e.g. by not talking to young men. However, as she explained, the situation for young people who have grown up in Denmark is complex, creating difficulty with living in two worlds: *'When at home one is Tamil, and when at school one is Danish'*.

However, women who came to Denmark as adults and who broke social conventions and conformities also have to deal with questions of loyalty and cultural identity. Iraqi Samia came to Denmark to live with her husband of Iraqi descent but was now divorced. She also found herself in a difficult position in relation to cultural loyalty and cultural identity:

> When one is stuck between two cultures it is difficult to know what is right. People from my culture say that I am a bad woman – I am divorced and live alone. Danes understand me much better. But it is hard for me to be a Dane. I would like to, but I cannot ... because I always come back to my culture.

Samia came from an urban liberal family and was shocked at how her life was restricted from the outset when she moved in with her husband and in-laws. She was worried about her daughters' future and while Samia thought it acceptable for her daughters to have boyfriends when they grew up, she was concerned about what her ex-husband, other family members and others in the Iraqi community would say and if they would resort to violence.

Threats of physical violence, including murder threats and attempts were the second main reason why women did not report the violence. This combined with the fear that the violence would worsen if they talked about it to professionals, such as teachers or social services. If they suspect or even have experienced that an attempt to get help with leaving the violence did not lead to a wholehearted effort, it can, as several of the women's stories show, be a very risky endeavour. Nada from Iraq is a case in point. When she finally revealed, in school, how bad things were at home, she was forcibly removed from the home. However, the family moved to another municipality that would not pay for her stay in a foster family, and she was sent back home to an unusually violent mother who got her into a forced marriage at the age of 14.

Women who speak out reflect on questions of loyalty, culture and identity: Am I supposed to put up with violence to be a true Tamil or Iraqi woman? Or should I seize the opportunities offered in Denmark to live a life free of violence? They also make a kind of risk calculation: Is it more dangerous to speak out than to stay? Will anyone believe and support me in breaking out of the violence?

Family honour and the ideal of protection

Most of the interviewees talked about family honour and its importance to their families. As women they were central to the maintenance of family honour, which, according to some of the young interviewees, meant that they were *'living in a kind of open prison'* with their every step watched and scrutinized. Rumours and gossip within their community seemed to have a devastating effect on the women's lives (cf. Eldén 2003). No matter how well they behaved and the extent to which they adopted a 'good girl' position, it was seen to never be enough. 'People' or 'they' were recurrent terms in the interviews. Both seemed to refer to the ever-watching community.

Emine, a young woman of Turkish background, reflected on her family's reaction to her escape from home to a shelter, saying that her mother was only worried about what she had told the staff and about any gossip. She explained: *'My mother is so concerned about what other people might say. It is a matter of honour. If people can talk about me and put my family down ... that is what they live for. They live to humiliate one another'.* It was Emine's perception that people in her community constantly sought to put others down. Within this, young women embody the battle of honour and recognition that is fought among families: *'Ask every girl of ethnic [minority] background ... they are all afraid that someone might say something about them, or that their family might hear something about them. That is the problem they face in their everyday life'.*[11]

Most of the other young interviewees' stories confirm these remarks. They speak about strict rules administered by their parents, and how the prohibitions serve to set them apart from their classmates or colleagues because they were only allowed to go directly to school and/or work and back again. Every little transgression was punished with violence by either parent. Although they went to school and sometimes were allowed to go to work, they

11 The young woman says 'they' when she refers to her own ethnic community, but this is probably no coincidence. It appears from the interview that she feels abused by her family and does not expect anything good from the Turkish community, which she tends to describe in monolithic terms. She even considers 'going Danish', skipping all relations to 'foreigners' as she calls them, taking a typical Danish name and becoming blond, etc.

led secluded lives and were expected to stay at home whenever possible. The usual reason given for the seclusion was *'girls carry the family honour'*. For one of the young women, Noha, the concept of family honour came down to one thing, namely an intact hymen: *'They see you as a sex organ somehow, only with legs'*. The maintenance of virginity was recurrent in many of the young women's stories, suggesting that it is an important cultural issue for some (cf. Aamand & Uddin 2007; Mørck 1998).

Seen from an internal perspective, protecting the family honour can mean protecting women against the dangers of the outside world, and against their own desires. Papanek (1973) writing about purdah, the institutional practice of female seclusion in much of South Asia, has coined the concept of 'symbolic shelter'. She suggests that female seclusion is centred on a strongly felt tension between the kin unit and the outside world, which is seen as a difficult and hostile place. Thus what is implied in the concept is that something and someone needs to be protected from forces originating elsewhere. This task, in turn, requires a profound differentiation between persons who need protection and those who provide it. According to Papanek, it is here that the deepest inequality is assumed because the entire system of seclusion is based on certain assumptions about the nature of women and men.

Our material shows clearly that the interviewees were neither expected nor trusted to be able to protect themselves. Whilst the unmarried women were subjected to many rules and regulations and parental control over their whereabouts, the married women were subjected to the control of their husbands and families-in-law. It is also evident that men are assumed to be the natural protectors of women and that protection is hard to separate from control. Papanek's question, 'What are these women being sheltered from?' may have an ironic undertone, because what happens when it turns out that the outside world is much less dangerous to women than the sheltered one? Discussing honour-based violence, Gill (2009) argues that it has the patina of social respectability, yet paves the way for other forms of gender-based violence and that honour, far from being a celebration of women's dignity and social importance, actually leads to their victimization and abuse. Numerous examples from our material confirm the vulnerability of women whose protectors were also their abusers; the following two examples are typical.

Fadia, an Iraqi woman, came to Denmark with her parents as a refugee when she was 15. At the age of 16 her father forced her to marry a man of Iraqi descent. Her father received 50,000 DKK for her. She fled her husband after just a few months, returning to her parents and began working in unskilled jobs. Her father collected the money she earned. When she was 21 her father traded her once more; this time to another Iraqi man who lived in Germany. She had a son in this short and unhappy marriage, but her husband kept the child in agreement to grant her divorce. Losing her child in that way caused a mental breakdown and she was hospitalized for a few months. When she got back to her parents, her father had another husband for her who was almost 40 years older than she was. Her protests were met with sanctions from her father who locked her up in a room and threatened that she would never come out alive. She stayed in the room for three days without food until she managed to escape through the window and found her way to a shelter. Her father controlled everything in the family; when she was asked to explain why her father beat her, she said '*They are Muslims with many rules*'. Her father had said that he would always control her, even when she married. He beat her whenever he thought she did something wrong or said something he did not like.

Samia who came to Denmark to live with her newly married husband of Iraqi descent soon found herself in a very strict environment, living with her husband, his younger brother and her mother-in-law. She faced social isolation and economic deprivation and, ultimately, was exposed to severe physical violence when she began thinking about getting a divorce. She was not allowed to talk to her family in Iraq or to have female friends, and he told her what clothes to wear. When she filed for divorce after years of physical and mental abuse, her husband abducted her one night and put her on a plane to Iraq where he intended to dump her after having taken her passport. She could not give up her children, however, so she went to the Danish embassy and managed to get back to Denmark. Her husband was angry about her return, believing that he had managed to get her out of the country. According to Samia, her husband and his family tried to dump her in Iraq because: '*They cannot have a divorced, single woman walking about in Denmark*'. Apparently a divorcee living on her own presents a threat to a man's honour and self-representations (Moore 1994), as the single woman is proof that women can protect themselves and be in control, which makes men redundant as protectors/controllers. The single or unsheltered woman also testifies to the fact that her ex-husband did not do his job well enough.

The game of suffering and care

When Adile came to Denmark as a marriage migrant she did not know her in-laws and she was unprepared for the life they forced on her. Her new mother-in-law told Adile that she was worn out by hard work in order to earn money and to establish a home in Denmark and a house back in Turkey. According to the mother-in-law, Adile was lucky to have it all ready for her and enjoy the fruit of their hard work. Consequently, Adile was expected to do all the housework in the common home and to care for her parents-in-law, including cutting their finger and toe nails and undressing them and put them to bed in the evening. Not until then could she rest herself. She ate her meals alone in the kitchen while the rest of the family ate together. She was not allowed to leave the apartment, and the only contact she had with the outside world was calling her parents in Turkey twice a year and speaking with them on the phone under the surveillance of the parents-in-law. She spent most of her time alone at home, crying in secret as her parents-in-law rejected the sight of any tears. Adile described her husband as a child obeying the words of his parents and not criticising them for how they treated her.

Many of the interviewed women had similar stories to tell about self-pity on the part of their abusers for their situations that legitimized exploitation and control of daughters-in-law. As Abu-Lughod and Lutz (1990) argue, emotions are often pragmatic acts and communicative performances rather than internal states of individuals. Adile's parents-in-law believed they had provided and suffered and that somebody had to compensate for all this. When her in-laws practiced dominance through demands for personal care, the dominance became even more humiliating. In Adile's case, the demand for care was extreme; however, in order to understand the violence that takes place in the intimate space of families, one has to consider the daily struggle to get recognition for suffering and corresponding care (Das 1997; Danneskiold-Samsøe 2006).

The ethnographic literature on the Middle East suggests a general strained relationship between wives and their in-laws (Choudry 1996; Fernandez 1997; Hegland 1999; Ghanim 2009). According to Hegland, in-laws feel that a daughter-in-law must be controlled and distanced from her husband. Whilst parents often rely on the income and labour of their son they consider it to be in their interest for their daughter-in-law to be cowed and submissive rather than a part of a decision-making husband-wife team. The daughter-in-law is seen as a potential competitor for (scarce) resources. This may be part of the explanation why none of our informants spoke nicely of their in-laws. When kinship, gender and generation intersect, daughters-in-law are in a weak position vis-à-vis their in-laws. In cases where they rebel – by disobeying, talking back or not performing the duties required of them – they are punished. Violence is used as a teaching device; a means for making women behave and accept dominance.

Parents, in-laws and husbands often legitimate dominance by referring to family loyalty (cf. Wikan 1996; Prieur 2002). They use notions of the 'common good' to confine the young women of the family, and violence often takes place with reference to alignment to the common good of the family.

The women described their families as social hierarchies determining not only who could force their will on others, but also who was in a position to have his or her sufferings acknowledged and consequently claim the right to be cared for. Young women, daughters and wives, were placed at the bottom of such a hierarchy of violence, suffering and care: they were victims of violence and at the same time they found little understanding for their predicaments.

However, few positions are unequivocal and most positions exist somewhere in a continuum of absolute dominance and complete subordination. Adile's husband exemplifies the position of intermediary pinched between the dominance of his parents on the one side and (expectations of) sympathy for his wife on the other. He does not beat her physically and he does not approve of his parents' exploitation of his wife, yet he does nothing to change her conditions and by not taking a stand he is a passive accomplice.

Noha's Moroccan parents maltreated and beat her throughout her entire childhood while she grew up in a little town near Copenhagen. Physical violence was part of everyday life and Noha heard her father brag about how he had beaten her since she was three days old. He was trained in martial arts and knew where to hit without it showing. Usually he would use his fist on her scalp or lash her bottom with his belt (and the buckle when he wanted it to really hurt). Noha's father did not beat her as often as her mother did though as he was more absent. Instead, Noha's mother would hit her more often, usually two or three times a week, slapping her face or pulling her hair. The worst part, for Noha was not the physical violence but the derogatory language of her mother who talked badly about Noha in front of friends and family. According to Noha, *'words hurt more than strokes'*. Even though she did her best to fulfil the expectations and demands of her parents, she was made to feel she was never good enough. She had to be a good daughter doing housework and looking after her brothers, being a studious and able student, and looking pretty, presentable and virtuous.

When Noha was 9 years old, her younger brother died of an illness and her mother became depressed. At that time, her mother slept all day and was not able to do any housework and Noha took over entirely. Noha became the one her mother would talk to about her lost son. Being preoccupied with her own concerns Noha's mother did not recognise any of Noha's problems; Noha's uncle abused her sexually for years, she started excessive eating that turned into bulimia, and she tried to escape the control at home. Noha's mother finally rebelled by claiming her right to the deed of some property she and her husband had built in Morocco. During this dispute Noha's father eventually left her mother. Noha's father moved abroad and was only able to maintain threats of violence and Noha's mother stopped her usual slapping altogether.

As Noha's story illustrates, mothers as intermediaries can be significant in the continuation or termination of violence. When the mother rebels against domination she may also reject passing on domination on her daughter. Being a victim of violence herself, Noha's mother feared the reactions and violence of her husband and she assisted in maintaining order in the family through warnings, threats and scorn, whereas the father was a more distant, but not less intimidating, authority. As an intermediary the mother became a victim and perpetrator at the same time. Like Noha's mother some mothers were merely an extension of a father's or husband's power. Other mothers tried to mediate between fathers and daughters, passing on orders, but interceding with the father as well. The interviewees expressed a tacit expectation – or at least hope – that their mothers would understand, protect and care for them. Hence, when mothers could not live up to that expectation, some interviewees expressed great resentment. Noha was left alone with her problems and suffered low self-esteem. She and some of the other interviewees directed their frustrations towards themselves and became self-destructive, and they told us about eating disorders, cutting and suicide attempts.

Abusive mothers and mothers-in-law do not fit easily into our feminist inspired definition of gender-based violence. However, women's violence towards other, usually younger, less powerful women can be seen as part and parcel of maintaining a gender order by putting the younger women in their right place and installing an expectation in them that they, in turn, can look forward to an increase in power within the gender order as they get older (Brown 1999; Brown and Kerns 1985).

Conclusion

Our interviewees' stories of violence have shown a common underlying pattern in that the women's lives have been controlled to such a degree that they have been left with no alternative but to leave their husbands and/or families. Some of the women presented their decision to leave as a matter of life and death. The women expressed disappointment and resentment. Their expectations of marriage and family life had not been met. The ideal and promise of protection and care – aspects of the symbolic shelter – turned out to be more rhetoric than reality as real life tipped towards isolation, control and violence, and women were reduced to pawns in the hands of the more powerful who demand care for themselves. Still the women have been reluctant to let go of their families and communities; a conflict of family and cultural loyalty seem to be ever present, and some women tend to get stuck. This ambivalence towards a stand on violence is the Gordian knot for the shelters to untie.

The Danish welfare state has been described as 'woman friendly' (Hernes 1987). To ethnic minority women who have realised that the inside world is more troublesome and dangerous than the outside world it does present a kind of external protection against internal restrictions (Kymlicka 1999). Shelters and economic independence for women make it possible to take the first step towards greater control of their own lives, bodies and sexuality.

References

Aamand, Kristina/Uddin, Asif (2007): Mødom på mode. Beretninger om skik og brug blandt indvandrere. Copenhagen: Gyldendal.

Abbink, Jon (2000): Preface: Violation and Violence as Cultural Phenomena. In: Aijmer, Göran/Abbink, Jon (2000): Meanings of Violence. A Cross Cultural Perspective. Oxford and New York: Berg, pp. xi–xvii.

Abu-Lughod, Lila/Lutz, Catherine A. (1990): Introduction: Emotion, Discourse and the Politics of Everyday Life. In: Lutz, Catherine A./Abu-Lughod, Lila (1990): Language and the Politics of Emotion. Cambridge: Cambridge University Press, pp. 1–23.

Ahmed, Leila (1984): Early Feminist Movement in the Middle East: Turkey and Egypt. In: Hussain, Freda (ed.): Muslim Women. New York: St. Martin's Press, pp. 111–123.

Aijmer, Göran/Abbink, Jon (2000): Meanings of Violence. A Cross Cultural Perspective. Oxford and New York: Berg.

Barlach, Lise (2009): LOKK voksenstatistik 2008. Copenhagen: Servicestyrelsen & LOKK.

Baumann, Gerd (1996): Contesting Culture. Discourses of Identity in Multi-Ethnic London. Cambridge: Cambridge University Press.

Brown, Judith K./Kerns, Victoria (1985): In Her Prime. A New View of Middle-Aged Women. Massachusetts: Bergin & Garvey Publishers.

Brown, Judith K. (1999): Introduction: Definitions, Assumptions, Themes, and Issues. In: Counts, Dorothy A./Brown, Judith K./Campbell, Jacquelyn C. (1999): To Have and to Hit. Cultural Perspectives on Wife Beating. Urbana and Chicago: University of Illinois Press, pp. 3–26.

Burman, Erica/Smailes, Sophie L./Chantler, Khatidja (2004): 'Culture' as a Barrier to Service Provision and Delivery: Domestic Violence Services for Minoritized Women. In: Critical Social Policy 24, 3, pp. 332–357.

Choudry, Salma (1996): Pakistani Women's Experience of Domestic Violence in Great Britain. Research Findings no. 43, Home Office Research and Statistics Directorate, London, Great Britain, October 1996.

Counts, Dorothy A./Brown, Judith K./Campbell, Jacquelyn C. (1999): To Have and to Hit. Cultural Perspectives on Wife Beating. Urbana and Chicago: University of Illinois Press.

Crenshaw, Kimberlé W. (1994): Mapping the Margins: Intersectionality, Identity Politics, and Violence Against Women of Color. In: Fineman, Martha A./Mykitiuk, Roxanne (1994): The Public Nature of Private Violence. The Discovery of Domestic Abuse. New York and London: Routledge, pp. 93–118.

Danneskiold-Samsøe, Sofie (2006): The Moral Economy of Suffering. Social Exchange among Iraqi Refugees in the Danish Welfare State. Copenhagen: University of Copenhagen.

Das, Veena (1997): Language and Body: Transactions in the Construction of Pain. In: Das, Veena/Kleinman, Arthur/Lock, Margaret (1997): Social Suffering. Berkeley: University of California Press, pp. 67–91.

Eldén, Åsa (2003): Heder på liv och död. Voldsomma berättelser om rykten, oskuld och heder. Uppsala: Uppsala University.

Fernandez, Marilyn (1997): Domestic Violence by Extended Family Members in India. Interplay of Gender and Generation. In: Journal of Interpersonal Violence 12, 3, pp. 433–455.

Ghanim, David (2009): Gender and Violence in the Middle East. Santa Barbara: Praeger Publishers.

Gill, Aisha K. (2009): South Asian Women's Experiences of Rape: Analysis of the Narrative of Survival. In: Horvath, Miranda/Brown, Jennifer (2009): Rape: Challenging Contemporary Thinking. Devon: Willan Publishing, pp. 161–183.

Harvey, Penelope/Gow, Peter (1994): Sex and Violence. Issues in Representation and Experience. London and New York: Routledge.

Hegland, Mary Elaine (1999): Wife Abuse and the Political System: A Middle Eastern Case Study. In: Counts, Dorothy A./Brown, Judith K./Campbell, Jacquelyn C. (1999): To Have and to Hit. Cultural Perspectives on Wife Beating. Urbana and Chicago: University of Illinois Press, pp. 234–251.

Hernes, Helga (1987): Welfare State and Women Power. Oslo: Norwegian University Press.

Jenkins, Richard (1997): Rethinking Ethnicity. Arguments and Explorations. London: Sage.

Kymlicka, Will (1999): Liberal Complacencies. In: Cohen, Joshua/Howard, Matthew/Nussbaum, Martha C. (1999): Is Multiculturalism Bad for Women? New Jersey: Princeton University Press, pp. 31–35.

Lundgren, Eva (1995): Feminist Theory and Violent Empiricism. Aldershot, UK: Avebury.

Moore, Henrietta (1994): The Problem of Explaining Violence in the Social Sciences. In: Harvey, Penelope/Gow, Peter (1994): Sex and Violence. Issues in Representation and Experience. London and New York: Routledge, pp. 138–155.

Mørck, Yvonne (1998): Bindestregsdanskere. Fortællinger om køn, generationer og etnicitet. Frederiksberg: Forlaget Sociologi.

Mørck, Yvonne (2000): Hyphenated Danes: Contested Fields of Gender, Generation and Ethnicity. In: YOUNG, Nordic Journal of Youth Research 8, 3, pp. 2–16.

Nielsen, Sissel Lea (2005): Projekt ikke-dansktalende kvinder på krisecenter – en evaluering og erfaringsopsamling. Copenhagen: VFC Socialt Udsatte & Danner.

Papanek, Hanna (1973): Purdah: Separate Worlds and Symbolic Shelter. In: Comparative Studies in Society and History 15, 3, pp. 289–325.

Petersen, Rasmus Bilde et al. (2009): Tal og fakta – befolkningsstatistik om indvandrere og efterkommere 2009. Copenhagen: Ministeriet for Flygtninge, Indvandrere og Integration.

Prieur, Annick (2002): Magt over eget liv: om unge indvandrere, patriarkalske familieformer og nordiske ligestillingsidealer. In: Borchorst, Anette (ed.): Kønsmagt under forandring. Copenhagen: Hans Reitzels Forlag, pp. 149–167.

Riches, David (1986a): The Phenomenon of Violence. In: Riches, David (ed.): The Anthropology of Violence. Oxford: Blackwell, pp. 1–27.

Riches, David (1986b): The Anthropology of Violence. Oxford: Blackwell.

Schmidt, Bettina E./Schröder, Ingo W. (2001): Anthropology of Violence and Conflict. London and New York: Routledge.

Schröder, Ingo W./Schmidt, Bettina E. (2001): Introduction: Violent Imageries and Violent Practices. In: Schmidt, Bettina E./Schröder, Ingo W. (2001): Anthropology of Violence and Conflict. London and New York: Routledge, pp. 1–24.

Sørensen, Bo Wagner (1998): Explanations for Wife Beating in Greenland. In: Klein, Renate C.A. (ed.): Multidisciplinary Perspectives on Family Violence. London and New York: Routledge, pp. 153–175.

Sørensen, Bo Wagner (2001): 'Men in Transition': The Representation of Men's Violence Against Women in Greenland. In: Violence Against Women 7, 7, pp. 826–847.

Wikan, Unni (1996): Kultur, makt og smerte. In: Kvinden & Samfundet 112, 1, pp. 8–12.

In the Name of 'Rights' – BAMER Women, Terrorism and Violence Against Women

Amrit Wilson and Sumanta Roy

In the various writings about violence against minority ethnic women and children, particularly the activism and state policies aimed at combating it, comparatively little has been said about the 'war on terror', and the new rights-based agenda and their impact on BAMER[1] women facing violence in the UK. In this chapter, we examine just one area of this impact – the effects of this policy on specialist BAMER services and routes to safety for BAMER women. Ever since the beginning of the debate on forced marriage and the proposal for a specific criminal law in 2005, the British state has carefully developed a public image of being concerned about gender-based violence in BAMER families and communities. But in the same period the state has implemented a number of policies which have impacted enormously on women from the same groups. Here we shall examine the policies of 'community cohesion' which have served to justify the closure of specialist refuges and even threatened women-only refuges; the so-called 'war on terror' with its justification and establishment of widespread surveillance and profiling; and the shift towards criminal justice responses to violence against women (VAW), favouring a punitive approach, under the Domestic Violence, Crime and Victims Act 2004, at the expense of preventative work, as well as changes in the Race Relations legislation at a time of increasing racism and Islamophobia.

British racism and Islamophobia

A strand of Islamophobia has long been a part of British racism, with its roots in the crusades, orientalism and colonialism (Said 1978). But when did the comparatively recent phase of virulent anti-Muslim racism really start? While the media and various 'common-sense' views suggest that Is-

1 BAMER stands for Black, Asian, Minority Ethnic and Refugee women.

lamophobia began with the horrific attacks of 9/11, the experience of BAMER women tells a different story. They invariably emphasize that while 9/11 led to an enormous escalation of Islamophobia, for the majority of Muslims of all communities (and other South Asian groups), deep-rooted racism had impacted on their lives throughout the era of multiculturalism, shaping immigration laws, welfare state policies, the attitudes of the police, discrimination in employment and spilling over into violent attacks on the streets.

Working-class South Asian communities in the North of England, most of them Pakistani and Bangladeshi, which had faced the worst effects of deindustrialization in the 1980s, remained, in the 1990s, locked in a limbo of poor educational opportunities and unemployment. In towns such as Burnley, Accrington, Oldham, Blackburn and Bradford, a generation has grown up in communities, white and South Asian, which are among Britain's most impoverished one percent. These communities were kept apart not by difference but by racism; at the same time South Asian encounters with the police and other agencies too were often shaped by racism. In the 1990s, the last phase of the multicultural era, the demonisation of Islam in America's global strategy had begun to feed into the British media, and into the ways in which minority ethnic communities were constructed, generating a specifically anti-Muslim racism. The construction of the 'Muslim' man as fanatical, fundamentalist, violent and owing allegiance to forces external – and hostile – to Europe came to the foreground in racist imagery (Kundnani 2007). Particularly since 9/11, these images have become much more widespread and the notion of all Muslims as suspect and dangerous has been consolidated by the media and by anti-terrorism policies which target whole communities. So intense is this politics of fear that even children as young as eleven are being asked to report their peers to their teachers and to the Police should they be identified as holding potentially extremist attitudes (BubblieKang 2010).

The images of Muslim women, which have been deeply inscribed in popular consciousness in this period, have a specific dichotomy. On the one hand, they are seen as victims, horrifically oppressed by the cruel and backward men in their families, with the newspapers often reporting 'forced marriages', brutal parents and victimized daughters. On the other, and increasingly, they are seen as aiding terrorism or else being terrorists themselves. All these factors have contributed to the rise in the numbers of attacks on Muslims – men, women and children-recorded by the police. A recent report also points out that many of these crimes remain hidden: *'The majority of anti-Muslim hate crimes are not reported to police either because of a lack of confidence in the police or because victims are unaware of a police interest'* (Githens-Mazer and Lambert 2010: 11).

In the last twenty years or so, culture and religion have also been conflated and populations which had earlier been categorised according to language or region of origin are now categorised by their religion above all else, even where those who identify with a religion, for example Islam, are from a diversity of groups. In the same period, the heightening Islamophobia and racism increased the ghettoisation of many working-class communities, particularly South Asian Muslim, and this, together with the acceptance by the state of South Asian patriarchy, led to the collusion of statutory and voluntary organizations in upholding patriarchal stipulations. At the same time, the focus on religion and culture made it possible for the state to ignore social and economic factors, power imbalances and institutionalized discrimination, which all contribute to women's marginalization (Dustin n.d.). This made South Asian women's struggles against violence and oppression far harder. They were hampered too by the extreme racism of media reportage of gender violence. It was against this background and under pressure from South Asian women's groups to respond to the sometimes extreme violence they faced that the state began to propose policies that appeared to confront 'Muslim' patriarchy (Siddiqui 2006). While multiculturalism had allowed the state to consolidate and strengthen both South Asian patriarchy and the construction of South Asian women as victims, state agencies and government statements began to now appear to confront it, reacting with shock and horror as though patriarchy was a monster unknown, which had suddenly appeared from an 'alien' and 'backward' land.

The first effects of this new confrontation were to be found in the enactment of the Forced Marriage Civil legislation which was brought in despite the opposition by the majority of the BAMER VAW sector. These groups argued that it was unnecessary because existing laws on abduction and domestic violence were adequate to deal with forced marriage, and what was required instead was the revision and proactive enforcement of these laws. It was also pointed out that forced marriage is a very broad category which includes nebulous issues such as emotional pressure which can be hard to evidence. The debate around the new law and its implementation was accompanied by the state and media's increasing obsession with forced marriage on another level which undoubtedly increased racism and Islamophobia. However, the revised protection orders stemming from the Act have been used by some women and have helped them escape forced marriages (Ministry of Justice 2009). They have also encouraged better informed debate within the generic VAW sector on an issue that was previously dealt with only by the BAMER sector.

The Forced Marriage Act was followed closely by the raising of the permitted age of entry to Britain of wives joining their husbands, making it apparent that immigration control was part of the reason for the sudden interest in this area. Not surprisingly, many South Asian women were able to see behind this smoke screen of 'concern'. As a woman user of the dwindling specialist services in Rotherham in North East England asked – *'What is the Forced Marriage agenda really about, is it about offering protection or keeping people out of this country?'* (Service User 2010).

Community cohesion

In the summer of 2001, a series of violent confrontations in northern towns led to the worst riots in England since 1981. Racist gangs had long and almost routinely invaded Asian areas attacking men, women and children, and the police themselves had targeted these areas, with the local media long sensationalising Asian crimes against whites and interpreting them as 'racially motivated' (Kundnani 2007: 53, 196). In every case in the 2001 riots, the violence was begun by racist gangs either going on a rampage or attempting to march through Asian areas and the police responding by donning riot gear and invading these areas themselves (Kundnani 2007). The riots in Bradford resulted in injuries to hundreds of police officers and the destruction of many buildings. The press and a variety of commentators argued that the over tolerance inherent in 'diversity' policies had encouraged Muslims to live by their own values, and that the riots were the result of the innate separateness of Islamic culture and that these communities had 'self-segregated' (see for example, Toynbee 2004; Phillips 2005).

Amidst these developments, the government assertions made it clear (Home Office 2002) that the concept of institutional racism, acknowledged in February 1999 (Macpherson 1999), was to be abandoned in favour of integration. Simultaneously, the Human Rights Act (1998) also virtually abandoned the whole question of racism or racial discrimination. The law made it plain that what was of concern in this era, when 'regime change' was carried out in the name of 'human rights', was not 'race' but 'human rights'. The 9/11 attacks provided the state with the ideal launching pad for policies like Community Cohesion. In fact, we argue that 'Community Cohesion', despite its name, can best be understood as an essentially racist framework of policies which stand for assimilation and is based on the politics of fear and the state's concern with national security and immigration.

The notion of community cohesion also provides the state with a 'moral' justification for its neoliberal economic policies of cuts in public expenditure. It urges the closure of certain services and organizations, whose very existence, it claims, undermines the 'glue' (CLG 2008a) [of Britishness] which holds the nation together. The policies of community cohesion, we argue, rule that funds be withdrawn from specialist BAMER projects or that these organizations be merged with mainstream services. In fact, it tries to erase the concept of specific needs altogether (Worley 2005). Further, despite the fact that UK government statistics indicate that women were the victims in nearly 8 out of 10 incidents of domestic violence (Home Office 2009), state policy has also begun to emphasize that men too face violence. In other words, that it is a question of gender, not women's oppression. Thus the systemic nature of women's oppression has increasingly been sidelined in state policy.

The Supporting People Programme (SP) implemented from April 2003 also paved the way for a series of cuts in the BAMER women's sector. SP claimed to offer *'vulnerable people the opportunity to improve their quality of life by providing a stable environment which enables greater independence'* (CLG 2005) but in reality, it has become a cost cutting exercise which, in the name of 'best value', has done away with a large number of BAMER refuges or merged them with mainstream organisations, drastically reducing such services (Thiara and Hussain 2005). With the increasing use of competitive tendering processes and 'best value' service evaluations, long-established BAMER services are now being routinely asked by their Local Authority to re-apply for funding, deliver their services with less funds while targeting more women from other communities, and in some cases to consider how their services cater for men. Consequently, funding for the women's sector has been re-distributed to make room for a monopoly of state-run services and generic 'super-providers' with a lack of expertise or history in delivering services for women and children.

The struggle against the decimation of this sector has intensified since early 2008, when Imkaan[2] launched a national campaign, publishing a report (Mouj 2008) which highlighted the closure of essential services, and the reduction in safe spaces for women and children as a consequence of the lack of recognition of the needs of BAMER women and children by Local Authorities. Imkaan reported 50% of BAMER women-led services had been taken over by large non-specialist providers, 70% of existing BAMER services for women and children were under threat of being decommissioned under the move towards area-based grants and value for money assessments (Mouj 2008). Since the 1980s, the BAMER sector has been crucially important in saving lives, providing safety to BAMER women facing domestic

2 Imkaan is a national second tier organisation that provides a strategic voice, research, training for BAMER refuges supporting women and children escaping violence.

violence, countering their total isolation from family and community networks, meeting their linguistic and cultural needs and those of their children and providing a space free from racism and Islamophobia. Yet Local Authorities have shown little recognition of the needs of BAMER women, brushing aside the ways of working which have been fought for and established over a considerable period. Their assessments of best value – on the basis of which refuges are asked to close or merge – ignore the well-established fact that BAMER women and children facing domestic violence need greater advocacy, and often need interpreters and outreach and therapeutic work (Thiara 2005). Despite the government's proclamation about investing in services, this does not appear to address the reality of women's needs particularly in the areas of housing-based support. More than 300 women a day are still unable to access a refuge which equates to 78,000 women per year in the UK (Women's Aid 2009). Shockingly, over 40% of BAMER women have been in the abusive relationship for 5 years or more and over 90% experienced abuse on a weekly basis (Thiara and Roy 2010). These figures speak for themselves, demonstrating that current approaches offer partial solutions to addressing violence, clearly signifying the importance of a holistic approach through early and crisis intervention, counselling, advocacy, advice, outreach and peer-support.

BAMER women's experiences of VAW services in this era of Community Cohesion and SP highlight the deep contradictions between the state's proclamations and the policies it implements. As many in the South Asian women's refuge movement are asking, if the state is concerned about South Asian women's lives being endangered by Forced Marriage and Honour Crimes (singling out South Asian and Middle Eastern women in this respect) why is it closing down the very organisations and services which support and strengthen South Asian women? And these organisations are shockingly few and far between anyway: for instance, Black women facing domestic violence had to contact an average of 17 agencies before finding help (for white women the number is 11) (Brittain et al. 2005). Imkaan's 2008 report also pointed out a key contradiction between these proposals for the future funding and delivery of domestic violence services and the government's own Gender and Race Equality Legislation:

> The Race Relations (Amendment) Act 2000 Section 2(2) holds public authorities to account where they are charged to rebuild trust and demonstrate fairness by eliminating racial discrimination and promoting equality of opportunity and good race relations... The Gender Equality Duty [requires that] public bodies… take pro-active steps to promote equality between women and men [and] take account of the different needs of women and men in policy and service planning rather than react to complaints when things go wrong. (Mouj 2008: 3)

This contradiction led to a remarkable victory for the BAMER women's sector, when Southall Black Sisters, facing cuts in their core funding from Ealing Council, took the Local Authority to court and won. The case established an important precedent which some BAMER refuges may well be able to use to fight back. However, without a shift in government policy and ring-fenced funding for VAW services, local groups will not be in a position to challenge local commissioning decisions.

The criminal justice system and violence against women

Changes in funding have been accompanied by a shift in the nature of work expected of domestic violence services. There is a greater emphasis on punitive action to tackle domestic violence through the CJS than on preventative work. The rhetoric behind this is that those who face violence will have the 'rights' needed to punish the perpetrators by taking them to court. This punitive CJS approach is institutionalized in the Domestic Violence, Crime and Victims Act 2004. The infrastructure consists of MARACS[3], often police-led multi-agency panels which discuss high risk cases of domestic violence with the aim of reducing repeat victimization; Independent Domestic Violence Advocates (IDVAs) often placed within the statutory sector or in large voluntary sector organisations, and Specialist Domestic Violence Courts (SDVCs). Although MARACs do not deal with low or medium risk cases, these comprise the majority of domestic violence cases supported by refuges (Gill and Banga 2008). As may be expected, MARACs have all the drawbacks of crisis management, since of about 1.5 million people who suffer domestic violence a year, they target only around 150,000, (10%) of the most high risk cases in any authority. The rest are expected to be catered for by domestic violence services increasingly under threat of funding cuts.

Since 2005, 127 SDVCs have been established across the UK, providing trained lawyers and judges and 'a more supportive environment' for women to pursue CJS routes. However, research by Imkaan shows that of 37% of women willing to report to the Police, with the support of a BAMER worker, only a fifth (20%) were willing to support a prosecution. The reasons given for not taking any formal action were wanting to access the safety of a BAMER service prior to approaching the Police. Respondents felt too scared of repercussions and did not want to have parents or family arrested (Thiara and Roy 2010). Despite neoliberalism's frequently stated aim of making the

3 Multi-Agency Risk Assessment Conferences (MARAC) are not strictly within the criminal justice system

individual 'independent', a system based on MARACs, also, inevitably disempowers women facing domestic violence. As Nicola Harwin of Women's Aid puts it, MARACS in most areas *'are not survivor-led. The victim is informed that a referral is happening. In a sense they are in direct conflict with the principle of empowerment'* (Hansard, 2008). In addition, while based in areas with sizeable BAMER communities, only 8.45% of cases reviewed at MARAC between July 2008-July 2009 involved BAMER women (Howarth et al. 2009). According to a worker in a generic advice centre, this is because these cases are deemed too complex and therefore there is *'an assumption that these so-called 'honour'-based violence cases 'take too long'* (Advice Centre worker 2010). In another interview, a BAMER outreach manager told us:

> We know of a generic organisation working with a South Asian woman who was referred to the MARAC – their support to her involved using an interpreter to call her over the phone 3 or 4 times. In our experience, if women do not feel they can build up a trusting face-to-face relationship with the organisation they will remain isolated for longer and are unlikely to leave the abuse. This is not about language only. (Outreach Manager 2010)

MARACs are not at present statutory provision, and are set up at the discretion of each local authority. The Association of Police Officers (ACPO) has proposed that they be made statutory, commenting that they: *'... do not consider it acceptable that effective public protection systems should be left to the whims of local agencies to decide upon ... there is a clear requirement that all areas shall have in place MARAC capability by a date to be determined'* (Hansard 2008). While there may be advantages in making MARACs statutory, before this is done their weaknesses need to be addressed if they are going to be useful, particularly for BAMER women.

There is also a further move towards criminalisation which is discussed in the ACPO document – this time of women facing domestic violence being prosecuted if they decide to withdraw their cases. In fact, the state had made provision for this in earlier legislation. In a Kafkaesque allocation of neoliberal 'responsibilities' accompanying neoliberal 'rights', the right to safety has been accompanied by a responsibility to take the perpetrator to court (ACPO 2009). Clearly, women, and particularly BAMER women can be pressurised into withdrawing support for a prosecution but an entirely legalistic approach will make it harder for them to speak out at all against violence. As the Director of Imkaan states:

> Imkaan will support any initiative that will make a difference to vulnerable women and children. However, the government's excessive focus on criminal justice outcomes and its isolationist approach to Violence Against Women policy is problematic – each new development somehow being the solution rather than another

> potential building block. In practice, this creates an 'either/or' context which limits women's routes into safety, support and empowerment (2010).

Increasingly, a picture is emerging of a system, we argue, which ties in with the security agenda and is focused mainly on pursuing and punishing perpetrators, as reflected in ACPO's recent response to a Home Office consultation, *Together we can end violence against women and girls*, which reinforced a 'perpetrator focus' (ACPO 2009). Would it not be more helpful if the police could also explore ways in which they can become more accessible to a larger number of women, since, according to the Home Office statistics, only 13% of women who told someone they were facing domestic violence approached the police (Povey et al. 2008).

Currently Sanctuary Schemes are being promoted as one of the key ways of addressing violence. At its basic level, the former provides women in danger with a secure room in the house to flee to. However, without an adequate risk assessment and links to support services women could feel isolated and essentially become prisoners in one room. In addition, the Government has invested £15 million in Family Intervention Projects (FIPs): (Home Office), which seek to address a wide variety of issues, including domestic violence. Apart from the underlying authoritarian approach here which blames families and parents for failing to cope with the disintegrating welfare state and the encroachment of market values into all areas of life, these programmes are, as one FIP worker told us:

> … problematic because it places untrained workers in highly complex and often dangerous situations. In one ongoing case in a family where the woman has been subject to a violent assault during pregnancy, despite interventions from the police and social services the woman remains in the home and I am then expected to work with the family to resolve a highly complex situation placing both the woman and worker at risk. (FIP worker 2010)

Under the Government's new policies, women are ultimately presented with fewer choices. Without the ability to secure a place of safety and emotional and peer support within a refuge setting, they are increasingly expected to manage their risk and rebuild their lives on their own. In addition, the ways in which cases are handled day to day suggests that the culture of surveillance and fear created by the 'War on Terror' has become deeply ingrained in VAW work in BAMER communities. A worker at a mainstream West London women's centre commented, for example:

> The only training on offer on issues affecting BME women is led by the community safety officer who is based at the local police station and whose whole focus with reference to forced marriages and honour killings is not on what rights and resources the woman can access but on profiling the perpetrators (Bubblie Kang 2008).

Given the climate of racism and the intensifying surveillance which is a part of the 'War on Terror', this profiling will inevitably target Muslim communities. While the state is profiling whole communities in the name of the 'War on Terror', in the name of the 'right' to live free of violence it is profiling perpetrators who we are increasingly told come from the same communities of 'organised criminals'. For example, Nazir Afzal, a Director of the Crown Prosecution Service (CPS), speaks enthusiastically of 'hotspots' of radicalism and honour-based violence. In a speech given at Imkaan's roundtable discussion, 'Responding to violence against women in the name of '*honour'* on 22 November 2006, he stated:

> The Forced Marriage Unit have a lovely map on their wall and it basically identifies where most of their referrals are from and, if you went in the Special Branch of the Terrorist Unit and looked at their map, you would see significant links, significant correlation… There was one case where I could actually evidence it, so how many others are there . . . I have been talking to ministers for the last few months. I mentioned radicalism hotspots and the map of honour-based violence hotspots – then they really listened!

While it may be assumed from Mr. Afzal's track record that this statement would not have been intended to reinforce negative perceptions of Britain's Muslim communities, nevertheless making this link is problematic. It presents a position which is at best over-simplified and at worst potentially dangerous.

The anti-terrorism agenda and violence against women

The deprioritisation of VAW is once again demonstrated by the National Indicators set by the government to shape the funds allocated to local authorities. Only one National Indicator out of 198 is related to domestic violence and it concerns 'repeat violence' by perpetrators. However, there is a new indicator about Preventing Violent Extremism (PVE)[4] and engaging with PVE has also become a statutory duty. It is expected that by April 2011, the budget for PVE will increase by a further £100million (Kundnani 2009).There can be no doubt that the anti-terrorism agenda, along with the sensational and often inaccurate media coverage, constantly escalates racism and Islamophobia. Even Police statistics show that the numbers of faith and race/hate

4 The PVE agenda is a part of PREVENT which is one of the four 'workstreams of 'CONTEST' part of the government's wider counter terrorism strategy (HM Government, 2009).

crimes have risen from 261 incidents in 2002–03 (Parry, Chowdhury and Tucker 2003) to 9,946 in 2009 (MPS 2009).

In Rotherham, a northern English town, for the Muslim community intimidation and violence are everyday experiences. During confidential interviews (2010, 13 January), women told us: 'People are scared living in Rotherham. We are wondering and anxious about what might happen next to the Muslim community': *'I was walking out one day – when a car full of English men who were wearing suits in a very nice car started swearing, shouting abusive words in English and some in broken Punjabi*' (Service User 2010). In addition, it has led to profound changes in the welfare framework (which directly affect BAMER women facing domestic violence) because it draws statutory bodies into:

> … the 'securitisation' agenda thereby dismantling the traditional relationships of trust and confidence between public bodies and service users…. And the community cohesion policies which are an integral part of it have led to 'the abandonment of funding for traditional community development, capacity building and empowerment work with BME communities (Lacman 2009).

Given these changes, it is hardly surprising that VAW has risen in the period 2009–2010 (MPA 2010). We are not arguing that PVE programmes have been used to divert money away from women's groups to religious groups but that they have created a group of Muslim spokespersons who acquiese with government policies on the 'War on Terror'. If community cohesion has led to the closure of organisations, the PVE strategy has set up new ones of a very different kind – working, it is claimed, with 'Muslim community leaders, youth and women'. In 2007, the CLG 'Preventing Violent Extremism Pathfinder Fund' (PVEPF) was established. This has led to the setting up and funding of local Muslim organisations, a part of whose role, in the words of the CLG, will be to empower Muslim women by giving them 'a stronger voice, increased confidence and the knowledge to challenge and tackle violent extremism' (CLG 2008b).

In Ealing, for example, two Muslim women's groups were being set up while Southall Black Sisters faced cuts. When Southall Black Sisters questioned this they were told by Ealing Council that these Muslim women's organisations were in a different funding stream under which they must 'link to the overarching objective of creating a situation where Muslim communities reject and actively condemn violent extremism and seek to undermine and isolate violent extremists. A condition of the grant is that it is not used for the furtherance or propagation of a faith' (Ealing Council 2008). Thus, it would appear that in the new state and media discourses, the measure of Muslim women's 'empowerment' is not whether they are able to confront or escape domestic violence but whether they can be involved as the state's allies in the surveillance which is central to the 'War on Terror' (Da Costa and Dubey 2008). In April 2008, the CLG launched the 'Community Leadership Fund' (CLF) aiming to 'support work that will build the capacity of individuals, organisations and communities to take the lead on tackling violent extremist influences' (CLG 2008: 3). The CLF prioritises five areas of voluntary work, including 'Supporting Muslim women'. What does CLF mean in reality? A Manager from Rotherham told us that CLF had not led to improvements in all services for local women and communities, while a community worker from Leeds said *'Its not about women at all but about supporting those who do not criticise government policies'*.

Clearly, this points to the problematic way in which Community Cohesion has been used, together with the Prevent agenda, to demonise whole communities, including women facing violence, while the same local authority questions the existence of a BAMER women's service. In Bradford, a largely Muslim working-class town in the North of England, home to a population which has been reduced to poverty by deindustrialisation and now neoliberal policies, local authorities have received £1,425,000 in one year alone (Kundnani 2009). How has this affected the situation of women whom PVE wishes to 'empower'? For a start, few women's organisations have even been informed of this funding, let alone drawn into its programmes. A project in Bradford providing the only service for single young women dealing with many cases of forced marriage among other related problems, has been told nothing about the Prevent strategy or funding. A refuge manager told us:

> We were recently reviewed and felt that the Local Authority had no overall interest in the outcomes of the service. Since then I have learnt that the Local Authority has set up its own service for homeless women including those fleeing violence – it is well resourced and they control all referrals and as a consequence we have seen a major drop in referrals from the Council.

Workers at the project say they know that women have actively chosen their services but now both they and the local generic Women's Aid are likely to be told that there is no demand for their services and hence penalised. In Nottingham, the Council was allocated £965,000 in pathfinder funds as part of the East Midlands region encompassing Derby, Leicester and Nottingham (Hansard 2009) in PVE money between 2007 and 2009, as well as funding under the strand of community cohesion. The Manager of the only BAMER women's refuge in the area told us:

> I have heard nothing at all about the Prevent Agenda or funding – but am aware that at one time the Council were offering pots of money for Muslim specific voluntary sector services, which we could not apply for because we are not Muslim

> only although 90% of the women we support are from the Muslim, Pakistani community! (Refuge Manager 2010)

This service is facing closure, despite various representations from its service users stating that they need, want and value a South Asian service. What is particularly significant is that this service deals with many forced marriage and so-called honour based violence cases, and despite the government's much publicised concern for women, it has no hesitation in ruthlessly causing its closure.

Conclusion

At a time when a rights-based agenda is said to be a primary aim, BAMER women are losing their rights to the welfare services which serve their needs best. Places and routes of safety are being closed down while immigration imperatives and the security agenda are completely eroding the relationships of trust which have been traditional in the welfare sector. On an everyday level, the politics of suspicion and fear, the rise of far-right groups and escalating racism and Islamophobia are creating an atmosphere of intense intimidation. The underlying rationale is clear enough – vulnerable people are costing the state too much and they will be increasingly abandoned as Britain moves towards American-style welfare provision. The ideological message is that the withdrawal of the state from all responsibility is actually empowering for the individual, even if their survival is threatened.

References

Association of Police Officers (2009): Tackling Perpetrators of Violence Against Women and Girls: ACPO review for the Home Secretary. London: ACPO. http://www.acpo.police.uk/policies.asp (04.02.2010)

Brittain, Emily/Dustin, Holly/Pearce, Caroline/Rake, Katherine/Siyunyi-Siluwe, Mamusa/Sullivan, Fay (2005): Black and Minority Ethnic Women in the UK. London: Fawcett Society.

BubblieKang (2010): 'Catching the Future Terrorists Young' Blog response. Evening Standard, 3 February. http://www.thisislondon.co.uk/standard/article-23801913-catching-the-future-terrorists-young.do (04.02.2010)

Communities and Local Government (2005): Supporting People. CLG. http://www.spkweb.org.uk (06.08.2008)

Communities and Local Government (2008a): Cohesion Guidance for Funders: Consultation. London: CLG. http://www.communities.gov.uk/publications/communities/cohesionfundersconsultation (06.08.2008)

Communities and Local Government (2008b): Empowering Muslim Women: Case Studies. London: CLG. London. http://www.communities.gov.uk/documents/communities/pdf/669801.pdf (06.08.2008)

Da Costa, Ana N./Dubey, Siddhartha (2008): 'Britain Targets Muslim Women to Fight Extremists'. Reuters. 26 March. http://www.reuters.com/article/latestCrisis/idUSL19739136 (06.08.2008)

Dustin, Moira (n.d.): Gender Equality, Cultural Diversity: European Comparisons and Lessons. London: Gender Institute.

Ealing Council (2008): Agendas, Minutes, Reports: 26.02.08 Grants Equality Impact Assessments and Grants Criteria, Item 4b – Appendix E1: Southall Black Sisters comments and the Council's response regarding the IEIA on community cohesion. Ealing: Ealing Council. http://www.ealing.gov.uk/ealing3/export/sites/ealingweb/services/council/committees/ agendas_minutes_reports/cabinet/15may2007-19may2008/_26_feb_2008/_26_feb_2008/Item_4b_-_Appendix_E1.doc (30.10.2008)

El-Salahi, Zaki (2009): Preventing Violent Extremism Through Community Work: Essentialism and Manipulation (Essay for Postgraduate Diploma in Community Education Course, Moray House School for Education, University of Edinburgh). Edinburgh: Scotland Against Criminalising Communities.

Gill, Aisha/Banga, Baljit (2008): Better Housing Briefing 9: Black Minority Ethnic and Refugee Women, Domestic Violence and Access to Housing. London: Race Equality Foundation.

Githens-Mazer, Jonathan/Lambert, Robert (2010): Islamophobia and Anti-Muslim Hate Crime: A London case study. Exeter: European Muslim Research Centre.

Hansard (2008): Select Committee on Home Affairs Sixth Report: 10 Partnerships. London: House of Commons. http://www.parliament.the-stationery-office.co.uk/pa/cm200708/cmselect/cmhaff/263/26314.htm#n371 (23.01.2010)

Hansard (2009): 16 June 2009 Written Answers: Communities and Local Government. London: House of Commons. http://services.parliament.uk/hansard/Commons/ByDate/20090616/writtenanswers/part015.html (06.02.2010)

HM Government (2009): Pursue Prevent Protect Prepare: The United Kingdom's Strategy for Countering International Terrorism. London: HM Government.

Home Office (n.d.): Tackling Anti Social Behaviour and its Causes: What is a family intervention project? London: Home Office. http://www.asb.homeoffice.gov.uk/members/article.aspx?id=8678 (04.02.2010)

Home Office (2002): Secure Borders, Safe Haven: Integration with Diversity in Modern Britain. London: Home Office.

Home Office (2009): Violent Crime Mini Site: Domestic Violence. London: Home Office. http://www.crimereduction.homeoffice.gov.uk/violentcrime/dv01.htm (04.02.2010)

Howarth, Emma/Stimpson, Louise/Barran, Dianna/Robinson, Amanda (2009): Safety in Numbers: A Multi-Site Evaluation of Independent Domestic Violence Advisor Services. London: CAADA.

Imkaan (2008): Herstory: Snapshot survey. London: Imkaan.

Kundnani, Arun (2007): The End of Tolerance: Racism in 21st Century Britain. London: Pluto Press.

Kundnani, Arun (2009): How Not to Prevent Violent Extremism. London: Institute of Race Relations.

Macpherson, William (1999): The Steven Lawrence Enquiry: Report of an Inquiry by Sir William Macpherson of Cluny. London: The Stationary Office. http://www.law.cf.ac.uk/tlru/Lawrence.pdf (06.08.2008)

Metropolitan police authority (2010): MPS Monitoring Statistics: Crime Statistics. London: MPS. http://www.mpa.gov.uk/statistics/crime-stats/ (February 2010)

Metropolitan Police Service (2009): Latest Crime Figures for London. London: MPS. http://www.met.police.uk/crimefigures/index.php (04.02.2010)

Mouj, Anjum (2008): A Right to Exist: A Paper Looking at the Eradication of Specialist Services to BAMER Women and Children Fleeing Violence. London: Imkaan.

Ministry of Justice (2009): One Year On: the initial impact of the Forced Marriage (Civil Protection) Act 2007. London: Ministry of Justice.

Parry, Laura/Chowdhury, Tanweer/Tucker, Dave (2003): Long Term Trends in Racist and Homophobic Crime Performance, Report 12 of the 17th July 2003 Meeting of the Equal Opportunities & Diversity Board. London: Metropolitan Police Service.

Povey, David/Coleman, Kathryn/Kaiza, Peter/Hoare, Jacqueline/Jansson, Krista (2008): Homicides, Firearm Offences and Intimate Violence 2006/07: Supplementary Volume 2 to Crime in England and Wales 2006/07 (3rd ed.). London: Home Office.

Phillips (2005): Speech to Manchester Council for Community Relations, September 22, 2005.

Said, Edward W. (1978): Orientalism. London: Penguin Books.

Siddiqui, Hanana (2006): 'There is no 'Honour' in Domestic Violence, Only Shame! Women's Struggles Against 'Honour' Crimes in the UK'. In: Welchman, Lynn/Hossain, Sara (eds.): 'Honour': Crimes, paradigms, and violence against women. New Delhi: Zuban.

Thiara, Ravi K./Hussain, Shamshad (2005): Supporting Some People: Supporting People and Services for Asian Women and Children Affected by Domestic Violence. London: Imkaan.

Thiara, Ravi K./Roy, Sumanta (2010): Vital Statistics: The Experiences of BAMER Women and Children Facing Violence and Abuse. London: Imkaan.

Toynbee, Polly (2004): 'Why Trevor is Right'. The Guardian. 7 April. http://www.guardian.co.uk/politics/2004/apr/07/society.immigration (06.12.2009)

Wilson, Amrit (2006): Dreams, Questions, Struggles – South Asian Women in Britain. London: Pluto Press.

Women's Aid (2009): Women's Aid Annual Survey. London: Women's Aid.

Worley, Claire (2005): 'It's Not About Race, it's About the Community': New Labour and 'Community Cohesion'. In: Critical Social Policy, 25, 4, pp. 483–496.

How Violence Against Women is Addressed in Social and Public Action for 'Women in Immigrant Communities': Mixed Standards and a Logic of Suspicion

Marion Manier

Introduction

The continuing invisibility[1] of women in immigration, both in research and in political preoccupations, has been deplored for more than 20 years (Morokvasic 1976; 2008). Now, however, the question of 'women in immigrant communities'[2] has acquired a high profile in the French media and politics as a 'public issue' in its own right. The question of 'women in immigrant communities' has mainly arisen in debates over the wearing of headscarves and measures taken in that connection (the first 'headscarf affair' in Creil in 1989, the secularity law of 2004), polygamy (1991) and, since 2000, forced marriages, violence against and social control of women and girls living on suburban social housing estates[3] (Condon/Hamel 2007; Mucchielli 2005 on gang rapes). These debates have largely helped to make the issue a priority for public action and social action and, more recently, to anchor the issue firmly in the paradigm of gender equality and sexist violence. This article considers some of the main ways in which the issue of women in immigrant communities is addressed in public and social action as a problem of 'violence'. Public and social action are important as spheres in which norms and categories are produced and reworked, and in which institutional and voluntary sector actors interact with women from immigrant communities.

I will start by briefly describing how the question of women in immigrant communities emerged as a 'public problem' and a target for social action.

---

1 This invisibility has been largely due to the economic and 'androcentric' terms in which immigration was long considered, both in research and in policy agendas. (Morokvasic 1997, 2008).

2 '*Femmes de l'immigration*' (translated here as 'women in immigrant communities') is an institutional category that includes women migrants of foreign nationality and French women from immigrant backgrounds, whether naturalised or of the 'second generation'. See the *Femmes de l'immigration* report by the Ministry of Labour (*Ministère du travail, des relations sociales, de la famille, de la solidarité et de la ville*) and the Ministry of Prefessional Equality and Parity (*Ministère de la parité et de l'égalité professionnel*), and the 2003 and 2007 framework agreements to foster the integration of '*femmes de l'immigration*', etc.

3 E.g. the success of the *Ni Putes Ni Soumises* ('Neither tarts nor submissive') movement.

The next part is based on material gathered during my doctoral research into social action organizations and institutions running programmes for women in immigrant communities[4]. I will use this material to examine (a) the ethnic and gender-based analyses made of these women's condition and (b) the ways in which social welfare actors frame the problem of violence and seek to address it. To close, I suggest some avenues for reflection on the social impact of these responses.

I will not, of course, be calling into question the usefulness of these organizations or the sincere concern of those who work in them, nor the very real violence sometimes inflicted on women in immigrant communities[5] (Condon and Hamel 2007). But it will be useful to examine the discourses and the interpretative framework within which the problem of violence against women in immigrant communities is understood and constructed. This will involve analyzing the way ethnic and gender categories are interwoven. Violence against women in this context tends to be construed (a) by reference to other concepts such as 'integration' that reflect the social treatment of immigration in general and (b) from a standpoint that ethnicizes social problems (Fassin, 2006) and matters of sex and sexism such as 'sexist violence on the estates' (Delphy 2008; Condon and Hamel 2007). Doubly categorized, as women and as members of an 'ethnic minority', women in immigrant communities are at the receiving end of sometimes paradoxical and often particularizing actions, usually based on the idea of their otherness. The question then is whether the treatment of violence against women, by aiming to be specific, does not symbolically produce another form of violence: stigmatization.

4 Field work was done in the Alpes Maritimes département from 2004 to 2008, in mainly voluntary-sector welfare units for the induction, training, mediation and integration of immigrant clients, especially women. Many of these units have specific missions and functions for immigrant women, particularly combating gender inequality and preventing sexist violence, although they do not specialise in caring for women victims of violence. I shall also use data on 'women on the estates' collected from a network of official and voluntary sector actors. I provide extracts from interviews and personal observations of meetings and situations recorded in these units using an inductive, participatory method (since I was once, myself an assistant trainer in the voluntary sector and also worked with these units).

5 Studies have shown that foreign women or those with immigrant parents are more vulnerable to certain forms of violence (Condon and Hamel 2007) and that situations of dependence, particularly administrative dependence in the case of foreign women, accentuate their dependence on their families. (See issue No. 75 of *Revue Plein Droit* (2007), 'Femmes, étrangers: des causes concurrentes ?').

Women in immigrant communities: new issues

In France in the 1960s and 1970s, the subject of women in migrant communities was marginal and not a matter of public debate. Nonetheless, social action organizations were formed to assist North African migrant women, seen primarily as wives coming to join husbands working in France (Golub, Morokvasic and Quiminal 1997). As Anne Golub (1997; 2000) points out, this mainly involved helping families obtain local authority housing. They aimed to take a hand in the 'social adaptability' of families, and of women:

> 'women' were never considered separately from 'families'. With the women, measures for the male worker's economic adaptability [previously ensured by their employers] were replaced by 'social adaptability' measures which were seen as an endless preliminary to any form of mobility (Golub et al. 1997: 24).

New migration policies introduced in the mid-1970s (official halt to worker immigration, family reunification procedures) focused on 'managing stocks rather than flows' (Taravella 1984). Social demand now focused on the 'social problems' connected with immigration, mainly seen in terms of the families' integration. So the question of migrant women emerged mainly through the prism of family, with representations of female and family roles that Catherine Quiminal calls 'archaic': 'It really is the family with the woman as mother and guarantor of Christian family values, but with no provision of the social and economic conditions for such families to become a reality' (Golub et al. 1997: 24). The question of women's occupational integration was gradually raised, but usually set aside until 'after' their cultural and social integration. The training proposed would often prepare them for domestic employment (cooking, cleaning, sewing etc.). As Morokvasic writes, 'the training proposed for immigrant women was limited to adapting them to a female role which was in any case completely outdated, being called into question in every social class our societies' (Golub et al. 1997: 25). As to the second generation, which was becoming visible in the 1980s, they were often seen as 'agents of change' and integration.

The standards of adaptability and integration is still sometimes based on somewhat rigid, victimizing representations of 'immigrant women' in which they are seen as traditional housewives, passive, isolated and particularly far removed from integration and 'employability'. But other registers have entered public discourse and are affecting public action and social action. Since the 1980s the question of 'migrant women' (and 'third-world women' more generally) has become much more visible; the World Bank, the United Nations and Europe (at the instigation of the Council of Europe) have declared their status a matter of global concern. The theme has gradually been taken up by campaigns against violence (particularly at the 1995 Peking conference and by Unicef and Amnesty International), female genital mutilation and human trafficking (e.g. by the *Office des Migrations Internationales*, the French government's immigration bureau). In France since 2000, 'women in immigrant communities', both 'mothers' and 'daughters', have become a major focus of public action, located as they are at the intersection between the issues of integration (with a tightening of immigration and integration policies and the application of the 'induction and integration contract'), the keeping of religious expression out of public space (*laïcité*) and gender equality. They have been made a priority for various government departments under the revived theme of combating violence against women.

This institutional and media categorization of women in immigrant communities and their problems has led to the creation (mainly by social action organizations) of integration programmes and targeted actions for 'women in immigrant communities', 'women on the estates', 'mothers', etc. Below I describe some of the main features of these actions.

An example of social action organizations

An ethnic and gender-based analysis

Amongst official and voluntary sector social action circles working – exclusively or not – with immigrant women, there is a growing tendency to consider women's 'integration' as a problem of emancipation and of combating sexist violence and dependence on the husband. These topics are now included in the social action organizations' mission statements through institutional directives (former FASILD, ACSE, DDASS, CAF[6], municipal policies). They are presented as essential priorities. In response to what is constructed as a worrying 'public problem', associations dealing with integration, literacy or other services for migrants have taken preventive action. Neighbourhood initiatives are springing up on the housing estates. Networks, partnerships and federations of smaller NGOs, working closely with local political circles, are forming around the issue of 'women in immigrant communities'. In the Alpes Maritimes local authority area, two networks have

6 FASILD: *Fond d'Action et de Soutien pour l'Intégration et la Lutte contre les Discriminations* (which works for integration and against discrimination); ACSE: *Agence nationale pour la cohésion sociale et l'égalité des chances* (responsible for social cohesion and equality of opportunity); DDASS: *Direction Départementale des Affaires Sanitaires et Sociales* (the welfare authority in each department of France); CAF: *Caisse d'allocations familiales* (child benefits department).

been formed in the last three years on the issue of 'women in immigrant communities' or, depending on the local situation, 'women on the estates'. These networks include dozens of social action organizations and associations. The launch project for one of these networks suggests the general thrust of these action programmes:

Extract from the initial project for the Femmes des Quartiers network.7 The network is composed of people from local politics, the family allowance authority, associations and welfare bodies in a neighbourhood on the northern edge of Nice.

Many partners are concerned about the situation of women on the estates, which also raises the question of intercultural relations. Several partners have expressed the wish to work together on these questions and share their working experience, so as not to be alone in confronting complex situations.
The main difficulties women on the estates encounter are

- The language barrier. There is strong demand for literacy groups.
- Conjugal violence/risk of forced marriages.
- Access to entitlements.
- The weight of culture/community introversion. Some women stay at home to raise their children and the number of women wearing the veil is increasing.
- Cohabitation between the different communities is still difficult (difficult to mix groups of residents of different ethnic origins).
- Discrimination in the labour market.
- Isolation/exclusion from the labour market.

Women in this neighbourhood have difficulty integrating because their level of French is poor and their sociocultural references are often very different from French cultural patterns. Despite official efforts to fund new literacy groups, there is still unmet demand. These problems seem to add to their isolation and their difficulties in educating their children. However, this group is still the driving force in these 'problem' neighbourhoods; although they suffer violence and discrimination they are still the best placed to call for change. That is why it is important to work in concert on this topical issue.

This analysis, though it does not give an exhaustive summary, is fairly representative of the terms in which institutional and voluntary sector discourse frames the question of 'women in immigrant communities'. The project has formally identified the issues facing welfare actors in relation to 'women on

7 The network's use of the term *femmes des quartiers* (translated here as 'women on the estates', referring to the public housing estates on which a high proportion live) may seem like a euphemism to avoid any reference to ethnic origin. It reflects the prudence of welfare staff and voluntary sector community workers who wish to avoid giving their actions ethnic or community connotations. Nonetheless, they clearly identify the main target of their actions as women of North African origin.

the estates' and has sought to analyze their situation. It has explained the problem in terms of ethnicity and gender and focused simultaneously on integration and gender issues.

Given that 'women on the estates' essentially refers here to women in North African immigrant communities, their situation is considered through the prism of 'cultural influence', cultural distance (De Rudder 1994) and the resulting difficulty of integrating. This is addressed around three gendered themes. Firstly, women in immigrant communities are categorized as being *particularly isolated*, more subject to 'the weight of culture' and tradition. This reflects a view of gender relations that makes women essentially the guardians of culture, values and social mores (Gaspard 2001: 12) while men are the breadwinners. Women continue to be thought of in terms of *emigration*: they are supposed to have stronger links with the culture of origin than the men, whose situation is often seen more in terms of *immigration*, i.e. their role in the host country (Sayad 2006). Institutionally and in social action, the women's situation tends to be categorized in terms of culture while their occupational and economic integration is seen as secondary. Secondly they are also categorized as being *particularly vulnerable to sexist violence* and under strict social control by their family/community. Lastly, and again through the prism of family, the women are seen as 'mothers' facing *particular problems in educating their children*. Cultural origin is seen as closely entwined with the social control or sexist violence suffered by immigrant women. This can be seen in the order of priorities the project presents: language, conjugal life, violence, culture, with employment last. It also presents the problems in pairs: conjugal violence/forced marriage; weight of culture/community introversion; children's education/housewives/the veil. The women's lack of adaptation and the sexist violence and community oppression they are thought to suffer also tends to be attributed to their ethnic and cultural origin.

In the goals and discourse of the associations interviewed in our survey, whether network members or not, the women's integration is generally correlated with their 'emancipation as women'. Emancipation is understood not only as a way of breaking out of their isolation and achieving independence and integration; it is also seen as emancipation – or indeed liberation – *as women*. Hence, the theme is helping these women to combat sexism, community self-segregation and violence. This way of framing the issue is more the result of a consensus among welfare actors than a response to demands formulated by their clients. These, as we shall see, are more often of an economic order: to learn French, to access entitlements, to obtain benefits, housing, or a job.

Framing social action against violence

In this context, violence against women and provision for victims are increasingly prominent questions. Not only specialist organizations but also social centres and associations working on integration, literacy, and social and cultural aspects are taking action on this issue. Preventive actions and information drives are introduced on such subjects as gender equality (e.g. distribution of the *Guide de l'égalité entre les hommes et les femmes issues de l'immigration*, published in 2007 by the Ministry of labour and social affairs), women's rights, the history of women's struggles, contraception, abortion, sexuality, virginity and sexist violence. Campaigns against forced marriage and intimate partner violence are organized. Different organizations collaborate to coordinate events (e.g. on 8 March) promoting women's careers or showing films about women's condition and Islam. There is an increasing number of awareness raising activities about gender equality, often pointing particularly at the supposedly 'specific sexist violence' of 'North African' culture or Islam (forced marriages, gang rapes, genital mutilation, Islamic headscarves) and run by local associations that do not directly specialize in caring for women victims of violence[8].

The Femmes des Quartiers network mentioned earlier is an example. Its very creation was a response to increasing anxiety among welfare actors about what they see as a deterioration in women's condition on the estates. The topics chosen and the cases described by network members at meetings reflect their desire to make sexism and violence priority issues[9]. Many organization members or representatives highlight situations of dependence or oppression of women by their husbands or their community. A social centre representative, for example, said that 'their husbands' reticence still puts a brake on their self-fulfilment (whatever their age or origin)' and asked that the network deal with 'the problem of 'family' pressure in the broad sense, the weight of tradition on women's day-to-day behaviour: emotional blackmail, gossip, the person's image in public space' The representative of a sociocultural association described the following case:

> A young woman married in her country of origin joins her husband, who has a visa. To keep his hold on her, he refuses to go with her to the immigration office to have her presence in France made official. Then the violence begins, because the wife is afraid of being in breach of French law.

8 Associations that have no expertise in matters of violence, legal aspects, procedures or direct contact with emergency accommodation facilities, etc., but who direct clients to the specialist organisations.

9 The data presented here are from observation notes on the network's meetings.

The report of the client's request, which we obtained from the association representative, showed that what she mainly wanted was economic and legal help and accommodation to enable her to separate from her husband: minimum State benefit, family allowance and medical aid, work, housing and information about French law. This is a typical case of the double violence – administrative and sexist – that foreign women may encounter. But in the same report the association representative reformulates it. Although she mentions the material and administrative dependence, she presents the problem as being primarily 'the strong hold of traditions, the strong impact of the husbands, the lack of freedom, failure to share responsibility, conventional wisdom linked to tradition, culture and religion.' This over-interpretation stems from a culturalizing characterization of the situation (note that it refers to 'the husbands' in the plural, moving from the particular to the general). It shows the gap there can be between the local associations' goals and their clients' demands. In meetings, network members regularly raised the issue of forced marriage, saying it was urgent to address the issue before the summer (a high-risk period in this regard), even though few cases had been identified by organizations in the network.

Similarly, situations or anecdotes seen as symptomatic of an *'upsurge in community self-segregation'* with tighter social control over women and worsening relations between men and women were regularly recounted at the network meetings: Imams at the school gates; teenagers disseminating religious books promoting women's submission; shocked reactions from boys, girls and women on seeing the film *Un été à la Goulette* (Férid Boughedir 1996) with a scene showing a young woman in her knickers. One association representative reacted in these terms:

> there were shock reactions (…) Some women were shocked by the nudes (…) but it isn't a risqué film! There's really a regression among the women, the parents (...) But that's what we told them: 'the images are meant to make you react'. We shouldn't spare them, we have to shock them. Even the young people are less liberated about nudity, sex, flirting etc.

The 'general impression' the participants seek to talk about in the network is one of widespread violence and worsening conditions for women. The following extract from a network meeting on violence further reflects this.

At a meeting of some fifteen representatives, mainly women, from different organizations, the chair of the meeting suggested everyone express their views about problem situations and particularly the question of violence.

S., representing a work integration association: 'Well, for example, there's commonplace violence (several people signal agreement). Male violence against women, women against their children and even fathers against their daughters. It has become commonplace (…) even in the way they talk to their children, insults and screaming are frequent …'

R., representing an official body, steps in: 'Yes, there's no need to ask why the youngsters insult each other, it's because the parents do that…'
[…]

Chair: 'At any rate we can identify a first type of problem to consider together: conjugal violence'.

B., on the staff of a non-profit body: 'Underlying these problems there's a problem of communication. These are women who never went to school and have difficulty communicating. That's where the violence comes from in the mother-children relationship. It comes from problems of communication and understanding between the kids and their mothers…'

C., prevention educator: 'It's a major trend. Everyone screams at everyone. It's a constant provocation for the youngsters. There's a gap. Work needs to be done with the young women to teach them to say no. Many are prepared for what's coming, in fact they wait and they don't know how to say no'.

R: 'Those of them from violent backgrounds'.

F., association worker: 'The women don't put themselves forward. It's the men who speak'.

R: 'It's a question of education (…) The question is how can they position themselves (…) without being violent themselves? Because even the young girls are violent, the hardened delinquents anyway'.[10]

B: 'We need to work on a whole set of messages. Outside of violence there's tenderness (…) These are people who've been raised by violence, they need to give themselves the right to be happy (…) And there's not only aggressiveness. Some youngsters learn that too…'

F: 'We have to work on raising the women's consciousness, so they become aware of being women and not just wives or mothers (…) because they only live through that, through their husbands. We have to work on them becoming self-aware. Women first and foremost. And find out what it means to them to be a woman. 'And for ourselves?' Because they ask for nothing. They want nothing for themselves. If you ask them what it means to them to be a woman, they say 'it's to be a wife, a mother', etc.'

C: 'Yes, it's an educational task (…) we must educate the mothers (…) and the children.

R: It's not necessarily a question of culture. I don't think it's only a question of culture. It's more a question of space, of place, family, work…'

Chair/project leader: 'What does each organization do for a woman to be a woman?'

10 '*Les crapuleuses'*, the delinquent ones, is an expression used by these violently rebellious girls themselves.

> C: 'We start from their needs. We try to convey the message: OK, you are good mothers but, just between us women, what does it mean to be a woman? We encourage them to take time for themselves, to dare to take time for themselves. But the question is, what's the legitimacy of these messages? We need to be able to check that we're not off-track. That's another reason why the network is important. To recharge our batteries'.

Here, 'violence against women' has been diluted in other paradigms. 'Commonplace violence' is attributed not to cultural practices explicitly but to a type of family which the welfare actors here seem to identify in the same way: a communication gap between parents and children and a vicious cycle of violence that is thought to explain the 'young people's violence' in particular. Both B and R link the responsibility of the parents (the mothers particularly) for their children's potential violence with the sexist education and patriarchal model characteristic of these women's lives and the lives of the daughters ('the hardened delinquents'). The violence in question here seems to be a vague family phenomenon rooted in the fact that girls are brought up to submit to violence from men, and to reproduce it. Thus some actions or practices are aimed at educating 'the women' to break out of their subjection – through education, prevention and provocation ('they have to be shocked!') – and to help 'normalize' the family unit.

This goal appears particularly in some parenting education initiatives where the women, who are 'the best placed to call for change', are encouraged to help 'modernize' the family by involving the fathers in educating the children, making their daughters aware of female issues (gynaecology and sexuality), teaching the boys non-violence (allowing them to express themselves, free their emotions, with 'preventing violent behaviour' as the underlying goal). These tendencies reveal sometimes paradoxical expectations of the target group women; sometimes they are seen as victims who must be helped to free themselves, to 'be women and not just wives and mothers',[11] sometimes responsible, as mothers, for passing on a better education to their children and achieving a better balance in the family. These paradoxical gender assignments are themselves derived from stereotyped traditional gender roles.

Implicit in all this is the idea that 'violence' is a feature of culture, and violence against women an epiphenomenon of ethnicized violence. This is often based on rigid representations of the North African family and its members: the 'submissive wife', the 'resigned father' or 'violent father' and the 'violent/delinquent children'. Thus the tendency to culturalize or 'racialize' (Hamel 2005) sexist domination provides justification for two types of action. There are ac-

11 To this end some associations set up beauty workshops (hairdressing, makeup) or bodywork sessions ('reclaiming our bodies').

tions designed to emancipate women and others designed to encourage mothers to take responsibility for halting the reproduction of their culture's sexism (Manier 2009), which is constructed as 'typically North African'.

Of course, participants' discourses on these models and norms are not entirely uniform. They criticize, express doubts and raise questions. In the extract above, one participant calls for vigilance ('it's not necessarily a question of culture') and doubts are expressed about the legitimacy of models and practices. The very way this network operates is based on the participants' desire to 'take a step back' and reflect on their practices and representations. This extract makes no claim to be fully representative of the different forms of social action aiming to improve the status of migrant women. However, it does reveal a shared underlying discourse, or at least a general tendency to culturalize social problems and issues of sexuality and sexist violence in particular. The phenomenon of 'violence' gives rise to discourses in which the subject shifts from gender relations to 'the weight of tradition', revealing the integrative and culturalist attitudes behind the social action organizations' objectives and practices in the field.

Besides the mismatch between the participants' expectations and those of their clients, social action in relation to a particular form of violence can itself be riddled with injunctions laden with symbolic violence.

By way of conclusion: logic of suspicion and danger of a 'double segregation'

In social action, the question of sexist violence is raised not only through measures to combat physical violence but also in the 'suspicion' of symbolic violence against women. Whether the issue is emancipation, family, parenting, violence or children's education, there are two trends in institutional discourses and social action. On the one hand, 'women in immigrant communities' are seen as victims of sexist oppression or violence; on the other, actual sexism is seen in terms of culture and a failure to integrate. This places these women in a double bind. As the target of actions aimed at integration *and* actions aimed at emancipation they are faced with 'contradictory racist and sexist injunctions that bid the dominated to simultaneously erase and uphold their difference' (Delphy 2008: 148). And these injunctions tend to open up other areas of symbolic violence. Institutional and social action for 'women in immigrant communities' fails to deal effectively with violence and this is partly due to the essentialist use of gender and cultural/ethnic categories. This dual essentialism – implying otherness and inferiority (Guillaumin 1992) – gives rise to paradoxical expectations of these women: a family role in the 1960s and 1970s, then integration and, more recently, female emancipation. They are sometimes seen as traditional women who must be helped on their way towards 'a better femininity', sometimes as victims of violent behaviour seen as inherent in 'the family', sometimes as mothers with special responsibility for helping to modernize the family unit. At the same time they are called upon to emancipate themselves from their exclusive assignment to the home, from family control and even from 'the men of their culture'. Two gender norms, or ideal social figures, alternate: the 'good mother' and the 'emancipated woman.

This blurring of registers has social effects and sometimes creates divisions between teams working in the field and their clients. This paper cannot fully analyze how the women concerned receive these messages and react to them. However, imputing a sexist 'culture' or violent behaviour as intrinsic to their families tends to provoke defensive reactions, in men and women alike. They will be tempted to use the women's status as a symbol of the respectability and morality of the incriminated group. Some women will comply with the expectations made of them; others will want to combat the stigmatization of 'Muslims' or 'North Africans'. They will renounce, resist or respond to stigmatization of the group they are being classed with by taking pride in membership of that group; this is the 'double segregation'.

This can be seen particularly clearly in the matter of headscarves. The wearing of the Muslim veil is a veritable 'invitation to suspicion' and acts as a catalyst of divisions within social action organizations that count many veiled women among their clients. During my surveys I observed that the field workers, the women especially, saw the veil as the archetypal symbol of the supposed sexist violence and traditionalism of 'Muslim-Arab culture'. It crystallized their concerns about women's oppression and increasing community self-segregation. It was the subject of tensions between associations that present women's emancipation more or less as an obligation and women from North African immigrant communities, whether or not they wear the veil. In response to anti-veil arguments or injunctions, these women generally reject the image of them that is presented, as oppressed, submissive or withdrawing into a community identity. Instead they present a positive image of the identity the veil represents. While in most cases conflict situations are solved by compromise, sometimes communication breaks down over issues around the veil and the status of women. Pressured to take off their veil or suspected of proselytizing, some women simply leave; others resist or claim the right to wear it. In one association, a young Egyptian woman was vigorously enjoined to remove her veil; she first checked that the association had no right to forbid her to wear it and then threatened to sue the association leader for discrimination.

References

Condon, Stephanie/Hamel, Christelle (2007): Contrôle social et violences subies parmi les descendantes d'immigrés maghrébins. In: Chetcuti, Natacha/Jaspard, Maryse (dir.): Violence envers les femmes. Trois pas en avant deux pas en arrière. Paris: L'Harmattan, pp. 201–222.

De Rudder, Véronique (1994): Distance (sociale, culturelle, ethnique). In: Pluriel Recherches, Cahier n° 2, pp. 10–11.

Delphy, Christine (2008): Classer, dominer, qui sont les autres? Paris: La Fabrique.

Fassin, Didier/Fassin, Eric (dir). (2006): De la question sociale à la question raciale? Représenter la société française. Paris: La Découverte.

Gaspard, Françoise (2001): La visibilité des femmes dans l'histoire de l'immigration. In: Les femmes de l'immigration face aux discriminations sexistes, racistes, culturelles. Actes du colloque national du 22 novembre 2001. Paris: Fasild, pp. 9–12.

Golub, Anne (2000): Un itinéraire – Propos recueillis par Jules Falquet. In: Cahiers du Cedref, n° 8–9, pp. 361–382.

Golub, Anne/Morokvasic, Mirjana/Quiminal, Catherine (1997): Evolution de la production des connaissances sur les femmes immigrées en France et en Europe. In: Migrations Société, vol XI, n°52, juillet-août 1997, pp. 19–36.

Guénif-Souilamas, Nacira/Macé, Eric (2004): Les féministes et le garçon arabe. Paris: Ed. de l'Aube.

Guillaumin, Colette (1992): Sexe, race et pratique du pouvoir: l'idée de nature. Paris: Côté-femmes.

Hamel, Christelle (2005): De la racialisation du sexisme au sexisme identitaire. In: Migrations Société, vol. 17, n° 99–100, pp. 91–104.

Manier, Marion (2009): L'engagement en faveur de l'émancipation des «femmes de l'immigration» dans les associations d'action sociale. Frontières interethniques et de genre. In: Sala Pala, Valérie/Arnaud, Lionel/Ollitrault, Sylvie/Rétif, Sophie (dir.): L'action collective face à l'imbrication des rapports sociaux. Classe, ethnicité, genre. Paris: L'Harmattan, pp. 75–95.

Morokvasic, Mirjana (2008): Femmes et genre dans l'étude des migrations: un regard rétrospectif. In: Falquet, Jules/Rabaud, Aude/Freedman, Jane/Scrinzi, Francesca: Femmes, genre, migrations: un état des problématiques. In: Cahier du Cedref, Université Paris Diderot, Paris, pp. 33–56.

Mucchielli, Laurent (2005): Le scandale des «tournantes». Dérives médiatiques, contre-enquête sociologique. Paris: La Découverte.

Sayad, Abdelmalek (2006): L'immigration ou les paradoxes de l'altérité. Paris: Raisons d'agir.

Taravella, Louis (1984): Les femmes migrantes, bibliographie analytique internationale (1965–1983). Paris: L'Harmattan.

Intimate Partner Violence and the Process of Seeking Help: Im/migrant Women who Approached Anti-Violence Centres in Emilia-Romagna (Italy)

Guiditta Creazzo, Emanuela Pipitone and *Anna Maria Vega Alexandersson*

Introduction

In recent years, a strong racialization of the problem of gender violence has occurred in the public domain in Italy. The overexposure by the media of episodes of sexual violence committed by immigrant men has tended to reduce the problem of male violence against women to the phenomenon of 'rape in the street' perpetrated by the 'foreigner'. In spite of the growing body of available evidence that partners or ex-partners and people known to the victims are the most common types of perpetrators of violence against women (ISTAT 2007), the major part of the Italian mass media, the government and most political parties have promoted a public discourse on gender-based violence as a problem of im/migrant men's criminal behaviour, to be tackled with public order measures. The institution of citizen patrols, the militarization of urban areas and the criminalization of irregular immigration have been proposed as the necessary measures to protect 'our' women – the Italian women – from the 'brutality of foreigners'. In this cultural and political context, strongly characterised by exploitation and distortion, raising the problem of violence committed by im/migrant men against their wives or girlfriends is difficult. However, the question of violence suffered by foreign born im/migrant women at the hands of their partner (or ex-partner), who frequently – not always – come from the same country, needs to be confronted. Im/migrant women find themselves located at the intersection of systems of power – race, class and gender – that belongs to different geographical and cultural contexts and might produce in their lives further and unexpected tensions and conflicts (Raj and Silverman 2002; Sokoloff and Dupont 2005). From a number of studies they often emerge as being at in higher risk of intimate partner violence than the women born in the countries in which they have settled and as having additional obstacles to overcome in order to flee from the violent situations[1]. The pertinence of focussing

1 See also 'Migrant women: at particular risk from domestic violence', Parliamentary Assembly, Doc.11991, 15 July 2009.

on the position and vulnerability of im/migrant women in relation to intimate partner violence has been recently recognised and reported on for the Council of Europe (Woldseth 2009).

This chapter explores the experiences of violence and the process of help seeking of im/migrant women victims of intimate partner violence, through the analysis of data collected by antiviolence centres in the region Emilia-Romagna. These data concern the whole population of women seeking help at these centres[2]. In Italy, according to what emerged from the national violence against women survey, conducted by ISTAT (2007) on a representative sample of 25,000 women between the ages of 16 and 70, 2.8% of those who suffer repeated or serious violence by a partner asked for help from such centres. This survey also indicates that in Emilia-Romagna 38.2% of women between 16 and 70 years of age had been victims of physical or sexual violence during their lifetime and that 17.8% had been victims of physical or sexual violence at the hands of a partner. Amongst the latter group, 5.1% press charges against their partner (ISTAT 2007: 35–40). Unfortunately, no statistics on im/migrant women are available from this survey. All women counselled and/or housed have suffered violence. Previous studies have shown that the concrete act in itself is not enough to define the overall severity of the experience of violence (CAHRV 2006; Dobash and Dobash 2004). From this standpoint, the aims of our study were to analyse the types and severity of violence they suffered, considering multiple victimisation, the severity of violence and its impact on women's health; the referral sources; their needs and initiatives, highlighting similarities and differences between im/migrant and Italian women. Since in Italy the problem of violence by (ex)-partner and im/migrant status or ethnicity is a little investigated topic[3], we frame our results by referring to the international literature.

Statistics on prevalence of intimate (ex)-partner violence according to ethnicity and/or im/migrant status are not univocal; they vary from study to study depending especially on the methodology used (Tjaden and Thoennes 2000; Rennison and Welchans 2000; Grossman and Lundy 2007). Menijiver and Salcido, on the basis of their review of scholarship, affirm that rates of (ex)-partner violence amongst im/migrant women are not higher than in the rest of the population (Menijìver and Salcido 2002: 901), while Raj and Silverman report studies attesting that immigrant women are at a higher risk of

2 The large majority of shelters and antiviolence centres in the region.

3 Italian research and studies on im/migrant women's experience of violence principally concentrate on trafficking, forced prostitution and female genital mutilations. We take the opportunity of mentioning here a research project on im/migrant women and violence – intimate partner violence included – launched in 2010 at the University of Padua Department of Sociology, directed by Prof. Franca Bimbi.

(ex)-partner violence (Raj and Slverman 2002: 367). In the European context, several prevalence studies on violence against women conducted in different countries find higher rates of intimate (ex)-partner violence against im/migrant women. In Spain, from the national survey conducted in 2006, 17.3% of im/migrant women compared to 9.3% of Spanish women were victims of on-going abuse, mainly perpetrated by (ex)-partner (Instituto de la Mujer 2006: 162)[4]. Condon and Schröttle's analysis of French and German data reveals not only higher rates of intimate partner violence against Turkish women in Germany and North African women in France (2006; also Condon 2005: 67), it also reveals that im/migrant women report higher levels of severity of violence, significantly higher rates of male dominance and control, and higher rates of threats of violence (p.42–44).

It is commonly recognised, however, that im/migration brings with it specific difficulties and vulnerabilities, linked to the fact of being a migrant, and to the conditions of reception in the host country. Several studies demonstrate that im/migrant women victims of intimate partner violence may have to overcome specific barriers to leave a violent partner and seek help. These include:

- legal barriers, particularly when the women are undocumented, worsened by the women's fear of deportation or other state sanctions;
- family and community barriers, as immigrant women may lack alternative support networks (extended families) or may more often encounter community and family resistance if they try to leave their partner;
- economic barriers, as they are likely to have an illegal job and face threat of deportation, or they more often have unstable and insufficiently paid jobs;
- language barriers, as they may not speak the native language and depend on official interpreting services that are not routinely available;
- institutional barriers, such as living far away from where services are located, or because of the professional background and/or lack of specific training of staff. (Narayan 1995; Dutton et al. 2000; Shetty and Kaguyutan 2002; Raj and Silverman 2002; Shettey and Kaguyutan 2002; Erez 2000).

All these conditions are consistently identified as barriers to help seeking also with regards to im/migrant women's use of shelters (Sullivan and Gillum 2001). On the basis of a systematic review of published literature, Raj and Silverman (2002) affirm that 'battered immigrant women are less likely

4 These women are defined as 'technically ill-treated', and suffered sometimes or frequently at least one type of physical, psychological, sexual, economic, spiritual or structural violence, at the time when the survey was conducted.

than non-immigrant battered women to seek both informal and formal help for IPV' (2002: 381; see also Erez 2000; Menjivar and Salcido 2002). Studies also suggest that shelters are a difficult resource for im/migrant women because they are perceived as being a 'point of no return', a refuge following an irreconcilable breakdown of the marriage (Erez 2002: 32). Our data suggest a different picture. In Emilia-Romagna, im/migrant women counselled and/or housed represent a minority group that has grown constantly over the years. Relevant and partially unexpected differences between im/migrant and native women appear during the help-seeking process and in the point in time when women ask for help at a centre. After describing these differences – which are the focus of our contribution – we discuss some factors that may have produced these results, the severity of violence suffered by women, their economic status and the consequent range of needs and requests they brought to the centres.

The national and local context of the study

Before the presentation of our findings, it is important to briefly contextualize the activities of antiviolence centres and the main characteristics of the im/migrant population in Emilia-Romagna. Antiviolence centres[5] are a fundamental resource for abused women and an important source of knowledge on gendered violence, on abused women's needs and claims, on the actions they take to flee from violence (Dobash and Dobash 1992; Creazzo 2003; 2008a; Lyon and Lane 2008; Sullivan and Gillum 2001). They flourished in Italy at the end of the 1980s and beginning of the 1990s, 10–15 years later than in other countries, and mainly developed in the central – northern regions of the country (Creazzo 2008b). With few exceptions, Italian centres are run by women's associations that are part of the women's movement, and have been instrumental in the public recognition of male violence against women as a multidimensional social problem. Each centre has its own telephone help line, usually functioning during working hours[6], and publicised in local newspapers, TV and radio. It is important to underline that Italian centres operate mainly through intensive counselling, mostly without housing the women. In 2005, for example, of a total of 1271 women who contacted the centres, only 78 (6.1%) stayed in a shelter. Since 2006, a national tele-

5 It is important to notice that in Italy antiviolence centres do not always have a shelter. In Emilia-Romagna 6 out of 10 antiviolence centres provided also shelter.

6 Sometimes they guarantee 24 hours availability.

phone help-line for women victims of violence has been funded by the state Equal Opportunities Department.

The first Italian shelter was opened in Bologna (region capital) in 1991. Today Emilia-Romagna is amongst the regions with the highest number of antiviolence centres: one in each capital of its respective province. Most of them are partially funded by local authorities though much of the work relies on unpaid activists. They support women through a range of different activities (information giving, counselling, legal and psychological consultancy and sheltering) which mostly take place at the centre, whose address is publicly available. Centre workers avoid proactive interventions: women who need help usually contact the centre directly. They can phone or drop in – if in a crisis – during the centre working-hours. Emergency services working 24 hours a day are rare. Usually, health and social services, police forces and hospital emergency workers refer battered women to the centres. These agencies might be part of formally established local networks (multi-agency work).

As far as the im/migrant[7] population residing in Italy is concerned, Emilia-Romagna is the fourth Italian region for numbers of im/migrant (about 421,000) after Lombardia, Veneto and Lazio (Caritas e Migrantes 2008)[8]. The estimated foreign born population regularly residing in the region has almost quadrupled since 1996. In 2005, the incidence of im/migrants in the whole regional population was 7.5%[9]. To estimate the presence of irregular foreign born im/migrants is obviously difficult. Considering the regulations of 2002, that followed the immigration amnesty (4 years after the previous one), that figure corresponded to about 30% of documented immigrants in that year (Regione Emilia-Romagna 2007: 19–20). On 1st January 2006 there were 289,019 immigrants legally registered residing in Emilia-Romagna, among which 48% (138,997) were women, 6.5% of the whole female resident population. 70% of foreigners come from Africa and Eastern Europe, the rest from Asia and Latin America. The increase in foreigners from Eastern Europe in the last years has been influenced in particular by the arrival of women working as house-keepers and care givers (Regione Emilia Romagna 2009: 12–15). About 75% of foreign residents are less than 40

7 The term 'im/migrant' identifies foreign born population residing in the country. The numbers results either from the Ministry of the Interior, responsible for the residing permit (permesso di soggiorno) or from the ISTAT (National Institute of Statistcs).

8 As clarified by the authors, the National Institute of Statistcs (ISTAT) estimates are usually lower, because they consider only legally registered resident im/migrant population (registered at the *anagrafe*) at 1st January of each year. Data from Caritas/Migrantes consider also foreigners with a permission of stay legally in Italy (*permesso di soggiorno*) which is counted at 31st December of each year.

9 This data include minors.

years old, compared with the 43% of the general population. Among foreign born im/migrant women over two-thirds (69.4%) of women are aged 15–49, while for the total female population this percentage is only 43.8%. The number of residence permits issued in Emilia Romagna has constantly grown: 50,450 were issued for women in 2001 and 111,073 in 2005. During this period, the proportion of permits issued to women for work rose from 37% (18,799) in 2001 to 47% (52,575) in 2005[10]. This indicates that women's migration is increasingly work motivated rather than simply for family reunification.

Methodology and objectives of the research

The gathering of statistical data concerning women counselled and/or housed in antiviolence centres is a routine activity for these centres in Italy. In Emilia-Romagna it has been supported and financed by the regional body and three surveys were carried out in 1997, 2000 and 2005[11]. The number of centres that took part in the studies were 15 in 1997, 10 in 2000 and in 2005[12]. A questionnaire common to all centres was used in order to collect data concerning both women who seek help and the activities performed by centre-workers supporting them. The adopted methodology was participatory action research, a strategy based on the direct participation of the parties involved in the subject to be investigated, and gives the opportunity of a guided and shared thinking process that is in itself the starting point of change (Gatenby and Humphries 2000; Wadsworth 1998). A working group of representatives from antiviolence centres who participated in all the research phases, from the questionnaire elaboration to the discussion of the final results, was established. The core of the data presented in this chapter concerns women victims of intimate partner violence counselled and/or housed in 2005. We decided to concentrate on this group because intimate partner violence is the most common form of violence suffered by women who sought

10 Data available from ISTAT website http://demo.istat.it/altridati/permessi/index.html. The 'motivazioni' are the reasons for the permission request, stated in documents.

11 A new survey started this year 2010.

12 A large group of workers belonging to regional antiviolence centres took part in this research project these researches. The centres who promoted research activities and have been involved in it were: Casa delle donne per non subire violenza, Bologna; UDI, Bologna; SOS Donna, Bologna; Centro donne e Giustizia, Ferrara; Linea Rosa, Ravenna; Casa contro la violenza, Modena; Nondasola, Reggio Emilia; Gruppo di lavoro contro la violenza alle donne, Forlì; Centro Antiviolenza, Parma; SOS Donna, Faenza; Casa Amica, Imola; Donne e Giustizia, Modena; Telefono donna, Piacenza.

help from antiviolence centres[13]. Data were collected between 1st January and 31st December 2005 by centre-workers[14]. Some of them were specifically trained for this purpose and then in turn trained their colleagues. Information was acquired in the context of counselling and/or housing and the questionnaires compiled after one or more interviews, in the absence of the woman, in order to avoid interfering with the counselling process. The questionnaire was compiled for every 'new'[15] woman counselled and/or housed in the mentioned period of time. It comprises 89 questions that cover the following areas: the characteristics of the first contact of the woman with the centre; demographic and social characteristics of victims and perpetrators; the relationship between victims and perpetrators (which means different types of perpetrators and contexts of violence – father, mother, uncle, brother, employer, stranger, friend etc.); types (up to 43), duration and frequency of violence; consequences of violence at a social, psychological and physical level; violence suffered by children and the level of their wellbeing/unease; actions undertaken by women before/after the contact with the centre; results, and responses obtained; actions of the centre-workers and their results.

Women's experiences of violence were categorised in the questionnaire through a range of 43 items grouped under four macro-categories: physical, economic, sexual and psychological violence. The definition of types of violence was discussed with centre-workers that took part in the research and reflected the experiences of the women as perceived by them. The overall criteria followed in items definition was behaviourally specific as is recommended and commonly practised in representative national prevalence studies on violence against women (CAHRV 2006). The frequency of violent acts was measured considering whether they occur once or more than once; the severity of violence[16] was measured through the construction of levels characterized by specific behaviour, to which was assigned a 'weight': highest levels correspond to higher severity. As far as sexual violence is concerned – for example – rape, attempted rape or to be forced to have sexual

---

13 A constant result of these surveys is that the large majority of women who seek help from these centres are victims of partner (ex) partner violence: 81.3% (959) of all women seeking help in 1997; 78.9% (847) in 2000; 80.1% (1 001) in 2005 (Creazzo, 2008).

14 The total number of antiviolence centres active in the region was 13. 10 centres took part to the research, 3 of them couldn't because of financial or organisational constraints. Of the 10 centres participating 6 had also a shelter.

15 This means that women counselled or sheltered in 2005, but in contact with a centre before 01.01.2005 were excluded.

16 We are aware that the severity of a violent event may depend on a number of variables: the context of the violence, the motivation and intention of the perpetrator, the physical and psychological differences between the perpetrator and the victim, the differences of social and economic power (Dobash and Dobash 1988; 2004).

intercourse with other men correspond to weight 3 (maximum severity); undesired sexual intercourse weight 2 (medium severity); verbal sexual harassment weight 1 (low severity). Then the weights were grouped into levels; so for example, women who suffered sexual violence at 'level 3' (the highest for sexual violence) have suffered at least one act of weight 3, alone or with others at a lower weight; all women who suffered at 'level 2' have suffered at least one violence at weight 2, alone or with others of a lesser weight. Physical violence is comprised of four levels of severity; sexual violence of three levels; economic violence, four; psychological violence, five.

Research findings

The comparison of data collected in 1997, 2000 and 2005 show a non linear increase in the total number of women asking for help from antiviolence centres in the region (table 1)[17]. However when the women's birthplace is considered, we see that the proportion of foreign born im/migrant women have grown constantly: there were 172 in 1997, 307 in 2000 and 464 in 2005. Even if some of them ask for help following experiences of trafficking and forced prostitution, the large majority suffer other types of violence, usually at the hand of known men: 134 in 1997, 199 in 2000 and 377 in 2005. Among all sheltered women the proportion of foreign women is even greater: 42.6% (23 women) in 1997; 64% (62 women) in 2000; and 78.2% (61 women) in 2005. The core of our data analysis, focused on women victims of partner or ex-partner violence, counselled or sheltered in 2005, offers some significant elements in order to understand this relevant result emerging from comparison.

Origins and demographic information

In 2005, a total of 986 women asked for help because of (ex)-partner violence[18], 77.6% of all housed and/or counselled women (1271) in antiviolence

17 A detailed analysis of the possible reasons of the decrease of the number of counselled or housed women in 2000 was made in a previous work (Creazzo 2003). It shows that the decrease mainly concerns antiviolence centres that either couldn't guarantee full time work because of a reduction in financial or human resources available or centres that mainly function as telephone line.

18 Women forced to prostitution that also suffered violence by partners or ex partners were excluded due to the peculiarity of their situation. They were in total 15: 14 foreigners and 1 Italian.

centres. Of these 986 women, 652 were Italian (66.1%) and 334 were foreigners (33.9%). The perpetrators of violence originating from different countries number 236. From the cross-referencing between the country of origin of the perpetrators and the country of origin of the women, it emerges that a significant percentage of foreign women suffer violence from Italian partners or ex-partners: 36.8% (117). A lower percentage of Italian women are victims of violence from foreign partners: 5.8% (35). In 42.6% of cases they are mixed couples.

Im/migrant women counselled or sheltered in 2005 came from different geographical areas and had very different cultural and ethnic backgrounds. The most represented areas reflect the origins of female foreign born population in the regions mentioned above – Central Eastern Europe (39.5%, 132 women) and North Africa (22.5%, 75 women). Central Southern America counts for 14.1% (47), Africa for 13.8% (46) (with the exclusion of Northern Africa), Asia for 6.9% (23) and the European Community for 3.3% (11). As expected, im/migrant women were significantly younger than Italian women: 79.8% (241) of them were less than 40 years old compared with 47.1% (278) of Italians, and 46.4% (140) were between 30 and 39 compared with 34.1% (201) of Italians. Even more relevant is the difference between those within the under 29-year-old group: 33.4% (101) of the im/migrants and 13.1% (77) of the Italians belong to this age group.

Just as for Italian women, im/migrant women who suffered partner or ex-partner violence were most often married. Italian women, however, were significantly more often separated (17.9%, 115 Italian compared with 7.3%, 24 foreign women). Very similar is the percentage of those who had children (85.1%, and 87.2% Italian women), bearing in mind that the children of one in seven of the im/migrant women (14.6%) live in the women's country of origin, a separation that is often painful for all concerned.

Legal immigrant status, language and education

Most (86.8%) of the im/migrant women have a residence permit, among which 39% were issued for working reasons, a lower percentage compared with the one recorded for the regional female immigrant population in the same year (47%). When asked to give the main reason for leaving their country of origin, a promise of marriage or a love relationship was stated by 59.2% (164) of women[19]. Over one in ten (13.2%) im/migrant women were

19 On 250 women with a residing permit, we know the reasons documented in the permit in 207 cases.

undocumented at the time they sought help, almost half were from Central Eastern Europe. It is not surprising that undocumented women counselled or staying in shelters represent a smaller proportion than regional estimate (as stated above, 30% of the regular im/migrant population). Some centres cannot shelter undocumented im/migrant women because of local authority restrictions, and women who find themselves in this situation may be more isolated because of fear of deportation and limited knowledge of Italian. In our research, 79.7% (251) of im/migrant women had a good knowledge of Italian language, 20.3% (64) did not speak Italian or spoke very little. Their education level was quite similar to the education level of Italian women (Table 2). This result mainly depends on the large percentage of women coming from Eastern Europe, who have a high level of education (data not shown).

Income, job and housing

A very high proportion of im/migrant women, 78.5%, declared they had an insufficient or non-existent income to support themselves and their children. Italian women declared themselves to be in the same situation significantly less often, yet a large number of them (63.2%) were in this situation. Since only 30% of Italian or im/migrant women live in households whose income is stated as insufficient or non-existent, the distressful economic conditions of so many individual women could be considered as a consequence of violence and as an indicator of the situation in which they find themselves when contacting a centre rather than a feature of their previous situation. They are in fact women restructuring their lives, changing house, work and sometimes locality. Congruent with this interpretation is the high percentage of women unemployed or looking for a new job: 33.3% of im/migrant women and 20% of Italian women (table 2). The majority of both im/migrant women and Italian women had a job (53.5% and 58% respectively). For im/migrant women, however, working conditions as well as housing conditions were more disadvantaged: more often they do casual, undocumented or unrecognised domestic work and they are less often home owners (data not shown).

Violence suffered by im/migrant women

Women victimised by their intimate (ex)-partner often suffered different forms of violence that overlap considerably. This is a well known pattern that also emerges from this research. Considering all macro-categories of violence –

physical, economic, sexual and psychological – only 168 (17%) women were victims of just one form of violence (26 victims of physical, 12 of economic, 130 of psychological violence). Im/migrant women, however, suffered more frequently from physical and economic violence than Italian women: 83.2% of foreign women suffered physical violence versus 64.9% of Italian women; 65.6% of foreign women suffered economic violence versus 48.3% of Italian women. They are therefore more often victims of multiple violence than Italian women: 91.2% (300) of foreign women versus 51.4% (495) of Italian women suffer different forms of violence ($p<0.0001$).

Our analysis shows that im/migrant women suffer higher levels of violence more often than Italian women; these differences however are not always statistically significant (Table 3). Im/migrant women suffered physical violence of level 4 more often, like being injured by weapons or suffering attempted murder (15.5% versus 12.9% of Italian women); and of level 3 like being locked indoors or thrown out of the home (21.2% versus 12.2% of Italian women); they suffered less often violence of level 1 and 2 like being slapped, pushed or having their hair pulled. Im/migrant women were more often subjected to psychological violence of level 4 like being victims of threats of violence or of serious intimidation (36.7% versus 29.4%) and less often violence of level 1 like a total lack of sharing everyday work and responsibilities, adultery, deception, constant lack of communication (6.7% versus 13.4% of Italian women) and of level 2 like jealousy, limitation of personal freedom or other forms of control, (28.3% versus 33.2%). Foreign women more often reported sexual violence of level 3 than Italians: rape and attempted rape (35.5% versus 27.5% of Italian women) and less often sexual violence at level 1 (verbal and physical sexual harassment). They also suffered specific forms of violence, like strict forms of exclusion from their community or confiscation of documents.

These findings are confirmed by those concerning the impact of violence on women's health and well-being (Table 5): foreign women significantly more often than Italian women feel fear (57.8% versus 43.1% of Italian women); suffer bruises, burns and cuts (30.8% versus 21.8% of Italian women); are admitted to hospital (9% versus 4.6% of Italian women) and miscarry their child due to violence (3.9% versus 1.5% of Italian women). Less often than Italian women, however, they reported to suffering from depression and suicidal tendencies (12% versus 19.6%).

The process of help seeking

Im/migrant women were significantly more often victimised by a husband and significantly less often victimised by an ex-partner than Italian women (Table 3). This means that they tend to contact a centre at an earlier stage of the process of help seeking – when the decision of breaking the relationship is not yet taken. They also tend to ask for help significantly sooner than Italian women: 26.3% of im/migrant women compared to 15.4% of Italian women asked for help within 0–1 year after they suffered the first physical or sexual violent episode; 43.2% of im/migrant women compared to 30.5% of Italian women asked for help after 2–5 years; while 39.4% of Italian women compared to 16.3% of im/migrant women asked for help after 10 years[20]. The average duration of physical or economic violence for foreign women seeking help is half the length reported by Italian women (five and ten years respectively), as it is for sexual or psychological violence (six and twelve years respectively).

Relevant and partially unexpected differences between the two groups were found also in relation to referral sources, in the needs expressed and in the intensity of the help seeking process. Im/migrant women significantly more often than Italian women arrived at centres because of the information received from the institutional sector: social and health services, police forces and hospitals; and less often, through informal contacts. Before asking for help from an antiviolence centre, they had in fact more contacts with the institutional sectors than Italian women: 40.7% of foreign women compared to 20.2% of Italian women had already made contact with a social worker; 23.7% had made contact with the emergency room at the hospital, compared to 12.6% of Italian women; 31.7% with the police forces compared to 22.7% of Italian women. This is not surprising considering the more disadvantaged economic situation of im/migrant women, on the one hand, and the more severe levels of violence they suffered, on the other. The range of needs brought by im/migrant women when they arrived at a centre tended in fact to be broader. They more frequently asked for an interview than Italian women (54.8% versus 42.2%) and were more numerous in a situation of crisis and asked for a room in a shelter (29.1% of foreign women versus 11.5% of Ital-

20 Considering the duration of violence – counted at the moment of the first contact with the centre – in class (0–1 year, 2–5 years, 6–10 years, more than 10 years) the differences are highly significant ($p<0.0001$) for both physical-sexual violence and psychological-economic violence. We underline that out of 286 in/migrant and 440 Italian women who reported physical or sexual violence, we know the duration of violence for respectively 190 im/migrant women and 246 Italian women; out of 320 im/migrant and 616 Italian women who reported economic or psychological violence, we know the duration of violence for 231 and 393 women respectively.

ians) or sought help for housing or finding a job (19.2% versus 7.2% respectively). Less often they asked for professional psychological support or to take part in self-help or another type of support group. Finally, im/migrant women reported violence to the police significantly more often than Italian women: the 24.3% of the former against the 14.6% of the latter (<0.0001). Controlling for the severity of physical and of sexual violence, im/migrant women pressed charges against their partners more often than Italian women except for physical violence of level 1. The difference, however, remains significant only for sexual violence of level 3[21]: 72.7% (16) im/migrant women and 17.9 (5) Italian women reported these types of violence to the police (<0.0001).

Discussion and conclusions

In Emilia-Romagna, im/migrant women counselled and/or housed at antiviolence centres represent a minority group that has grown constantly over the years, a fact that cannot be explained by the increase in the foreign female population residing in the region. Even considering that among im/migrant women, 13% are undocumented, and others might have a resident permit but not be locally registered, there is still a difference that needs to be explained[22]. Im/migrant women counselled and/or housed undergo more severe violence, and come to the antiviolence centres sooner than Italians. Moreover, they had contacts with formal and informal agencies – like social workers, police forces and hospitals – and press charges against their (ex)-partner, more often than Italian women. In other words, they appear to be more active and more intensely seeking institutional help than Italian women. The most surprising of our research results is that of the higher proportion of im/migrant women who press charges. Studies in other countries have highlighted how much police reactions are often racist and affected by strong prejudice towards both victims and perpetrators from different countries (Mama 2000: 49–50). In consequence, women from discriminated, stigmatized groups do not trust the police and hesitate before denouncing violent partners.

---

21 This includes rape, attempted rape or sexual aggression, coercion to have sex with others and was reported by 50 women: 22 im/migrants and 28 Italians.

22 All im/migrant residing in Emilia-Romagna (*soggiornanti*) counted for the 7.5% of the regional population in 2005 – the 48% being female – (at 31.12.2005; Regione Emilia Romagna, 2007, 12). Registered im/migrant population counts for the 6.9% of the regional population (at 01.01.2006; idem 15).

As stated above, surveys conducted in Spain, Germany and France show that im/migrant women are victims of intimate partner violence more often than native women. The higher proportion of im/migrant women contacting antiviolence centres in Emilia-Romagna might then be the result of them being victims of partner violence more often than Italians, an hypothesis that can not be verified as we have no prevalence data available on the im/migrant female population. A different line of interpretation – not necessarily in contrast with the previous one – emphasising the role of economic/social conditions and of the severity of violence can be considered. Hence, the more economically disadvantaged conditions and the more severe violence suffered by im/migrant women – also resulting in the broader range of needs they described to workers at the centres – together with the paucity of familiar and/or informal resources characterising the im/migrant status, could become 'push factors'. That is, rather than acting as 'retaining factors' these factors encourage im/migrant women to seek help more often and more intensely than Italian women both from antiviolence centres and the institutional sector. The research results of some United States studies seem to support this hypothesis. Strauss and Gelles (1995) and Johnson and Leon (2005; see also Johnson 1995) suggest that victims of violence who seek help may experience more abuse than those who do not and that, on average, the number of protective strategies that a woman uses increases with the severity of the violence experienced (Hamby and Gray Littke 1997). Others studies show that women with a lower income are more likely to ask for help from a shelter (Cattaneo and De Loveh 2008). As Sullivan and Gillum (2001) highlight most women decide to enter a shelter at a time of extreme crisis, because living collectively with many other women and children, having no or little privacy, and abiding by numerous rules is something they choose only as a last resort (2001: 248).

Some of these factors, especially the more severe violence reported by im/migrant women, are responsible for the higher proportion of those who press charges against their partner or ex-partner. Several studies conclude that the seriousness of the offence is the most important factor influencing victims' decisions to report crime (Tarling and Morris 2010). There are, however, differences that remain. Considering how often im/migrant women have contacts with institutions, before approaching a centre, it is possible that reporting crime represents a positive action, making them appear as 'reliable mothers' and 'faithful battered women' to agencies that can offer them crucial resources to survive the violence (Creazzo 2009). Furthermore, the paucity of family and/or informal bonds available to them in Italy and a different perception of love and marriage (which for some have been arranged marriages), might contribute to making it easier for im/migrant women to break the relationship with their partner and/or to consider intervention by family support institutions an acceptable solution.

In conclusion, our findings challenge the common stereotype depicting im/migrant women as more passive, helpless and subjugated to their violent partners and patriarchal relations than Italian women. The findings also do not give support to the idea that shelters are a difficult option for foreign born im/migrant women and suggest that, in the Italian context, there might be no need for specific services for this group of women. They tend to challenge a common stereotype that depict im/migrant women as more passive, helpless and subjugated to their violent partner and patriarchal traditions than Italians. At the same time, however, they suggest the possible existence of a 'submerged reality' of im/migrant women completely cut out from service provision. A reality made up of those who do not speak Italian, who are undocumented and/or are more severely controlled and isolated by their partners. We know that it exists from several testimonies, such as from cultural mediators working in hospital emergency rooms or elsewhere and from foreign women's associations (Creazzo 2009). Most im/migrant women counselled or housed were in fact legal immigrants, speaking Italian and with a medium/high level of education, similar to those of Italian women. A crucial question raised by our results then is how to reach, to inform and to sustain im/migrant women who find themselves in the most dramatic situation as regards resources. And this is a situation exacerbated by the recent immigration laws approved by the Italian parliament (Romito et al. in this Reader).

Table 1: Im/migrant and Italian women by year of survey

Origin of the Women	**1997**		**2000**		**2005**	
italy	1046	87.2%	790	72.0%	807	63.5%
Other countries	172	12.8%	307	28.0%	464	36.5%
Total	1218	100%	1097	100%	1271	100%
Im/migrant Women Type of Violence						
Forced prostitution	38	22%	108	35%	87	19%
Other types of violence	134	78%	199	65%	377	81%
Total	172	100%	307	100%	464	100%

Table 2: Social and economic condition of women by country of origin: 2005

Work Status	**Other countries**		**Italy**		
Employed	167	53.5%	349	58.1%	
Unemployed/In search of work.	104	33.3%	120	20.0%	
Housewife	34	10.9%	69	11.5%	
Pensioner	0	0.0%	41	6.8%	
Disabled or unable to work	1	0.3%	11	1.8%	
Student	3	1.0%	6	1.0%	
Other	3	1.0%	5	0.8%	
Total	312	100.0%	601	100.0%	<0.0001
Income of the Woman**					
Non existent	122	40.9%	146	25.2%	
Insufficient	112	37.6%	220	38.0%	
Sufficient	64	21.5%	213	36.8%	
Total	298	100.0%	579	100.0%	< 0.0001
Income of Family **					
Non existent	5	2.0%	8	1.6%	
Insufficient	68	27.0%	90	18.3%	
Sufficient	179	71.0%	393	80.0%	
Total	252	100.0%	491	100.0%	< 0.01
N	*334*		*652*		

*Percentages derived from the total number of employed women 349 Italian. 167 im/migrants.
**According to women's perception.

Table 3: Importance of current partners and ex partners among perpetrators of violence by country of origin of women: 2005

	Other countries		**Italy**		
Husband	231	69.2%	364	55.8%	<0.0001
Live-in partner	61	18.3%	119	18.3%	
Boyfriend	7	2.1%	22	3.4%	
Lover	1	0.3%	2	0.3%	
Ex partner	34	10.2%	145	22.2%	<0.0001
Total	334	100.0%	652	100.0%	
N	*334*		*652*		

References

Caritas e Migrantes (2008): Immigrazione. Dossier statistico 2009, XIX Rapporto sull' immigrazione. www.dossierimmigrazione.it

Condon, S. (2005): Violence Against Women in France and the Issues of Ethnicity. In: Smeenk, W./Malsch, M.: Family Violence and Police Response. Learning from research, Policy and Practic in European Countries, Ashgate, pp. 59–82.

CAHRV (Schröttle, Monika/Martinez, Manuela/Condon, Stephanie/Jaspard, Maryse/Piispa, Minna/Westerstrand, Jenny/Reingardiene, Jolanta/Magnus, Vytautas/Springer-Kremser, Marianne/Hagemann-White, Carol/Brzank, Petra/May-Chahal, Corinne/Penhale, Bridget) (2006): Comparative reanalysis of prevalence of violence against women and health impact data in Europe – obstacles and possible solutions. Testing a comparative approach on selective studies, December 2006.

Cattaneo, L.B./DeLoveh, H. (2008): The role of socioeconomic status in help seeking from hotlines, shelters, and police among a national sample of women experiencing intimate partner violence. In: American Journal of Orthopsychiatry, 78 (4), pp. 413– 422.

Condon, S./Schröttle, M. (2006): 'Violence against immigrant women and their daughters: a first comparative study using data from the French and German national surveys on violence against women', CAHRV, Comparative reanalysis of prevalence of violence against women and health impact data in Europe – obstacles and possible solutions. Testing a comparative approach on selective studies, December 2006, pp. 40–45.

Creazzo, G. (2008a): La costruzione sociale della violenza contro le donne in Italia. In: Studi sulla questione criminale, Anno III, 2, pp. 15–42.

Creazzo, G. (2008b) (ed.): Scegliere la libertà: affrontare la violenza. Indagini ed esperienze dei Centri antiviolenza in Emilia-Romagna. Franco Angeli, Milano.

Creazzo, G. (2003): Mi prendo e mi porto via. Le donne che hanno chiesto aiuto ai Centri antiviolenza in Emilia Romagna. Franco Angeli, Milano.

Creazzo G. (2009): Il caso italiano: Bologna. In: Creazzo G./Bianchi L. (eds.): Uomini che maltrattano le donne: Che fare? Sviluppare strategie di intervento con uomini che usano violenza nelle relazioni di intimità. Carocci, Roma, pp. 81–114.

Dobash R./Dobash R. (1992): Women, violence and social change. London: Routledge.

Dobash R./Dobash R. (1988): The nature and antecedents of violent events. In: The British Journal of Criminology, Vol. 24, n. 3, pp. 269–88.

Dobash R./Dobash R. (2004): Women's violence to men in intimate relationships. Working on a puzzle. In: British Journal of Criminology, n. 44 (3), pp. 324–349.

Dutton, M.A./Orloff, L.E./Aguilar Hass, G. (2000): Characteristics of help-seeking behaviours, resources and service needs of battered immigrant Latinas. In: Georgetown Journal of Poverty Law & Policy, 2(2), pp. 245–305, cited in Shetty et al. (2000).

Erez (2000): Immigration, culture conflict and domestic violence/woman battering. In: Crime Prevention and Community Safety: An international Journal, Vol 2, N. 1, pp.27–36

Johnson, M.P. (1995): Patriarchal Terrorism and Common Couple Violence: Two forms of Violence Against Women. In: Journal of Marriage and the Family, Vol. 57, May, pp. 283–294.

Gatenby/Humphries (2000): Feminist Participatory Action Research: Methodological and Ethical Issues. In: Women's Studies International Forum, Vol. 23, N. 1, pp. 89–105.

Grossman, Susan F./Lundy, Marta (2007): Domestic Violence Across Race and Ethnicity. Implications for Social Work Practice and Policy. In: Violence against Women October 2007, Vol. 13, No. 10, 10:29–10:52.

Hamby, S.L./Gray-Little (1997): Responses to partner violence: Moving away from deficit models. In: Journal of Family Psychology, 11, pp. 339–350.

Instituto de la Mujer (2006): III Macroencuesta sobre la violencia contra mujeres. Informe de resultados.http://www.inmujer.migualdad.es/MUJER/mujeres/estud_inves/violencia%20 final.pdf

ISTAT (2007): La violenza e i maltrattamenti contro le donne dentro e fuori la famiglia. Anno 2006. http://www.istat.it/salastampa/comunicati/non_calendario/20070221_00/ testointegrale.pdf

Johnson, Michael e Leone (2005): The differential effects of intimate terrorism and situational partner violence: Finding from the National Violence Against Women Survey. In: Journal of Family Issues, 26 (3), pp. 322–349.

Lyon E./Lane S. (2008): Meeting Survivors' Needs: A Multi-State Study of Domestic Violence Shelter Experiences, [Original Report Title: Domestic Violence Shelters: Survivors' Experiences] Final Report, October, 2008, No 225025, Washington D.C.: Prepared for National Institute of Justice.

Mama, Amina (2000): Violence against black women in the home. In: Hanmer, J./Itzin, C.: Home Truth About Domestic Violence. Feminist Influence on policy and practice, Routledge, London, pp. 44–56.

Menijiver/Salcido (2002): 'Immigrant Women and Domestic Violence. Common Experience in Different Countries'. In: Gender and Society, Vol. 16, N. 6, pp. 898–920.

Narayan, U. (1995): 'Male Order' Brides: Immigrant women, domestic violence and immigration law. In: Hypatia, 10(1), pp. 104–19.

Raj, A./Silverman, J.: 'Violence Against Immigrant Women: The Roles of Culture, Context, and Legal Immigrant Status on Intimate Partner Violence'. In: Violence Against Women, Mar 2002, vol. 8, pp.367–398.

Rennison/Welchans (2000, May): Bureau of Justice Statistics special report: Intimate partner violence. http://www.ojp.usdoj.gov/bjs/

Regione, Emilia-Romagna, Osservatorio regionale sul fenomeno migratorio (2009): L'immigrazione straniera in Emilia-Romagna Dati al 2007 A cura dell'Osservatorio regionale sul fenomeno migratorio (art. 3, L.R. n. 5, 24 marzo 2004), CLUEB, Bologna.

Shettey S./Kaguyutan J. (2002, February): Immigrants Victims of Domestic Violence: Cultural challenges and available legal protections. Harrisburg, PA: VAWnet, a project of the National Resource Center on Domestic Violence/Pennsylvania Coalition Against Domestic Violence. http://www.vawnet.org

Sokoloff, Nathalie/Dupont, Ida (2005): Domestic Violence and the Intersection of Race, Class and Gender: Challenges to Understanding Violence against Marginalized Women in Diverse Communities. In: Violence against Women 11, 38, pp. 38–63.

Straus M.A./Gelles R.J. (1995): Physical violence in American families: risk factors and adaptations to violence in 8,145 families. New Brunswick, NJ: Transaction, cited in Grossman, S.F./Lundy, M. (2007): Domestic Violence Across Race and Ethnicity: Implications for Social Work Practice and Policy. In: Violence Against Women, Vol.13, n.10, pp.1029–1052.

Sullivan, C.M./Gillum, T.(2001): Shelters and Other Community-Based Services for Battered Women and Their Children. In: Renzetti, C./Edleson, J.L./Kennedy Bergen R. (eds.): Sourcebook on Violence Against Women, SAGE, pp. 247–260.

Tarling/Morris (2010): Reporting Crime to the Police. In: British Journal of Criminology, 50, pp. 474–490.

Tjaden, P./Thonnes, N. (2000): Extent, nature, and consequences of intimate partner violence: Findings from the National Violence Against Women Survey. Washington, DC, US Department of Justice. http://www.ncjrs.org/pdffiles1/nij/181867.pdf

Wadsworth, Y. (1998): 'What is Participatory Action Research?' Action Research International, Paper 2. http://www.scu.edu.au/schools/gcm/ar/ari/p-ywadsworth98.html

Woldseth, K.S. (2009): Migrant women: at particular risk from domestic violence, Report, Committee on Equal Opportunities for Men and Women. Parliamentary Assembly, Doc.11991. http://assembly.coe.int

Part 5:
Is It a Question of (Their) Culture and (Our) Honour?

'They' Rape 'Our' Women: When Racism and Sexism Intermingle

Alice Debauche

Introduction

Throughout Europe, the gradually increasing recognition of violence against women and sexual violence in particular has gone hand in hand with a systematic othering of rapists. In other words, although men in Western societies such as France are now prepared to acknowledge that women are victims of male violence, they are not ready to accept the corollary: that men in these societies commit violence against women. But in that case who can the perpetrators be? How is the paradox between recognising male violence against Western women and denying the collective responsibility of Western men in this violence to be resolved? The approach to this, I argue, has been to distinguish the perpetrators of the violence from the men of our societies so that they are seen as different, special, as 'other'. Two processes are at work in the construction of the 'other' who commits violence. When the perpetrator is a man of our modern societies, his violence is treated as pathological and exceptional, so that violent men can be considered as 'monsters' or 'madmen' who are not responsible for their actions. In short, they are 'other' by virtue of their psychological problems. But if the perpetrator is a member of a minority group, the violence is attributed to his culture and the perpetrator can be identified with his minority group, viewed in terms of race and according to migratory and cultural history.

The aim of this article is to describe precisely the way that perpetrators of sexual violence are represented in terms of ethnicity and to show that there are no quantitative data on which to base this scientifically. The first part demonstrates the social construction underlying the marking out of certain groups as especially liable to sexual violence. The second part compares statistical facts with social representations and shows how far apart they are. In conclusion, I consider the consequences for women victims from these minority groups, who are called on by the host country to reject their 'community' if they want the violence they have suffered to be recognised.

The rapist as 'other'

Let's first review the two ways in which perpetrators of sexual violence are 'othered' (Delphy 2009). Violence by members of the dominant group is viewed as pathological, while that by members of minority groups is viewed as an aspect of their culture. But both these rationales have the same function: to make as sharp a distinction as possible between the figure of the rapist and that of the dominant figure in society – the white, heterosexual, middle or upper-class male. In the one case, the finger is pointed at the minority groups the rapists are supposed to belong to; in the other, if the rapist is a member of the dominant group, his acts are explained in terms of individual vice. The two processes complement each other.

Othering violence by dominant-group men by classifying perpetrators as pathological

Classic sociology proposes a gender-blind interpretation of sexual violence, treating this type of violence as part and parcel of interpersonal violence in general. This has helped to fabricate a protective distance between the figure of the rapist and that of the male member of the socially and culturally dominant classes. From this perspective, sexual violence is analysed as a deviant practice (Becker 1985) in the same way as other delinquent or criminal acts. But the notion of deviance is necessarily based on that of a norm. In this way, sexual violence is seen as a deviant practice compared to a social norm of consensual, non-violent sexuality. This postulate suggests that the perpetrators of sexual violence have either failed to interiorise this norm or have been socialised in societies or sub-cultures that have different norms for sexual behaviour.

The failure to adequately interiorise the norm is seen as an innate individual failing. It may be a genetic defect, an exaggerated propensity for violence or an unnatural sexual compulsion. It can also be acquired as a result of trauma. The trauma is usually connected with an experience as victim of or spectator to violence against women or sexual violence. This hypothesis (routine in psychology) that child victims of violence reproduce violence, removes the blame from the perpetrators *as men*, by treating them as victims or diminishing their responsibility for their acts. Thus, a lawyer speaking in defence of a man accused of raping a mentally deficient woman explained the facts as being due to sexual aggression the accused had suffered as a child:

> 'Normality does not apply to this case. My client's life was turned upside down when he came across a friend of his father's who did not entirely want the best for him. Since then, he has not wanted to be confronted with others.' He then emphasised the notion of consent: 'For there to be rape, there must be absence of consent. The victim appears to be capable of saying no. That day she did not say no, or my client did not perceive it. This man is not a sexual predator. He respects women, he cannot commit rape.' (Midi Libre 29/10/10)

Thus the perpetrator of sexual violence is not simply an individual involved in social relations of power and domination but is identified either with the figure of the 'monster' or that of the victim. This procedure is used almost routinely when the victim is a child. The perpetrator of sexual violence on children has for several decades now embodied absolute evil and is routinely associated with this figure of the 'monster' (Lits 2008). Thus the paedophile (and also the serial killer-rapist) is seen above all as sick, a psychiatric case: bibliographical research in one of the human and social sciences portals with 'paedophile' as the keyword gives 422 results in psychology or psychoanalysis reviews but only 152 in sociology[1]. But in the social construction of the 'monster' figure, the person is a monster by nature: a biological or genetic mistake, in other words Nature's mistake (Foucault 1999). Viewed in this way from the standpoint of his abnormality, the perpetrator of sexual violence is blamed on nature, obviating any analysis of the social processes underlying sexual violence.

This approach to the rapist as psychologically or naturally abnormal is often used when the violence cannot be attributed to culture because the perpetrator is too close to the mainstream/dominant group. As regards rapes of adult women and adolescent girls, the rapist is othered by assigning him to a group whose membership of the national mainstream is already contested, and of which it is said that the use of violence is characteristic.

Sexual violence as a cultural practice of minority-group men

Sexual violence by members of minority groups is not interpreted in the collective imagination or explained in social science research in the same way as sexual violence by men of the mainstream population. While the argument of madness is used for the latter, quite different arguments are used for the former.

To consider sexual violence as *social deviance* is to postulate that there is a norm of sexuality based on consensus and equality between the sexes, and that this norm defines Western societies in contrast to others (Fabre & Fassin 2003). Equality between men and women is supposed to have been achieved,

1 Search carried out on CAIRN, 15/09/2010

particularly in sexual matters, and there is supposed to be a *process of behavioural civilisation* in Western societies (Elias 2002), marked by a drop in the threshold of tolerance of violence but also by greater self-control and therefore fewer manifestations of violence. As a result, sexual violence is considered something external, belonging to an *elsewhere* or a *before.* A characteristic of this *before* and *elsewhere* is the absence of an egalitarian norm in matters of sexuality, this norm being seen as a criterion of modernity, or Westernness, since modernity is seen as synonymous with the West. Sexual violence can thus only be committed by groups that are less modern, less civilised, less Western. This may mean non-Western national groups and, in France particularly, the former colonies or groups in France that are inferiorised *through social relations of class or race.*

The social construction of a hierarchy of groups requires the idea of 'natural' differences, of groups that are different in essence. The very principle of stigmatising minority groups is based on the principle of differentiation: they exist as minority groups because they are different (and they are different because they are minorities). The social construction of 'racial' groups is, historically, based on an argument from nature (Guillaumin 1992), but as this *natural difference* now seems highly suspect it has been replaced by an argument from *culture* (Volpp 2006). The argument from cultural difference does not simply assert that there are differences between groups: it also implies a hierarchy between groups, with one culture being better than another. It may even apply the term 'culture' only to one group while defining the other in terms of 'civilisation'.

Forms of the culturalist argument about sexual violence

Sexual deprivation

Violence can be treated as a natural characteristic in several ways, the most developed being the argument from culture. Numerous studies refer to *sexual deprivation* as an explanation for violence: if men commit sexual violence, it is because they have sexual needs and urges they cannot resist.

> The industrial revolution had disastrous effects on young country dwellers, who were suddenly penned into the confined atmosphere of the factory with an imposed pace of work, abandoned in neighbourhoods that were urban only in name, crowded into furnished rooms and under forced sexual segregation. These robust, uprooted young men in the full force of youth and desire usually arrived alone,

> either because they were single or because they had left their partners in their home villages. They suffered sexual deprivation and assuaged their frustration by brutal attacks on women and often even small girls. (Chesnais 1981: 183–184)

The argument from nature is obvious here: men's sexual instinct is a survival from the animal stage which can only be brought under control by 'culture'. Obviously 'culture' in this case means culture/civilisation and not 'barbarian' culture: educated/middle-class/Western men can resist these instincts, but men from minority groups, like the men of the colonies, are closer to nature and instinct and are not capable of sublimating their drives through forms of culture such as art and religion.

There is an updated version of this view based on the idea of a sexual market. In this view, men of the minority groups are disqualified by their lack of social and economic capital, or even human capital. For these reasons they do not have access to sexual partners and are reduced to using prostitution – if they can afford it – or sexual violence. In this version, the instinctual aspect of sexuality is less obvious and the argument from nature less direct. However, there is still an underlying notion of sexual *need* that cannot be regulated other than by immediate satisfaction, including by means of violence. The argument from *sexual deprivation* and its variants thus implies that sexual violence is natural to the groups to which it is attributed. These groups commit sexual violence because they are less *civilised* than *us*, their culture is less advanced or *developed*, *they* are closer to their drives and instincts. While the minority cultures are not directly blamed in this version, that blame is implicit since it seems to be an absence of culture (or an underdeveloped culture) that is involved.

'Culture clash'

Arguing in terms of a *culture clash, o*ther analyses of sexual violence offer a more directly culturalist interpretation. This argument directly targets minority 'racial' groups on the supposition that there is a tension between the culture of the host country's mainstream population and the culture 'imported' from the migrants' country of origin. This tension is based on a supposed wide gap between the two 'cultures' as regards their norms concerning sexuality and relations between men and women. The mainstream culture is associated with a norm of gender equality, the 'sub-culture' with norms involving separation or relations of domination between the sexes. Hugues Lagrange asserts that 'it is in this narrow stratum of youths from poor backgrounds, who are doing badly at school, that we frequently find sexual violence' (2001: 263). He continues: 'On the housing estates, the tension observed in relations between boys and girls is heightened' (p. 272). He connects this with 'tensions between Muslim norms, which for many are a vector for their sense of pride and identity, and egalitarian norms' (p. 272–273) and with the fact that 'boys on the estates tend to be thrown towards an aggressive culture that is nostalgic for a golden age of virility' (p. 275). This approach makes it easy to take for granted that sexual violence and male domination are external to the mainstream culture, and to think of the minority group as a culturally uniform whole, as when Lagrange assumes a homogeneous *Muslim* culture.

This argument can also be instrumentalised to excuse some perpetrators (depending upon their origins) of sexual violence. They are sometimes presented *victims of their culture*. A Peruvian on trial for rape in France in September 2010 stated: 'I come from a different country. At home, when a woman invites a man to her flat, it's because she wants sex' (Midi Libre 11/09/2010). This man's argument would be almost comical had a woman not been its victim and had the psychiatrist called in to examine the accused not adopted it himself:

> There is a relation to informal women that is based on need; the man's desire comes first. This is not perverse; it is a heavy cultural heritage. (...) He even told me 'The French ought to give me classes so that I understand that women are equal to men.' (Midi Libre 11/09/2010)

This example also shows how benevolently this argument is viewed in the case of South American macho culture. One wonders what conclusions the same expert witness would have presented if an attacker from a North African immigrant background had offered the same explanation. It can be posited that there is a hierarchy among minorities in which South American 'culture' is seen as closer to European 'culture', particularly through language and religion.

Only culture

For some observers, particularly journalists and some people in NGOs, *minority culture* and sexual violence or gender violence quite simply go together. It is striking to note the increasing, indeed predominant, space given to so-called 'traditional' forms of violence (honour killings, forced marriages, genital mutilation) in some denunciations of violence against women. The chairwoman of the *Coordination Française pour le Lobby Européen des Femmes*, speaking about the creation of a UN Women's agency, said: 'Many harmful traditions defended on pretext of customs or religion, prevent equality between men and women and deny women any independence' (Libération 15/09/2010). Presented in this way one might think that only 'harmful traditions' prevent equality between men and women and forget that there are 'Western' or French social phenomena that also restrict equality – sexual violence being one of them.

The foreigner within

The argument from *culture* adapts its target to social circumstances. The minority groups accused of purveying a sexist culture and sexist behaviour that lead to violence are considered 'foreigners within'. In the 19th century the threat was seen as coming from young men moving from the countryside to city outskirts, which were considered dens of iniquity where promiscuity was rife and sexual boundaries erased. These young men belong to the 'barbarian' classes (Chevallier 1958), this term clearly reflecting the idea of civilisation as progress on a scale from barbarity to modernity. The 'barbarian' classes at home echoed the 'barbarian cultures' attributed to the colonised peoples.

The 20th century identified the sexual threat as coming from young manual workers in working-class neighbourhoods. These were now the 'barbarian' classes blamed for every ill. In the 1930s media denunciations of gang rapes focused on the *apaches*; in the 1960s, the target was the *blousons noirs*. In both cases this meant idle youth in working-class neighbourhoods (Mucchielli 2005). Some of the young *blousons noirs* of the 1960s were descendants of migrants who arrived in the first half of that century from Italy, Poland, Portugal, and Spain but that was not the factor focused on; at the time, the social debate was built around issues of class struggle. The media and sociologists of the time reported on the gang phenomenon:

> Rape today is gang rape, perpetrated by gangs before a carefully selected audience – and the participants are increasingly frequently under twenty years of age. It is happening in the housing estates on the outskirts of Paris (...) and big major provincial cities (...) ('Les viols collectifs ou l'amour dans les tribus de l'hexagone', *Le nouvel Adam*, No. 6, January 1967)

Here the finger is pointed mainly at the perpetrators' young age: youth chimes with impulse, weak self-control and greater sexual need. The 1960s was also the decade when youth first became a subject of sociological study (Galland 2002), so that 'the young' were viewed as a homogeneous group with its own culture, referred to as a counter-culture or sub-culture. The 'young' referred to here are implicitly young men and as such members of the dominant group, but they are a minority because they have their own culture, different from the mainstream culture.

The context of the 2000s is very different. The resurgent media focus on gang rapes identifies the main perpetrators as the *'jeunes des cités'*. Literally 'youths from the estates', the term implies that these are youths from immigrant backgrounds, more specifically African and mainly North African backgrounds. The shift that occurred between the 1960s and the 2000s is a shift from focus on groups identified in terms of social class[2] to groups identified in terms of migration status and perceived as *racially* specific (Hamel 2005). Furthermore, the media campaign on gang rape in the 2000s, resuscitating the argument about the newness and spread of the phenomenon, has allowed sociologists who remember the similar campaign of the 1960s to recognise it as artificial and expose its xenophobic basis:

> The way the gang rapes are treated in public debate has tended to attribute it to the supposed 'barbarity' of young men from immigrant backgrounds and above all, because of the connection made with male domination and sometimes with Islam, those with parents from North Africa. Our inquiry has shown that these are mistaken interpretations and false associations. But they are now commonplace and most people taking part in the public debate (journalists, politicians and others) do no see them as stigmatisation. (Mucchielli 2005: 85)

An example is the following extract from an article published in *Libération* on 9th March 2001. Although like Laurent Mucchielli, the article's author notes that the phenomenon is not new, it has not avoided the trap of stigmatising minorities:

> Practices as old as the hills, which, according to police, were even more widespread in the late 1980s. Those were the days of the *Requins vicieux*, the *Requins juniors*, the *Derniers salauds*. Those gangs of black youths committed rape as an initiation rite. (Libération 2001)

Social representations versus statistics

How do these representations compare with the available empirical data? As regards sexual violence, two main types of data exist in France: administrative data on the work of the police and law courts, and survey data, whether surveys of victims or socio-demographic surveys focusing on broader issues.

2 Although the criterion is not the one we are considering here, the othering phenomenon is the same. These working-class youths were seens as 'foreigners within the gates', 'barbarians' whose culture was intrinsically dangerous for social order.

Administrative statistics (police and law courts)

The 'foreigner' category in administrative statistics

The administrative statistics of the police and law courts record the annual number of persons charged[3] (police data) and the number convicted (courts) for each type of offence. The data are broken down by category, including age, sex and nationality. The *nationality* category is the only one from which an (inaccurate) idea of origin or 'race' can legally[4] be obtained from administrative statistics in France (De Rudder 1997). This is because the use of ethnic and racial categories is completely prohibited in the French Republic. In practice, can these figures be usefully compared with representations that see the perpetrators of sexual violence in ethnic terms?

The 'gang rapes scandal' has firmly established the image of gang rapists from immigrant minorities, and no administrative source is able to confirm or contradict this image. The category *foreigner* is unrelated to the migration status, residency status or origin of the person or their parents and is useless for pinning down the facts about crime among the *immigrants* or *young people from immigrant backgrounds*[5] whom the media constantly claim are preponderant in the delinquency figures. *Foreigners* include any foreign national who is in the country for a short time (business trip, tourism etc.), those who have taken up residence in France long-term, children of the latter who were born abroad, and children of born in France to two foreign parents (a) until their eighteenth birthday and (b) after that date if they have not taken steps in advance to acquire French nationality[6]. It is thus a very mixed category and, although it has an essential legal meaning for crime statistics, it is not a reflection of social reality in France and is not well suited to sociological research on the issue.

Sexual violence committed by foreigners

Unhelpful as the 'foreigners' category in administrative statistics may be, these data can be compared with those of the census, which gives the percentages of immigrants[7] and resident foreigners. Of persons charged with rape in 2009, 13.4% were foreigners, but according to the census foreigners represent only 5.7% of the population. But there is a spectacular difference

3 I.e.suspects referred to a *juge d'instruction* for investigation, which may or may not lead to their being brought to trial (Translator's note].
4 Act of parliament No. 78–17 of 6 January 1978 on electronic records and freedom of information.
5 Not to mention the category *youths from the estates*.
6 I.e. the majority of children born in France to two foreign parents.
7 Persons born of foreign nationality in a foreign country and resident in France.

between rapes of minors and rapes of adults: 20.9% of those charged with rape of an adult were foreigners compared to only 7.4% of those charged with rape of a minor. This connects with our assertion that the child rapist is othered through the figure of the 'monster' while the rapist of adult women is mainly seen in ethnic terms.

The data for convictions are more precise but the categories used are different from those used by the police so it is impossible to compare the two data sets. The table below shows the percentages of foreigners among those convicted of different classes of rape in 2008:

Type of rape	French	Foreign	Percentage of foreigners
All types	1449	154	9.6%
Gang rape	123	24	16.3%
Rape with aggravating circumstances[8]	538	40	6.9%
Rape of minor aged 15 or less	460	17	3.6%
Rape by an ascendant or person exercising authority	78	7	8.2%
Ordinary rape	250	66	20.9%

Source: Ministry of Justice 2008

Although prudence is called for when comparing such small numbers, we find a sharp difference between convictions for rape of adults and those for child rape. Very few foreigners are convicted of rape of minors under 15 years of age, rape with aggravating circumstances or rape by an ascendant or person exercising authority. But the proportion of foreigners among those convicted of gang rape or ordinary rape is very high. As regards gang rape, the numbers are too small for conclusions to be drawn, especially as it concerns the number of persons convicted and not the number of cases tried[9]. As we do not know the number of perpetrators involved in each case, or the composition of the groups of rapists – which could be mixed groups of French and foreign perpetrators – these figures are scarcely meaningful, but they suggest that foreigners are seriously over-represented.

Looking now at estimates based on the national census, we see that at that time foreigners made up 5.7% of the population living in France (Regnard 2009), slightly less than the percentage of foreigners among those convicted of rape. It does seem, therefore, that foreigners are over-represented among perpetrators of rape, suggesting that foreigners are more inclined to sexual violence. However, it must be remembered that the 'foreigners' category is not identical with that of 'youths from African and North African immigrant

8 For the list of aggravating circumstances see the *Code Pénal*, art. 222–24 à 222–26
9 Which is necessarily less than the 61 total cases tried.

backgrounds' on which social representations are based. The 2008 criminal court records were the first to give a breakdown of the 'foreigners' category of convicted persons by main country of origin. They show that of 24 foreigners convicted of gang rape, 12 were of North African origin, 1 Turkish and 4 Zairian, the nationalities of the other 7 not being specified. Of the 66 persons convicted of ordinary rape, 29 were of North African origin, 5 Turkish, 1 Zairian, 3 Portuguese, 1 Italian and 27 of other nationalities. This sheds a different light on the preponderance of ethnicised groups from former colonies and the French overseas territories in social representations. In particular, the figures show that foreign rapists include men born in European Union countries.

Also to be borne in mind is the fact that police and judges are not impervious to social stereotyping and it is likely that a process of selection and discrimination against members of minority groups is at work during police work and criminal proceedings (Jobart and Névanen 2007). It may therefore be postulated that those who best correspond to the popular representation of perpetrators of sexual violence are more likely to be charged and convicted and that the administrative statistics over-represent minority groups. This hypothesis can only be verified by studying criminal proceedings as a whole very closely and comparing the proportions of persons from minority groups among those charged and among those convicted. Furthermore, the effect of representations probably also has an impact on victims and it may be supposed that they are more inclined to lodge a complaint if their attacker matches the stereotype of the 'rapist'.

Evidence from survey data

Since the data on convictions do not provide an empirical basis for concluding that men of minority groups are more likely to commit rape, what do the survey data tell us? And above all, what are the facts that allow some to assert that sexual violence is more prevalent in working-class neighbourhoods?

Rapes are more often committed by a member of the family than by a stranger

The first thing we learn from surveys on experience of sexual violence is that they mostly take place within the family or friendship network. A 2008 survey[10] shows that of women aged 20–59 reporting having suffered sexual violence (rape or attempted rape) by a person acting alone, 21% were victims

10 *Contexte de la Sexualité en France*, INED-INSERM (Bozon et Bajos eds.), 2009

of a family member (8% by the father or stepfather), 34% a spouse or friend, 27% another person known to them and 18% a stranger (Bajos and Bozon 2008). The traditional representation of a night-time attack by a (minority group) stranger in a public area is thus very far from typical. Cases of sexual violence in the family are thus very numerous. However, from the data on convictions we find that 'rape by an ascendant or person exercising authority'[11] account for only 5.3% of convictions and that these include a relatively small proportion of foreigners.

Gang rapes account for only a small proportion of sexual violence

Rapes and attempted rapes by several men together account for 2.7% of the sexual violence declared by women aged 18–69 and 2.5% of those declared by men of the same age bracket, but they amount to 9.2% of convictions. Gang rape seems to give rise to convictions more often than other forms of rape, whether because it is more often reported to the police or because the courts convict more readily for this type of crime.

Not all types of rape are equally likely to result in a complaint to the police

In the Enveff survey, women who reported having been victims of sexual violence were asked what steps they had taken in response. Of women reporting rape or attempted rape, 9.5% said they had reported it to the police (12.2% for those who were victims before aged 15 and 9% for victims after aged 15), and more than half of these cases gave rise to criminal proceedings. Of all sexual violence cases declared in the survey, only 5% gave rise to criminal proceedings, and it seems that the closer the attacker is to the victim, the harder it is to report the offence (Fougeyrollas-Schweibel and Jaspard 2002).

Analysis of calls to a free helpline for rape victims confirms this point; 41% of calls concerning rape by strangers had been reported to the police compared to 32% of calls concerning rape by a known person, a spouse or a partner and 22% of calls concerning rape by a family member. These results confirm the hypothesis that victims are more likely to report to the police if the rapist is a stranger or in cases of gang rape. Thus the survey data neither confirm nor disprove that rapes committed by minority group men are disproportionate. However, the facts that do emerge undermine traditional representations of rape, particularly those conveyed by the media.

---

11 This category is broader than 'father, stepfather'; it may include grandfathers, teachers, sport instructors etc.

Conclusion

From this overview of the ways in which perpetrators of sexual violence are represented in ethnic terms it can be seen that these representations exist because they distance the perpetrators of sexual violence from men of the dominant group. They can persist because it cannot be shown from existing statistics that they are unfounded. The othering of the perpetrators of sexual violence makes it possible to deny the sexism of French society. Because the perpetrators of sexual violence are identified as belonging to minority groups, defined among other things by a minority culture different from mainstream French culture, it is logical to conclude that men of the mainstream group do not commit sexual violence, or if they do, it is purely an accident. In those cases, the argument of individual madness is used to disculpate mainstream men as a whole. The second implication is that these representations put minority group women in a situation of great tension. They are called on to choose between the supposedly non-sexist (but racist) culture of the French mainstream and the 'archaic' and non-egalitarian culture of the men of their own group. In this regard the law against wearing the full veil stems from the same reasoning that imputes ethnic causes to rape: minority group women must be 'freed' from the burden of their culture and traditions perpetuated by the men of their group.

References

Bajos, Nathalie/Bozon, Michel (dir.) (2008): Enquête sur la sexualité en France. Pratiques, genre et santé. Paris: La Découverte, 609 p.

Becker, Howard S. (1985): Outsiders. Paris: Métailié, 248 p.

Chevallier, Louis (1958): Classes laborieuses et classes dangereuses. Paris: Plon, 566 p.

Davis, Angela (1983): Le viol, le racisme et le mythe du violeur noir. In: Femmes, race et classe. Paris: Editions des femmes, pp. 217–254.

Delphy, Christine (2008): Classer, dominer, qui sont les autres? Paris: La Fabrique, 227 p.

De Rudder, Véronique (1997): 'Quelques problèmes épistémologiques liés aux définitions des populations immigrées et de leurs descendants'. In: Aubert, France/Tripier, Maryse/Vourc'h, François: Jeunes issus de l'immigration, de l'école à l'emploi. Paris: L'Harmattan, pp. 17–44.

Elias, Norbert (2002): La civilisation des mœurs. Paris: Calmann-Levy, 509 p.

Equipe, Enveff (2002): Les violences envers les femmes en France. Une enquête nationale. Paris: La documentation française, 370 p.

Fabre, Clarisse/Fassin, Eric (2003): Liberté, égalité, sexualité. Actualité politique des questions sexuelles. Paris: Belfond, 270 p.

Fassin, Eric (2009): Le sexe politique: genre et sexualité au miroir transatlantique. Paris: Edition EHESS, 313 p.

Foucault, Michel (1999): Les anormaux. Paris: Gallimard,.

Fougeyrollas-Shweibel, Dominique/Jaspard, Maryse (2002): Violences envers les femmes: démarches et recours des victimes. Les apports de l'enquête Enveff. In: Archives de politique criminelle. 2002/1, n° 24, pp. 123–146.
Galland, Olivier (2002): Les jeunes. Paris: La découverte, 124 p.
Guillaumin, Colette (1992): Sexe, Race et pratique du pouvoir. L'idée de Nature. Paris: Edition Des Femmes, 239 p.
Hamel, Christelle (2003): Faire tourner les meufs'. Les viols collectifs: discours des médias et des agresseurs. In: Gradhiva, 2003, n°33, pp. 85–92
Jobart, Fabien/Névanen, Sophie (2007): La couleur du jugement. Discriminations dans les décisions judiciaires en matière d'infractions à agents de la force publique (1965–2005). In: Revue Française de Sociologie, Vol. 48, n° 2, pp. 243–272.
Lagrange, Hugues (2001): De l'affrontement à l'esquive: violences, délinquances et usage de drogues. Paris: Syros, 300 p.
Lits, Marc (2008): La construction médiatique d'un monstre criminel: l'affaire Dutroux. In: Caiozzo, Anna/Demartini, Anne-Emmanuelle: Monstre et imaginaire social: approches historiques. Paris: Creaphis, pp. 341–356.
Ministere de la Justice (2009): Les condamnations en 2009. Paris: La Decouverte, 124pp.
Mucchielli, Laurent (2005): Le scandale des tournantes. Paris, La Découverte, 124 pp.
Régnard, Corine (2009): La population etrangère résidènt en France. Infos Migrations, 10. 4pp.
Volpp, Leti (2006): Quand on rend la culture responsable de la mauvaise conduite. NQF, Vol 25, n° 3.

Violence Against Women in Minoritised Communities: Cultural Norm or Cultural Anomaly?

Khatidja Chantler and Geetanjali Gangoli

Introduction

Violence perpetrated against minoritised[1] women in the UK and elsewhere in Europe is frequently cast as a cultural issue without an adequate interrogation of what culturally based violence is, which aspects of violence against women count as cultural and what the implications are of using a cultural frame to understand and respond to domestic violence in minoritised communities. More recently, the 'cultural' in relation to minoritised communities has been re-formulated and more tightly specified as 'honour based violence'. This chapter seeks to address four key debates. Firstly, we question the notion of how and why gender based violence is perceived as a cultural phenomenon in minoritised communities (i.e. as a cultural norm), but constructed as an individual action (i.e. as cultural anomaly) in majority communities. Secondly, we briefly highlight the role of cultural relativism in understanding abuse; thirdly we outline the difficulties of responding to minoritised victims of gender based violence within a cultural frame. Lastly, we return to the theme of honour and offer a critique of over determining violence against women through the trope of honour and challenge the notion of violence against minoritised women as a cultural norm. We argue instead for a multi-layered analysis which incorporates the structural and cultural in conceptualising any form of violence against women whether in majority or minoritised communities.

1 We use the term minoritised throughout the chapter to indicate that one is not a minority purely on the basis of numbers, religion, language etc, but is positioned as such through a socio-historic process.

Violence against women and the role of culture

We are troubled by the trend to cast violence against women in minoritised communities as purely cultural. To begin this debate we briefly compare the construction of two forms of violence against women: forced marriage and date rape. These two forms of violence serve as examples to illustrate our key points rather than offering a detailed analysis of forced marriage or date rape. Forced marriage debates within the UK are firmly positioned within cultural discourses, the chief lexicon being 'honour based violence' with honour and shame the key markers. So although forced marriage currently sits within the UK Government domestic violence definition, it is also conceptualised as honour based violence pertaining mostly to minoritised communities. In addition, the concept of honour is usually presented as only concerning minority cultures, so within this construction, forced marriage comes to be seen (erroneously) as a characteristic and normal part of certain cultures. A recent report on honour based violence in the UK argues that forced marriage and domestic violence particularly in South Asian and Middle Eastern communities are 'not isolated practices, but are instead part of a self-sustaining social system built on ideas of honour and cultural, ethnic and religious superiority' (Brandon and Hafez 2008:1).

On the other hand, to our knowledge date rape is never explicitly formulated as a cultural issue in majority communities. Feminist writers on sexual violence (e.g. Kelly 1988) highlight how male sexual violence is made possible because of unequal gender relations. This means that, at least in part, sexual violence is explained at a structural and cultural level, yet this analysis seems to disappear when we compare the treatment of date rape with forced marriage. Date rape, which has largely been analysed in Anglo-American contexts, is constructed as an individualised aberrant or abnormal behaviour and therefore is not seen as part of the culture. So the representation of Anglo-American culture remains intact and 'honourable' with date rape behaviour being seen as outside of this. In contrast, when we consider the case of violence against women (including forced marriage) in minoritised communities this is frequently constructed as an intrinsic part of the culture.

We must, therefore, ask ourselves what processes are in play to allow these differing constructions to exist. We argue that the key difference is the way in which culture is called upon as an explanation of certain anomalies, for example, forced marriage in minoritised communities but is occluded in the case of date rape. In the instance of date rape, no reference is made to culture and an individualistic focus is instead offered as an explanation. The differences in the manner in which date rape and forced marriage are treated leads one to mistakenly assume that forced marriage is endemic within minoritised communities and hence a central part of their cultures whilst date rape is an unusual occurrence and therefore not endemic to western culture. How have these constructions taken hold given that there are no reliable figures in the UK for either form of violence? What veracity do they hold and should we accept these assertions without question? The culturalist formulation buttresses the view that forced marriage is the inevitable fate of young women in minority communities, particularly in South Asian and middle-eastern communities. It also paints a portrait of these (young) women as pathetic and hapless victims who only exist through culture, thus undermining agency and autonomy (Shachar 2001). Indeed, agency and autonomy do not sit comfortably with the stereotypical view of South Asian women as passive. Patriarchy in minoritised communities is thus allowed to flourish in the safe knowledge that 'culture' can be used as a foil to prevent the protection of women. This in turn feeds into the view that minority communities are more patriarchal than western communities. What fails to be acknowledged is that the West's construction of passive women, together with an insistence that forced marriage is 'part of their culture', fails to protect minoritised women.

Razack (2004) argues that perceptions of cultural superiority inherent in some western feminisms is problematic and highlights the work of Wikan (2002) as an example of this. Razack (2004) critiques Wikan's work on the following three grounds: Firstly, Wikan implies that Westerners have values (liberal, democratic, egalitarian) whilst Muslims have cultures, inevitably constructed as oppressive and patriarchal. This creates a dichotomy between individual autonomy and freedom versus the oppressive forces of culture which are seen to be an inherent part of the 'other'. Secondly, Razack argues that the over-determining manner in which culture is used by Wikan obscures structural relationships based on race and class and neglects the historical basis of the power relations (often based on colonisation) between majority and minoritsed communities in European contexts. Thirdly, Razack points out that implicit in Wikan's work is the self-image of the West as outside of culture, privileging instead personal autonomy. In turn, this is seen as a more 'civilised' way of living, and further that this civilised way of living needs to be taught to migrants. Thus 'barbaric' others need to be instructed in the values of the West.

Further, in the case of forced marriage, there are a range of other factors that precipitate forced marriage including structural factors such as poverty, particularly in trans-national marriages (Chantler et al. 2009). Within essentialist culturalist discourse, these factors are overlooked and this position contributes to a limited understanding of violence against women in minoritised communities and places them in a vulnerable position (Siddiqui 2005). The issue of how culturalist thinking contributes to the increased vulnerability of minoritised women is discussed further below. For now, it should be noted that it is the differences in the power relations between majority and minority communities that allow violence against women to be cast as 'cultural' in minority communities but as 'abnormal' in majority communities. These differences are not just semantic, as they tend to have an important effect in how we respond to domestic violence in minoritised communities.

The double-edged sword of relativism

One of the key theoretical positions in relation to explaining violence against minoritised women is cultural relativism. According to cultural relativism, there can be no definitive view as to what violence against women is, as this depends on the socio-cultural contexts and understandings of different communities. This means that what is considered abusive in some contexts will not necessarily be viewed as such from the vantage point of a different community. This position has the advantage of attending to different cultural contexts in framing violence against women, and enables us to explore the specificities of the forms of violence perpetrated against women in diverse communities, thus allowing for a more nuanced understanding of violence against women. The other major advantage of relativism is that it readily accepts changing definitions and understandings. An example of this can be seen in the current UK definition of domestic violence which is quite different from previous ones. The key difference is that the definition has shifted from its previous conceptualisation of domestic violence as only occurring in intimate, heterosexual relationships to a conceptualisation that includes violence perpetrated by family members as well as violence within gay relationships. Notwithstanding these advantages, a key factor which is frequently glossed over in relativist debates is the issue of power. In what follows, we interrogate relativism and illustrate the complex relationship between culture and power in the context of violence and abuse.

We argue that relativism is also a double-edged sword as it can work against protecting women and children from abuse in minoritised communities in the West. Principally this is achieved by suggesting that what happens in such communities is unique and embedded within those communities, and therefore a special case. This can have serious repercussions by making certain principles, such as violence against women, seemingly irrelevant to minoritised communities as these are framed only within culturalist discourses and practices, rather than within a (universal) human rights framework (Gill 2006). In the next section, we discuss some key concepts and dynamics that work to deny minoritsed women the protection they are entitled to, particularly when working from a relativist position.

Protecting minoritised women from violence

Drawing on research on minoritsed women and violence against women (Chantler et al. 2001; Batsleer et al. 2002), we argue that in relation to protecting minoritised women from abuse, there are three key inter-related ideas that need to figure in our conceptualisation, understanding and practice. These are: race anxiety, cultural privacy and the tendency to privilege culture over gender. The inter-relationship between these are important to understand as they serve to obscure sensitive responses to minoritsed women and need to be guarded against if the state is to offer relevant protection to minoritised women.

Chantler et al. (2001) use the term 'race anxiety' to refer to individual and collective (institutional and state level) anxiety about how to intervene in relation to minoritised peoples, particularly in the context of abuse and other sensitive topics. The anxiety is generated through a fear and shame of being labelled racist or culturally insensitive and it is this anxiety that appears to over-ride sound assessment and decision-making in relation to protecting vulnerable women in abusive situations. Such anxiety has a silencing effect, for to speak might bring accusations that the practitioner or institution is culturally insensitive. Importantly, institutions do not want to be 'named and shamed' as being institutionally racist. Hence, maintaining the institution's honour becomes paramount. However, cultural sensitivity frequently entails the exclusion of issues of gender and other marginalised groupings, so that being 'culturally sensitive' in effect serves largely to uphold traditional, conservative readings of communities. Race anxiety, therefore, contributes to the conditions which allow for abuse in minoritised communities to go unchallenged.

The desire to be culturally sensitive and the requirement to be seen as 'non-racist' prevents the speaker or institution from challenging practices based on unequal power relations *within* minoritised communities. The failure to intervene when it is required is further underpinned by the notion of 'cultural privacy' (Batsleer et al. 2002). Cultural privacy refers to the manner in which self-appointed 'community leaders', often powerful men within minoritised communities, draw the boundaries over their community domains (Gangoli et al. 2006). It is community leaders who thus influence what can and cannot be talked about and further it is community leaders who are normally consulted by the government and local authorities. Sensitive issues such as domestic violence and childhood abuse are unlikely to be discussed openly as these would shatter the romanticised notion of strong, nurturing families within minoritised communities. Here, the interests of minoritised women and children are rarely seen as important, and the security of the patriarchal family, representing male interests, takes priority. Hence community leaders are more likely to draw a veil of silence over sensitive issues and insist on a level of cultural privacy. Black feminists working on domestic violence within minoritised communities, e.g. Imkaan and Southall Black Sisters, are often seen as working against community interests, as they pose a challenge to patriarchy. Feminists (including black feminists) have long pointed out that an essential step to combating violence against women is to move away from the notion that what happens in the home is a private matter. It is, therefore, the movement of domestic violence from the privacy of the home into the public domain that is essential, as it is the public consideration of abuse and violence which leads to legislation and support for victims. This shift from private to public is also what is required in relation to minoritised communities, that is, a shift is required from 'cultural privacy' to a more public contestation of sensitive issues such as violence and abuse within minoritised communities (see also Kukathas 1998; Sachar 1998).

Cultural privacy together with race anxiety makes for a powerful cocktail that act as barriers to the detection and appropriate intervention in abuse situations. Inevitably, this leads to a privileging of cultural issues over gender. The desire to be culturally sensitive overlooks issues of abuse as this is wrongly formulated as being 'part of their culture' and the anxiety stops the interrogation that is required. To break this cycle, we argue that a consideration of gender within minoritised communities is essential. However, this position is also fraught with problems. If one were to work only with gender issues at the expense of cultural and structural issues, such as poverty, racism, and immigration controls, the resultant gender analysis would be devoid of context and of the lived experiences of minoritised women. This is a point that has been made forcefully by black feminists over a number of years (e.g. Amos and Parmar 1984) and is worth reiterating in the context of recent anti-immigration legislation in Europe to supposedly combat forced marriage. Hence the gender analysis which is required is one that is fully cognisant of other dimensions of oppression and disadvantage (Thiara and Gill 2010). Thus, several studies that focus on domestic violence in minoritsed communities in the UK have been at the forefront of highlighting the problems of 'no recourse to public funds' (Chantler et al 2001; Sundari et al. 2008; Rai and Thiara 1997). These can be thought of as largely focussing on structural issues, whilst other literature, discussed below has focussed almost exclusively on cultural issues such as honour.

Understanding honour

It has become fashionable within policy and academia to understand violence against minoritised women as arising from an honour based culture (Brandon and Hafez 2008). Feminist activist organisations such as Southall Black Sisters have consistently pointed out that there is no honour in committing crimes of violence against women. This has led, in the British context, to the labelling of these crimes as 'so-called crimes of honour' to signify their inherent lack of honour. In this section of our chapter, we pay particular attention to the construction of so called honour based crimes and interrogate the differences between this and crimes of passion. These two paradigms are positioned as binaries, with crimes of passion attributed to the west and honour based crimes attributed to Muslim communities in particular. These terms and their attributions have been much contested and in our view this needs to continue as some of the thinking around these terms has been described as 'tortuous' (Razack 2004: 152).

Honour and shame have been treated as motifs of otherness, and attributed almost entirely to minoritised communities. However, there is much literature on how being the victim of any violent crime can cause overwhelming feelings of shame (World Society of Victimology 2005); the role and consequences of shame experienced by adult survivors of child sexual abuse (Feiring et al. 2002) and abusive family environments (Hoglund and Nicholas 1995); and women experiencing sexual violence (Kelly 1988). There is also literature on how certain stigmatised members of society, including prostitutes, can feel a sense of shame due to their occupation (see Tomara 2009; Pheterson 1990). While some of this shame is individualised, rather than collective, we argue that ideas of honour and shame in South Asian contexts can also be both collective and individual. For example, women's bodies are frequently read as repositories of community honour (Sanghari and Vaid 1989), but shame can also be experienced individually by women who may have experienced sexual violence (Gangoli et al. 2006). Hence, shame is much more widespread than is commonly articulated in western contexts. Acknowledging this helps to prevent shame being perceived as a marker only of cultural others.

Discourses of honour and shame in the literature in some non western contexts, and minoritised women in the west, understand honour as vested in the bodies and actions of women (and to a lesser extent men) with loss of control over women potentially leading to shame (Araji 2000). Unlike the examples cited above, shame may be vested in the bodies of individual women, but is shared by the community, which is embodied by the men. There is a rich corpus of literature that looks at ways in which women's bodies are seen as symbolically representing a community, nation or race, and how dishonouring a women can lead to a symbolic dishonouring of the community or nation (Jayawardena and De Alwis 1996; Gangoli 2006). Research on domestic violence within specific minoritised communities in the UK, particularly South Asian, has pointed to the importance of culturally specific concepts of *izzat* (honour) and *sharam* (shame) in preventing women from articulating their experiences of violence in domestic situations (Bhopal 1997). *Izzat* and *sharam* are based primarily on the notion that the bodies and actions of women and girls represent community or individual honour. South Asian young women and girls in the UK are often vulnerable to such control, as there can be a high premium attached to ideas of sexual purity and chastity for young unmarried girls, especially in the context of taboos around premarital sexuality, loss of virginity and fears of young women being 'corrupted' by western values (Gangoli et al. 2009). This can sometimes be manifested in forced marriage of girl children, as a method to prevent such transgressive sexual behaviour.

However, it should be noted that until very recently chastity and sexual purity have also been features of many western industrialised nations. 'Shotgun' marriages in the west are a good example in the recent past of the pressure on women pregnant outside of marriage to marry their lovers since sexual relations outside of marriage were not culturally acceptable. Alternatively, such pregnancies were concealed and young women sent away to have their babies in alternative parts of the country where the babies were placed for adoption. In part, the free availability of contraception combined with state welfare support for lone mothers has enabled more permissive sexual mores. This illustrates the centrality of material resources in shaping what is considered to be culturally acceptable. Another more recent example is the case of marital rape. It was only in 1991 that rape within marriage in the UK was recognised as a violation, highlighting the cultural acceptance that a husband was entitled to sex with his wife whenever he wanted, thus throwing into question the notion of the progressive rights of women in the west.

Moreover, in religious communities in the west (of whatever faith), sexual purity is still highly prized. A recent case in point is the Christian movement's reaffirmation of sexual purity before marriage, for example the 'silver ring thing' initiated by Pastor Denny Pattyn in Arizona, USA in 1996 and which was launched in the UK in 2003 (times online June 22 2007, accessed 21/08/09). It preaches chastity and the silver ring is to remind the wearer that they have pledged to be virgins until they marry. Interestingly, if the wearers are unable to keep their promise they are advised to flush the ring down the toilet rather than wear it and dishonour the community. These examples (pregnancy outside marriage, marital rape and religious emphasis on sexual purity) illustrate how ideas of collective shame and honour are not the exclusive domain of minoritised non-Christian communities.

It has been argued that honour crimes are different from other forms of violence against women, including sexual jealousy. Purna Sen has identified six key features of crimes of honour, including: gender relations that problematise and control women's behaviour and sexuality; women policing other women's behaviour; collective decisions regarding punishments; women's participation in killings; ability to reclaim honour through killings or enforced compliance; and State sanction of such killings through recognition of honour as motivation and mitigation (Sen 2005). She suggests that honour crimes have more in common with dowry related murders in countries like India and femicide in various contexts than those involving sexual jealousy or what she terms 'individualistic fit of fury' (Sen 2005: 51). Seen thus, the focus is more on collective honour and shame, as reflected in the behaviour of women, rather than the individual.

However, we argue that while different forms of violence against women are contextually different, discourses of honour and shame are not restricted to specific ethnic communities or to particular forms of violence against women. Recent work also argues that contrary to Sen's assumptions, the links between dowry and domestic violence are neither obvious nor automatic but that domestic violence in India, as in the west, has other important social and economic causes and manifestations and that reducing Indian experiences of domestic violence to dowry can be essentialist and can lead to exoticising domestic violence in India (Talwar Olbenburg 2002). Therefore, seeking cultural explanations for violence against women in Third World countries when similar research conclusions are not made for violence against women in Western countries can be dangerous and counterproductive (Talwar Oldenburg 2002). Further, we argue that dowry related murders often have strong individualist and/or relational aspects (for example, financial reasons or strife between mothers-in-law and daughters-in-law), in addition to ideas of honour. Further, violence against women in ethnic white groups in the west can also demonstrate some of the features identified as symptomatic of honour crimes above and this is discussed below.

Whilst accepting many of Sen's arguments, we depart with the analysis that domestic killings in majority communities are merely crimes of passion committed in a moment of rage. While this may be the case in some domestic killings in both the majority and minoritised communties, we argue that crimes of passion cannot explain all domestic murders or violence in any community. There have been several cases in the UK media concerning domestic violence in majority communities where ex-spouses or partners have murdered their partners (and often children) on pre-arranged contact visits. In this situation, it is hard to argue that the violence committed during such visits is not premeditated or part of a pattern of violence perpetrated against the victim. It is also worth noting that the level of violence meted out to all women, including majority white women who leave abusive relationships, is significant (Hester and Westmarland 2005), highlighting the pressure on majority women to stay in violent relationships as leaving can exacerbate the violence. Many feminists (Stark 2007) working in this field have long argued that violence against women is not an individual act, but is part of a system of domination and control based on unequal gender and other social relations. What puzzles us is that this feminist analysis clearly acknowledges the role of structure and culture in shaping unequal gender relations, yet somehow this gets obscured when comparing violence against women in majority communities versus violence against women in minoritsed communities. It seems to us that this is a retrograde step as it performs its own kind of double violence. The first kind is to transfer the unit of analysis in relation to majority women from the structural/cultural to the individual level, thus directing attention to the 'few bad apples' rather than to the structures and culture which maintain violence against women in majority communities. The second kind of violence is to only see the cultural in relation to violence against minoritised women, thereby invoking essentialist thinking and pathologising minoritised communities.

Research on the relationship between sexual jealousy and intimate partner violence in USA has found that controlling for cultural variations, intimate partner violence is a common behavioural result of sexual jealousy among American couples, and this is based on the degree of intimacy between the partners, which in turn owes much to 'symbolic' practices such as sexual exclusivity as a commitment (Paik et al. 2000). Sexual jealousy appears to manifest most strongly where sexual exclusivity or monogamy is seen as challenged, and this can have a strong gendered element, with men more likely to be violent, based on the belief that violence is justified when they suspect that their partners are unfaithful or in other situations where they believe that their honour is being threatened. Further, far from being individualistic fits of fury, many of these murders are planned meticulously (Polk 1994). There is also evidence that suggests that there is a tolerance for physical and sexual violence against women by young people in the UK, especially where the violence happens within a marriage and where the woman is seen as sexually promiscuous or cheating on her partner (Burton et al. 1998). It would appear, therefore, that for white majority communities as well as minoritised communities, wives are considered the property of their husbands, and cheating on them can be seen as justifying physical retribution.

This may not be articulated as collective honour and shame but seen as individual loss of face (Araji 2000). As Araji also points out, this individualisation of shame and honour can be seen to be closely tied to the more individualistic focus of western industrialised societies so it is not surprising that the collective ideas which are in circulation in the west get subordinated to the individual level. Further, following Sen's definition of honour crimes, there is evidence that such violence, deemed as 'crimes of passion' are often treated leniently by western judicial systems (Mullen 1995). Regarding such acts of violence, Araji (2000) further notes that in some non-western 'traditional' societies, women's sexual transgressions are often not punished if they are not made public, for instance if a woman in India is pregnant out of wedlock, a discreet abortion can prevent further repercussions. In contrast, in Western societies women are mostly abused or killed for transgressions that are both known or suspected privately as well as those that are public. While this may also happen in minoritised communities, it could well be the fear of disclosure and the resultant loss of honour that may be a contributory factor to abuse in such cases.

Conclusions

We contend that violence against women in minoritised communities cannot be understood purely in terms of the cultural or in terms of honour based violence. We also argue that violence against women in majority communities cannot be understood as merely individual acts of violence. To persist in seeing them as such compounds the violence experienced. Race anxiety, cultural privacy and the privileging of culture over gender in minoritised communities will continue to leave women unprotected. Black feminist organisations, such as Southall Black Sisters, have also attacked unthinking multi-culturalism as contributing to violence against women in minoritised communities going unacknowledged. Dustin and Phillips (2008) point out that both doing nothing as a consequence of this unacknowledgement, as well as doing 'something' is problematic if that something does violence to minoritised cultures via its misrepresentation.

Feminist analyses emphasise patterns of power and control and unequal social relations as an explanation for violence against women (Hague and Malos 1998). We have illustrated how violence against all women is part of structural and cultural arrangements. The slide to a more individualistic focus that is gaining ground in explaining violence against women in majority cultures is problematic. This slide is particularly noticeable in discussions when violence against majority women is juxtaposed with violence against minoritised women and works to position majority communities as culturally superior. Lessons from over thirty years ago do not appear to have been heeded as yet by liberal western feminists. Liberal feminists have increased their spheres of influence and are now more powerfully positioned to act to protect all women from violence. Instead, some of their interventions have been taken on by nation states to increase surveillance, regulation and control of minoritised communities often through the use of immigration control in the name of protecting minoritsed women from 'honour based violence'. This chapter urges for an approach that utilises multidimensional levels of analyses: individual, cultural and structural in understanding and responding to violence against women and to stem the tide of culturalist explanations of violence against women in minoritised communities.

However, as we have reiterated throughout the chapter, we cannot ignore culture and have focussed on honour as a key motif. This chapter discusses the limitations of constructing violence against women in minoritised communities as only constituting the cultural. Our key argument is that ideas about culture influence all forms of violence against women, including women from majority communities, yet this often goes unacknowledged. Central to our concerns is the manner in which a focus on culture alone in relation to minoritised women has the double effect of leaving minority women unprotected from violence, and at the same time sediments the view that minority cultures are 'backward' in relation to gender relations. We also suggest that by drawing attention to the way in which honour and shame can influence particular behaviours need not necessarily lead to cultural relativism, but can possibly lead to a greater understanding of contexts. For example, even if we start by accepting that sexual jealousy in intimate heterosexual relationships in both white mainstream and minoritised communities is based on ideas of hurt honour and shame, we might then begin to understand how its formulation may differ in both contexts. To illustrate, in white mainstream communities, these ideas may be more individualised or linked to ideas of individual masculinity while in some minoritised communities, they may be more community or family based, or based on ideas that women's behaviour can discredit familial pride and honour. Our argument is, therefore, not that culture is irrelevant in violence against women but that it is relevant to both majority and minoritised communities, and exoticising particular forms as cultural and others as aberrant can have tragic consequences for all women who are victims of violence.

References

Amos, Valerie/Parmar, Pratibha (1984): Challenging Imperial Feminism. In: Feminist Review 17, pp. 3–20.

Araji, Sharon, K. (2000): Crimes of Honor and Shame: Violence against Women in Non-Western and Western Societies. In: The Red Feather Journal of Postmodern Criminology, 8. http://www.critcrim.org/redfeather/journal-pomocrim/vol-8-shaming/araji.html (23.07.2009)

Batsleer, Janet/Burman, Erica/Chantler, Khatidja/Mcntosh, Shirley/Pantling, Kamal/ Smailes, Sophie/Warner, Sam (2002): Domestic Violence and Minoritisation: Supporting Women to Independence. Manchester: Women's Studies Research Centre.

Bhopal, Kalwant (1997): Gender, 'Race' and Patriarchy: A Study of South Asian Women. Aldershot: Ashgate.

Brandon, James/Hafez, Salam (2008): Crimes of the Community: Honour based violence in the UK. London: Centre for Social Cohesion.

Burton, Susan/Kitzinger, Janet/Kelly, Liz/Regan, Linda (1998): Young people's attitude towards violence, sex and relationships: a survey and focus group study. Glasgow: Zero Tolerance Charitable Trust, Glasgow City Council and Fife Council. Research Report 002.

Chantler, Khatidja/Burman, Erica/Batsleer, Janet/Bashir, Colsom. (2001): Attempted Suicide and Self-harm: South Asian Women. Manchester: Women's Studies Research Centre, Manchester Metropolitan University.

Chantler, Khatidja/Gangoli, Geetanjali/Hester, Marianne (2009): Forced Marriage in the UK: Religious, cultural, economic or state violence? In: Critical Social Policy, 29, 4, pp. 587–612.

Dustin, Moira/Phillips Anne (2008): Whose Agenda is it? Abuses of Women and abuses of 'culture'. In: Britain Ethnicities Vol 8 (3), pp. 405–424.

Feiring, Candice/Deblinger, Esther/Hoch-Espada, Amy/Haworth, Tom (2002): Romantic Relationship Aggression and Attitudes in High School Students: The Role of Gender, Grade, and Attachment and Emotional Styles. In: The Journal of Youth and Adolescence, 21, 5, pp. 373–385.

Gangoli, Geetanjali/McCarry, Melanie/Razak, Amina (2009): Child Marriage or Forced Marriage: South Asian Communities in North East England. In: Children and Society 23, 6, pp. 418–429.

Gangoli, Geetanjali/Razak, Amina/McCarry, Melanie (2006): Forced Marriages and Domestic Violence Among South Asian Communities in North East England. Newcastle and Bristol: Northern Rock Foundation and University of Bristol.

Gill, Aisha (2006): Patriarchal Violence in the Name of 'Honour''. In: International Journal of Criminal Justice Sciences, 1, 1, pp. 1–12.

Hague, Gill/Malos, Ellen (1998): Domestic Violence: Action for Change. Cheltenham: New Clarion Press

Hester, Marianne/Westmarland, Nicole (2005): Tackling domestic violence: effective interventions and approaches. Home Office Research Study 290. London: Home Office.

Hoglund, C.L./Nicholas, K.B. (1995): Shame, Guilt and Anger in College Students Exposed to Abusive Family Environments. In: Journal of Family Violence, 10, 2, pp. 141–155.

Jayawardhane, Kumari/de Alwis, Malathi (1996): Embodied Violence: Communalising women's sexuality in South Asia. New Delhi: Kali for Women.

Kelly, Liz (1988): Surviving Sexual Violence. Cambridge: Polity Press.

Kukathas, Chandran (1998): Liberalism and Multiculturalism: The Politics of Indifference, Political Theory Vol 26 (5), pp. 686–699.

Mullen, Paul, E. (1995): Jealousy and Violence. In: Hong Kong Journal of Psychiatry, 5, pp. 18–24.

Paik, Anthony/Laumann, Edward O./Haitsma, Martha Van. (2000): Sexual Jealousy, Violence, and Embeddedness in Intimate Relations: A Social Structural and Cultural Explanation. Society for the Scientific Study of Sexuality. Orlando, FL.

Pheterson, Gail (1990): The Category 'Prostitute' in Scientific Inquiry. In: The Journal of Sex Research, 27, 3, pp. 397–407.

Polk, Kennett (1994): When Men Kill. Scenarios of Masculine Violence. Cambridge: Cambridge University Press.

Rai, Dhanwant/Thiara, Ravi (1997): Redefining Spaces: The needs of Black women and children in refuge support services and Black workers in Women's Aid. Bristol: Women's Aid Federation England, 82 pp.

Razack, Sherene (2004): Imperilled Muslim Women, Dangerous Muslim Men and Civilised Europeans: Legal and Social Responses to Forced Marriages. In: Feminist Legal Studies, Vol. 12 (2), pp. 129–174.

Sachar, Ayelet (2001): Multicultural Jurisdictions: Cultural Differences and Women's Rights, Cambridge: Cambridge University Press.

Sangari, Kimkum/Vaid, Sudesh (1989): Recasting Women. Essays in Colonial History. New Delhi: Oxford University Press.

Sen, Purna (2005): 'Crimes of honour', value and meaning. In: Welchman, Lynn/Hossain, Sara (eds.): 'Honour' Crimes, Paradigm and Violence Against Women. New Delhi: Zubaan, pp. 42–63.

Siddiqui, Hanana (2005): There is no honour in domestic violence, only shame! Women's struggles against 'honour' crimes in the UK. In: Welchman, Lynn/Hossain, Sara (eds.): 'Honour' Crimes, Paradigm and Violence Against Women. New Delhi: Zubaan, pp. 263–281.

Stark, Evan. (2007): Coercive Control: How Men Entrap Women in Personal Life. New York: Oxford University Press

Sundari, Anitha/Chopra, Priya/Farouk, Waheeds/Huq, Qamar/Khan, Saliya (2008): Forgotten Women: domestic violence, poverty and South Asian Women with no recourse to public funds. Manchester: Oxfam and Saheli.

Talwar Oldenburg, Veena (2002): Dowry murder. The imperial origins of a cultural crime. New Delhi: Oxford University Press.

Thiara, Ravi K./Gill, Aisha K. (2010): Violence Against Women in South Asian Communities: Issues for Policy and Practice. London: Jessica Kingsley

Times online June 22, 2007 http://www.timesonline.co.uk/tol/news/uk/article1971937.ece, (21.08.2009)

Tomura, Miyuki (2009): A Prostitute's Lived Experience of Stigma. In: Journal of Phenomenological Psychology, 40, 1, pp. 51–84.

Wikan, Unni (2002): Generous Betrayal: politics of Culture in the New Europe. Chicago, London: University of Chicago Press.

World Society of Victimology (2005): World Society of Victimology Urges a Practical Vision for Victims. Press Statement from the World Society of Victimology on the Occasion of the 11th UN Congress on Crime Prevention and Criminal Justice Bangkok, Thailand. http://www.worldsocietyofvictimology.org/ (12.1.2010)

Women's Rights, Welfare State Nationalism and Violence in Migrant Families

Suvi Keskinen

Introduction

During the last decade, the Nordic countries have experienced heated public debates about issues of gender, sexuality and ethnicity. The focus of attention has been especially on 'forced marriages', 'honour-killings' and 'female genital cutting'. With reference to gender equality and women's rights arguments have been formulated to promote anti-immigration politics, as well as to create dichotomous divisions between the perceived gender equal majorities ('us') and patriarchal minorities ('them') (see Keskinen 2009a). Gendered violence has become a site of negotiation and conflict regarding national belonging, national boundaries and ethnic relations. Violence in minority families has become a core issue and one through which boundaries for the national collective (Anthias and Yuval-Davis 1992) are (re)produced. Gendered violence and women's rights have also been used to legitimate hegemonic transnational projects, such as the US-led 'war on terror', notably in connection with the attack on Afghanistan in 2001 (Russo 2006).

In this chapter, I focus on the contested meanings of women's rights and gender equality when dealing with violence in migrant[1] families in present-day Finland. I am interested in how gender and sexuality shape the construction of national boundaries, as well as how gendered violence figures in the processes of creating divisions on the basis of 'race' and ethnicity. I will use empirical data from ongoing research on gendered violence in migrant fami-

1 In general, I use the term 'violence in ethnic minority families' since this is a common way to address the phenomenon in international literature. However, when writing about the empirical data drawn from Finland I use the term 'migrant', as this is the prevailing terminology in Finland and describes the focus of my research. I want to point out that the term 'migrant' is embedded in a problematic distinction between those who have the unquestioned right to belong to the nation and those who do not, as well as being a broad and homogenizing category. However, I use this term as there are no better alternatives, and the term 'ethnic minority' would require me to discuss also the 'old' minorities in Finland, such as the Roma and the Sami, which is not possible here. The term 'immigrant' is applied when citing interviewees who use it.

lies to develop the theme of women's rights as a multifaceted issue and as a site of continuous struggle. This data thus serves to destabilize the dichotomous constructions described above. I argue that in the current political and social situation it is essential for feminist researchers to engage in developing conceptualisations that provide alternatives to the culturalist understandings of violence circulating in European societies today, and that the narratives of abused migrant women provide a fruitful starting point for such (re)conceptualisations.

The chapter starts with an analysis of current debates on multiculturalism in Europe and the role of violence in minority families in these debates. I then discuss the Finnish welfare state context, and show how nationalist and culturalist discourses shape welfare professionals' speech about violence against minority women. In the last part of the chapter, I contrast the views presented in public debates and professional speech with the narratives of abused migrant women, in order to bring in elements that are often bypassed in the discussions on the topic.

The crisis of multiculturalism and debates on gendered violence

In several European countries, public attention on gendered violence in ethnic minority families during the past decade has intensified (see Phillips and Saharso 2008; Bredström 2003; Bredal 2005; Teigen and Langvasbråten 2009). From being a marginal issue raised mainly by minority women's organisations, the topic has become the focus of broad debates in the media and in politics, and, along with the 'head-scarf issue', has achieved a symbolic value well beyond the scope of the initial problem. Few other topics have so powerfully represented the perceived subordination of women in minority, notably non-Western and Muslim, communities. In the course of these debates, culture has been used as a static and monolithic concept to construct differences between the ethnic majorities and minorities.

This process has occurred at the same time, and *as part of,* what has been called the 'crisis of multiculturalism' (Modood 2007) or the 'backlash against difference' (Grillo 2007). Multiculturalism has been under severe pressure from critics who claim that Europe suffers from an 'excess of alterity' and that multiculturalism promotes ethnic segregation – and ultimately terrorism. This position has gained strength in the period following the attack on the World Trade Towers in New York on 11 of September, 2001. One of the clearest examples of this critique is to be found in the upsurge of populist and right-wing parties with anti-immigration agendas in recent elections, but also in broader debates articulated in the media, on the internet and in politics regarding different ways of living in present-day societies and the limits of tolerance (Gingrich and Banks 2006). The 'crisis of multiculturalism' is also a highly gendered discourse. The figure of the 'immigrant woman' plays a central role in the imaginaries of what the nation should be about, who can be included and what values are to be regarded as constitutive of the nation (Lewis 2005, 2006). The body of the 'immigrant woman' becomes the imaginary battlefield on which these definitions are debated and played out. 'Honour-related violence' and 'female genital cutting' have frequently been used as examples of the negative effects of multiculturalism and to show that certain cultural backgrounds, especially Third World and Muslim, are incompatible with what are understood to be European values (freedom, equality, democracy) (Razack 2004).

Debates on multiculturalism in the Netherlands and Denmark have been especially intense and polarised, with the topic of violence in minority families feeding into discussions about the lack of integration of Muslim minorities (Korteweg and Yurdakul 2009; Siim and Skjeie 2008). By invoking Dutch patriotism and appealing to 'ordinary people' who were said to know from their daily experiences the problems of multi-ethnic societies, the politics of 'new realism' gained a strong foothold within a short time in the Netherlands (Prins and Saharso 2008). 'Forced marriages' and 'honour-killings' have been used as an examples *par excellence* of the backward culture of Muslim 'immigrants', and on the basis of these practices arguments are made for the superiority of purportedly 'Western' values. In Denmark arguments related to the prevention of 'forced marriages' have legitimated the tightening of immigration policies, leading to some of the strictest legislation on immigration in Europe (Bredal 2005)[2].

While debates on gendered violence in minority families have been somewhat less polarised in other European countries, similar trends appear in most of them (Phillips and Saharso 2008). However, less clear-cut constructions of violence in minority families also circulate in the public sphere. Boundaries between ethnic majorities and minorities appear more blurred in such constructions: minority communities are described as heterogeneous entities and connections are made to violence in majority families (Dustin and Phillips 2008; Korteweg and Yurdakul 2009). This has been especially

2 This includes for example strict rules for family reunification including a stipulated age for both spouses (24 years), national affiliation (both spouses need to prove they have closer ties to Denmark than to any other country), and requirements regarding housing and maintenance.

the case in situations and contexts where minority women's organisations have managed to make their voices heard in public arenas, such as in the UK.

Welfare state nationalism and gender equality

The Nordic countries (Sweden, Norway, Denmark and Finland) base their national self-images on being culturally homogeneous countries and leading nations with regard to establishing gender equality (Hilson 2008; Magnusson, Rönnblom and Silius 2008; Mulinari et al. 2009). Such national images exclude differences in relation to class, 'race', ethnicity, religion, language and gender that have existed even before the migration flows of recent decades. The images also establish the nation as an entity based on common origin and distinguish between those who have a self-evident right to belong (based on ethnic origin) and those who do not. The emphasis on achieved gender equality seems to turn a blind eye to enduring gendered inequalities and provides an efficient tool for creating hierarchies among the majority and minorities.

As argued by Verloo and Lombardo, gender equality is an 'empty signifier that takes as many meanings as the variety of visions and debates on the issue allow it to take' (2007: 22). The broad consensus about the importance of gender equality in the Nordic countries makes it especially liable to several kinds of uses – among these are the nationalist and racialising discourses of interest to this chapter. In Finland, gender equality is regarded as deeply grounded in national history: it is linked to the agrarian tradition in which, it is claimed, Finnish women had equal social standing and they worked on an equal footing with men (Rantalaiho 1994). A recent analysis of Finnish parliamentary discussions shows that gender equality is presented as beneficial for the whole nation and is used to define Finnishness in relation to other nationalities (Raevaara 2008). In multicultural women's politics (which involves women's movement activists, as well as politicians and authorities), gender equality is so closely linked to Finnishness that migrant women are expected to adopt it as a value and practice in order to become 'Finnish' (Tuori 2007).

In the Finnish, as well as in the Nordic context, the state and municipalities play a central role in providing welfare services. While integration policies in, for example the UK, favour and require the active role of migrant organisations, the Finnish system relies heavily on authorities and public institutions (Wahlbeck 1999). Authorities, such as the social office and the employment office, perform the main part of the integration work. The welfare state is in many ways beneficial for women which has led Nordic feminists to call it 'women-friendly' (Borchorst and Siim 2002). However, a view of the welfare state as solely women's ally fails to address the question of how it is part of the (re)production of social inequalities, and to which women it is beneficial. The welfare state is a site of complex power relations based on gender, ethnicity, 'race', class and sexuality, which means it is also a site of exclusions and creation of hierarchies.

I use the concept *welfare state nationalism* to grasp the specificities of nationalism in the Nordic countries (see also Mulinari et al. 2009). With it I refer to four interrelated aspects. Firstly, of relevance is the important role of welfare state policies and practices in performing nationalism in the Nordic countries, as described above. Secondly, I refer to the central role of the gender equality discourse in nationalist rhetorics and politics. Thirdly, I show that an emphasis on the countries' cultural, linguistic and ethnic homogeneity is characteristic of this kind of nationalism. The fourth aspect of welfare state nationalism is the narrow space given to discussion about racism and colonial legacies in present-day Nordic societies. As Keith Pringle (2005) has suggested, the same characteristics – egalitarianism, collectivism and an emphasis on consensus – that enable commitment to welfare and equal rights in the Nordic countries may limit the ability to recognise inequalities related to 'race' and ethnicity. These countries also perceive themselves as innocent bystanders to colonialism. It has been claimed that cultural racism is especially prominent in the Nordic countries (Hilson 2008), and often is not even recognized as racism.

The Finnish context

Finland is among the EU countries with a relatively small foreign-born population: 3.4% of the total population in 2005[3]. The largest migrant communities are the Russians, Estonians, Swedes, Somalis, Iraqis, Iranians, Turks and ex-Yugoslavians.[4] After approximately fifteen years of political consensus on integration policies, along with a strict asylum policy, issues related to migration and multiculturalism have recently become politicized in a new way. In the municipal elections in September 2008 and the European Union (EU) elections in June 2009, anti-immigration forces gained a notable rise in support, led by the populist party *True Finns,* but affecting the politics

3 Migration Policy Institute http://www.migrationinformation.org/DataHub/charts/1.1.shtml , accessed 23.5.2008

4 Migration Institute http://www.migrationinstitute.fi/db/stat/img/ef_06.jpg, accessed 3.7.2009

of other parties as well (see Keskinen 2009b). However, the Finnish debates have been more focused on asylum seekers and border control than on gendered violence.

Finland has been a latecomer to the public concern on gendered violence in families (Keskinen 2005). When the topic was raised at the end of the 1970s, it was discussed in gender-neutral terms as 'family violence'. Since the 1990s, the term 'violence against women' has been used, and several means to tackle gendered violence through legislation and social and health care initiatives have been introduced. Victimisation surveys directed at Finnish women show that gendered violence in families is a broad and persistent problem: while in 1997 8.6 per cent of women living in partnerships reported being subjected to violence during the last year, the figure was 7.9 per cent in a follow-up survey eight years later (Piispa et al. 2006).

Violence in migrant families became a topic of public interest in the aftermath of the national Programme to Prevent Violence Against Women (1998–2002) which strove to combat domestic violence and prostitution. Policy measures in relation to violence in migrant families have been introduced gradually since 2005, but are still scarce. Violence has been discussed mainly in terms of 'immigrant women' and 'immigrant families', bypassing 'older' ethnic minorities, such as the Roma and the Sami. The focus has been on domestic violence, with a growing interest in so-called honour-related violence. The discussions related to violence in migrant families have not been as heated as in the other Nordic countries, but many discursive structures, such as those related to 'honour-related violence', have been adopted from other countries, notably Sweden (Keskinen 2009a).

The study

The empirical data in this chapter was collected during recent research[5] which analysed the way in which abused migrant women negotiated their identities, the spaces for agency made available to them in a welfare state context, as well as the constructions of violence, gender and ethnicity by welfare professionals and authorities. The term 'violence in families' was used to cover both violence by partners and by other close relatives (parents, siblings, uncles etc.).

---

5 The project *Violence in families, migrancy and the Finnish welfare state* (2006–2009) was funded by the Finnish Cultural Foundation, the University of Tampere Centre for Advanced Study (UTACAS) and Scandinavian Research Council for Criminology.

The data consists of semi-structured interviews with abused migrant women and representatives of central agencies working with violence in migrant families. Thirty five interviews were conducted with the police, social workers, representatives of shelters (for victims of violence) and NGO driven projects. In addition, twenty interviews were conducted with women who had been abused by their partners, other close relative(s) or both. The women had moved to Finland from three geopolitical areas: (1) Russia (six interviewees); (2) an area I call the 'Middle East' – Turkey, Iraq, Iran, Afghanistan, Pakistan – (ten interviewees); and (3) North, West or Central Africa (four interviewees). Some of the interviewees had come to Finland as refugees, others had migrated due to marriage or as 'remigrants'[6]. The largest group of the interviewees had migrated from countries labelled as 'Muslim countries' in the Middle East or North Africa (twelve interviewees). However, this does not mean that all of them were Muslims which shows the problematic nature of making such generalising categorisations. Several of the interviewees from 'Muslim countries' either had another religion or were not committed to religious thinking.

Despite the homogenising effects of broad categories like 'Middle East' and 'Africa', I use these here in order to protect the anonymity of my interviewees. Migrant communities in Finland, except for the Russian and Estonian ones, are small and the interviewees could be distinguished if detailed information about their ethnicity, nationality or migration histories was presented. In places where I consider it safe I have provided more precise information. The interviewed women were contacted through NGOs and shelters working with abused women, as well as through one municipality (social work and family counselling), and asked whether they were willing to participate in an interview. The professionals and authorities were contacted in five big cities (Helsinki, Espoo, Vantaa, Turku, Tampere) in Southern Finland and interviewed individually, in pairs or as a group. The interviews were anywhere between one and three and a half hours long. The data was analysed thematically. Poststructuralist discourse analysis (Winther Jörgensen and Phillips 2002; Wilkinson and Kitzinger 1995) was used to locate the central discourses, in addition to which a more detailed reading of the interviews focusing on the use of language and power relations embedded in it was made.

6 The term 'remigrant' refers to Ingrians and others with a classification of 'Finnish ethnic origin' who were scattered to different locations in the Soviet Union during Stalin's repressions. These groups were given the right to permanent residence in Finland at the beginning of the 1990s.

Professionals teaching and guiding 'immigrant women'

In the interviews with authorities and professionals the most common way to explain violence in migrant families was to refer to 'culture'. Many authorities and professionals perceived the problem to be rooted in 'their culture' and the 'low position of women in immigrant families'. Women were said to 'accept violence as part of their life' and to presume it to be a normal part of marriage. Authorities and professionals also claimed this to be the reason why migrant women did not turn to authorities, such as the police, when they were abused. Thus, gendered violence in migrant families was in many cases culturalised. Culturalisation is a problematic process in several ways (Ghorashi et al. 2009), not least because culture is given precedence over social and economic considerations. Furthermore, culture is used in a static and homogenising way. All migrants or members of an ethnic minority community are presented as similar, thus rendering differences within groups invisible.

In culturalist speech, positions could also be created for professionals, in which they performed the task of teaching and guiding 'immigrant women' to the realm of gender equality. This seemed especially to be the task of female professionals in social work and NGO projects, some of whom emphasised how migrant women did not know how to behave in the Finnish welfare system or were not familiar with the rights Finnish women have come to regard as self-evident. Thus, these professionals were taking took the position of more educated women teaching and guiding less fortunate fellow sisters, and becoming experts through this process. This resembles very much the results of Jaana Vuori's study (2009) in which she analysed official guidebooks produced within Finnish integration policies. She found that the guidebooks constructed gender equality as a state of existence and characteristic of what Finns are like: 'in Finland women and men are equal'. Family issues featured very centrally in the guidebooks and were always linked to gender equality.

Such speech shows how the figure of the Finnish woman is created as a contrast to the figure of the immigrant woman. In fact, it is the figure of the Finnish woman that is central here. It is her strength and capacity for action that is highlighted and praised when the professionals and authorities express their views on how migrant women behave. In the gender equality context the 'Finnish woman' often turns into the norm in relation to which 'other' women are measured (Tuori 2009).

> And these cultures are very male dominated [...] where the man is the head of the family, and the woman's role is different from what we're used to... so it must be related to this, that people experience things... somehow differently. The way we

> have it, a Finnish woman just packs up and leaves [a violent husband], but an immigrant woman doesn't… (A13, NGO-project)

> The cases are often a bit different compared to violence in majority families. The situations have often gone further, since immigrant women have a higher threshold for contacting the police. Whereas a Finnish woman may call the police already when she's being slapped for the first time, like 'I'll show you old man.' (B5, police)

Needless to say, many 'Finnish' women who have been abused by their partners also find it difficult to contact the police or leave their partners. However, this fact totally vanishes from sight in such dichotomous and homogenising constructions.

Some professionals saw migrant women as having strength in themselves and the capacity to change their lives. However, here too the yardstick was often the way of life understood as Finnish. If migrant women followed patterns labelled as Finnish they could be regarded as strong and resourceful. Empowerment and freedom of will were not located in women's life histories or in the countries from where they came, but were thought to be found in Finland or the West. These professionals described migrant women as oppressed by their culture with no choice but to stay at home and bring up many children. But after living in Finland for several years women could, according to the professionals, become independent, take a language course and prepare themselves to seek employment.

> I mean this woman, it has clearly been the case that… she has been in Finland for over ten years and I have known her for about six years, and what has clearly happened is that she has turned from someone who adopts this traditional role for women, in which there's actually no other choice than to have a big herd of children and stay at home… so I think this new environment in Finland has made this mother realise that she has other options as well. (B14, social worker)

The normative model against which migrant women were measured was deeply embedded in notions of gender, heterosexuality, nation and modernity. Migrant women were seen to embody traditional femininities, but had the chance to adopt the 'Finnish way of life' and thus to become modern. Tradition and modernity were connected through an evolutionary frame of progress (McClintock 1995). Time was spacialised: certain parts of the world, and particular the Third World countries, were presented as living in pre-modern times, while modernity was located in the Western countries. This distinction was constructed on the basis of gender and heterosexuality: becoming modern required performing gender and heterosexuality in the 'proper' way.

Although I have here, for the sake of argument, focused on ways of constructing power hierarchies based on gender, nation and ethnicity, it should be noted that the professionals also used other, less dichotomous ways of discussing violence in migrant families. Culture could be used to articulate differences on a broad scale, ranging from habits and language to social circumstances. In such speech culture was used to make distinctions, but not to order hierarchically. The position of universalising speech was also rather strong, with connections both to the welfare state principles (everyone should be treated equally) and views that emphasised commonalities between violence in majority and minority families. There was also some recognition of differences within migrant communities, for example when it was noted that women's rights and human rights were fought for by actors within the communities, including men who had become refugees because they devoted their lives to such activities.

Migrant women struggling for their rights

Against this background, it is striking how differently the interviewed women narrated their experiences of violence. Women spoke about being subjected to violence and other hardships in life, but also about their struggles to gain rights, and to have opportunities to make their own decisions. The narratives of the interviewed women were thus, in many ways linked to questions of power. They were struggling with their abusive husbands and/or family members (parents, siblings, parents and siblings of the husband) who exercised control over their lives. The interviewees were also struggling to navigate the 'women-friendly' Finnish welfare state: trying to find an apartment in the racialised housing market, looking for a way to deal with the bureaucratic and exclusionary immigration rules, and coping with indifferent authorities and professionals.

The women I interviewed did not seem to fit very well into the distinction between individual and collectivist cultures, commonly made in scientific and professional speech. According to such thinking, the West is characterised by an individualist culture in which autonomy and independence are the defining features, while non-Western countries share a collectivist culture in which loyalty to family and community are the main features[7]. Many of my interviewees, coming from all three geographical areas, however stressed that they wanted to take care of their business themselves, not to ask for help from their relatives or friends, or to wait for the authorities to solve the problems for them. Thus, they were presenting themselves in a position that

7 For a more thorough discussion see for example Bredal (2006), especially chapter five.

could be regarded as individualist. On the other hand, some of them were rather worried about how their families, relatives and neighbours (either in Finland or transnationally) would react to their possible divorce or living alone in a European country. Some interviewees also spoke of the importance of their parents and of receiving their approval in order to stay (psychologically) well. This position can be interpreted as a familist, or if one so wishes, collectivist.

I argue that it is not a question of two distinct cultures that one is born with or trajectories to follow through one's life, but should rather be seen as different positions that one moves between in time and space. A person can adopt the position of an individual – that is, act in a way that emphasises her own will and choices – at a certain time and in specific contexts, while at other times emphasising loyalties to the family or negotiating how to balance her own wishes and those of her family's. Ethnicity is not irrelevant for such processes, but instead of being regarded as something that automatically leads to individualism or collectivism, it should be regarded as a part of the context that, together with gender, class and age, shapes the possibilities of moving between these positions. The struggles that my interviewees mentioned can also be interpreted in this context, as efforts to try out and widen the boundaries of the possibilities that have opened for them.

Not all the women I interviewed struggled with their families. Some spoke about the broad support they received from their families, for example, when going through disputes over custody of their children in a 'Middle Eastern' or North African court. Other interviewees were not particularly concerned about how their families would relate to them leaving abusive husbands. A few even questioned my interest in how their families reacted to their choices saying that their families would not interfere in their life and regarded them as adult persons. This response came from women from Russia, 'Middle Eastern' and 'African' countries.

Neither does it seem as if the women underwent a metamorphosis when arriving in or living in Finland or the West, as some of the professionals suggested. One of my interviewees who had escaped war and persecution from Afghanistan said she had always wanted to be free, but was not able to live in such a way earlier. She had been abused and controlled by her husband, but also denied peace and freedom by the government of her previous home country. Another woman from Iran told me how she fought to get her husband sentenced by the local court for his violent acts, but was not successful and had to flee abroad to escape his violence. It is clear that many of the women struggled to gain rights and to enable life without violence, but that their social environments were not always beneficial for these struggles. The interviewed women had at times encountered situations in which violence in the family was connected to institutional violence and torture. By comparison, Finland could be viewed as a country in which legislation and the authorities supported women's rights and enabled them to live the kind of life they had been struggling for.

The role of religion also seems to be multifaceted. Since many religions value highly the heterosexual family and present it as the cornerstone of society, religious discourses may be used to argue for continuance of marriage despite existing violence. Some of my interviewees referred to this, when they spoke about their family members opposing divorce or about their own difficulties in reaching a decision about what to do. Both Christianity and Islam were mentioned in these instances. On the other hand, one of my interviewees pointed out that it was Islam that gave her the right to leave her violent husband and to protect herself from violence. She told me that during the marriage ceremony it was emphasised that women should be treated well and violence was to be avoided. She also said that according to Muslim thinking personal consideration and forming one's own opinion is important, and that one is not meant to just follow the views presented by religious leaders.

It is often claimed in public discussions, and even in professional speech, that Western or Finnish values provide protection for abused migrant women. In the light of my interviews, it seems that it was more Finnish laws and egalitarian social benefits that were appreciated by the interviewed women rather than the values or ideas as such. Nor does it seem to be the case that values such as freedom, women's rights or democracy are the sole property of the Western world. On closer examination, it is evident that both the Western and the non-Western parts of the world are heterogeneous entities within which struggles occur on an everyday basis about issues related to these values. The Finnish welfare state with its institutions can, at best, provide support and security to abused migrant women. But this requires many favourable conditions to be fulfilled, and thus cannot be considered self-evident.

Many of my interviewees had received practical help and support from welfare professionals and authorities. However, not everyone is entitled to welfare services and personal security. For example, asylum seekers are placed in what I call a 'space of uncertainty' with limited rights. Most importantly, they face the threat of deportation. They can also be transported from one Finnish asylum centre to another thereby breaking up their support networks in a geographically vast country. In addition, asylum seekers only have the right to some of the existing welfare services. For example, psychological therapy, essential for some women due to their (sometimes multiple) experiences of violence, is not necessarily available for asylum seekers. Furthermore, those who have formal rights are not always able to exercise them in practice. Categorisations related to 'race' and ethnicity can lead to differentiated treatment by authorities and professionals (de los Reyes 2006). For example, the culturalisation of violence in migrant families is likely to have effects on welfare practices and the kind of help deemed relevant for abused women. It also seems that navigating in and finding help within the complicated and bureaucratic welfare system requires considerable experience, otherwise one may not receive all essential information or the services one is entitled to. Thus, the promises of equal rights in the welfare state are not always fulfilled.

Conclusions

In this chapter my aim has been both to deconstruct static and homogenising constructions characterizing much of the current discussions on violence in minority families, and to offer ideas of how to analyse and conceptualise the issue in a more nuanced and multifaceted way. I have argued for an approach that regards women's rights as *a site of struggle* and aims to capture the *complexities and the multiplicity of positions* in migrant women's lives. What are often perceived as two opposite and excluding elements, such as belonging to an individualist or collectivist culture, should be understood as movement between different positions and as continuous processes in time and space. Neither should women's rights be regarded as an either-or element that some nations or parts of the world can claim ownership of and completely achieve. Rather, women's rights are the object of continued struggles both within nations and transnationally.

The Nordic welfare states with their legislation and social benefits can provide support for abused migrant women. It is not incorrect to say that the welfare state is to some extent 'women-friendly' for these women, but its role can better be characterized as *paradoxical* (Ålund and Schierup 1991). While the welfare state on the one hand provides benefits and services on a universal basis (for its citizens and others deemed entitled to them), on the other hand it serves as a locus for welfare state nationalism, entwined in many ways with discourses of gender and sexuality. The emphasis on universalism and collectivism conceals the fact that these are built on a narrow and normative definition of similarity, excluding in multiple ways those who do not have the right to belong on the basis of a common origin. For abused migrant women this means that they can find support in the legislation and egalitarian benefits of the welfare state to claim their rights, and to leave abusive partners and families. However, there are also several exclusionary discourses and practices that hinder the realisation of those rights.

References

Ålund, Alexandra/Schierup, Carl-Erik (1991): Paradoxes of Multiculturalism. Aldershot: Avebury.

Anthias, Floya/Yuval-Davis, Nira (1992): Racialized Boundaries. Race, Nation, Gender, Colour and Class and the Anti-Racist Struggle. London: Routledge.

Borchorst, Anette/Siim, Birte (2002): The Women-Friendly Welfare States Revisited. NORA (Nordic Journal of Women's Studies) 10, 2, pp. 90–98.

Bredal, Anja (2005): Tackling Forced Marriages in the Nordic Countries: Between Women's Rights and Immigration Control. In: Welchman, Lynn/Hossain, Sara (eds): 'Honour'. Crimes, Paradigms, and Violence Against Women. London: Zed Books, pp. 332–353.

Bredal, Anja (2006): 'Vi er jo en familie'. Arrangerte ekteskap, autonomi og felleskap blant unge norsk-asiater. Oslo: Unipax.

Bredström, Anna (2003): Gendered Racism and the Production of Cultural Difference: Media Representations and Identity Work Among 'Immigrant Youth' in Contemporary Sweden. NORA (Nordic Journal of Women's Studies) 11, 2, pp. 78–88.

de los Reyes, Paulina (2006): Välfärd, medborgerskap och diskriminering. In: de los Reyes, Paulina (ed.): Om välfärdens gränser och det villkorade medborgerskapet. SOU 2006:37. Stockholm: Edita, pp. 7–31.

Dustin, Moira/Phillips, Anne (2008): Whose Agenda Is It? Abuses of Women and Abuses of 'Culture' in Britain. Ethnicities 8, 3, pp. 405–424.

Ghorashi, Halleh/Hylland Eriksen, Thomas/Alghasi, Sharam (2009): Introduction. In: Alghasi, Sharam/Hylland Eriksen, Thomas/Ghorashi, Halleh (eds): Paradoxes of Cultural Recognition. Perspectives from Northern Europe. Farnham: Ashgate, pp. 1–15.

Gingrich, Andre/Banks, Marcus (eds.) (2006): Neo-Nationalism in Europe and Beyond. New York: Berghahn Books.

Grillo, Ralph (2007): An Excess of Alterity? Debating Difference in a Multicultural Society. Ethnic and Racial Studies 30, 6, pp. 979–998.

Hilson, Mary (2008): The Nordic Model. Scandinavia Since 1945. London: Reaction Books.

Keskinen, Suvi (2005): Commitments and Contradictions: Linking Violence, Parenthood and Professionalism. In: Eriksson, Maria/Hester, Marianne/Keskinen, Suvi/Pringle, Keith (eds.): Tackling Men's Violence in Families. Nordic Issues and Dilemmas. Bristol: Policy Press, pp. 31–48.

Keskinen, Suvi (2009a): 'Honour-Related Violence' and Nordic Nation-Building. In: Keskinen, Suvi/Tuori, Salla/Irni, Sari/Mulinari, Diana (eds.): Complying With Colonialism. Gender, Race and Ethnicity in the Nordic Region. Farnham: Ashgate, pp. 257–272.

Keskinen, Suvi (2009b): Pelkkiä ongelmia? Maahanmuutto poliittisen keskustelun kohteena. In: Keskinen, Suvi/Rastas, Anna/Tuori, Salla (eds.): En ole rasisti, mutta… Maahanmuutosta, monikulttuurisuudesta ja kritiikistä. Tampere: Vastapaino, pp. 33–45.

Korteweg, Anna/Yurdakul, Gökce (2009): Islam, Gender, and Immigrant Integration: Boundary Drawing in Discourses on Honour Killing in the Netherlands and Germany. In: Ethnic and Racial Studies 32, 2, pp. 218–238.

Lewis, Gail (2005): Welcome to the Margins: Diversity, Tolerance and Policies of Exclusion. In: Ethnic and Racial Studies 28, 3, pp. 536–558.

Lewis, Gail (2006): Imaginaries of Europe. Technologies of Gender, Economies of Power. In: European Journal of Women's Studies 13, 2, pp. 87–10.

Magnusson, Eva/Rönnblom, Malin/Silius, Harriet (2008): Introduction. In Magnusson, Eva/Rönnblom, Malin/Silius, Harriet (eds): Critical Studies of Gender Equalities. Nordic Dislocations, Dilemmas and Contradictions. Göteborg: Makadam, pp. 7–23.

McClintock, Anne (1995): Imperial Leather: Race, Gender and Sexuality in the Colonial Contest. New York: Routledge.

Modood, Tariq (2007): Multiculturalism: A Civic Idea. Cambridge: Polity.

Mulinari, Diana/Keskinen, Suvi/Irni, Sari/Tuori, Salla (2009): Introduction: Postcolonialism and the Nordic Models of Welfare and Gender. In: Keskinen, Suvi/Tuori, Salla/Irni, Sari/Mulinari, Diana (eds): Complying With Colonialism. Gender, Race and Ethnicity in the Nordic Region. Farnham: Ashgate, pp. 1–16.

Phillips, Anne/Saharso, Sawitri (2008): The Rights of Women and the Crisis of Multiculturalism. In: Ethnicities 8, 3, pp. 291–301.

Piispa, Minna/Heiskanen, Markku/Kääriäinen, Juha/Sirén, Reino (2006): Naisiin kohdistunut väkivalta 2005. Publication Series no. 51. Helsinki: Oikeuspoliittinen tutkimuslaitos/HEUNI.

Pringle, Keith (2005): Neglected Issues in Swedish Child Protection Policy and Practice: Age, Ethnicity and Gender. In: Eriksson, Maria/Hester, Marianne/Keskinen, Suvi/Pringle, Keith (eds.): Tackling Men's Violence in Families. Nordic Issues and Dilemmas. Bristol: Policy Press, pp. 155 .171.

Prins, Baukje/Saharso, Sawitri (2008): In the Spotlight. A Blessing and a Curse for Immigrant Women in the Netherlands. In: Ethnicities 8, 3, pp. 365–384.

Raevaara, Eeva (2008): In the Land of Equality? Gender Equality and the Construction of Finnish and French Political Communities in the Parliamentary Debates of Finland and France. In: Magnusson, Eva/Rönnblom, Malin/Silius, Harriet (eds.): Critical Studies of Gender Equalities. Nordic Dislocations, Dilemmas and Contradictions. Göteborg: Makadam, pp. 48–74.

Rantalaiho, Liisa (1994): Sukupuolisopimus ja Suomen malli. In: Anttonen, Anneli/Henriksson, Lea/Nätkin, Ritva (eds.): Naisten hyvinvointivaltio. Tampere: Vastapaino, pp. 9–30.

Razack, Sherene (2004): Imperilled Muslim Women, Dangerous Muslim Men and Civilized Europeans: Legal and Social Responses to Forced Marriages. In: Feminist Legal Studies 12, 2, pp. 129–174.

Russo, Ann (2006): The Feminist Majority Foundation's Campaign to Stop Gender Apartheid. In: International Feminist Journal of Politics 8, 4, pp. 557–580.

Siim, Birte/Skjeie, Hege (2008): Tracks, Intersections and Dead Ends: Multicultural Challenges to State Feminism in Denmark and Norway. In: Ethnicities 8, 3, pp.322–344.

Teigen, Mari/Langvasbråten, Trude (2009): The 'Crisis' of Gender Equality: The Norwegian Newspaper Debate on Female Genital Cutting. In: NORA (Nordic Journal of Feminist and Gender Research) 17, 4, pp. 256–272.

Tuori, Salla (2007): Cooking Nation. Gender Equality and Multiculturalism as Nation-Building Discourses. In: European Journal of Women's Studies 14, 1, pp. 21–35.

Tuori, Salla (2009): The Politics of Multicultural Encounters. Feminist Postcolonial Perspectives. Åbo: Åbo Akademi University Press.

Verloo, Mieke/Lombardo, Emanuela (2007): Contested Gender Equality and Policy Variety in Europe: Introducing Critical Frame Analysis Approach. In: Verloo, Mieke (ed.): Multiple Meanings of Gender Equality. A Critical Frame Analysis of Gender Policies in Europe. Budapest: Central European University Press, pp. 21–49.

Vuori, Jaana (2009): Guiding Migrants to the Realm of Gender Equality. In: Keskinen, Suvi/Tuori, Salla/Irni, Sari/Mulinari, Diana (eds): Complying With Colonialism. Gender, Race and Ethnicity in the Nordic Region. Farnham: Ashgate, pp. 207–223.

Wahlbeck, Östen (1999): Kurdish Diasporas. A Comparative Study of Kurdish Refugee Communities. London: Macmillan.
Wilkinson, Sue/Kitzinger, Celia (eds.) (1995): Feminism and Discourse. London: Sage.
Winther Jörgensen, Marianne/Phillips, Louise (2002): Discourse as Theory and Method. London: Sage.

Culture-Based Violence Against Immigrant Women in German Federal Court of Justice (BGH) Decisions

Erol Rudolf Pohlreich

In this paper I will show the material problems of judicial assessments of violence based on foreign culture.[1] These are elaborated from a sample of the Federal Court of Justice's decisions on homicides and sex-related crimes. Subsequently, possible alternatives to existing judicial assessments of culture-based violence by the Federal Court of Justice (BGH) are discussed.

The increasing number of reports on culture-based violence against immigrant women in the German media has led to a change in public opinion within the general debate on integration. Forced marriages, so-called 'honour killings' or female genital cutting now serve as a projection screen for criticism of integration policies to date. The growing attention that people pay to these forms of violence against women in Germany coincides with a discussion about the introduction of new or modifications to existing criminal provisions,[2] in order to reflect the public's abhorrence of such violent behaviour in case law. This paper examines the current approach of case law to violence identified as culture-based in the German case law at the Federal Court of Justice, demonstrated on sex-related crimes and homicides according to valid legal provisions.[3] There are no extant decisions by the Federal Court of Justice on the criminality of forced marriages or customary female genital cutting in Germany. The German case law, on the other hand, has found ways of considering cultural evidence in the offender's favour with regard to

1 The term 'culture-based violence' is viewed critically by the author but used within this article referring to the terms of court lanaguage. The exact German term 'Gewalt mit fremdkulturellem Hintergrund' means in word-by-word translation 'violence with a foreign cultures background' but would be too complicated for the English chapter and was replaced by 'culture-based violence'.

2 This has for some years concerned mainly the penal repression of forced marriages. For further details on currently applicable legal regulations and the reform discussion cf. Kalthegener 2007; Schubert/Moebius 2006.

3 A more comprehensive investigation of the punishment of so-called 'honour killings' and other homicides with cultural motivation can be found in Pohlreich 2009.

homicides and sex-related crimes, even though the German criminal code does not expressly admit it as a mitigating circumstance. The decisions under investigation do not exclusively refer to immigrant women, but they still allow for conclusions to be drawn about the criminal justice's way of dealing with violence against immigrant women.

Based on these decisions the study shows the circumstances under which the German criminal justice system at the Federal Court of Justice uses foreign cultural motives for offender-friendly determination of punishment and whether this results in immigrant women being protected differently by the law than German women. Seeing that the German criminal justice system assesses cultural motives for a crime inconsistently and even stereotypically, the question arises what alternatives are there when dealing with culturally-based violence. In the author's opinion, reference to the offenders' culture of origin is generally not necessary for determining an appropriate sentence. In the interest of legal certainty and a uniform application of the law it is, therefore suggested that cultural evidence should be considered when determining the sentence, but only within the framework of such criteria which may apply to offenders of any origin. Wherever these criteria do not apply, cultural evidence cannot be taken into consideration.

Sex-related crimes

When considering cultural evidence of sexual offences in the offender's favour, the Federal Court of Justice postulates varying requirements. In particular, the extent to what the offender's diverging perceptions must be reflected in their native culture in order to be considered in their favour remains unclear. Sometimes the offender's perceptions to be in unison with their native legal system is required, and sometimes this requirement seems to be dispensed with. Another decision from the recent past, presented in the following paragraphs, is even more difficult to place, as here the offender's immigrant background was not considered in his favour when determining the sentence but a decision made to the contrary.

Immigrant background as mitigating circumstance

In general, an offender's foreign cultural perceptions work in their favour when it comes to determining the sentence for a sexual offence. The Federal Court of Justice, however, contests general assumptions of the accused being most probably absorbed in sexist images of women in his native country. Irrespective of the fact that the German criminal code applies in Germany, foreign perceptions can only be regarded as mitigating factors if they are in line with the other country's legal system.[4] The Federal Court of Justice does not, however, regularly raise the question of whether an offender's sexual morals are in line with the criminal code of their country of origin. In a recent decision,[5] it was apparently sufficient for the Federal Court of Justice to see that the offender's sexual morals were in line with the religious values of his culture of origin. The case dealt with a Kurdish Yazidi, whose family tried to force her to marry her cousin. He abducted her and repeatedly coerced her into sexual intercourse. The Federal Court of Justice confirmed the conviction for second degree kidnapping as well as a single count of rape. This was reasoned on the offender's and the victim's cultural background and the family's 'high expectations'. Pointing out that the victim's cultural background was Yazidi is peculiar, as this may lead to the inappropriate impression that Yazidi women must submit to sexual violence more than other women. Additional concerns are raised as now, apart from the – relatively – clear touchstone of the legal system of the country of origin, the criterion of religious background is introduced, which may tempt to make stereotyping assessments.

A decision from 2001[6] also did not take the criminal code of the offender's country of origin into account. The offender had been living in Germany for 30 years and had been married to his wife from the same origin since 1975. As a result of marital problems, the wife moved out and filed for a divorce petition with the Family Court, but, when urged by her sons, returned to the accused. He coerced her into sexual intercourse by threatening her with a knife. The wife moved out of the flat after frequent altercations and further incidents of physical violence, and pressed charges for bodily harm. After the divorce, the situation calmed down, which is why the woman repeatedly asked for a lenient sentence during the trial. The Federal Court of Justice assumed a less severe case, the assertion of which is generally possible if individual facts of the case deviate significantly from the regular case and therefore call for less severe punishment.[7] Such conditions were, in the assessment of the judges, the long years of marriage with the victim, his desire for her affection as well as the assumption that he was less inhibited than a German offender. Also the common origins of the spouses and their being

4 BGH NStZ-RR 1999, 359; 1998, 298f.
5 BGH decision dated 1st February 2007 – 4 StR 514/06, unpublished to date.
6 BGH StV 2002, 20f.
7 BGH StV 2002, 20f. with further references.

deeply rooted in common values, which supposedly demand submission and obedience of the wife, were considered in his favour.

In fact, it was a case of rape involving the use of a dangerous instrument, which § 177 par. 4 of the German Criminal Code penalises with a minimum prison term of five years. If, however, an unspecified less severe case, as defined by § 177 par. 5, applies, the term is one to ten years in prison. The Federal Court of Justice elaborated that in the case of concurrence of aggravated rape, as defined by § 177 par. 4 of the German Criminal Code (StGB) and a less severe count, the minimum term must not remain below the statutory minimum for rape, i.e., two years.

Foreign cultural background as aggravating circumstance

Interestingly enough, in the Federal Court of Justice considerations, the victim's origins and their cultural background sometimes are disadvantageous for the offender. Aggravating circumstances are, for instance, if a devout Turkish Muslim returns to her parents' home after multiple rapes, is no longer respected by her cultural community as a divorcee and is burdened by the reduced chances of entering into a suitable marriage.[8] As the woman and the perpetrator have the same cultural background, it could have been assumed that, as in the case of the Yazidi Kurd, the cultural aspect would have been considered a mitigating factor. There is no information to the effect that the Yazidi culture is particularly sensitive or open about experiences of rape. The Yazidi Kurd woman, however, intended to calm the situation and 'extend a hand' to the accused by having her attorney declare that she would agree to a suspended sentence. It was the good fortune of the accused that she had, in the meantime, married her secret boyfriend and apparently did not have especially close ties with the Yazidi culture, thanks to which he received his mild sentence. Otherwise it could have been quite possible for the sentence to shift to the other extreme.

The question is, should the respective cultural background (be it a constructed or an actual one) be considered in the assessment of the severity of the punishment at all? The severe consequences for the repeatedly raped wife described in the latter decision should be clear to those without intimate knowledge of her culture as well, and should justify a comparably severe punishment, even when considered individually. As far as the cases described earlier are concerned, a more lenient punishment seems possible even without taking cultural evidence into account. This is why these decisions, by

8 BGH ruling dated 20/06/2007 – 1 StR 167/07.

emphasising cultural aspects, are conducive to a far too stereotypical perception of non-Western cultures.

Crimes against life

If the Federal Court of Justice's decisions on sex-related crimes with a foreign background appear inconsistent, this applies even more so to how the Federal Court of Justice deals with homicides committed by offenders with a non-German cultural background. Here case law in its sometimes contradictory and often confused causistry in individual cases refrains from the presumption of base motives for a crime and convicts the offenders of manslaughter (prison terms up to 15 years) instead of murder (life imprisonment), if no other criteria for murder apply.

According to case law, a motive is base, if '*according to general moral values it is at the lowest moral level, determined by uncontrollable, driven selfishness and therefore particularly condemnable, even contemptible.*□[9] In the case of killings motivated by so-called foreign cultures, the question arises: according to what set of moral values should the motives be judged? It is imaginable to focus solely on the foreign morals. Current case law, however, asks objectively, whether the motive was base, i.e. without considering the perpetrator's origins or socially determining factors. The yardstick for assessing a motive is, moreover, to be derived from the values of the general legal community in the Federal Republic of Germany and not from the perceptions of ethnic communities that do not accept this legal community's moral and legal values.[10] This in no way anticipates a negative result for the perpetrator, as long as perceptions, which initially appear foreign, are questioned critically to the effect of whether they indeed diametrically oppose the values in this country or whether they are universally comprehensible.[11]

When it comes to culture-based killings, case law for once does not presume base motives, if the perpetrator at the time of the crime was not aware of the fact that these could be weighted as aggravating, or if he was not able to exercise will-power to control the passions determining his physical acts. This implies that a perpetrator allegedly determined to a large degree by his cultural perceptions, who due to his personality or living situation, was not able to disengage himself from them at the time of the offence, as an excep-

9 BGHSt 3, 132f.; 42, 226; 47, 128.

10 BGH NStZ 2006, 284; 2002, 369; 1995, 79; BGHR StGB § 211 II base motives 41; BGH NJW 2004, 1466ff.; BGH NStZ-RR 2004, 361f.

11 Cf. BGH NStZ 2006, 286.

tion to the rule can be convicted of manslaughter in spite of the objective baseness of his motives.[12] The same applies to the perpetrator still very much attached to his culture of origin, who cannot comprehend the meaning of baseness of the motive.[13]

Implications of cultural pressure

In the Federal Court of Justice's first decision on the authority of the country's values,[14] the rejection of base motives was accounted for by the fact that the Eastern Anatolian accused acted on pressure exerted by his family. The length of his stay in Germany is not revealed, and neither is the sort of pressure exerted on him. Apart from his simple character, the Federal Court of Justice found it sufficient that the accused was *'caught up in the idea of 'vendetta' and 'chosen' by his family for carrying out the deed'*. This allegedly reduced his freedom of choice at the time of the offence.

A more recent decision by the Federal Court of Justice[15] on the other hand, did not allow any kind of pressure on the perpetrator to be seen as a mitigating factor. This case dealt with the killing of a member of the Kurdish Workers' Party, PKK, and his mistress by three other members of the party on the orders of the regional leader, as he deemed this relationship to be dishonourable. The Federal Court of Justice affirmed the assumption of base motives in its decision. Pressure would only be considered a mitigating factor for the perpetrator if they were threatened with physical violence or death. It was apparently of no importance for the Federal Court of Justice in this case that two of the accused had already been severely beaten up in Turkey for not adhering to PKK orders – the possibility of torture cannot be ruled out – and the third accused suffered from extreme fear of physical violence after an imprisonment in Turkey.[16] It might be conclusive not to consider these kinds of pressures nor the social consequences; but to be consistent, then, neither family exerted pressure nor an imminent social isolation must be counted as mitigating factors for the perpetrator per se, but only qualified pressure.[17]

---

12 BGH NStZ 1995, 79 with further references

13 BGH NJW 2006, 1008 (1012).

14 BGH NStZ 1995, 79.

15 BGH StV 2003, 21.

16 Cf. Momsen 2003: 238.

17 Partially different in Valerius 2008: 916, who questions the particular reprehensibility of the motives for the killing, if the loss of respect and honour in the perpetrator's social environment leads to social ostracism.

Implications of the perpetrator's social integration

Case law only intends to consider different moral values in a perpetrator's favour, if his fixation on values narrows his mind. As such, a fixation on values regularly decreases with the progress of integration it should only be taken into account in exceptional cases. Consequently, the consideration of base motives requires a comprehensive evaluation of the individual process of integration. Supposedly 'informative cues' in this question are a long stay in the host country, a working life, circles of friends and acquaintances, commitment to societies and political organisations, language difficulties as well as preferences in food and drink.[18] For the Federal Court of Justice, the duration of stay does not directly translate into how well the perpetrator is integrated. But if the Federal Court of Justice does not pay attention to the time of stay, this begs the question why it emphasises it at all and with contradicting results.

In the PKK case, the Federal Court of Justice contested that the judgement of two of the accused was still affected after their fourteen-year stay in Germany, as they had already been convicted as joint offenders in a case of attempted vendetta killing in this country. It did, however, also affirm that the third accused was capable of rational judgement, notwithstanding the fact that he had only been in Germany for two years, as he had felt connected to *'the 'people's' cause'* but did not want to commit any further to the society or the PKK. As evidenced in a later decision, on the other hand, even after a ten-year stay in Germany and naturalisation, the assertion of rational judgement was not a given.[19] In another decision, the accused pleaded his attachment to his culture of origin after a twenty-year stay in Germany and naturalisation, which was refuted as counterfactual.[20] In a decision dating from 1977[21], the Federal Court of Justice elaborated that during the period of cultural adaptation a foreigner's judgement may be affected, as they may relapse into a 'Sicilian way of thinking' when committing a crime and not be able to fully comprehend the disproportion between the killing and its occasion. Apparently, the Federal Court of Justice assumes that immigrants increasingly adapt throughout their stay in this country. It is not taken into consideration that immigrants do not, as a rule, entirely assimilate and shake off their enculturation. Also the reference in one 2003[22] decision by the Federal Court of Justice to an *'accused incapable of integration'* says a great deal about the

18 Schneider 2003: Paragraph 95; cf. also Fischer 2008: § 211 Paragraph 29.
19 BGH sentence dated 5th September 2007, 2 StR 306/07, unpublished to date.
20 BGH NStZ-RR 2007, 86.
21 BGH in Holtz 1977: 809.
22 BGH NStZ-RR 2004, 44 (commented by Trück 2004: 497).

judges' understanding of integration. Apparently there are not only those perpetrators who are unwilling to integrate, but those that are incapable of integration, so that in some cases, the rational judgement of perpetrators with foreign enculturation may still be affected after decades of living in Germany.

A more convincing decision stems from the year 2004[23] which dealt with a man originally from Turkey who had killed his wife, a German citizen who was born and raised in Germany, by stabbing her 48 times with a knife. She wanted to separate after being humiliated and abused by him and was not willing to support him in extending his residence permit. The Federal Court of Justice contested that his judgement was affected, seeing that members of the family had informed him about the relationship between men and women in German society; also the sister had threatened to call the police on him. Furthermore, it was to be doubted that the accused could have felt justified by his Anatolian values to continuously abuse and eventually kill his wife. Rather, turning up the volume on the radio before the act so as to make sure the neighbours could not hear what was going on, as well as denying the charges towards his parents, might indicate that he very well understood the German assessment of his motives. The Federal Court of Justice also affirmed his ability to control his passions, notwithstanding some indications that the crime was committed on impulse, as a perpetrator's growing passion cannot exonerate him if he, as in this case, consciously lets his controllable emotions drive him to completion of the act.

Implications of the law in the perpetrator's country of origin

Recently, the Federal Court of Justice has been referring to the law valid in the perpetrator's country of origin as an indicator for foreign perpetrators' subjective attitudes to their motive for killing. In a decision dating from 2004[24], the Federal Court of Justice affirmed the perpetrator's capacity for rational judgement, i.e. by referring to the perpetrator's country of origin and its laws. Motives not reflected in their native country's laws are pure sectarian convictions and therefore not to be considered when assessing the perpetrator's capability of judgement. In the case of the attempted killing of a former wife, who wanted to separate from her husband, the Federal Court of Justice emphasised that foreign behavioural patterns, convictions and notions were, as a rule, to be considered only, if they are in accordance with the for-

23 BGH NStZ 2004, 332.
24 BGH NStZ-RR 2004, 361.

eign legal system, something that did not apply in the case of the Turkish perpetrator.[25]

The Federal Court of Justice does not intend to give a conclusive evaluation of the subjective part by referring to the law in the country of origin. It, therefore, proceeds along the lines of its regular decisions on the range of punishment, which at times do refer to the law in the country of origin, but at other times do not.[26]

Preferably, considerations of the law applicable in the perpetrator's country of origin should be excluded altogether. More often than not, the law in the perpetrator's country of origin is not as unequivocal as to do away with any doubts about the perpetrator's original culture's leniency towards the crime committed by him. Moreover, a great number of states are made up not by a – relatively – homogeneous population, as it is the case in Germany. Particularly in multinational states like, for instance, Turkey, the Turkish criminal code cannot be expected to reflect all ethnic communities' values. This issue is even more complicated where states like Nigeria are concerned, where the applicable criminal code varies according to place of residence, ethnicity and religion.

Alternative solutions for the punishment of culture-based homicides

If the Federal Court of Justice's consideration of the assumed effects of foreign cultures in the case of sex-related crimes is questionable, it is even more so in the case of homicides, such as the so-called 'honour killings'. For culpable homicides, constitutional issues arise out of the mandatory lifelong prison sentence, as demanded for murder in § 211 StGB, because according to the Federal Constitutional Court's case law the sentence must be proportional to the severity of the crime and must not exceed the perpetrator's culpability.[27] On the other hand, the mandatory link between elements of murder and life imprisonment serves legal certainty and a uniform application of the law.[28]

25 BGH NStZ-RR 2007, 86.

26 For the foreign legal code's authority cf. BGH in Pfister 1999: 359; BGH NStZ-RR 1998, 298. For a merely indicative effect of the foreign legal code cf. BGH NStZ 1996, 80; BGH NStZ-RR 2007, 86 (87).

27 BVerfGE 45, 187 (259 f.) with further references.

28 BVerfGE 45, 187 (260).

The Federal Constitutional Court infers from art. 103 par. 2 of the *Basic Law* (GG*), the German constitution,* that criminal provisions *defining* the more severely penalised crimes must be worded with the greatest precision.[29] Certain unspecified elements, however, are admissible as constitutional, provided a uniform case law accounted for the content.[30] Such a provision for base motives has yet to be worded. In case law the content of such murder criteria, however, has only been determined insufficiently by a casuistic as yet. The published decisions by the Federal Court of Justice on taking foreign cultural determination into consideration when evaluating subjective requirements for whether base motives apply show significant inconsistencies, resulting in understandable confusion for the judiciary. In fact, the assessment of whether base motives apply in cases of culpable homicides is reversed in 71% of the cases between indictment and conviction of the perpetrators.[31] For no other element of murder do the assessments vary as significantly between judges and courts of appeal as they do for the element of base motives.[32] It is, therefore, hardly to imagine how members of the public are supposed to make informed decisions, when judges themselves are often at a loss when faced with this question.

Criminal law responses to an offence dependent on cultural evidence must, when consistently applying this, lead to a discussion of circumstances, which often cannot be safely proved. Some of the questions arising from the consideration of foreign cultural influences are: whether certain views actually played a significant role in the perpetrator's socialisation; whether these views are only held by sectarians in the culture of origin; how the culture of origin is to be defined and to be limited; whether the crime is based on individual or psychological reasons and less on reasons determined by culture or socialisation;[33] whether the criminal behaviour was induced by compulsion; whether the perpetrator was already integrated and from what moment an immigrant can be considered sufficiently integrated; and whether the view reflected in the crime is in fact diametrically opposed to German views.

Another question is the difference between a perpetrator influenced by foreign culture – when culture is defined on the basis of similarities amongst all those who belong to it – and a person influenced by a subculture. In other words, why is the question of whether deviating views should be considered not posed for subcultures or members of a sect? It is certainly a misconception to believe that all Germans were brought up according to the same moral

29 BVerfGE 75, 329 (342f.).

30 BVerfGE 28, 175 (183); 37, 201 (208); 45, 363 (372); 73, 206 (243).

31 Kargl 2001: 368.

32 Eser 1981: 384.

33 On these issues cf. the paper by Gloor/Meier in this Reader.

code and that subculturally motivated perpetrators willingly cede this uniform socialisation and turn towards their subculture. For those who are part of a subculture, this belonging can be fateful as well, for instance, German perpetrators, who grow up in parts of Germany that are particularly infamous for their xenophobia or in such a family, who then go on to kill a foreigner out of racial hatred. Even if such a German perpetrator was socialised in an ordinary environment, they could have become involved with a subcultural community that had such a strong hold on them that the question of considering these ties when examining their capability of mastering their passions and controlling themselves should also arise here. This applies also to fanaticised members of a sect. If such consideration is demanded for perpetrators from different cultural backgrounds, then the exclusion of other (German) perpetrators whose ability to exercise will power or to control themselves must also be carfully considered, is not entirely convincing.

Limiting the consideration of cultural values to foreign cultures is not convincing, either, when examining the Federal Court of Justice's decision dating from the year 1956, in which it presumed base motives in the case of a grandmother and grandfather, who in an exaggerated sense of honour killed their grandchild soon after birth, because it was born out of wedlock.[34] It is easily imaginable that the grandparents at the time were not able to control their feelings, given that they lived in the country, found out about their unmarried daughter's pregnancy only when she entered labour and carried out the crime straight after finding out. As is well known, an illegitimate child born in 1950s rural Germany could mean social ostracism and complete isolation. The unexpected confrontation with this circumstance they regarded as shameful may have overwhelmed the couple and led them to commit the crime. Nevertheless, the Federal Court of Justice at the time did not even question their ability to control their passions. Moreover, reading between the lines it becomes clear that it, quite rightly, did not at all see a need to discuss the grandparents' ability to act in a controlled and rational manner. With regard to foreign perpetrators, on the other hand, the Federal Court of Justice – with the exception of premeditated murder – does feel the need to discuss whether the perpetrators were able to control themselves at the time of the offence in view of their socialisation and the ties following on from it. The Federal Court of Justice, therefore, applies double standards in considering the socialisation of German and foreign perpetrators, as it demands a higher measure of control of German perpetrators than of foreign offenders. Using the 'cultural impulse' to explain offences committed by perpetrators with a foreign cultural background in effect works in their favour, it reproduces and

34 BGHSt 9, 180; crit. Dreher 1956: 501.

perpetuates un-reflected, stereotypical perceptions of the non-Western 'Foreigner'.

Limitations of questioning the ability to exercise rational judgement

The question of the rational judgement of perpetrators with a foreign cultural background should only arise if their motive for killing is privileged in the case law of their country of origin. It is, furthermore, to be assumed that all cultures in principle disapprove of the premeditated killing of a person. A specific provision for reduced punishment in the criminal code of the perpetrator's country of origin, as Turkey's former criminal code provided in its article 462 up until 2003, for some 'honour killings', does not in itself point to a lack of ability of rational judgement, as a reduced sentence does not exonerate the perpetrator from the crime they are charged with. Irrespective of the provision in article 462 of Turkey's former criminal code, the 'honour killings' covered by it were still punished.

In any case, it can be expected that immigrants seeking permanent residence in Germany should inform themselves of the core provisions of the criminal code on entering this legal community. Even if they fail to do so and remain ignorant of the law, they can not be cleared of their responsibility in spite of their foreign cultural backgrounds.[35] It is not the perpetrator's conduct they are charged with but the crime itself. Indeed, reproaching the perpetrator for their conduct would not be permissible,[36] as a perpetrator's guilt must always refer to an individual crime. It is, for instance, not permissible to reproach perpetrators for something that happened through no fault of their own. Case law, however, does in certain cases link into wrongdoing before the actual crime was committed,[37] provided that perpetrators knowingly did not inform themselves of certain specific legal regulations, which they could not then learn at the time of the offence. This applies, for instance, to some-

35 Cf. Lesch 1996: 609.

36 According to the national socialist concept of criminal conduct, the determination of punishment could directly refer back to the perpetrator's lifestyle before the crime. The guilt concept has luckily been replaced by the concept of responsibility for a crime. According to this concept, the punishment depends primarily on the question to what extent the individual perpetrator is to be blamed for the concrete crime. The perpetrator's conduct must only be considered as an exception, and only if it is directly connected with the crime, cf. e.g. BGHSt 5, 132; BGH NStZ-RR 2001, 295.

37 BGHSt 2, 208 f.; critically on this decision, which deals not really with the avoidability but an actual error concerning the prohibited nature of an act, Roxin 2006: 949.

body with an occupation regulated by certain penal provisions or public order offences acts, of which they knowingly fail to get information. The argument in case law here is that it does not refer to all of the perpetrator's conduct in life, but to concrete violations of the duty of care. For it is still the actual crime the perpetrator is charged with, as long as the charge is founded on a clearly specified violation of the duty of care before the committal of the crime (e.g. lack of information about job-related penal provisions), which from the outset suggested a later violation of the regulation (e.g. a violation of job-related penal provisions).[38]

Also it cannot be assumed that immigrants just ended up somewhere through no fault of their own, as specified in the concept of 'criminal conduct', if they knowingly and of their own volition determined to immigrate into a country like Germany. Somebody from a society bindingly applying tribal customary law or Islamic law to the individual members of that society cannot presume that the notions behind it coincide entirely with those in Western industrialised societies. At the least they can be expected to take note of the limited number of provisions of the core criminal code as from the time of entering the country it can be surmised that certain behaviour, more or less approved of or tolerated in the perpetrator's country of origin, will be disapproved of or even penalised in the host country. It goes without saying that immigrants must not ignore the opinions held in the host country, especially as they are not even required to share these convictions. Whoever assumes that perpetrators with a supposed foreign cultural background have an awareness of wrongdoing determined by fate in effect denies them any learning ability, which after all is an important aspect of a person's individual qualities and therefore their dignity.

Considering impaired mental responsibility

The assessment that an impaired mental responsibility reduces the wrong committed by the perpetrator, makes sense. Raising the fact that a perpetrator is from a different country to determine, whether they were able to exercise control results in an untenable, stereotyped image of non-German nationals. The Federal Court of Justice no longer considers cultural evidence in the same way as in its first pertinent decision[39], when it claimed that personality defects would have to be pleaded for *'psychopathic personalities'* and conse-

38 Roxin 2006: 949f.; Rudolphi 2008: Paragraph 44f. with further references.; Puppe 2004: 238 with further references.

39 BGH GA 1967, 244.

quently all the more for foreigners, if they are deeply rooted in the divergent values of their countries of origin. On the other hand, the question of impaired mental responsibility only marginally applies to perpetrators with a foreign cultural background, if we take a closer look at Paeffgen's example of substantiating this requirement: *'Same as a shackled person cannot be reproached for remaining inactive, someone wrapped up in their motivation cannot, in excess, be reproached for their inability to master their motives.'*[40]

A person with an immigrant background is as rational an individual as anyone else and not so deeply wrapped up in their motivation so as not to be able to control themselves. Whoever wishes to consider diminished responsibility or lack of self-control based on cultural backgrounds in the perpetrator's favour, must at the same time take note of standards tolerating violence within the German culture and regard them in the German perpetrator's favour. Quite rightly, though, the Federal court of Justices show no signs of doing so.[41] Here the constitutional requirement of the punishment's proportion to the crime is overemphasised for immigrants and – for very good reasons, nonetheless – subordinated for those perpetrators motivated by German culture. Besides, the consideration of foreign cultural ties depends on a tangle of factors not provable, thus favouring unpredictable court decisions. With regard to the predictability and uniformity of state penalisation this approach thus appears to be highly questionable.

It would, therefore, make sense to weigh the impaired mental responsibility of perpetrators with a foreign cultural background to the same extent as that of perpetrators socialised in Germany to presume diminished responsibility only for those reasons that potentially apply to anyone, e.g. overfatigue, paraphilias or spontaneous reactions to sudden uncontrollable passions[42]. Thus, the original cultural background of the perpetrator should not in itself become a reason for questioning their ability to exercise control over their passions.

Conclusion

When punishing violent crimes against immigrant women, the victim's ingrained cultural values carry any weight only in exceptional cases in the Fed-

40 Paeffgen 1982: 271.

41 Cf. BGHSt 9, 180.

42 BGH NJW 1989, 1739 (1740) with further references; NStZ-RR 1998, 67f.; NStZ-RR 2004, 108; BGHR StGB § 211 II base motives 10; Eser (2006): Paragraph 39; Schneider (2003): Paragraph 98.

eral Court judges' decisions. The question of whether or not to consider cultural evidence usually arises from the perpetrator's position and not their victim's. It is, however, highly problematic to consider foreign cultural elements without questioning whether these elements should also be taken into account for perpetrators without a foreign cultural background. Not explicitly considering cultural evidence to determinate the sentence would allow for a more consistent punishment of perpetrators with foreign cultural backgrounds, something that is not currently done.

Refraining from directly connecting cultural evidence with mitigating factors does not constitute a violation of art. 103 par. 2 GG setting out the constitutional right to a fair hearing. The judge's knowledge of the particularities of the other culture can and should help them qualify the evidentiary facts and the perpetrator's personality in line with criteria for determination of punishment that apply to all perpetrators of any origin or culture. Where, however, cultural evidence cannot be assigned to any generally acknowledged criterion of determining punishment, it goes beyond the limits of what can be taken into consideration.

References

Dreher, Eduard (1956): Anmerkung zu BGH Urteil vom 27.1.1956. In: MDR 1956, S. 499–501.

Eser, Albin (1981): Die Tötungsdelikte in der Rechtsprechung zwischen BVerfGE 45, 187 und BGH-GSSt 1/ 81. In: NStZ 1981, S. 383–388.

Eser, Albin (2006): Kommentierung zu § 211 StGB. In: Schönke, Adolf/Schröder, Horst (Begr.): Strafgesetzbuch. Kommentar, München: C.H. Beck.

Fischer, Thomas (2008): Strafgesetzbuch und Nebengesetze, München: Verlag C.H. Beck.

Gloor, Daniela/Meier, Hanna (2011): The police's use of 'culture' in (re-)constructing domestic homicides. In this Reader.

Holtz, Günter (1977): Aus der Rechtsprechung des Federal Court of Justices in Strafsachen. In: MDR 1977, S. 807–811.

Kalthegener, Regina (2007): Strafrechtliche Ahndung der Zwangsverheiratung: Rechtslage – Praxiserfahrungen – Reformdiskussion. In: Bundesministerium für Familie, Senioren, Frauen und Jugend (Hrsg.): Zwangsverheiratung in Deutschland, Forschungsreihe Band 1. Baden-Baden: Nomos Verlag, S. 215–228.

Kargl, Walter (2001): Gesetz, Dogmatik und Reform des Mordes (§ 211 StGB). In: StraFo 2001, S. 365–375.

Lesch, Heiko (1996): Die Vermeidbarkeit des Verbotsirrtums. In: JA 1966, S. 607–612.

Mezger, Edmund (1938): Die Straftat als Ganzes. In: ZStW 57, S. 675–701.

Momsen, Carsten (2003): Der Mordtatbestand im Bewertungswandel? – Abweichende soziokulturelle Wertvorstellungen, Handeln auf Befehl und das Mordmerkmal der ‚niedrigen Beweggründe' (§ 211 StGB). In: NStZ 2003, S. 237–242.

Paeffgen, Hans-Ulrich (1982): Einmal mehr – Habgier und niedrige Beweggründe. In: GA 1982, S. 255–275.

Pfister, Wolfgang (1999): Aus der Rechtsprechung des BGH zu materiellrechtlichen Fragen des Sexualstrafrechts 1998–1999 – 2. Teil. In: NStZ-RR 1999, S. 353–359.

Pohlreich, Erol Rudolf (2009): ‚Ehrenmorde' im Wandel des Strafrechts. Eine vergleichende Untersuchung am Beispiel des römischen, französischen, türkischen und deutschen Rechts. Berlin: Duncker und Humblot.

Puppe, Ingeborg (2004): Bemerkungen zum Verbotsirrtum und seiner Vermeidbarkeit. In Rogall, Klaus/Puppe, Ingeborg/Stein, Ulrich/Wolter, Jürgen (Hrsg.): Festschrift für Hans-Joachim Rudolphi zum 70. Geburtstag. Neuwied: Luchterhand Verlag, S. 231–241.

Roxin, Claus (2006): Strafrecht Allgemeiner Teil Band 1. Grundlagen. Der Aufbau der Verbrechenslehre. München: Verlag C. H. Beck.

Rudolphi, Hans-Joachim (2008): Kommentierung zu § 17 StGB. In: Rudolphi, Hans-Joachim/Horn, Eckhard/Samson, Erich (Hrsg.): Systematischer Kommentar zum Strafgesetzbuch, Loseblattsammlung, Bd. 1 Allgemeiner Teil, Neuwied: Luchterhand Verlag.

Schneider, Hartmut (2003): Kommentierung zu § 211 StGB. In: Joecks, Wolfgang/ Moebach, Klaus (Hrsg.): Münchener Kommentar zum Strafgesetzbuch, Bd. 3, München: Verlag C.H. Beck.

Schubert, Karin/Moebius, Isabella (2006): Zwangsheirat – Mehr als nur ein Straftatbestand: Neue Wege zum Schutz der Opfer. In: ZRP 2006, S. 33–37.

Trück, Thomas (2004): Die subjektive Komponente beim Mordmerkmal der niedrigen Beweggründe. Anmerkung zu BGH Beschluss vom 10.9.2003 – 5 StR 373/03. In: NStZ 2004, S. 497–499.

Valerius, Brian (2008): Der sogenannte Ehrenmord: Wertvorstellungen als niedrige Beweggründe? In: JZ 2008, S. 912–919.

Culture and Ethnicity in (Re-)Constructing Domestic Homicides

Daniela Gloor and *Hanna Meier*

Introduction

This article is based on a multi-year study on police (re-)construction of domestic homicides.[1] The purpose of this study was to examine how and according to what criteria the police force analyses and documents accomplished and attempted homicides in intimate partner relationships and families. A special focus was given to the question: in what way does the police investigate couples' histories and to what extent is domestic violence preceding the crime included and documented in the investigation. While the researchers' questions were not primarily focused on issues of ethnicity, during the analysis 'ethnicity' and 'culture' proved to be interpretive patterns, which are of unexpected importance in police work. The results indicate that, when investigating the context of the homicides and giving explanations for the incidents, the dimensions of ethnicity and culture become important concepts (of understanding) for the police.

Our text analyses of police documents illustrate an approach which Leti Volpp (2000) reveals to be a typical construction pattern. She shows that a local or dominant ('own') culture is often not registered and consequently 'culture' is not used as a means of explaining or understanding certain behaviours. Thus, the actions of members of an autochthonous society are not set in a context of culture. When the behaviour of members of 'other' cultures is addressed, however, Volpp notices a change such that for foreign, immigrant ethnic groups attributions of culture are used, often in combination with moral valuations. Through this approach, essentialist differences are constructed. In her investigation of texts on teenage marriages in the US, Volpp writes:

---

1 The qualitative-empirical study was conducted at the University of Basel, Switzerland, Center for Gender Studies. Research was supported by the Swiss National Science Foundation (01/01/2005–30/04/2008) and published as a doctoral thesis (Gloor/Meier 2009a). A summary of the main findings has also been published (Gloor/Meier 2009b).

> These narratives suggest that behavior that we might find troubling is more often causally attributed to a group-defined culture when the actor is perceived to 'have' culture. Because we tend to perceive white Americans as 'people without culture', when white people engage in certain practices we do not associate their behavior with racialized conception of culture, but rather construct other, non-cultural explanations. The result is an exaggerated perception of ethnic difference that equates it with moral difference from 'us'. (Volpp 2000: 89)

This paper discusses how ethnicity is dealt with by using an example of police work. It is presumably one of the 'commonalities across Europe' that a culture, which in a national context can be regarded as 'foreign', is called upon as a factor for understanding and constructing events and actions that are viewed as negative and contentious. To illustrate such processes, the paper uses a concrete example (homicides and domestic violence) within a concrete institution (police force) and a specific country (Switzerland). It highlights the symptomatic, casual and routine presence of culturalising attributions in institutional contexts.

Data, context and methods

The database comprises 38 completed legal cases of accomplished and attempted homicides that were brought to court in the canton of Aargau, Switzerland, within a period of 10 years (1995–2004). The study includes files on homicides in intimate partner relationships – comprising two in three cases, they make up the large majority – as well as homicides in nuclear and extended family relationships, the killing of children by relatives and killings in the context of intimate partner relationships, where non-related persons are affected (the so-called rival as prototype). The analysed documents are so-called 'Final Police Reports', comprising between 5 to approximately 100 pages; texts dealing with accomplished homicides are significantly longer than those dealing with attempted homicides. The 'Final Police Report' collects and condenses the police's results of the investigation phase, which usually extends over a few months. All facts and evidence considered relevant for the definition, understanding and the assessment of the homicide are collected in this document and are subsequently submitted to the public prosecutor's office and the court. The police as well as the prosecutors confirm that the 'Final Police Reports' constitute key documents, which shape a criminal case for the first time, and this first time is of eminent importance within the whole process (Innes 2002). The (re)constructed content of the criminal case – the first written and condensed version of the incident – constitutes a substantial basis for the entire process of jurisdiction.

Even though the documents differ greatly in their individual makeup and structure, the information on the investigated homicide is roughly structured along the following issues and chapters. At the outset, we find formal identification data on offender and victim (1). This is followed by separate chapters on the victim and the offender respectively, containing information on how the police found the victim and the offender. In a further step, the investigation approach is detailed as well as the offender's behaviour during the investigation and during questioning, and the biographies of victim and offender are included here as well (2). Information on the crime, the course of action of the case, the investigation results and material information on the context of the incident make up the body of the report (3). A chapter enquiring the question of motive completes the Final Police Report (4).

Our in-depth text analysis is based on the methodological fundamentals of Grounded Theory Methodology (Strauss and Corbin 1996). Texts – and especially those written within institutions – offer an ideal starting point for decoding institutional logics and lines of reasoning as well as underlying patterns of the cases' problem definition by the police. As Silverman states *'Texts document what participants are actually doing in the world [...]'* (2006: 157). As Final Police Reports are addressed at other institutions following down the line (public prosecutors and courts), they must hold detailed information and comprehensible arguments and deliberations for them (Gloor/Meier 2012, to be published in: Klein/Kelly). This makes it possible to reconstruct, for instance, 'foreign culture' as a meaningful line of interpretation of an investigated homicide in such texts. In the following, we refer to texts on accomplished homicides, as they are considerably more elaborate and include more detailed information than those on attempted killings.

Results and discussion: the 'culture' concept as an omnipresent subtext

We notice that the police, when reporting on homicides within intimate partner relationships and families, very often and as a matter of course refer to the foreign origins of those involved. Whenever non-Swiss nationals are involved in a homicide, be it as a victim or an offender, their background is a factor repeatedly emphasised in the police (re)construction of events and used to create a foundation for understanding the offence. Indications of the unfamiliar culture and culturalising arguments run as a subtext through the police reports, thus establishing the ethnic origins of offender and/or victim successively as a relevant context of the crime. For Swiss nationals, on the other hand, their cultural origins and background are not specifically mentioned in the texts.

In the following, we examine the mentioned police practice based on text examples and demonstrate how, in the reports, ethnic origin comes into play and acquires a negative meaning in interpretation. We arrange our text along the structure of the police reports. To begin with, we examine the 'offender chapter', where, inter alia, the offender's behaviour during pre-trial detention is brought up. We then discuss paragraphs on 'biographic details', which are shown in the reports for the offender as well as for the victim. Subsequently, we refer to the 'history' of the homicide and point to the central role played by violent incidents, which, are linked with 'foreign' culture. Finally, we illustrate the presentation of the 'motive' for the crime. Overall, it becomes clear that culturalising arguments run through the whole of police reporting and that ethnicity is repeatedly implied as an important factor.

'Culturally determined' behaviour of the offender during proceedings

The chapters 'Offender' and 'Victim' in the Final Police Reports present the offender and the victim as objects of the proceedings to the readers and only become tangible as 'alleged offender' and 'dead victim', respectively. Whereas the victim is presented as an object throughout, the analysis for the offender shows a more varied picture. In describing the investigation and proceedings, the offender is simultaneously presented as the object of various police and/or judicial actions as well as an actor taking part in these actions as a specific person. Deliberations on investigation proceedings include *how* the offender behaved during remand and descriptions of the offenders' character as well as his ways of thinking and personal traits. According to the findings, such personal traits are usually discussed in the texts if the police perceive them as problematic deviations from certain, implicit expectations. It becomes clear that, apart from mental illness and addiction, primarily one attribute is repeatedly emphasised: the offender's ethnic origin and culture and this always refers to foreign, non-Swiss cultures, which are constructed as an important, behaviour determining attribute.

The following quotations from Final Police Reports on completed homicides demonstrate how culture is made out to be a determining, essential feature of the offender:

> 4.5. Course of the investigation; questioning
>
> [...] Towards the reporting officer [surname, given name; male offender] always behaved correctly and decently. Most of the time he was also ready to openly answer the questions put to him. Certain parts he found more challenging than others. What broke through again and again with him was his descent. Thus from my subjective point of view, for him his family's uncertain future was harder to take than the bloody deed itself. He repeatedly pointed out that his wife was to blame for her own fate; she neglected her family and drove it apart. [Report 38, Par. 158]
>
> 5.20.8. Personal assessments
>
> [Surname, given name; male offender] always behaved correctly and very decently in every way during his stay at the Telli pre-trial detention centre. I noticed that his children, especially [given name; daughter] were very close to him. He only showed feelings of grief and guilt in respect to his children. The role of women, on the other hand, he does not regard very highly. Towards his divorced wife he rather developed certain feelings of hatred.
> It was difficult to enter into close contact with [surname, given name; male offender]. He was quite withdrawn. [Report 11, Par. 682–684]
>
> 3.9.2. Personal remarks
>
> [Surname, given name; male offender 1] from a subjective point of view does not exactly conform to the image of a Kosovo Albanian as it is generally accepted in Switzerland, something that is also reflected in his extract from the judicial record, dated 08.09.1995, and in his character reference, dated 16.10.1995. [Surname, given name; male offender 1] also behaved correctly and relatively openly towards the police officers, although under special circumstances his Albanian roots naturally came to light again and again. [Report 23, Par. 348–349]

Repeatedly, the texts communicate to the reader 'foreign', culturally determined characters. For instance, it is 'his descent', which 'broke through again and again' (report 38). The verb 'break through' invokes an uncontrolled, force taking on a life of its own. This means that the origin (or cultural background) acquires its own (dangerous) potential – it breaks through. According to the construction, it is the alleged offender's culture (descent), which lays the foundation for why he does not repent the crime and blames his wife. The offender is denied any respect for women. This means that the cultural attributions are at the same time interlinked with gender attributions (Jäger 1999). The alleged offender is constructed as a person, whose character is determined by his cultural origin, which again is characterised by patriarchal conditions. For assessment, this places the offender in a negative light. In the second quote (report 11) the construction is a little less obvious – without the use of the term 'descent', however, it centres on culture just the same. Again, the offender is attributed a family and offspring oriented attitude, according to which the children are awarded primary importance and the wife/partner considered lesser. This is stressed by the intimation that the offender *'does not regard the role of women [...] very highly'*. The stereotype behind this statement is: 'Foreigners' love their children and do not respect their wives. Disrespect for the wife becomes a culturally defined behaviour determining feature of the offender. This interpretation is underlined, when talking about 'feelings of hatred', which the alleged offender developed for the woman. In the third quote, we also recognise the interpretive pattern, which essentially establishes the culture of non-Swiss offenders as a defining characteristic (report 23). Initially, the offender is introduced as an atypical 'foreigner', which, especially due to the deviation, is to be understood as characterising him favourably; the alleged offender has a flawless criminal record and an excellent reputation. By deviating from the implicit mould of perception – 'men of this origin breach *our* laws and act uncooperatively' – the offender is highlighted as an exception, and thus the underlying stereotype is upheld. The following, however, clearly qualifies the description. The writer opposes the positive picture with statements about the offender still acting *'again and again'* – *'under special circumstances'* – as a person with a different background, a 'foreigner', and that his *'cultural roots came to light'*. Even though the offender does not fulfil certain (negative) cultural expectations in the writer's description, his personality remains determined by his ethnic origins nonetheless. Culture of origin is postulated as determining the offender's character and behaviour, without substantiating this. However, the statement is underlined with the word 'naturally' – i.e. 'naturally' the roots came to light – making it even clearer to the reader that culturally fixed behaviour is 'normal' and inevitable and nothing else can be expected; it is 'natural' and corresponds with this person's nature. The strategy of culturalising the offender – notwithstanding missing substantiation – becomes very clear, and a culturally determined character is emphatically constructed. This proves to be disadvantageous for the offender, as the character description contributes to the explanation of the offence.

Biographies of offender and victim: stereotype versus individual

The chapters 'Offender' and 'Victim' as a rule contain a subchapter 'Personal details'. This records the investigation results on the offender's and the victim's biographies, respectively. The information on the offender and victim usually comprises the following areas: family of birth and growing up; schooling, training and jobs; relationship, marriage, family and children; leisure activities, interests, skills and character. As the findings show, the details of offender and victim are shown according to an implicit norm of a male/female 'standard biography' (Swiss middle classes) and respectively measured by it. The biographic details of the investigation are supposed to give an impression of the two main persons involved: offender and victim. Furthermore, as the analysis finds, the underlying question of the texts is to what extent a connection can be established between biography and crime.

Reduced information on non-Swiss nationals

The analysis shows that complete, elaborate biographies in the police's representation of the victim's and the offender's lives are reserved for Swiss nationals. Remarkably, none of the examined reports comprises the biographic details for non-Swiss nationals in all the required areas. Leisure activities of immigrants, for instance, are systematically excluded from the texts. We interpret the lack of description of leisure activities – or the readiness to include such details in the details of Swiss nationals – as an expression or a result of social or cultural distancing or closeness, respectively, between the police and the subjects under investigation. The description of leisure activities, however, must not be underestimated, particularly with regard to how a person is contoured. If such interests, leisure activities or social commitment are shown, the reader gets a clearer, more elaborate picture of the described person. If the person, however, is only described based on details when they were growing up, as well as their work and family, this person remains colourless and comes less to the fore as an individual.

In general, with regard to the biographic details, in the reports on non-Swiss nationals (offenders and victims alike) individualising information is systematically excluded whereas this information is mentioned more frequently and descriptively for Swiss nationals (offenders and victims alike).

Foreign, married women without a biography of their own

Our analyses further found that biographic details for wives with immigrant origins, who fell victim to their husbands, do not contain any information on their childhood and adolescence. This period of their lives is excluded. In their biographies, the victims have neither a childhood nor a family of birth. The same exclusion applies to the questions of schooling and vocational training in these women's lives. One report even fails to mention date and place of birth of the female victim (report 37). This woman's life story, therefore, starts only on her arrival in Switzerland when taking up residence with her husband. What is reported is paid occupation and work in the home in Switzerland as well as her wedding date, and the children are listed in striking detail with names and dates of birth. The victims, and this is the result of the reconstruction, are primarily presented as wives and mothers. Their previous lives, when they had no connection with the offenders, are excluded from the police reports. Thus, for married, female victims of non-Swiss origins, the biographies – in stark contrast to Swiss-born wives – do not reconstruct an individual presence.

This biographic reduction, consequently, limits the representation of the relevance of those involved 'in their own right'. Whereas the description of Swiss wives victimised by their husbands reveals their personalities as individuals, thus granting them relevance in their own right, non-Swiss wives, who fell victim to their husbands, are consistently typified and de-individualised.

Investigation results on the background: previous violence against partner as a reference to 'foreign' mentality

The police reports record the time before the homicide and the context of the crime in various ways. On examining the paragraphs one result becomes obvious: 'domestic violence' does not appear as an independent subject for investigation in police reporting on homicides within the context of intimate partner relationships or the family. The fact that a history between offender and victim characterised by violence and control could form a setting for the crime hardly comes to the attention of the investigators. The killings are not discussed in the context of previous incidents of assaults or threats of emotional, physical or sexual abuse. The analysis found that such violent incidents and assaults during the time preceding the crime are investigated to a limited extent only. Thus, previous violent incidents are neither extensively documented or dealt with, nor are they included in the reports with regard to criminal proceedings.

Nevertheless, as we have found, the Final Police Reports often contain certain information and indications of previous violence. The indications of previous violent incidents – for the main part these are violent assaults by the man against the female partner – are generally used in reports to emphasise and illustrate a certain interpretive pattern regarded as most relevant by the police for understanding the crime. The text analyses reveal three interpretive patterns, which are repeatedly applied in the reports. Firstly, in elaborating on previous violent incidents the investigative concept of a 'bad relationship' is substantiated. Secondly, the indication of previous violence is used to illustrate the argument that the offender's 'personality' must be understood as a decisive factor in the crime, and finally, the description of violence establishes the 'cultural origins' of those involved as an interpretive pattern.

'Bad relationship' between offender and victim

In the contextual logic of the text, descriptions of violence in this pattern serve as an indicator and proof of the poor quality of the relationship between offender and victim. The passages serve to illustrate that the relationship as such was not a harmonious one and that this is to be understood as the decisive setting for the crime. Typically, violence is described without an active agent and only vaguely: the reader remains in the dark as to what the conflicts may have looked like and what kind of violence occurred ('attacks' suggest physical violence) and who assaulted whom. The simplified indications of violence are not meant to document the history of the crime but rather to emphasise the conceptual interpretive pattern of the 'bad relationship':

> From the 21 pages of the specific interrogation follows clearly that the relationship was not harmonious in any way. Altercations and separations alternated regularly with reconciliations. Apparently there were numerous reasons for the mutual attacks. [Report 8, Par. 948]

'Personality' and 'character' of the offender (rarely the victim)

In the reports making use of this interpretative pattern, the paragraphs containing statements on previous violent incidents are usually recorded in parts of the reports describing the character and personality of the offender in detail. The negative character – the described person's *being* – is evoked to the reader by way of the violent incidents – the description of the person's *doing*.

> The statements of the informants give a consistent impression of [surname, given name; male offender] […]. [Surname, given name; male offender] is therefore described as a brutal, egoistic, coarse, aggressive person with a very conservative way of thinking and always thinking of his own interests first. Various statements,

> however, allow the conclusion that the accused tended to be jealous. Before and after the divorce he followed [surname, given name; female victim], in order to control and check on her.
>
> The fact that the accused massively beat and hurt [surname, given name; female victim], does not emerge exclusively from the statements of friends and acquaintances […]. [Report 11, Par. 661–662]

'Cultural background' and 'mentality' of the offender

This construction pattern uses information on previous violence as an indicator for the offender's cultural background and mentality. The description of violence serves the purpose of revealing the cultural foreignness or 'otherness' of a person. In the textual record they are an expression of 'culture' and prove the deviation from local standards.

The following quotation – in this case, the victim is the male offender's father (the offender is therefore the victim's son) – shows the culturalising understanding of the violence preceding the killing. The statements first refer to the behaviour of the victim's wife and then turn to the separate members of the family:

> After [the] woman [surname; victim's wife] was informed of the violent death of her husband, […] she initially only presented to us the bright side, or emphasised without fail that the deceased had been a good father and husband and in general had been a very good person.
>
> Only when told of her son's [given name; offender] confession […], she was obliging enough to reveal […] also the negative side of family life. In this respect during the interview on 15.04.1996 (act. A2/6.1.5) she characterised the victim as a very conservative person and someone who, according to his origins, lived strictly by his cultural mentality. Within his family, he had been the absolute boss, never allowing any 'ifs and buts'. Thus it wasn't a rare fact that he beat her in front of the children because of altercations or other incidents, which he did not approve of. The children had also been subjected mercilessly and had to suffer all kinds of beatings. This had also been the reason for the daughters [given name] and [given name] to move out early. The son [given name] had only stayed in the family home, as this was, on the one hand, demanded by tradition and, on the other hand, so as not to leave her on her own to the brutal devices of the patriarch. As far as the son [given name] is concerned, he had never done right by his father and was forced to do all his biddings. On the outside, however, her husband had managed to act the loving, caring family man and person. Also in respect of the finances the husband had managed the whole of the family income at all times, and held all the necessary authorisations, even though he himself had not been working for years. [Report 22, Par. 331–335]

When asking about the conceptual logic, into which the violent incidents described above are embedded, our analyses show that it is the victim's cultural background (the 'otherness'), which supplies the textual mould for the description of violence. The victim (the offender's father) is, as reported, 'according to his origins' a 'very conservative' person, who lived 'strictly by his cultural mentality'. Subsequently, the victim's 'negative side', i.e. that he 'beat' and 'subjected' are set in the close context of his cultural background. The text sets 'mentality' and 'beating' in context by using the small word 'thus': *'Thus it wasn't a rare fact that [...].'* The violent behaviour according to this construction is to be understood as an expression and proof of the fact that the victim acted in obedience to a backward culture and his origins. What is shown here is not the individual, negative violent and domineering behaviour of one person, but rather a culturally determined, quasi-natural (violent) behaviour, which, according to the account, is typical of men of this origin. Another expression of the 'foreign culture' as an interpretive pattern for the incidents can be found towards the end of this paragraph, when the 22 year old son's staying on in his parents' home is explained as this 'being demanded by tradition'.

Culturalising descriptions of violence can exclusively be found in reports on homicides involving non-Swiss nationals. The autochthonous (local, national) culture, on the other hand, is never an issue in the reports and never discussed as a determining factor, which defines values and behaviour of a person and might be connected with a homicide.

What strikes the reader is that the style of describing violence in the police reports differs according to the investigation concept. In the case of the indications on previous violence functioning as proof of a 'bad relationship', elaborate and precise descriptions are usually not adhered to. Only very imprecisely do they lay down who carried out an assault, what the exact actions were, what kind of violence was used and what the consequences of the violent incidents were for those involved. This is merely described by vague statements and general indications. This gives the impression that the 'bad relationship', rather than one of the involved persons, is to blame for the killing. According to our analyses, this is the dominant pattern in reports on homicides within the context of intimate partner relationships.

Whenever previous acts of violence are used to illustrate the concept of the offender's 'personality', the descriptions are noticeably more detailed and concrete. Such paragraphs more frequently contain detailed statements on the violent acts and on those responsible as well as on the consequences of violent incidents. If previous violent behaviour is meant to prove a certain way of being, the character of the person involved, the incidents are included in the report more precisely. Also the descriptions of violence, which in the text construction serve as proof of the foreign and backward 'cultural origins' and mentality of the involved, are written in a way that an active agent comes into view. They specifically mention *who* became violent. However, the actual violent incidents are not described and documented in detail for each occasion, but mostly simply in a generic, generalising manner.

For both interpretive patterns, 'personality' as well as 'cultural origins', we therefore notice a description oriented on the agent. A remarkable difference is, however, where the violent behaviour is attributed to the individual as a 'personality' pattern where individual psychological (psychologising) interpretations are repeatedly used. Violence as an indicator of 'cultural origins', on the other hand, is attributed collectively. Certain behaviour is interpreted as a cultural (not as an individual) trait. In line with this culturalising construction, a collective cultural character defines the individual.

Patriarchal culture of origin as 'evident' motive

Asking *why* – the motive for the crime – or, respectively, offering a plausible approximation to *why* the crime was committed, is an important part of the police processing of the crime. Investigation on results on the potential background of the crime and its motives is information that is used in order to judicially assess the offender's actions. The reports, consequently, regularly offer possible explanatory contexts and a motive for the homicide. Usually, the chapter on the motive follows as supplementary and summarising information towards the end of the police report. The question *why* therefore follows the detailed asking of *who*, *what* and *how*.

When asking about the reasons for the crime, the police investigate by questioning the alleged offender. In the texts, the offender is, therefore, often quoted as the main source of information for the construction of a motive. On the other hand, the police include their own interpretation and view of things. It is the latter paragraphs that again bring up ethnicity and the foreign origins of the offender. The following example is taken from the motive chapter in a police report on a wife killed by her husband. In a first subchapter, the police refer to the offender's statements on his motive. The second subchapter then offers 'more potential motives'; and this, according to the police, includes 'humiliation by the wife's behaviour':

> 12.2.2. Humiliation by the wife's behaviour The sister-in-law [surname, given name; sister-in-law] and her toddler [given name] had stayed at the accused offender's home since 14/08/1999. [...] She therefore must have witnessed at least some of the incidents involving [surname, given name; male offender] and his

> wife, even though she denied this during the interview. According to her statement, the offender's family life was untroubled and without disputes. [Surname, given name; sister-in-law] does not even confirm that [surname, given name; male offender] consumed wine before leaving for Bremgarten on 21/08/1999.
>
> [Surname, given name; male offender] does admit that his wife's remarks concerning his alcohol consumption offended him. Nevertheless, as a motive for the crime he excludes the offence. It is doubtful that this is actually the case. The fact that males do not accept their female partners to answer back, reproach or reprimand them, should be widely known in connection with the Kosovo Albanian mentality. It must also be taken into consideration that the alleged offender may have felt even more offended by the presence of [surname, given name; sister-in-law] during the discussions with his wife about the said subject. [Report 37, Par. 930–932]

As an introduction, statements by the offender's and the victim's sister-in-law are recorded (she is the offender's brother's wife, visiting at the time of the crime). Subsequently, the police enter into their own deliberations, the style of writing in the second paragraph is characterised by arguments. It is the police officers' aim to come to a synthesis and to coherently and comprehensively lay out the incident. Whereas the police, in many cases, simply paraphrase the offender's statements for the description of the motive, in this case giving a reason for the crime is not left up to the offender only. Rather, the police intervene for the purpose of creating a motive. And they do it whilst referring to the offender's cultural origins. The cultural origins are drawn upon as a basis and motive for the offender's actions.

Let's take a closer look at the motive construction: what is noticeable is the introductory paragraph with the comments on the sister-in-law's statement. The police officers assume that she witnessed the altercations ('incidents') and her brother-in-law's (the offender's) use of alcohol on the day the crime was committed. However, the sister-in-law's statement is to the contrary and, in fact, disproves the police's findings rather than corroborating them. And still the person is mentioned in the text. The reason being, as we assume, is that the police can illustrate and reason *their* interpretation of the events and the motive by way of the sister-in-law's presence. The police assume that the offence and humiliation of the husband by his wife, the future victim, are the cause of the crime. Yet the offender, as recorded in the second paragraph, refutes the motive of 'offence' suggested by the police. The police, on the other hand, regard offence as a credible motive and doubt the offender's attitude when rejecting the attributions.

In order to substantiate their point of view – being insulted and humiliated as a motive – the police apply two culturalising arguments: firstly they refer to the fact that 'the Kosovo Albanian mentality' 'is widely' known and, secondly, they quote a specific sexist image of gender inherent in this mentality. According to this gender attribution, women in this culture do not tell men what to do and do not contradict them. Both arguments are entered into this case without factual reference to the case at hand. They are, in fact, connected generically to so-called known 'facts' about the foreign culture of Kosovo Albanians.

As already stated in the introductory paragraph, the sister-in-law was present during the incident at the time the crime was committed, which can now be construed as another argument corroborating the police's view of things and strengthening the weight of the cultural motive of 'offence'. The fact that the sister-in-law as an additional person was present increased the public character of the 'offence'. In the above-mentioned cultural context, this aggravates, according to the logic of the argument, the postulated offence and humiliation. The sister-in-law's presence is used as a textual means of corroborating the culture-based construction of the motive. In line with this construction, the motive lies in a mental, quasi-natural or culturally determined attitude. Thus, not certain objective or specific behavioural intents, but culture – an essentialist definition of behaviour – is constructed as a motive.

The quoted paragraph refers again to the already mentioned interlinking of discourses about ethnicity and gender or culture and gender relations and norms, respectively. The culturalising arguments are connected with gender attributions and the argument pattern of sexism. The empathy of the Swiss writer of the report for the 'Kosovo Albanian mentality' here is remarkable. By devising the motive of culture, he explicitly distances himself from the offender. At the same time, though, he takes the perspective of the accused. The victim's breach of foreign, so-called cultural norms is described convincingly in the text, and the aggravation of the breach by the sister-in-law's presence is described empathically and authentically. Though writing about a 'foreign mentality', the writer obviously does not have difficulty empathising with the offender's situation and experience. It is our hypothesis that this is made possible through the (common) male view on the fact that the wife supposedly resisted her husband.

Conclusion

As our qualitative text analysis of police reports has shown, whenever migrants are involved in homicides within the context of intimate partner relationships or families, the police frequently and regularly fall back on the 'foreign culture' of those involved when processing and interpreting events.

The ethnic origin of the involved become a decisive factor for understanding and is used as a setting and explanation of events. In doing so, other unfamiliar mentalities and cultural differences are established as a given, as collective traits of character of all the involved and blamed for these actions. Homicides committed by Swiss nationals, on the other hand, are in no way interpreted along a cultural mould. These results emphasise Volpp's hypothesis (2000) that merely the 'others' have a culture, whereas persons perceived as 'local' act individually, i.e., are not determined culturally. The study shows that this process runs through all of the investigating agency's reporting and it shows the various construction patterns of ethnicity as important as well as stereotypical interpretive pattern for the police.

Domestic violence as a history of the homicide and a context of the crime – and this is a second, material result of the study – is not recognised by the police. If the homicide involves immigrants, previous violent assaults against the partner are rather seen as an indicator of their foreign culture. Using the 'culture concept', we conclude, prevents domestic violence from being recognised and termed as such and it prevents its precise documentation.

References

Gloor, Daniela/Meier Hanna (2009a): ‚Von der Harmonie zur Trübung' – Polizeiliche (Re)Konstruktionen von Tötungsdelikten im sozialen Nahraum. Eine qualitativ-soziologische Aktenuntersuchung. Bern: Stämpfli Verlag.

Gloor, Daniela/Meier, Hanna (2009b): Tötungsdelikte im sozialen Nahraum. Ein von Behörden und Forschung vernachlässigtes Thema. In: FamPra.ch, Jg. 10, Nr. 4, S. 946–971.

Gloor, Daniela/Meier, Hanna: 'Clouds darkening the blue marital sky' – How language in police reports (re)constructs intimate partner homicides. Will be puplished in: Kelly Liz, Klein Renate: Just Words? – How language frames violence prevention.

Innes, Martin (2002): The 'Process Structures' of Police Homicide Investigations. In: British Journal of Criminology, Vol. 42, S. 669–688.

Jäger, Margarete (1999): Ethnisierung von Sexismus im Einwanderungsdiskurs. Analyse einer Diskursverschränkung. Presentation. [Zugriff 9. Mai 2008: www.diss-duisburg.de/Internetbibliothek/Artikel/Ethnisierung_von_Sexismus.htm#edn8]

Silverman, David (2006): Interpreting Qualitative Data. Methods for Analyzing Talk, Text and Interaction. Third Edition. London, Thousand Oaks, New Delhi: Sage.

Strauss, Anselm, Corbin Juliet (1996): Grounded Theory: Grundlagen qualitativer Sozialforschung. Psychologie Verlags Union, Weinheim.

Volpp, Leti (2000): Blaming Culture for Bad Behavior. In: Yale Journal of Law and Humanities, Vol. 12, Nr. 89, S. 89–116.

Author Biographies

Chantler, Khatidja is a lecturer and researcher in Social Work at the University of Manchester. She has undertaken a range of research projects including attempted suicide and self-harm (South Asian women); gender based violence in minoritised communities. She is interested in research at the intersections of 'race', gender and class. She is also a counsellor and supervisor and has worked in health and social care settings for over 25 years. Publications include: British, European and International journal articles; book chapters and co-authored books: *Attempted Suicide and Self-harm: South Asian Women (2001), Domestic Violence and Minoritisation (2002)* and co-edited book *Gender and Migration: Feminist Interventions (2010).*

Collet, Beate holds a PhD in sociology from the Ecole des Hautes Etudes en Sciences Sociales (EHESS) in Paris (France). Her PhD thesis explored 'Citizenship and mixed marriages in France and Germany' (1996). Her first lectureship post was at the University of Lyons in 1998 and before moving to the University Paris-Sorbonne in 2007, where she is member of the research unit GEMASS (social methods and research). She teaches social theory, sociology of family and of migration and methods. Her research interests are: mixed couples, mobility and migration, work-family balance, comparison in European societies. Several surveys on marital choice among people of immigrant descent, conducted with Emmanuelle Santelli, led them to look more closely at the social and political reality of 'forced marriages'. In 2008, they jointly coordinated a special issue of the journal *Migrations & Société* on this topic, with contributions from authors from a variety of national contexts (Germany, Norway, Tunisia and France).

Condon, Stephanie is full-time researcher at INED (National Demographic Studies Institute) in Paris. Her work mainly focuses on gender and migration, in particularly on migration from the Caribbean. In parallel, she conducts research on the topic of violence against women in Europe and on the links made with ethnicity. After working as a member of the team that carried out the first French national survey on the topic (Enveff, 2000), she participated in the CAHRV programme funded by the European Commission (2004–2007). Her recent publications on VAW include: Condon S et Hamel C, 2007, 'Etude du contrôle social et des violences exercés à l'encontre des descendantes d'immigrés maghrébins' in: M. Jaspard et N. Chetcuti, *Violences envers les femmes: 'trois pas en avant, deux pas en arrière!' Réflexions autour d'une enquête en France*, Paris, Harmattan, La bibliothèque du féminisme, pp. 201–222. Condon, S, Lieber M and F. Maillochon, 'Feeling unsafe in public places: Understanding women's fears', *Revue Française de Sociologie*, 48 *Supplément*, 5 (2007), pp. 101–128. Jaspard M et Condon S (eds), 2007, *Nommer et compter les violences envers les femmes en Europe.* (Proceedings of the conference organised by CAHRV/INED/IDUP in Paris, 2005), Paris: Idup.

Creazzo, Giuditta lives and works in Bologna. She is a free-lance researcher trained in law and criminology. She was initially involved in the field of crime prevention and urban safety. Since the beginning of the 1990s she has been working on the subject of violence against women. She directed several research projects on this topic, often in collaboration with women's anti-violence centres, and published various books and articles. From 2007 to 2009 she coordinated a Daphne project – MUVI – on programmes for men who use violence against women in intimate relationships. In 2010 she started a new Daphne project – WOSAFEJUS – on women's requests for justice and protection when getting victims of partner violence and the responses of the criminal justice system.

Danneskiold-Samsøe, Sofie is an Assistant Professor at the Department of Society and Globalisation, Roskilde University, Denmark. She received her Ph.D. in anthropology from the University of Copenhagen on the dissertation *The Moral Economy of Suffering: Social Exchange among Iraqi Refugees in the Danish Welfare State* (2006). Her research focuses on social suffering and gendered violence among Middle Eastern families in the context of the welfare state.

Debauche, Alice, following a degree in statistics and economics (ENSAE school), is about to defend a PhD thesis in sociology (Sciences Po-Cnrs/Ined) entitled 'Rape and gender relations. Emergence, recording and contesting of a crime against the person' supervised by Michel Bozon. She has taught statistics and survey methods at Paris 1 and Paris 7 Universities. She took part in the CAHRV programme and worked on a Daphne-funded research project on rape and attrition rates. She is a member of the editorial board of the journal *Nouvelles Questions Féministes*, of which she has coordinated the issues *Les lois du genre I* et *II* (the Laws of Gender).

Doniol-Shaw, Ghislaine is ergonomist. She is a research scientist at a CNRS unit attached to Paris-Est University. She studies the impact of technical and organizational changes on working conditions, safety and health and on the security and reliability of systems. Gender is an important focus in her work, particularly in relation to employment equality and on the skill levels of women's jobs. Research into domestic employment is directly related to these topics. She contributed to a pioneering publication in France along with doctors on violence against women at work: 'Évolution de l'emploi et des conditions de travail des femmes et effets sur leur santé', in Femmes au travail, violences vécues, SYROS, 2000, pp. 185–212.

Gangoli, Geetanjali works at the Centre for Gender and Violence Research, University of Bristol. She has previously taught at the University of Delhi, been a Sir Ratan Tata Visiting Fellow at the London School of Economics and Political Science and a Research Fellow at the International Centre for the Study of Violence Against Women Research Group, University of Sunderland. She has researched in the areas of domestic violence in the UK and China, on prostitution and trafficking in South Asia, Indian feminisms and law and forced marriage, perpetrators of domestic violence, honour based violence and domestic violence amongst Black and Minority Ethnic Women in the UK. She edits the journal 'Policy and Politics', published by Policy Press.

Gloor, Daniela and **Meier, Hanna**, Sociologists Dr. phil., cofounded and own the independent Social Research Institute 'Social Insight' in Schinznach-Dorf, Switzerland, see: www.socialinsight.ch. Their institute is specialized in the fields of violence, gender and equality. Since twenty years the two researchers conduct together numerous quantitative and qualitative research and evaluations in domains of violence against women and intervention pratices against domestic violence.

Hamel, **Christelle** is a sociologist and research scientist at the National Institute for Demographic Research (INED) in Paris. She specializes in gender issues within minorities in France. Her earliest research was into sexuality and the management of HIV related health risks amongst young people of North African parentage living in France. She now works on the formation of couples and partner choice amongst descendants of immigrants and also on the experience of racism and discrimination. She is currently studying forced marriages and is preparing a quantitative survey on VAW in France. She is a member of the editorial board of the journal *Nouvelles Questions Féministes.*

Højberg, Henriette is the head of the research and documentation center at Danner which also includes a shelter. Danner has more than 30 years of experience working with violence against women. She has 8 years of experience in working with violence against women. She started out as a volunteering as a counselor at the shelter Danner. Later she became the project manager of a programme working with aftercare and development of methods working with ethnic minority women at the shelter. In her former position she worked at Roskilde University, Denmark and has published articles regarding philosophy of science.

Keskinen, Suvi is a postdoctoral researcher and Adjunct Professor at Turku Institute for Advanced Studies, University of Turku, Finland. Her research interests include gendered violence, postcolonial feminism, media representations, multicultural politics, nationalism and racism. She has published widely in Finland and internationally. Among her publications are the co-edited book *Complying with Colonialism. Gender, Race and Ethnicity in the Nordic Region* (2009, Ashgate) and 'Borders of the Finnish Nation. Media, Politics and Rape by 'Foreign' Perpetrators' in Eide, E. & Nikunen, K. (Eds.) *Media in Motion. Cultural Complexity and Migration in the Nordic Region* (2011, Ashgate).

Khelaifat, Nadia has an MSc in Public Health from the University of Bielefeld. In her Master's thesis, she carried out a secondary analysis on the data of the study 'Living situation, safety and health of women, a representative study on violence against women in Germany' (Schröttle and Müller 2004) examining factors that correlate with partner violence among Turkish women. The study made recommendations for appropriate prevention and intervention, while differentiating between the first and second migration generation. In the UK, she completed a BSc (Honours) in Psychology with a focus on clinical and health psychology. She was a research assistant in the project 'Health – violence – migration: a comparative secondary analysis on the health situation of violence between women with and without migration background in Germany' at the University of Bielefeld (Schröttle and Khelaifat 2008). Nadia Khelaifat also worked on the special issue on health consequences of violence for the Federal Health Monitoring System (2008). She has substantial working experience in clinical and social settings, including a

Women's Counselling Centre, where her work focussed on outreach projects for migrant women affected by domestic violence. She has devised and carried out campaigns raising awareness about domestic violence, laws against it, health consequences, and sources of help and support with the aim of wider prevention.

Lada, Emmanuelle is a sociologist, assistant professor at Lausanne University (Switzerland) and member of a CNRS research unit on gender, work and migration (France), and attached to the Gender studies centre LIEGE (Lausanne). Her work centres on changing conditions of work and labour in the service sector and their impacts on employment, training, family and health trajectories. She is particularly interested in the links between these dynamics and public policy. The gender perspective cuts through this work, as well as focusing on an intersectionality approach. She has recently studied young people entering the labour market as well as low-skilled salaried workers in the public sector, the charity-funded organisations and in hotel sector. Her research into domestic employment was linked to this work.

Lehmann, Nadja is a freelance social scientist and accredited supervisor (DGSv) focusing on diversity issues, gender, development of democracy skills as well as on issues related to intercultural social work, child abuse prevention and adult education. She is a co-founder of the 'Interkulturelles Frauenhaus' in Berlin (Intercultural shelter and consultation for victims of domestic violence), where she is also a member of the executive board. In 2006 she graduated with a doctoral degree in sociology from the Freie Universität Berlin with a thesis focusing on 'Female migrants in shelters for domestic violence. Biographical perspectives on experiencing violence'. She is a frequent invited expert and speaker at workshops and events focusing on migrants and domestic violence. Since 2007 Nadja Lehmann also provides research guidance, supervision and consulting for projects focusing on social work in various domains. She is also an adjunct professor at the Alice-Salomon-University of Applied Science in Berlin.

Lesné, Maud is currently a PhD student at Paris 8 University/INED investigating the topic of measuring racist and sexist/gender discrimination. Before beginning her doctoral research, she was a Master's student in demography in 2005, with Maryse Jaspard at IDUP (Paris 1 University). She continued working with M. Jaspard on a number of VAW data collection projects, notably for the ONG *Fédération Nationale Solidarité Femmes* on women calling the emergency telephone number and for the IDUP (VAW surveys in the Seine-St-Denis suburb and in Martinique, survey on contraceptive practice).

During this period, she acquired a sound experience in collecting both quantitative and qualitative data on sensitive topics such as interpersonal violence, FGM, sexuality and racism. She has published "Discrimination: a question of visible minorities" with C. Beauchemin, C. Hamel and P. Simon (*Population et Sociétés*, monthly bulletin, INED, n° 466, April 2010), the results of the INED-INSEE survey Trajectories and Origins.

Logar, Rosa is Executive Director of the Domestic Abuse Intervention Program Vienna, a victim/survivor service that has been established with the new Domestic Violence Act (1997); she is lecturer at the University of Applied Sciences/Department of Social Work; member of the Austrian interministerial working group on the new Domestic Violence Act; co-founder of the European Network WAVE (Women Against Violence Europe, 1994); member of the UN Expert Group Meeting *Good practices in legislation on violence against women In Vienna (2008);* member of the Council of Europe *Task Force to Combat Violence against Women, including Domestic Violence* (2006–2008); currently member of the Council of Europe *Ad Hoc Committee on Preventing and Combating Violence against Women and Domestic Violence (CAHVIO)* having prepared a legally binding instrument to prevent violence against women in Europe; Rosa is a trained supervisor, she holds a bachelor in social work and master in social management.

Manier, Marion has recently defended her thesis on the topic of social work directed towards immigrant minority women at issues of intersectional – ethnic, gender, class – categorisation and its social effects. Her research themes, bringing together sociology of migration, interethnic relations and sociology of gender relations, led her to examine the institutionalisation of the struggle against VAW and its effects on public policy, in particular social work and local organizations.

Masson, Sabine is a sociologist, research scientist at the Institut des Hautes Etudes Internationales et du Développement (IHEID)-NCCR Nord-Sud. She works on gender and feminist theories, postcolonial theory, racism, colonialism, globalisation, citizenship and indigenous people's movements in Latin America. She is a member of the editorial board of the journal *Nouvelles Questions Féministes.* Her publications include: 'Le viol en temps de guerre: crime ou bavure? Avancées et résistances de la condamnation du viol contre les femmes'. *Nouvelles Questions Féministes*. Vol. 20, No 3/1999; 'Sexe/ genre, classe et race: décoloniser le féminisme dans un contexte mondialisé. Réflexions à partir de la lutte des femmes indiennes au Chiapas'. *Nouvelles Questions Féministes,* vol. 25, no 3/2006; 'Sexe, race et colonialité. Point de vue d'une épistémologie féministe postcoloniale latino-américaine', in Dorlin, Elsa (dir.): *Sexe, race et classe: Pour une épistémologie de la domination*. Paris: Presses Universitaires de France, coll. Actuel Marx/Confrontations.

Mørck, Yvonne is an Associate Professor at the Department of Society and Globalisation, Roskilde University, Denmark. She received her Ph.D. in anthropology from the University of Copenhagen in 1996. Her research focuses on sociological and cultural issues, e.g. migration, multiculturalism, globalisation, citizenship, youth education, gender, sexuality and violence against women. She has published the book '*Bindestregsdanskere. Fortællinger om køn, generationer og etnicitet*' (Hyphenated Danes. Narratives on Gender, Generation and Ethnicity, 1998) and many articles.

Paci, Daniela is an educator, a researcher and an anti-violence activist. She has collaborated to several national and international research projects on violence against women, sexual abuse against children, gender roles and violence among adolescents, as well as on the health of migrant women and adolescents, focussing also on the institutional responses to violence and discrimination. She has published articles and book chapters on these topics in Italian and English. With other colleagues (including P. Romito), she developed and is in charge of the first Italian Web site on Violence, addressed to adolescents 'No to violence' (www.units.it/noallaviolenza).

Patel, Pragna is a founding member of the Southall Black Sisters and Women Against Fundamentalism. She worked as a co-ordinator and senior case worker for SBS from 1982 to 1993 when she left to train and practice as a solicitor. In 2009 she returned to SBS as its Director. She has been centrally involved in some of SBS' most important campaigns around domestic violence, immigration and religious fundamentalism. She has also written extensively on race, gender and religion. Among her many publications have been like the 1992 'Citizenship: Whose Rights?' in *Women and Citizenship in Europe: Borders, Rights and Duties*, ed. A. Ward et al. (Trentham Books), the 1997 'The Time Has Come ... Asian Women in Struggle' in *Black British Feminism – A Reader*, ed. H. S. Mirza (Taylor & Francis), several essays in: *From homebreakers to jailbreakers* 2003 ed. R. Gupta (Zed Books), the 2008 'Faith in the State? Asian Women's Struggles for Human Rights in the UK', *Feminist Legal Studies,* Spring issue and R v Zoora (Ghulam) Shah in *Feminist Judgments from Theory to Practice* September 2010 ed. Rosemary Hunter; Clare McGlynn and Erika Rackley.

Pedersen, Bodil is currently employed as Associate Professor at the Department of Psychology and Educational Studies of the University of Roskilde in

Denmark. Furthermore she has taught psychology at the Copenhagen University College for Social Work and at the University of Copenhagen. She is a specialist in psychotherapy and supervision and has worked with family counselling, youth counselling as well as organisational psychology and counselling. She has participated in founding diverse counselling facilities such as a community based counselling, facilities for people living with HIV, facilities for women and for gays and lesbians. She has held diverse administrative positions and was a co-founder of the Studies of Health and Health Promotion at the University of Roskilde. She has worked with projects on parenthood and drug use, prostitution, psychosocial problems in living with HIV, burn-out, and rape and other forms of sexualised coercion. Her main interests are social psychological questions and dilemmas concerning subjectivity in the fields of gender, ethnicities, gendered violence, marginalisation, help facilities, health promotion, and methodology.

Pipitone, Emmanuela received a degree at the University of Bologna, Faculty of Statistical, Demographic and Attuarial Sciences, then she attended a one year specialisation course in bio-statistics at 'Mario Negri Institute – Clinical Research Centre on Rare Diseases' and she specialised in Epidemiological and Medical Statistic at the University of Verona, Faculty of Medicine and Public Health. Since obtaining her degree she has collaborated with the University of Bologna and then with the University of Modena and Reggio Emilia, where at present she is the tutor on the Health Planning course. In addition, she has been involved for health and health economy projects and as biostatistician for other Institutions. She has been involved in several studies concerning the violence against women, in particular for 'La casa delle donne per non subire violenza'. Since 1993 she has been a consultant of the Health Department of the Municipality and she has been involved in the development of the statistical and epidemiological area of European or local projects.

Pohlreich, Erol Rudolf studied law at the Humboldt University of Berlin, at the Pantheon-Assas Paris II University and at the University of Hamburg. Pohlreich received his doctorate in law at the Humboldt University of Berlin for his thesis on so-called 'honour killings'. Therein, he compares the reactions of various legal systems – namely Roman, French, Turkish, Islamic and German Criminal Law – to 'honour killings' and examines the relevant changes in each of these legal system's history. Pohlreich was granted a doctoral scholarship from the German National Academic Foundation (Studienstiftung des deutschen Volkes). Since 2007 he is a research assistant at Humboldt University focusing on Criminal Law, Comparison of Laws, Prison Law and Criminal Procedure. From 2008 to 2010, Pohlreich unterwent his legal practical training period (Referendariat) in Berlin and was i.a. assigned to the Federal Constitutional Court of Germany (department of Senior Judge, Prof. Dr. Gertrude Lübbe-Wolff). Since 2010, Pohlreich is preparing his habilitation thesis on Criminal Procedure at Humboldt University.

Pourette, Dolorès is research scientist at the IRD (Paris) and attached to the CEPED research centre. She works on gender issues, health and migration. She has been on the research team for several studies on VAW. Her most recent publications are: 'Sexualité et reproduction des femmes 'africaines' vivant avec le VIH/sida: stéréotypes culturalistes et expériences', *L'Autre*, 2010, 11 (3); 'Excision et chirurgie réparatrice: expérience personnelle et dynamiques familiales', *Sociétés contemporaines*, 2010, 77 (avec A. Andro et M. Lesclingand); *Violences envers les femmes à La Réunion. Poids des chiffres et paroles de victimes*, PUP, 2009 (with I. Widmer); 'Migratory Paths, Experiences of AIDS and Sexuality: African Women living with HIV/Aids in France', *Feminist Economics*, 2008, 14(4); 'Paroles et sexualité dans le couple à La Réunion et en Polynésie Française', in: M. Jaspard, N. Chetcutti (eds.), *Violences envers les femmes: Trois pas en avant, deux pas en arrière!*, L'Harmattan, 2007.

Romito, Patrizia, PhD, is a professor of Social Psychology at the University of Trieste, Italy, where she teaches courses on Research methods, Community psychology, and Violence against women. She is also an advocate of women's rights. She has extensive experience, as a researcher and as an activist, in the topics of women's mental health, and of violence against women. She is the author of many articles and of some books on motherhood, women's health, and violence. In English, she has published: 'A deafening silence: Hidden violence against women and children' (2008).

Romkens, Renée is a criminologist and holds the Chair on Interpersonal Violence at INTERVICT International Victimology Institute Tilburg at Tilburg University Law School in the Netherlands. As Visiting Professor she has been affiliated with various international Universities (New York Law School/Global Law Program, Columbia University – New York, Women and Gender Studies and the University of the Western Cape/South Africa). She has published widely on various aspects of violence against women in the home and its regulation. In the Netherlands, she conducted the first national in-depth survey on wife abuse and marital rape (1989). Her current research focuses on socio-legal aspects of regulation of and interventions in the field of violence against women, notably intimate partner violence. As independent expert adviser she served on the Council of Europe Commission that drafted the *Convention on Violence Against Women and Domestic Violence* (2011). She serves regularly as an expert on international commissions in the field of VAW of the UN, Council of Europe and the European Commission.

Roux, Patricia is professor and director of the Centre for gender studies LIEGE at the University of Lausanne (Switzerland). Since 2001, she has been co-editor responsible for the journal Nouvelles Questions Féministes. Her research focuses on processes of justification for inequality, intersections between sexism and structural racism and in lay society, as well as the instrumentalisation of women and feminism in racist practice and discourse in Switzerland, which have recently been targeting Muslem women and men (debate and votes on the outlawing of the construction of minaret towers, on the extradition of foreign criminals, forbidding of the wearing of the Islamic veil, for example, in schools). Her two recent articles on the topic are: Gianettoni, Lavinia et Patricia Roux (2010). 'Interconnecting Race and Gender Relations: Racism, sexism and the attribution of sexism to the racialized Other'. *Sex Roles: A Journal of Research, 62* (5–6), 374–386; Roux, Patricia, Lavinia Gianettoni et Céline Perrin (2007): 'L'instrumentalisation du genre: une nouvelle forme de racisme et de sexisme'. *Nouvelles Questions Féministes, 26* (2), 92–108.

Roy, Sumanta has worked in the field of gender, violence and cultural perspectives for over 14 years. She is the Research and Training Officer of Imkaan, responsible for developing sector-specific publications and helping in the delivery of accredited training programmes on forced marriage and honour-based violence. Sumanta's previous academic and work experience has included working at Newham Asian Women's Project as a Training Manager. She has also carried out research, public relations and fundraising for women's organisations committed to national and international grassroots perspectives. She is a freelance consultant and has carried out a range of projects, reviews and needs assessments for social care charities and housing associations. More recently, she has led on a study for the Greater London Authority on forced marriage, female genital mutilation and honour-based violence which aims to explore methods for improving service responses for women.

Santelli, Emmanuelle holds a degree in sociology and a PhD from the University of Lyon (France). Her PhD thesis was on trajectories of the descendants of North African migrants (1997). She has been a research scholar at France's National Centre for Scientific Research (CNRS) since 2000 at the

Centre Max Weber (research unit in Lyon) and, since 2005, an associate research scholar at the National Institute of Demographic Studies (INED) in Paris. Her research interests are: the second generation of Maghrebi migrants, upward mobility, transnationalism, conjugal and familial dynamics. As part of this research, she has worked with Beate Collet on the topic of 'forced marriage', leading to the coordination of a special issue of the journal *Migrations Société:* 'Entre consentement et imposition, réalités politiques et sociales des mariages dits 'forcés'' (2008).

Schröttle, Monika, PhD., is a political scientist and social researcher and has been researching in the field of gendered violence since 15 years. She is currently visiting professor at the University of Gießen. Since 2002 until 2011 she was leading research projects at the Interdisciplinary Center for Women's and Gender Studies, University of Bielefeld. Monika Schröttle is a specialist in the fields of violence, gender, health, disabilities and migration. From 2000 to 2001 she was involved in the creation of an information center for child abuse and neglect at the German Youth Institute (DJI). From 2002 to 2004 she conducted, together with Ursula Müller, the first national representative prevalence study on violence against women in Germany, funded by the German Federal Ministry for Women, Family Affairs, Senior Citizens and Youth (BMFSFJ). From 2005 up to 2009 this data set served as a basis for further analysis and evaluation in the areas of migration, health impact, levels and patterns of partner violence as well as risk and protective factors for violence against women. From 2009 to 2011 new national prevalence studies were conducted on violence against disabled women, violence against women and men and VAW in Europe. Together with Manuela Martinez, Monika Schröttle was coordinator of a European sub-network on violence prevalence research and health consequences, as part of the EU network CAHRV (Coordination Action on Human Rights Violations, see: www.cahrv.uni-osnabrueck.de) where standards and recommendations for European research on violence prevalence and monitoring systems were developed.

Siddiqui, Hannana has been involved in working on race and gender issues for over 25 years. She has worked at Southall Black Sisters for 21 years. Her work has ranged from undertaking casework, research, policy and campaigning on violence against black and minority women, and has included domestic violence; battered women who kill, in particular the famous case of Kiranjit Ahuwalia; immigration/asylum and no recourse issues, which included helping to reform the law on domestic violence and immigration in 1999 and in creating the pressure leading to the recent government introduction of a pilot project on address no recourse and announcement to develop a long-term solution to pay benefits to victims of domestic violence'; forced marriage, including helping to introduce the forced marriage guidelines and the Forced Marriage (Civil Protection) Act 2007, and was an original member of the Home Office Working Group on Forced Marriage in 1999; suicide and self-harm; and so called 'honour killings' or honour based violence. Hannana has also undertaken some international work, such as lobbying on the 'Convention of All Forms of Discrimination Against Women'. She was a founding member of 'Women Against Fundamentalism' and is currently involved in fighting the use of religious courts or tribunals on women's issues. She is currently developing a UK wide strategy on violence against black and minority women.

Sørensen, Bo Wagner is currently an Associate Professor at the Department of Society and Globalisation, Roskilde University, Denmark. He received his Ph.D. in anthropology from the University of Copenhagen in 1993. His dissertation *Magt eller afmagt? Køn, følelser og vold i Grønland* (Power or Powerlessness? Gender, Emotions and Violence in Greenland) was published in 1994. He has done extensive fieldwork in Greenland and published many articles. His main research interests are VAW, gender, ethnicity and nationalism, migration, urban anthropology, landscapes, museums, material culture, and representation. In recent years he has practiced anthropology at home.

Thiara, Ravi is Principal Research Fellow at the Centre for the Study of Safety and Well-being at University of Warwick, UK. Over the last 25 years, she has conducted extensive research and evaluation, training and service development in the violence against women field, in the UK and overseas. Ravi has a particular interest and expertise in violence issues for children, child contact and post-separation abuse, gendered violence within black and minority ethnic communities, and issues for abused disabled women. She has published widely on these issues. In addition, she has written and conducted research on the Indian diaspora in South Africa, bride price and marriage rights in Uganda, and black and minority ethnic youth in the UK.

Vega Alexandersson, Ana Maria was born in Chile, where she trained in medicine. She migrated to Italy in 1991 and she now lives and works as a doctor in Bologna. In 1993 she became a volunteer of the "Casa delle donne per non subire violenza", an autonomous feminist antiviolence centre, where she has continued to work since 1996. She has collaborated in different projects such as the shelter, the hotline and the project against trafficking. At present, she is responsible for the antiviolence centre's statistical data base. She also participates in the local studies into violence against women which are conducted regularly in Emilie Romagna region.

Wilson, Amrit is the chairperson of Imkaan and a writer and activist on issues of gender and race. Her books include 'Finding a Voice – Asian Women in Britain' published by Virago, London in 1978, which won the Martin Luther King Award and 'Dreams, Questions and Struggles – South Asian women, gender and race in Britain' published by Pluto Press in 2006. Between 1990 and 2003 she was Senior Lecturer in South Asian Studies at the University of Luton in which capacity she supervised research into the lives of South Asian women in Britain – particularly issues of Honour related violence and effects of British immigration legislation. She is/was a Visiting Research Fellow at the University of Huddersfield and an Honorary Research Fellow at the Royal Holloway College, University of London.